Pan was founded in 1944 by Alan Bott, then owner of The Book Society. Over the next eight years he was joined by a consortium of four leading publishers – William Collins, Macmillan, Hodder & Stoughton and William Heinemann – and together they launched an imprint that is an international leader in popular paperback publishing to this day.

Pan's first mass-market paperback was *Ten Stories* by Rudyard Kipling. Published in 1947, and priced at one shilling and sixpence, it had a distinctive logo based on a design by artist and novelist Mervyn Peake. Paper was scarce in post-war Britain, but happily the Board of Trade agreed that Pan could print its books abroad and import them into Britain provided that they exported half the total number of books printed. The first batch of 250,000 books were dispatched from Paris to Pan's warehouse in Esher on an ex-Royal Navy launch named *Laloun*. The vessel's first mate, Gordon Young, was to become the first export manager for Pan.

Around fifty titles appeared in the first year, each with average print runs of 25,000 copies. Success came quickly, largely due to the choice of vibrant, descriptive book covers that distinguished Pan books from the uniformity of Penguin paperbacks, which were the only real competitors at the time.

Pan's expertise lay in its ability to popularize its authors, and a combination of arresting design coupled with energetic marketing and sales helped turn the likes of Leslie Charteris, Eric Ambler, Nevil Shute, Ian Fleming and John Buchan into bestsellers. The first book to sell a million copies was *The Dam Busters* by Paul Brickhill, first published in 1951. Brickhill was among the first to receive a Golden Pan award, for sales of one million copies. His fellow prize winners in 1964 were Alan Sillitoe for *Saturday Night and Sunday Morning* and Ian Fleming, who won it seven times over. It was also given posthumously to Grace Metalious for *Peyton Place*.

In the Sixties and Seventies authors such as Dick Francis, Wilbur Smith and Jack Higgins joined the fold, and 1972 saw the founding of the ground-breaking literary paperback imprint, Picador. Then-Editorial Director Clarence Paget signed up the third novel by the relatively unknown John le Carré, and transformed the author's career. Pan also secured paperback rights in James Herriot's memoirs of a Yorkshire vet in 1973, and a year later fought off tough competition to publish *Jaws* by Peter Benchley. Inspector Morse made his first appearance in Colin Dexter's *Last Bus to Woodstock* in 1974.

By 1976 Pan had sold over 30 million copies of its books and was outperforming all its rivals. Over the ensuing decades they published some of the biggest names in popular fiction, such as Jackie Collins, Dick Francis, Martin Cruz Smith and Colin Forbes.

By the late Eighties, publishers had stopped buying and selling paperback licences and in 1987 Pan, now wholly owned by Macmillan, became its paperback imprint. This was a turbulent time of readjustment for Pan, but with characteristic energy and zeal Pan Macmillan soon established itself as one of the largest book publishers in the UK. By 2010, the advent of ebooks allowed the audience for popular fiction to grow dramatically, and Pan's bestselling authors, such as Peter James, Jeffrey Archer, Ken Follett and Kate Morton – not to mention bestselling saga writers Margaret Dickinson and Annie Murray – now reach an even wider readership.

Personally, my years working at Pan were incredibly exciting and a time of countless opportunities. The paperback market was exploding, and Pan was at the forefront. Sales were incredible – I remember selling close to a million copies of a Colin Dexter novella alone. I'm proud that today, Pan retains the same energy and vibrancy.

In the year that Pan celebrates its 70th anniversary its mission remains the same – to publish the best popular fiction and non-fiction for the widest audience.

David Macmillan

Born Free

Joy Adamson was a pioneer in the field of conservation. With her husband George, senior game warden in a huge area of the northern frontier province of Kenya, she established one of the world's first wild animal appeals. Now the Elsa Conservation Trust, it operates an education, training and wildlife retreat centre at the Adamson's former home of Elsamere, on the shores of Lake Naivasha.

BY THE SAME AUTHOR

Born Free

Living Free

Forever Free

for children

Elsa: The Story of a Lioness

Elsa and Her Cubs

JOY ADAMSON

Born Free

PAN 70

First published 1966 by Collins and Harvill Press as *The Story of Elsa*

This paperback edition published 2017 by Pan Books
an imprint of Pan Macmillan
20 New Wharf Road, London N1 9RR
Associated companies throughout the world
www.panmacmillan.com

ISBN 978-1-5098-6024-1

1 3 5 7 9 8 6 4 2

A CIP catalogue record for this book is available from the British Library.

Typeset by SX Composing DTP, Rayleigh, Essex
Printed and bound by CPI Group (UK) Ltd, Croydon, CR0 4YY

Visit **www.panmacmillan.com** to read more about all our books
and to buy them. You will also find features, author interviews and
news of any author events, and you can sign up for e-newsletters
so that you're always first to hear about our new releases.

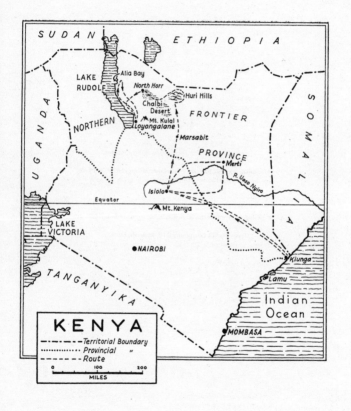

KENYA

- - - Territorial Boundary
········· Provincial "
- - - - Route

0   100   200
MILES

Preface

Whether fact or fiction lies at the root of tales which credit the Assyrians with having trained lions as cheetahs, greyhounds or retrievers are today trained to hunt in co-operation with man, the Adamsons can certainly claim to be the first for several thousand years to have made an approach to achieving that result with a lioness – and that, *not* by any deliberate attempt to do so, but merely by allowing the animal to grow up in their company and *never* allowing her nature to be subjected to the strains of being confined in any way.

The history of their lioness 'Elsa', reared from earliest infancy to three years old and finally returned to a wild life, forms a unique and illuminating study in animal psychology – a subject to which the last half-century has seen a wholly new approach. Partly, no doubt, in revolt against the tendency of nineteenth-century writers to attribute to animals anthropomorphic qualities of intelligence, sentiment and emotion, the twentieth century has seen the development of a school of thought according to which the springs of animal behaviour are to be sought in terms of 'conditioned reflexes', 'release mechanisms', and the rest of a wholly new vocabulary which is regarded as the gateway to a clearer understanding of animal psychology. To another way of thinking which cannot reconcile that mechanical conception with the diverse character, intelligence, and capabilities exhibited by different individuals of the same species, that gateway to understanding seems as far removed from truth as the anthropomorphism of a previous generation, and more apt to raise a further barrier to a sympathetic understanding of animal behaviour than a revelation of it.

To whatever way of thinking the reader of Elsa's history may lean, it provides a record of absorbing interest depicting the gradual development of a controlled character which few would have credited as possible in the case of an animal potentially as dangerous as any in the world. That such a creature when in a highly excited state, with her blood up after a long struggle with a bull buffalo, and while still on top of it, should have permitted a man to walk up to her and cut the dead beast's throat to satisfy his religious scruples, and then lend her assistance in pulling the carcass out of a river is an astonishing tribute no less to her intelligence than to her self-control.

If the most fanciful author of animal stories of the nineteenth century had drawn the imaginary character of a lioness acting in that manner it would assuredly have been ridiculed as altogether 'out of character' and too improbable to carry conviction – and yet Elsa's record shows that it is no more than sober fact.

If in her development Elsa has made her own commentary both on the 'anthropomorphism' of the nineteenth century and the 'science' of the twentieth, she has not lived in vain.

WILLIAM PERCY

Contents

Preface by Lord William Percy vii

PART ONE

1. Cub Life 3

2. Elsa Meets Other Wild Animals 15

3. Elsa Goes to the Indian Ocean 26

4. Safari to Lake Rudolf 33

5. Elsa and Wild Lions 52

6. The First Release 60

7. The Second Release 75

8. The Final Test 92

9. Postscripts 106

PART TWO

10. Elsa Mates with a Wild Lion 125

11. The Birth of the Cubs 136

12. We See the Cubs 153

13. The Cubs Meet Friends 161

14. The Cubs in Camp 171

15. The Personality of the Cubs 178

16. Elsa Meets Her Publisher 186

17. The Camp Is Burned 197

18. Elsa's Fight 210

Contents

19. Dangers of the Bush *221*

20. Cubs and Cameras *231*

21. Elsa Educates the Cubs *241*

22. A New Year Begins *256*

PART THREE

23. The Deportation Order *267*

24. Elsa Is Ill *278*

25. Elsa's Death *284*

26. Guardians of Elsa's Children *292*

27. Plans to Move the Cubs *299*

28. Have the Cubs Found a Pride? *306*

29. The Cubs in Trouble *311*

30. Crisis *315*

31. Preparations for Trapping the Cubs *324*

32. The Capture *329*

33. The Journey to the Serengeti *335*

34. The Release *344*

35. The Migration *349*

36. The Ravine *361*

37. I Become a Tourist in the Serengeti *371*

38. We See the Cubs Again *383*

39. The Long Search *391*

40. The Price of Freedom *404*

Maps *413*

List of Illustrations

SECTION ONE

The cubs, soon after their arrival.

Stalking practice.

The tyre game.

Elsa after her sisters had left for Rotterdam.

By the Indian Ocean.

Sharing my camp bed at Lake Rudolf.

Elsa resting in a tree.

Claw-strengthening exercises.

Elsa with Nuru Makedde and Ibrahim.

After the second release.

Elsa with the author.

Elsa on the Land Rover roof.

Elsa's favourite lookout rock.

Elsa in a hollow baobab tree.

Reunion after my return from England.

SECTION TWO

Elsa bringing the cubs over the river.

The cubs playing with their mother.

Claw exercises.

Elsa meets her publisher, Billy Collins.

Elephant at a watering hole.

xi

Crossing the river with the cubs.

Elsa suckling the cubs.

Elsa and Jespah.

The family together at the burnt camp site.

Little Elsa.

Siesta!

Buffalo.

The cubs' first Christmas.

One year old.

SECTION THREE

Elsa's grave.

My last day with the cubs at their original home.

The crates and arrival in the Serengeti.

Release of the cubs.

Jespah taking cod-liver oil.

Jespah with George in the Serengeti.

Jespah on the Land Rover.

A cheetah.

A leopard and its kill.

Zebra.

Elsa's grave after its repair.

Our last view of the cubs.

George winches the Land Rover out of a lugga.

Lions of the Serengeti.

George and Joy.

PART ONE

1. Cub Life

For many years my home has been in the Northern Frontier Province of Kenya, that vast stretch of semi-arid thornbush, covering some hundred and twenty thousand square miles, which extends from Mount Kenya to the Abyssinian border.

Civilization has made little impact on this part of Africa; there are no settlers; the local tribes live very much as their forefathers did, and the place abounds in wild life of every description.

My husband, George, is Senior Game Warden of this huge territory and our home is on the southern border of the Province, near Isiolo, a small township of about thirty Whites, all of whom are government officials engaged in the task of administering the territory.

George has many duties, such as enforcing the Game Laws, preventing poaching and dealing with dangerous animals that have molested the tribesmen. His work causes him to travel over tremendous distances; these journeys we call safaris. Whenever it is possible I accompany my husband on such trips and in this way I have had unique opportunities of coming to grips with this wild, unchanged land, where life is tough and nature asserts her own laws.

This story has its beginning on one of these safaris. A Boran tribesman had been killed by a man-eating lion. It was reported to George that this animal, accompanied by two lionesses, was living in some nearby hills and so it became his duty to track them down. This was why we were camping far to the north of Isiolo among the Boran tribesmen.

Early on the morning of 1 February, 1956, I found myself in

camp alone with Pati, a rock hyrax who had been living with us as a pet for six and a half years. She looked like a marmot or a guinea pig; though zoologists will have it that on account of the bone structure of its feet and teeth, the hyrax is most nearly related to rhinos and elephants.

Pati snuggled her soft fur against my neck and from this safe position watched all that went on. The country around us was dry with outcrops of granite and only sparse vegetation; all the same there were animals to be seen, for there were plenty of gerenuk and other gazelles, creatures that have adapted themselves to these dry conditions and rarely, if ever, drink.

Suddenly I heard the vibrations of a car; this could only mean that George was returning much earlier than expected. Soon our Land Rover broke through the thornbush and stopped near our tents, and I heard George shout: 'Joy, where are you? Quick, I have something for you . . .'

I rushed out with Pati on my shoulder and saw the skin of a lion. But before I could ask about the hunt, George pointed to the back of the car. There were three lion cubs, tiny balls of spotted fur, each trying to hide its face from everything that went on. They were only a few weeks old and their eyes were still covered with a bluish film. They could hardly crawl, nevertheless they tried to creep away. I took them on my lap to comfort them, while George, who was most distressed, told me what had happened. Towards dawn, he and another game warden, Ken, had been guided near to the place where the man-eater was said to lie up. When first light broke they were charged by a lioness who rushed out from behind some rocks. Though they had no wish to kill her, she was very close and the way back was hazardous; so George signalled to Ken to shoot; he hit and wounded her. The lioness disappeared, and when they went forward they found a heavy trail of blood leading upwards. Cautiously, step by step, they went over the crest of the hill till they came to a huge flat rock. George climbed on to it to get a better view, while Ken skirted around below. Then he saw Ken peer under the rock, pause, raise his rifle and fire both barrels. There was a growl; the lioness appeared and came straight at Ken. George could not shoot for Ken was in his line of fire; fortunately a Game Scout who was in a more favourable position fired his rifle and caused the animal to swerve; then George was able to kill her. She was a big lioness in the prime of life, her teats swollen with milk. It was only when he saw this that George realized why she had been so angry and faced them so courageously. Then he blamed himself for not having recognized earlier that her behaviour showed that she was defending her litter.

Now he ordered a search to be made for the cubs; presently he and Ken heard slight sounds coming out of a crack in the rock face. They put their arms down the crevice as far as they could reach; loud infantile growls and snarls greeted this unsuccessful manoeuvre. Next they cut a long hooked stick and after a lot of probing managed to drag the cubs out; they could not have been more than two or three weeks old. They were carried to the car where the two biggest growled and spat during the whole of the journey back to camp. The third and smallest, however, offered no resistance and seemed quite unconcerned. Now the three cubs lay in my lap, and how could I resist making a fuss of them?

To my amazement Pati, who was usually very jealous of any rival, soon came to nestle among them, and obviously accepted them as desirable companions. From that day onwards, the four became inseparable. During these early days Pati was the biggest of the company and also, being six years old, was very dignified compared with the clumsy little velvet bags who couldn't walk without losing their balance.

It was two days before the cubs accepted their first milk. Until then, whatever trick I tried to make them swallow diluted unsweetened Ideal milk only resulted in their pulling up their tiny noses and protesting: 'ng-ng, ng-ng'; very much as we did as children, before we had learned better manners and been taught to say, 'No, thank you.'

Once they had accepted the milk, they could not get enough of it, and every two hours I had to warm it and clean the flexible rubber tube which we had taken from the wireless set to serve as a teat until we were able to get a proper baby's bottle. We had sent at once to the nearest African market, which was about fifty miles away, not only for the teat but also for cod-liver oil, glucose and cases of unsweetened milk and had at the same time sent an SOS to the District Commissioner at Isiolo, about 150 miles away, announcing the arrival there within a fortnight of Three Royal Babies, asking him to be good enough to have a comfortable wooden home made in time for our return.

Within a few days the cubs had settled down and were everybody's pets. Pati, their most conscientious self-appointed nanny, remained in charge; she was devoted to them, and never minded being pulled and trodden on by the three fast-growing little bullies. All the cubs were females. Even at this age each had a definite character: the 'Big One' had a benevolent superiority and was generous towards the others; the second was a clown, always laughing and spanking her milk bottle with both her front paws as she drank, her eyes closed in bliss. I named her Lustica, which means the 'Jolly One'.

The third cub was the weakling in size, but the pluckiest in spirit. She pioneered all round, and was always sent by the others to reconnoitre when something looked suspicious to them. I called her Elsa, because she reminded me of someone of that name.

In the natural course of events Elsa would probably have been

6

the throw-out of the pride.* The average number of cubs in a litter is four, of which one usually dies soon after birth and another is often too weak to be reared. It is for this reason that one usually sees only two cubs with a lioness. Their mother looks after them till they are two years old. For the first year she provides their food; she regurgitates it, thus making it acceptable to them. During the second year the cubs are allowed to take part in the hunting, but they get severely disciplined if they lose their self-control. Since at this time they are unable to kill on their own, they have to rely for their food on what may be left over from a kill by the full-grown lions of the pride. Often very little remains for them, so they are usually in a bad, scruffy condition at this age. Sometimes they can't bear the hunger; then either they break through the line of gorging adults and are likely to be killed, or they leave the pride, in small groups, and, because they do not yet know how to kill properly, often run into trouble. Nature's law is harsh and lion have to learn the hard way from the beginning.

The quartet – Pati and the three cubs – spent most of the day in the tent under my camp bed; this evidently seemed to them a safe place and the nearest thing they could find to their natural nursery. They were by nature house-trained and always took great care to reach the sand outside. There were a few accidents during the first days, but afterwards, on the rare occasions when a little pool disgraced their home, they miaowed and made comical grimaces of disgust. In every way they were wonderfully clean and had no smell except for a very pleasant one like honey – or was it cod-liver oil? Their tongues were already as rough as

*A 'pride' is a loose term used to describe the association of more than two lions. It may consist of one or more families living together with some adults, or of a number of adults living together for the purpose of hunting in combination, in contradistinction to a pair of lions or a solitary lion.

sandpaper; as they grew older we could feel them, even through our khaki clothes, when they licked us.

When, after two weeks, we returned to Isiolo, our Royal Babies had a palace awaiting them, everyone came to see them and they received a royal welcome. They loved Europeans and especially small children, but had a marked dislike of Africans; the only exception was a young Somali, called Nuru. He was our garden boy; now we appointed him guardian and lion-keeper in chief. The post pleased him for it raised his social status; it also meant that when the cubs got tired of romping all over the house and its surroundings and preferred to sleep under some shady bush, he was able to sit near them for long hours, watching to see that no snakes or baboons molested them,

For twelve weeks we kept them on a diet of unsweetened milk mixed with cod-liver oil, glucose, bone-meal and a little salt. Soon they showed us that they only required three-hourly feeds, and then gradually the intervals became longer.

By now their eyes were fully opened, but they could not yet judge distances and often missed their target. To help them over this difficulty, we gave them rubber balls and old inner tubes to play with – the latter were perfect for tug-of-war games. Indeed, anything made of rubber, or that was soft and flexible, fascinated them. They would try to take the inner tube from each other, the attacker rolling sideways onto the possessor, pressing her weight between the end of the tube and its owner. If no success was achieved by this method, the rivals would simply pull with all their might. Then, when the battle had been won, the victor would parade with the trophy in front of the others and provoke an attack. If this invitation was ignored, the rubber would be placed in front of their noses, while the owner pretended to be unaware that it might be stolen from her.

Surprise was the most important element in all their games.

They stalked each other – and us – from the earliest age and knew by instinct how to do it properly.

They always attacked from the rear; keeping under cover, they crouched, then crept slowly towards the unsuspecting victim until the final rush was made at flying speed and resulted in the attacker landing with all her weight on the back of her quarry, throwing it to the ground. When we were the object of such an attack we always pretended to be unaware of what was going on; obligingly we crouched down and looked the other way until the final onslaught took place. This delighted the cubs.

Pati always wanted to be in the game, though, as the cubs were soon three times her size, she took good care to keep out of the way of heavy spankings and to avoid being squashed by her charges. In all other circumstances she retained her authority by sheer character; if the cubs became too aggressive she put them in their places by just turning round and facing them. I admired her spirit, for, small as she was, it needed a lot of courage to convince them of her fearlessness; the more so that her only defences were her sharp teeth, quick reactions, intelligence and pluck.

She had come to us when she was newly born, and had entirely adapted her life to ours. Unlike her cousin the tree hyrax, she was not a nocturnal animal, and at night she would sleep round my neck like a fur. She was a vegetarian but had a craving for alcohol and for the strongest spirits at that; whenever the opportunity arose she would pull the bottle over, extract the cork and swig the liquor. As this was very bad for Pati's health, not to mention her morale, we took every precaution to prevent any indulgence in whisky or gin.

Her excretory habits were peculiar; rock hyraxes always use the same place, for preference the edge of a rock; at home Pati invariably perched herself on the rim of the lavatory seat, and thus situated presented a comical sight. On safari where no such refinements were provided for her, she was completely bewildered, so we had eventually to rig up a small lavatory for her.

I never found a flea or a tick on her, so at first I was puzzled by her habit of constantly scratching herself. She had round toe-nails, like those of a miniature rhino, on her well-padded feet; four toes in front and three behind. On the inner toe of her hind legs there was a claw known as the grooming claw. With this she used to keep her fur sleek and her care for her coat explained her constant scratchings.

Pati had no visible tail; she had a gland along the middle of her spine, which was visible as a white patch in her otherwise brindled-grey fur. This gland discharged a secretion and the hair around it used to rise when she became excited by pleasure or alarm. As the cubs grew larger her hair stood up all too frequently owing to the fear which their playful but rough antics caused her. Indeed, had she not always been quick to seek refuge on a windowsill, a ladder or some other high object, she would often have been in danger of being mistaken by them for a rubber ball. Until the cubs came Pati had always been number one among our pets. So I was very touched that she should continue to love the little rascals even though they diverted our visitors' attention from herself.

As the lions became increasingly aware of their strength, they tested it on everything they could find. For instance, a ground-sheet, however large, *had* to be dragged about, and they would set to work in proper feline fashion, placing it under their bodies and pulling it between their front legs, as in later life they would drag a kill. Another favourite game was 'king of the castle'. A cub would jump on to a potato sack and keep her attacker at bay until she was suddenly dethroned by the other sister coming up from behind. The victor was usually Elsa who, seeing the other two locked in combat, made the most of her opportunity.

Our few banana trees were also regarded as delightful toys, and very soon their luxuriant leaves hung in tattered fringes. Tree climbing was another favourite game. The little lions were born acrobats, but often they ventured so high that they could not turn to come down, and we were obliged to rescue them.

When at dawn Nuru let them out, they shot out of doors with a whole night's pent-up energy, and this moment could be compared to the start of a greyhound race. On one such occasion they spotted a tent in which two men who had come to visit us were staying. Within five minutes it was a wreck and we were wakened by the cries of our guests who were vainly trying to rescue their belongings, while the cubs, wild with excitement, dived into the wreckage and reappeared with a variety of trophies – slippers, pyjamas, shreds of mosquito netting. We had to enforce discipline that time with a small stick.

Putting them to bed was also no mean task. Imagine three very naughty little girls, who like all children hated bedtime, but who could run twice as fast as those who were in charge of them and had the added advantage of being able to see in the dark.

We were often obliged to resort to subterfuge. One very successful trick was to tie an old bag to a length of rope and drag it steadily towards and then into the pen – usually they could not resist chasing it.

Outdoor games were all very well but the cubs also developed a fancy for books and cushions. So, to save our library and other possessions, we were eventually obliged to ban them from the house. To effect this we made a shoulder-high door of strong wire on a wooden frame and placed it across the entrance to the veranda. The cubs resented it very much, so to compensate them for their lost playground we hung a tyre from a tree, and this proved to be grand for chewing and also as a swing. Another toy we gave them was an empty wooden honey barrel which made a resounding boom when it was pushed. But best of all was a hessian bag. We filled it with old inner tubes and tied it to a branch, from which it dangled invitingly. It had another rope attached to it, and when the cubs hung on to the bag we pulled and swung them high up into the air; the more we laughed the better they enjoyed the game.

Yet, none of these toys caused them to forget that there was at all times a barrier in front of the veranda and they often came and rubbed their soft noses against the wire.

Late one afternoon some friends had arrived for a sun-downer. Intrigued by the sounds of merriment inside, the cubs soon turned up, but that evening they behaved in a disciplined fashion, there was no nose-rubbing against the wire, all three kept a foot away from it. This exemplary conduct aroused my suspicion, so I got up to investigate its cause. To my horror, I saw a large red spitting cobra between the cubs and the door. In spite of the presence of three lions on one side and of ourselves on the other, it wriggled determinedly across the veranda steps, and by the time we had fetched a shotgun it had disappeared.

No barricades, cobras or prohibitions made Lustica give up her intention of entering the house; repeatedly she tried all the doors. Pressing a handle proved easy enough, even turning a knob could be done, only when we quickly fitted bolts all round was she defeated, and even so I once caught her trying to push the bolt aside with her teeth. Thwarted in her purpose, she had her revenge upon us for about this time she tore the laundry off the clothes line and galloped off into the bush with it.

When the cubs were three months old they had teeth big enough to make it possible for them to eat meat. So now I gave them raw minced meat, which was the best we could do to imitate their mother's regurgitated food. For several days they refused to touch it and pulled grimaces of disgust. Then Lustica made the experiment, and found it to her taste. The others took courage from her and soon there was a fight at every meal. This meant that poor Elsa, who was still weaker than the others, had little chance of getting her fair share, so I kept the titbits for her and used to take her on to my lap for her meals. She loved this; rolling her head from side to side and closing her eyes, she showed how happy she was. At these times she would suck my thumbs and massage my thighs with her front paws as though she were kneading her mother's belly in order to get more milk. It was during these hours that the bond between us developed. We combined playing with feeding, and my days were happily spent with these charming creatures.

They were lazy by nature and it needed a lot of persuasion to get them to move from a comfortable position. Even the most desirable marrow bone was not worth the effort of getting up, and they would roll into position to get at it by the easiest way. But best of all they liked me to hold their bone for them while they lay on their backs, paws in the air, and sucked at it.

When the cubs went into the bush they often had adventures. One morning I was following them, for I had given them a worming powder and wished to see the result. I saw them a little way off asleep. Suddenly I noticed a stream of black soldier ants approaching them. Indeed some were already climbing up their bodies. Knowing how fiercely these ants will attack anything that lies in their path and how powerful their mandibles are, I was just about to wake up the cubs when the ants changed their direction.

Soon afterwards five donkeys approached and the cubs woke up. This was the first time they had seen such big animals, and they certainly showed the proverbial courage of a lion, for they all charged simultaneously. This put them into such good heart that when, a few days later, our forty pack donkeys and mules came near the house, the three little lions fearlessly put the whole cavalcade to flight.

At five months they were in splendid condition and getting

stronger every day. They were quite free except at night, when they slept in an enclosure of rock and sand which led off from their wooden shelter. This was a necessary precaution, for wild lions, hyenas, jackals and elephants frequently roam round our house and any of these might have killed them.

The more we grew to know the cubs the more we loved them, so it was hard to accept the fact that we could not keep for ever three fast-growing lions. Regretfully we decided that two must go and that it would be better that the two big ones, who were always together and less dependent on us than Elsa, should be the ones to leave. Our African servants agreed with our choice; when asked their opinion they unanimously chose the smallest. Perhaps they were influenced by visions of the future and thought: 'If there must be a lion in the household, then let it be as small as possible.'

As to Elsa we felt that if she had only ourselves as friends she would be easy to train, not only for life at Isiolo but also as a travelling companion on our safaris.

As a home for Lustica and the Big One, we chose the Rotterdam-Blydorp Zoo and made arrangements for them to make the journey by air.

Since they would have to leave from the Nairobi airfield, which was one hundred and eighty miles away, we decided to get them accustomed to motoring, and took them for short daily trips in my one-and-a-half-ton truck, which had a wired box body. We also began to feed them in it, so that they might get used to it and consider it as one of their playpens.

On the last day we padded the car with soft sandbags.

When we drove off, Elsa ran a short way down the drive and then stood with the most mournful expression in her eyes watching the car in which her two sisters were disappearing. I travelled in the back with the cubs and had armed myself with a small first-aid kit fully expecting to be scratched during the long journey. However, my medical precautions were put to shame, for, after an hour of restlessness, the cubs lay on the bags beside me, embracing me with their paws. We travelled like this for eleven hours, delayed by two blow-outs. The lions could not have been more trusting. When we reached Nairobi they looked at me with their large eyes, puzzled to know what to make of all the strange noises and smells. Then the plane carried them off for ever from their native land.

After a few days we received a cable announcing the safe arrival of our cubs in Holland. When I visited them, about three years later, they accepted me as a friendly person and allowed me to stroke them, but they did not recognize me. They live in splendid conditions and, on the whole, I was glad to know that almost certainly they had no recollection of a freer life.

2. Elsa Meets Other Wild Animals

While I was absent in Nairobi George told me that Elsa was very much upset, and never left him for a moment; she followed him around, sat under his office desk, where he was working, and at night slept on his bed. Each evening he took her for a walk, but, on the day of my return, she refused to accompany him and sat herself down expectantly in the middle of the drive. Nothing would move her. Could it have been that she knew I was coming back? If so, to what animal instinct can one attribute such fore-knowledge? Behaviour of this kind is difficult if not impossible to explain.

When I arrived alone she gave me a great welcome but it was heartbreaking to see her searching everywhere for her sisters. For many days to come she gazed into the bush and called for them. She followed us everywhere, evidently fearing that we too might desert her. To reassure her we kept her in the house, she slept on our bed and we were often woken by her rough tongue licking our faces.

As soon as we could make the necessary arrangements we took her on safari in order to break this atmosphere of waiting and distress and luckily she took to all that safari means and loved it as much as we did.

My truck, packed with soft luggage and bedding rolls, was ideal for her to travel in, since, from a comfortable couch, she could watch all that was going on.

We camped by the Uaso Nyiro river whose banks are lined with doum-palms and acacia bush. In the dry season the shallow waters flow slowly down to the Lorain swamp, passing some rapids and forming many deep pools, which are full of fish.

Near our camp there were rocky ridges; Elsa explored their clefts, sniffed among the rocks and usually ended by settling herself on the top of some rock from which she could survey the surrounding bush. In the late afternoon the sun turned the country into a blaze of warm colours, then she blended into the reddish stone as though she were a part of it.

This was the most enjoyable part of the day: everything and everyone relaxed after the great heat; the shadows lengthened and became a deep purple until, by the rapid sinking of the sun, all details were extinguished. A faint bird call died gradually away, the world grew silent, all was in suspense, awaiting the darkness and, with it, the awakening of the bush. Then the long-drawn call of the hyenas gave the signal and the hunt began.

I remember one particular evening I secured Elsa to a tree in front of the tents and she started to chew her dinner while I sat in the darkness and listened.

Pati hopped on to my lap and, nestling comfortably, ground her teeth – a habit which I knew indicated that she was happy. A cicada chirruped near the river where rippling waters reflected the rising moon. In the soft darkness above, the stars sparkled brilliantly – and in the Northern Frontier they always seem to me to be twice as big as anywhere else – now I heard a deep vibrating sound like that of distant aircraft – this meant that elephant were making their way to the river. Luckily the wind was in our favour; and the rumbling soon ceased.

Suddenly, the unmistakable grunts of lion became audible. At first they were very far away, then, gradually, they grew louder and louder. What could Elsa be thinking about all this? In fact, she seemed utterly unconcerned at the approach of her own kind. She tore at her meat, gnawing slices off with her molars, then she rolled on her back, all four paws in the air and dozed off, while I sat listening to the chuckling of hyena, the yelping of jackal and the magnificent chorus of the lions.

It is very hot at that season, so Elsa spent part of the day in the water; then, when the sun made this uncomfortable for her she would rest in the reeds, at intervals rolling lazily into the river, where she landed with a great splash. As we knew that crocodiles were plentiful in the Uaso Nyiro this caused us some concern, but none ever approached her.

Elsa was always full of mischief; sharing her fun with us she would splash us whenever she found us off our guard, or she would jump quickly out of the water, pounce on us, wet as she was, and we would find ourselves rolling in the sand with our cameras, field glasses and rifles pressed down by her heavy dripping body. She used her paws in a variety of ways. She would use them in gentle caresses, but she could also deliver a playful well-aimed smack at full speed, and she knew a little ju-jitsu trick which unfailingly laid us flat on our backs. No matter how prepared we were for the act, she would give just a small twist to our ankles with her paw and down we went.

Elsa was very particular about her claws; certain trees with a rough bark provided her with the means of sharpening them and she scratched away, leaving deep lines, until she was satisfied with the result of the operation.*

Elsa was not afraid of the sound of a shot and she grew to know that 'bang' meant a dead bird. She loved retrieving, especially guinea fowl, whose quills she crunched, though she very rarely ate the flesh and never the feathers. The first bird was always hers; she would carry it proudly in her mouth till she found this uncomfortable, then she placed it at my feet and looked at me, as though to say, 'Please carry it for me,' then, so long as I dangled it in front of her nose, she trotted good-naturedly after it.

Whenever she discovered some elephant droppings, she at once rolled in them. Indeed it seemed that she regarded them as an ideal bath powder. She hugged the big balls and rubbed the perfume well into her skin. Rhino droppings she also found attractive, in fact, she liked the droppings of most herbivorous animals, but preferred those of pachyderms. We often wondered about this behaviour – could it come from an instinct to disguise her own scent from the animals that, in a natural state, she would kill and eat? The habit, common to the domestic cat and dog, of rolling in excrement is no doubt a degenerate form of the same instinct. We never saw her roll in the droppings of carnivorous animals.

Elsa was very careful in placing her droppings always a few yards away from the game paths where we usually walked.

One afternoon Elsa rushed off into the bush attracted by the noise of elephant. Soon we heard loud trumpetings and screams and the cackling of guinea fowl as well. In great excitement we awaited the outcome of this meeting. After a while the elephant noises ceased but to make up for it, the guinea fowl raised a most

*In fact she was probably stretching her retractile claw muscles.

alarming clatter. Then, to our amazement, Elsa emerged from a thicket closely followed by a flock of vulturine guinea fowl who seemed determined to chase her away, for, whenever she made an attempt to sit down, they chuckled and cackled, so that she just had to keep going. Only after these bold birds became aware of our presence was she allowed some peace.

During one of our walks Elsa suddenly froze in front of a cluster of sansevieria bush, then leapt in the air and retreated hastily giving us a look which seemed to say, 'Why don't you do like me?' At this moment we saw a large snake between the pointed sword-sharp sansevieria leaves. It was well protected in the impenetrable thicket of blades and we thanked Elsa for her warning.

When we returned to Isiolo, the rains had started. The country was covered with little rivulets and pools. This provided fine fun for Elsa, she splashed in every one of them and, greatly invigorated, proceeded with pouncing leaps to cover us with what she evidently considered to be heavenly mud. This was beyond a joke. We had to make her realize that she had grown too heavy for such light-hearted flying jumps. We explained the situation to her by the judicious use of a small stick. She understood at once, and thereafter we very seldom had to make use of it, though we always carried it as a reminder. By now Elsa also understood the meaning of 'no' and she would obey even when tempted by an antelope.

Often, it was touching to see her torn between her hunting instinct and her wish to please us. Anything moving seemed to her as it would to most dogs, just asking to be chased; but, as yet, her instinct to kill had not fully developed. Of course, we had been careful never to show her her goat meat alive. She had plenty of opportunity of seeing wild animals, but as we were usually with her when this happened, she gave chase merely in play and always came back to us after a short time, rubbed her head against our knees and told us with a low miaow about the game.

We had animals of all kinds around our house. A herd of waterbuck and impala antelope and about sixty reticulated giraffes had been our neighbours for many years; Elsa met them on every walk and they got to know her very well and even allowed her to stalk them to within a few yards before they quietly turned away, and a family of bat-eared foxes got so used to her that we were able to approach to within a few paces of the burrows of these timid animals while their cubs rolled in the sand in front of the entrance holes, guarded by the parent foxes.

Mongooses also provided Elsa with a lot of fun. These little creatures, no bigger than a weasel, live in abandoned termite hills which, made as they are of cement-hard soil, constitute ideal fortresses. Standing as high as eight feet and built with many air funnels, they also provide cool shelters during the heat of the day. About teatime the mongoose comedians leave their stronghold and feed on grubs and insects until it becomes dark, when they return home. That was the hour at which our walks often made us pass them. Elsa would sit absolutely still in front of the anthill besieging them, apparently deriving great satisfaction from seeing the little clowns popping their heads out of the air funnels, only to give a sharp whistle of alarm and disappear like shadows.

But, if the mongooses were fun to tease, the baboons were infuriating. They lived in a leopard-safe dormitory, on a sheer cliff, near our house. There they would spend the night in safety, clinging to the slightest depression in the rock. Before sunset they always retired to this refuge, and the cliff appeared to be covered with black spots. From their safe position they barked and shrieked at Elsa, who could do nothing in retaliation.

It was an exciting moment when the cub met her first elephant, an anxious one too, for poor Elsa had no mother to warn her against these animals who regard lion as the only enemies of their young and therefore sometimes kill them. One day Nuru, who had taken her out for her morning walk, came back panting to say that Elsa was 'playing with an elephant'. We took our rifles and he guided us to the scene. There we saw a great old elephant, his head buried in a bush, enjoying his breakfast. Suddenly Elsa, who had crept up from behind, took a playful swipe at one of his hind legs. A scream of shocked surprise and injured dignity followed this piece of impertinence. Then the elephant backed from the bush and charged. Elsa hopped nimbly out of his way, and quite unimpressed began to stalk him. It was a very funny though an alarming sight, and we could only hope that we should not need to use our guns. Luckily, after a time, both became bored with the game; the old elephant went back to his meal and Elsa lay down, close by, and went to sleep.

During the next few months the cub took every opportunity that came her way to harry elephant, and there were many such occasions for the elephant season was beginning. This meant an annual invasion by herds numbering several hundred animals. The great beasts seemed to be very familiar with the geography of Isiolo and always went to the places where the best maize and Brussels sprouts grew. Apart from this and in spite of a dense African population and motor traffic they behaved very well and gave little trouble. As our home, which is three miles distant from Isiolo, is surrounded by the best browsing, a large number of the invaders come to visit us, and an old rifle range in front of the house has become their favourite playground. At this season, we have therefore to be very careful on our walks, for small groups of elephant are always about. Now, having to protect Elsa as well as ourselves made us all the more alert.

One day at noon Nuru and Elsa returned home followed by a large number of elephant; from our dining-room window we could see them in the bush. We tried to divert her attention but she had turned and was determined to meet the advancing herd. Then, suddenly, she sat down and watched them as they turned away and walked in single file across the rifle range. It was a grand parade as one after another emerged from the bush in which Elsa crouched giving them her scent. She waited until the last of about twenty elephant had crossed then she followed them slowly, her head held in a straight line with her shoulders, her tail outstretched. Suddenly the big bull in the rear turned and, jerking his massive head at Elsa, screamed with a high-pitched trumpeting sound. This war cry did not intimidate her, and she walked determinedly on; so did the big elephant. We went out and, following cautiously, saw glimpses of Elsa and the elephants mingling together in the undergrowth. There were no screams nor any sound of breaking branches, which would have indicated trouble. All the same, we waited anxiously till eventually the cub reappeared looking rather bored with the whole business.

But not all the elephants which Elsa met were so amiable as these. On another occasion she succeeded in starting a colossal stampede. The first thing we heard was tremendous thundering on the rifle range and when we reached the scene we saw a herd of elephant racing downhill, with Elsa close behind them. Finally she was charged by a single bull, but she was much too quick for him and in time he gave up the attack and followed his companions.

Giraffe provided her with great fun too. One afternoon, when we were out with her, she took on fifty. Wriggling her body close to the ground and shivering with excitement, she stalked them, advancing step by step. The giraffes took no notice of her, they just stood and watched her nonchalantly. She looked at them and then back at us, as though she wanted to say, 'Why do you stand there like candlesticks and spoil my stalking?' Finally she got really cross and, rushing full speed at me, knocked me flat.

Towards sunset, we ran into a herd of elephant. The light was failing rapidly but we could just see the shapes of elephant in all directions.

It has always seemed miraculous to me that these colossal animals can move noiselessly through the bush and are thus able to surround one without warning. This time there was no doubt that we were cut off. Wherever we looked for an opening to run through an elephant blocked the way. We tried to hold Elsa's attention, for it was not a moment for her to start one of her games with the giants. But all too soon she spotted them and dashed into their midst, then she was beyond our control. We heard screams and shrill piercing cries; my nerves were on edge, for, however carefully we manoeuvred through the dark bush, there stood an elephant confronting us. At last we managed to make our way out and reached home, but, of course, without Elsa. She only returned much later; apparently she had had great fun and certainly did not understand why I was a nervous wreck.

A euphorbia hedge borders our drive; no ordinary animal will break through it because it contains a caustic latex. If the smallest drop of this substance touches the eye it burns the membrane most painfully and will inflame it for many days. It is therefore given a wide berth by all animals except elephant, who love eating its juicy twigs and after a night's meal leave big open gaps.

Once, when I was feeding Elsa in her enclosure, I heard the unmistakable rumbling of elephant behind this hedge which borders her wooden house and there, sure enough, were five of the giants crunching loudly and making a meal of the only barrier which stood between us. Indeed, at the time I am writing about, the hedge was already a poor sight owing to their attentions.

To add to the excitement of Elsa's life there was now a rhino living close to our house. One evening at dark, when we were returning from a walk, the cub suddenly darted behind the servants' quarters. A tremendous commotion ensued. We went to find out what it was about and saw Elsa and the rhino facing each other. After a few moments of indecision, the rhino, snorting angrily, retreated with the cub in hot pursuit.

The following evening I was walking with Elsa and Nuru, we were late and it was getting dark, when suddenly the Somali grabbed my shoulder, thus preventing me from walking straight into the rhino, which stood behind a bush, facing us. I leapt back and ran. Luckily Elsa, who had not seen the rhino, thought I was playing a game and followed me. This was fortunate for rhinos are unpredictable creatures who are apt to charge anything, including lorries and trains. The next day, however, Elsa had her fun; she chased the animal for two miles across the valley, Nuru loyally panting behind her. After this experience the rhino took itself off to quieter quarters.

By now we had established a routine for Elsa. The mornings were cool; it was then that we often watched the impala antelope leaping gracefully on the rifle range and listened to the chorus of the awakening birds. As soon as it got light Nuru released Elsa and both walked a short distance into the bush. The cub, full of unspent energy, chased everything she could find, including her own tail.

Then, when the sun got warm, she and Nuru settled under a shady tree and Elsa dozed while he read his Koran and sipped tea. Nuru always carried a rifle to protect them both against wild animals but was very good about following our instructions to 'shout before shooting'. He was genuinely fond of Elsa and handled her very well.

About teatime the two of them returned and we took over. First, Elsa had some milk, then we wandered into the hills or walked in the plain; she climbed trees, appeared to sharpen her claws, followed exciting scents or stalked Grant's gazelle and gerenuk, which sometimes played hide and seek with her. Much to our surprise, she was fascinated by tortoises which she rolled over and over; she loved playing, and never did she miss an opportunity of starting a game with us – we were her 'pride' and she shared everything with us.

As darkness fell we returned home and took her to her enclosure, where her evening meal awaited her. It consisted of large quantities of raw meat, mostly sheep and goat; she got her roughage by breaking up the rib bones and the cartilages. As I held her bones for her I would watch the muscles on her forehead moving powerfully. I always had to scratch the marrow out for her; she licked it greedily from my fingers, resting her heavy body upright against my arms. While this went on Pati sat on the windowsill watching us, content to know that soon her turn would come to spend the night cuddled round my neck and that then she would have me to herself.

Till then, I sat with Elsa playing with her, sketching her or reading. These evenings were our most intimate time and I believe that her love for us was mostly fostered in these hours when, fed and happy, she could doze off with my thumb still in her mouth. It was only on moonlight nights that she became restless; then she padded along the wire, listening intently, her nostrils quivering to catch the faintest scent which might bring a message from the mysterious night outside. When she was nervous her paws became damp and I could often judge her state of mind by holding them in my hands.

3. Elsa Goes to the Indian Ocean

Elsa was now a year old, she had changed her teeth and I had been allowed to wiggle out one milk canine, while she helpfully held her head quite still. To gnaw off her meat she usually used her molars, not her incisors, but her very rough tongue, covered with minute quills, she employed for rasping it from the bone. Her saliva was rich and very salty.

Pati was now getting old and I kept her as quiet as I could.

Our local leave was due and we planned to spend it by the sea, on a remote part of the coast, close to a small Barjun fishing village and not far from the Somali border. The nearest white population was ninety miles south in Lamu. It would be a perfect place for Elsa, for we could camp on the beach, away from people, with miles of clean sand around us, and a bushy hinterland behind would provide shade.

We took two friends with us, one a young District Officer, Don, and the other, Herbert, an Austrian writer who was our guest.

It was a long journey over bad tracks and it took us three days. I usually went ahead with Elsa in my truck, George and the others following in two Land Rovers with Pati. The country through which we passed was dry, sandy and hot.

One day the road became a network of camel spoor. When it was getting dark I lost my way, ran out of petrol and, hoping that George would follow my tracks, waited for him. Only after several hours did I see his lights. When he arrived, he said that our camp was already pitched some miles away and told me we must hurry back as he had left Pati very ill with heat stroke.

He had given her some brandy to strengthen her but had little hope. The miles back to the camp seemed endless to me. I found Pati in a coma. Her heart was beating so rapidly that it was improbable that it would stand the strain much longer. Gradually she became semi-conscious, recognized me and made a weak attempt to grind her teeth. This had always been her way of showing her affection; it was her last message to me. Later she grew calm and her heart slowed down till it had almost ceased to beat; then suddenly her little body quivered in a last convulsion, stretched stiffly and collapsed.

Pati was dead.

I held her close. Her warm body took a long time to cool.

I thought of the many moments of happiness she had given me in the seven and a half years during which we had shared our lives. On how many safaris had she been my companion. She had been with me to Lake Rudolf, where the heat had been a great strain on her; to the coast, where she had spent many hours cramped in a dhow; to Mount Kenya, whose moorlands she had loved; to the Suguta valley and Mount Nyiro, where she had cleverly hung on to the mule which I rode across precipitous tracks; she had been with me to camping places all over Kenya, when I was painting the African tribes. Sometimes for months on end she had been my only friend.

How tolerant she was of the bushbabies, squirrels and mongooses which came and went in our household, and how she loved the lions. At meals she sat by my plate and took the titbits gently from my hand.

She had become part of me.

Now I wrapped her in a cloth, fastened her harness and leash round it, and carried her some distance away from the camp. Here I dug her grave. The night was hot and the moonlight softened the shadows in the wide plain around us. All was still and so peaceful.

The next morning we drove on and I was glad that the bad road held my attention.

It was late afternoon when we reached the coast and fishermen who came out to greet us told us that a lion was causing a great deal of trouble. Almost nightly it raided their goats and they very much hoped that George would kill it.

There was no time to make a proper camp, so we put our beds out in the open. I was the only woman among four Europeans and six Africans and I placed mine at a little distance away. Elsa was secured in my truck next to me. Soon everyone went to sleep except myself. Suddenly I heard a dragging noise and flashed my torch; there, a few yards from my bed, was a lion with the skin of the buck we had shot that afternoon in its mouth.

For a second I wondered if it might be Elsa, but then I saw her in the back of my car. I looked again, the lion was still staring at me and now he was growling.

I moved slowly towards George and, stupidly, turned my back on the lion. We were only a few paces from each other and I felt that he was following me, so I turned and shone my torch into his face; by then we were about eight yards apart. I walked backwards towards the campbeds where the men were snoring. Only George woke up. When I told him that a lion was following me he said, 'Nonsense, probably a hyena or a leopard'. All the same he picked up his heavy rifle and went in the direction I indicated and there, sure enough, he soon saw two eyes and heard the growl of a lion. He had little doubt that this was the troublesome lion we had been told about; so he tied a large piece of meat to a tree some thirty yards in front of the car and decided to sit up and wait for him.

After a short time we heard a clatter coming from behind the cars where our evening meal had been cooked.

George crept round, levelled his rifle and flashed his torch there; he saw the lion sitting amongst the pots and pans finishing off the remains of our dinner. He pressed the trigger, only a click sounded, he pressed it again with the same result. He had forgotten to load the rifle! The lion got up and sauntered off. Sheepishly George loaded the rifle and went back to his post.

Much later he heard something tugging at the meat and switched on the car lights; then he saw the lion brilliantly illuminated and shot him through the heart.

He was a young maneless lion, typical of the coast region.

When light broke we investigated his pugmarks and discovered that he had first seized the skin of the antelope, then dragged it to within twenty yards of my bed where he had eaten his meal. When replete he had made a leisurely round of the camp. Of all these goings-on Elsa had been an interested spectator, but she had never uttered a sound.

As soon as the sun was up the whole camp trooped down to the water's edge to introduce her to the Indian Ocean. The tide was receding; at first she was nervous of the unaccustomed roar and rush of the waves. Then she sniffed cautiously at the water, bit at the foam; finally, she put her head down to drink, but her first mouthful of salt water made her wrinkle her nose and pull grimaces of disgust. However, when she saw the rest of the party enjoying a bathe, she decided to trust us and join in the fun. Very soon she became quite water-crazy. Rain pools and shallow rivers had always excited and invigorated her, but this great ocean was a real heaven for her. She swam effortlessly, far out of her depth; ducked us and splashed the water with her tail and ensured that we too swallowed mouthfuls of salt water before we were able to escape from her antics.

She followed us everywhere, so I usually stayed behind when the others went fishing; otherwise she would have swum out after our boat.

But occasionally I could not resist the temptation to skindive through this world of luminous iridescent colours and fairy shapes, then I left Elsa with someone to keep her company. Usually they rested in the shade of a mangrove tree close to the camp. When passing fishermen got to know of this they made a big detour, hitched up their loin cloths and waded into the sea. They would have felt less reassured had they known what an amphibious creature she was.

She loved walking along the beach, where she chased the coconuts bobbing in the surf, getting splashed and swamped by the waves in the process. Sometimes we tied a string to a coconut and swung it in a circle above our heads while she jumped high up after it as it flew past. She soon discovered that digging in the sand was a most rewarding game, since the deeper the hole the wetter and cooler it became and therefore the nicer to roll in. Often she dragged long strands of seaweed along, entangling herself in it till she looked like some odd sea monster. But crabs provided her with the best fun of all. Towards sunset the beach became alive with these little pink creatures shuffling sideways in order to get from their holes to the water, only to be washed ashore again a moment later. Persistently they shuffled, only to be thrown back again, until finally their patience was rewarded and they grabbed some piece of delicious seaweed and pulled it into their hole before the next wave was able to carry it off. Elsa did not make things easier for the busy creatures; she would rush from one to the other, invariably getting nipped in the nose, but undeterred she pounced again, only to be nipped once more. To the crabs' credit be it recorded that of all Elsa's opponents they were the only ones, not excluding elephants, buffaloes and rhinos, which stood their ground. Sideways-on they waited in front of their holes, one pink claw erect, and, however cunningly Elsa tried to outwit them, they were always quicker than she was and her soft nose got punctured again.

Feeding Elsa became quite a problem, for the local fishermen were quick to recognize the source of income which she represented and the price of goats soared. In fact, for some time, she kept the villagers in luxuries hitherto unknown to them.

However, in the end, she had her revenge. The herdsmen never guarded their animals, which straggled along all day in the bush, an easy prey to leopard and lion. One evening, we were out on the beach, long after bedtime for goats, when Elsa suddenly darted into a bush; there followed a loud bleat and then silence. She must have scented a lone straggler, pounced on the goat and squashed it with her weight. But, never having killed before, she did not know what to do next and when we arrived she plainly asked us for help. While Elsa held the animal down George quickly shot the beast. As no complaint was made by the owner for its loss, which was no doubt credited to the usual kill of some wild lion, we kept quiet about the incident. Had we done otherwise every moribund goat from a day's march north and south of the camp would have been left out for Elsa to devour so that compensation might be claimed. We overcame our qualms of conscience with the thought that George had rid the district of its chief goat-eater and also with the recollection of the exorbitant prices we had paid for the most miserable little beasts which we had bought on Elsa's behalf.

Towards the end of our holiday George developed malaria; as he was anxious to go fishing he now dosed himself with mepacrine and, before he had given the drug time to work, he went skindiving, with the result that he became seriously ill.

Returning home one evening from a walk along the beach with Elsa, as I neared the camp I heard an alarming howling and screaming. After securing Elsa in my truck, I rushed to the tent, where I found George limp and collapsed in a chair. He was emitting frightful groans and yelling for his revolver, for me, cursing Elsa and shouting that he wanted to shoot himself. Even in his semi-conscious condition he recognized me, seized me with an iron grip and said that now that I was there he could relax and die. I was most alarmed; the boys stayed a few yards away looking very frightened. Our friend stood helpless, clutching a stick with which he proposed to club George if he should become violent.

In whispers, they told me that, quite suddenly, George had started to gesticulate wildly, shrieking for me and shouting for his revolver to kill himself. Luckily I had returned soon after he had collapsed. The main thing now was to carry him to his bed and try to calm him. He hung lifeless and icy cold in our arms as we moved him. Although my heart was heavy with fear, I began talking to him in a quiet voice, telling him about our walk along the beach, about the fish we were going to eat for dinner, about a shell I had found, and made fun of his strange behaviour. But all the time I wondered whether he were not going to die. Like a child, he responded to my efforts to soothe him and calmed down. But his temples grew grey, his nostrils fell in and his eyes closed. He whispered that an icy current was creeping up his legs towards his heart, that his arms were equally lifeless and cold, and that when both icewaves met at his heart, he would die. Suddenly he was seized by panic, clutched me with a desperate strength, as though hanging on to life. I poured brandy between his dry lips, stroked him gently and, trying to divert his mind towards some action associated with the near future, told him about his birthday cake which I had brought all the way from Isiolo, and said that we should eat it that night, as soon as he was well enough to get up.

Before he fell into an exhausted sleep, the night had passed; during that time he had had several relapses, during which his brain worked with frightening rapidity while he uttered sense-less words. The next morning I sent to Lamu for a doctor, but the competent Indian who came could do little for George except order sleeping drugs and give him confidence that he was going to recover provided he did not go goggling again.

When he had sufficiently recovered we returned to Isiolo.

4. Safari to Lake Rudolf

One day, soon after our return to Isiolo, I noticed that Elsa walked with difficulty, and was in pain. It was getting dark and a long distance of steep rocky slopes, covered with thornbush, lay between us and home. Soon Elsa could walk no farther. George thought that she might be suffering from constipation and suggested that I should give her an enema on the spot. That meant returning home and then driving to Isiolo to get what was needed. While I did this, he remained with Elsa.

By the time everything was ready it was dark, then I had to struggle up the hills, carrying warm water, an enema and a lamp. It is one thing to administer an enema in a vet's surgery, but it is quite another to do this amongst thorn-covered bush and in the dark, to a wildly scratching lion.

I congratulated myself when I had inserted a pint of liquid into poor Elsa, but that was all that she would tolerate and it was, of course, far too little to produce any results, so we had no choice left but to carry her home.

Again, I stumbled back to the house, where I collected a camp bed, to use as a stretcher, a few torches and six boys to act as porters. The procession then moved up the hill.

When we arrived, Elsa rolled at once on to the bed where, lying on her back, she showed that she was thoroughly enjoying this queer mode of transport. Indeed it seemed as though she had never travelled in any other way. But as she weighed at least 180 lb her pleasure was not shared by the porters as they sweated and panted, struggling down hill, stopping every few minutes to rest.

Elsa made no attempt to leave the stretcher, but she had great fun giving an occasional nip on the bottom to the nearest boy, as if to urge him on.

When, at last, we reached home, all of us – except Elsa – quite exhausted, we were obliged to roll her off the bed, for she had no intention of leaving it voluntarily.

Later we discovered that hookworm was the cause of her trouble. She must have got infected with it when we were on the coast.

It was not long after she had recovered that George had to deal with two man-eating lions which, during the past three years, had killed or mauled about twenty-eight people of the Boran tribe. Elsa and I accompanied George on this expedition which proved difficult and dangerous. Twenty-four days passed before he was able to kill the two lions. During this period the paradox of the situation often came clearly to my mind: here we were hunting dangerous man-eating lions by day and by night, yet, when we were returning exhausted and defeated we looked forward to being with Elsa who compensated us for the fatigue and the strain by her affection. Lion versus lion?

Elsa was now eighteen months old and I noticed, for the first time, that she had, temporarily as it proved, developed a strong smell. She had two glands, known as anal glands, under the root of her tail; these exuded a strong-smelling secretion which she ejected with her urine against certain trees and although it was her own smell she always pulled up her nose in disgust at it.

One afternoon, after we had returned to Isiolo, we met a herd of eland. Elsa instantly began to stalk them. These large antelopes were grazing on a steep slope and had several young amongst them. One eland cow waited for her and before she got too close to the calves distracted her attention from the young-sters by playing hide and seek with her in the bushes. In this way, she kept her engaged until the herd and the calves had safely disappeared beyond the hillside. Then the eland cow galloped off at high speed, leaving poor Elsa standing.

Another case of animal diplomacy was fascinating to watch. We had taken Elsa up a hill behind the house, from the top of which we saw a herd of about eighty elephants with many small calves feeding below. Elsa saw them too and before we could shout 'No' she went off downhill and, a few moments later, was advancing cautiously towards the herd.

Nearest to her was a cow with a small calf. Elsa stalked it with great cunning, but the mother elephant was well aware of her intention. We watched, tense with anxiety, expecting a charge, but to our surprise the mother elephant moved quietly between Elsa and the calf, pushing it slowly towards some big bulls, keeping our lioness on the far side. Disappointed, Elsa looked for the next best playmate and used careful cover to join two feeding bulls. But again she was ignored. Then she tried to provoke other small groups of elephants, advancing to within a few yards of them. Still nothing happened. The sun was getting low; we shouted to her but she obstinately disregarded our calls. Finally we had no alternative but to return home without her. She certainly intended to take her time and we could only rely on her intelligence to keep her out of trouble.

I waited for her inside the enclosure and became more and more worried. What could we do? Chaining Elsa up during the elephant season would only frustrate and infuriate her; indeed, it might end by making her dangerous. We had to let her learn her limitations by experience, allow her to weigh the fun against the boredom, or danger, of playing with these big animals. In doing so perhaps she would come to lose interest in them. By this time she was three hours overdue and I feared an accident, then suddenly I heard her familiar hnk-hnk and in she came, very thirsty indeed, yet before she went to her water bowl she licked my face and sucked my thumbs as if to tell me how glad she was to be with me again. She smelled strongly of elephant, and I could well imagine how close she had been to them, and that she had rolled in their droppings. By the way she flung herself with a crash to the ground, I could also judge how tired she was. I felt very humble; here was my friend just returned from a world that was utterly denied to me, yet she was as affectionate as ever. Did she have any realization of the extraordinary link she was between the two worlds?

Of all animals, giraffe were undoubtedly her favourites. Often she stalked them until both sides became tired. Then she would sit down waiting for the giraffe to return and sure enough, after a time they would approach again, advancing slowly step by step, facing Elsa, looking at her with their large sad eyes, while their slender necks arched in an inquisitive way. Then usually, browsing at their favourite acacia seeds as they went by, they would walk peacefully away. But, sometimes, Elsa would drive them in proper lion fashion. After spotting them, she would turn off at right angles down wind, crouching with her belly close to the ground, every muscle quivering, until she had encircled the herd, then she would drive it towards us. No doubt we were expected to wait in ambush and kill the victims she had so cleverly rounded up for us.

Other animals also attracted her attention; for instance, one day she sniffed the air and then dashed into a thick bush. Soon afterwards we heard crashing and snorting coming straight at us! Quickly we jumped out of the way as a warthog thundered past, with Elsa hot on his heels. Both disappeared at lightning speed and for a long time we heard them breaking through the woods. We were very worried for Elsa's safety, as the warthog has formidable tusks which he can use to kill, till she returned. The winner of the chase rubbed her head against our knees and told us about her new playmate.

Our next safari was to take us to Lake Rudolf, a stretch of

brackish water, some 180 miles long, reaching to the Ethiopian frontier. We were to be away for seven weeks and most of the time we should travel on foot with pack donkeys and mules. It would be Elsa's first experience of a foot safari in the company of donkeys and we could only hope that both sides would accept each other. We were quite a party: George and myself; Julian, a Game Warden from a neighbouring territory; Herbert, who was again our guest; as well as Game Scouts, drivers and personal servants; six sheep to feed Elsa on the way; and thirty-five donkeys and mules. The pack animals were sent off three weeks ahead to meet us on the shores of the Lake, while we travelled the distance of about 300 miles by motor transport.

It was a big convoy: two Land Rovers, my one-and-a-half-ton truck with Elsa in the back of it, and two three-ton lorries. The latter were necessary to enable us to carry, as well as the men, sufficient food and petrol for the weeks we should be away, also eighty gallons of water. Our first 180 miles led us through the sandy, hot and dusty plains of the Kaisut desert. Then we ascended the volcanic slopes of the Marsabit mountain, an isolated volcanic mass rising to 4,500 feet out of the surrounding desert. Clothed in thick, cool, lichen-covered forest, and often enveloped in mist, it presented a welcome contrast to the hot arid country below. It is a game paradise and harbours elephant carrying some of the finest ivory in Africa, besides rhino, buffalo, the greater kudu, lion and lesser game. Here was the last administrative post.

From now on we made our way through practically uninhabited country and were cut off from any contact with the outside world. Nothing broke the monotony of the sand gullies and lava ridges. The only incident was a crash which nearly broke my car in half. One back wheel left us and we came to an abrupt stop. Poor Elsa; it took hours to repair the damage and she had to spend the time inside the car, since it provided the only shade from the fierce sun which she hated. However, she was most co-operative and although she did not like strange Africans, obligingly put up with the jabbering crowd of our people, who pressed close to the car trying to be helpful. When we were mobile again, we climbed up the most shocking track into the Hurri hills on the Ethiopian border. These are desolate and, though higher than Marsabit, attract less moisture. An enervating gale blows across their slopes and, in consequence, they are barren of forest. Elsa was quite bewildered by the fierce wind and had to spend the night in the truck, well protected with canvas curtains from its icy blast.

George's purpose in visiting these hills was to examine the game situation and to see whether there were any signs of poaching by the Gabbra tribesmen. After a few days spent in patrolling the country we turned westwards, crossing the most depressing, desolate lava country, where sharp rocks jerked the car mercilessly, and Elsa had a tough time as we pushed the vehicles through deep sandy river beds or ground our way carefully between boulders, jostling against the large stones. At last we came out on to the Chalbi desert, a dry ancient lake bed some eighty miles in length, with a smooth fairly firm surface on which a vehicle can travel at full speed. Mirages are the most remarkable feature of this area: great expanses of water with palm trees reflected in their surface appear but swiftly vanish as one approaches them. Here, too, gazelles assume the proportions of elephants and appear to be walking on the waters. It is a land of thirst and grilling heat. At the western end of Chalbi lies the oasis of North Horr, where there is a police post, and where thousands of camels, sheep and goats belonging to the Rendile tribe come to water. Another remarkable sight to be seen there in the morning is that of thousands of sand grouse flying in to drink at the few pools. Soon, as there was nothing to keep us at North Horr, we filled our water containers and continued on our way.

At last, after two hundred and thirty miles of hustling and bumping, we reached Loyongalane, an oasis of fresh-water springs in a grove of doum-palms near the south of Lake Rudolf. Here we found our donkeys waiting for us. We took Elsa at once to the lake, which was two miles distant. She rushed into the water as though to throw off the strain of the journey and plunged in right among the crocodiles, which are very plentiful in Lake Rudolf. Luckily they were not aggressive, but all the same we tried to scare them away. During our safari, their floating, horny shapes, silhouetted all along the shore, were to make bathing, at least for us, a dubious pleasure.

At Loyongalane we established our base camp and spent the next three days in repairing saddlery and packing donkey loads. Each load weighed approximately fifty pounds, two to each donkey. At last all was ready. There were eighteen donkeys loaded with food and camping gear, four with water containers, one riding mule for anyone who went weak or lame, and five spare donkeys. I was worried about what Elsa's attitude towards the donkeys was going to be. She watched all our repacking with restrained interest, then when we started loading she had to be chained up, for the sight of so much lovely meat braying and kicking and rolling in the sand in an endeavour to throw off unwanted burdens, with shouting Africans rushing about trying to bring order into the chaos, made her tense with excitement. The main cavalcade started off in the morning and we followed with Elsa later in the day when it was cooler. Our march was northwards along the shore line. Elsa was very excited and rushed like a puppy from one to the other of us, then she dashed in among the flocks of flamingoes, retrieved a duck we had shot, and finally went swimming in the lake, where one of us had to cover her with a rifle on account of the crocodiles. Later, when we passed a herd of camels, I was obliged to put her on the chain; this made her furious and her efforts to meet these new friends nearly pulled my arms off. I, however, had no wish to see a stampeding, panic-stricken herd of camels falling over each other, bellowing, gurgling, legs intertwined, and Elsa in their midst. Fortunately these were the last livestock we met along the shore.

When night fell, we saw the fires of the camp by the lake. Again I put Elsa on the chain for fear that she might have enough energy left to chase our donkeys. When we arrived we found camp already pitched and everything laid out for dinner. While we had a belated sundowner we decided that at dawn each morning the lion party – George and I, Nuru, a Game Scout as guide – and Elsa would start off, while camp was being struck and the animals saddled and loaded. In this way, we would benefit by the cooler hours and the animals would follow at a safe distance, dispensing us from any need to keep Elsa on the chain. Then about nine thirty, we would look for a shady place where we could rest during the heat of the day and where the donkeys could get some grazing. As soon as these were sighted, we would put Elsa on the chain. In the afternoon we would reverse our routine, the donkey party leaving two hours before the lion party and pitching camp before dark. We kept to this routine during the whole safari and it worked out very well, for it kept Elsa and the donkeys apart, except during the midday rest, when she was chained up and very sleepy. As it turned out, both parties soon learned to take each other for granted and to accept that everything which formed part of the safari must be tolerated.

We found that Elsa marched well until about nine in the morning, then she began to feel the heat and kept stopping wherever a rock or bush gave shade. In the afternoon, she was reluctant to move before five; after that, once her pads had hardened, she could have gone on all night. On an average she trotted from seven to eight hours daily, and kept in wonderful condition. She dipped herself in the lake and swam as often as possible, often only six or eight feet from the crocodiles; no shouting or waving on my part would bring her back till she felt like doing so. Usually we reached camp between eight and nine in the evening; often the donkey party would fire Very lights to guide us.

The second day out we left the last human habitation behind us; it was a small fishing village of the primitive El Molo tribe. This tribe numbers about eighty souls who live almost entirely on fish, varied occasionally by crocodile and hippo meat. As a result of this badly balanced diet and of inter-breeding many of them are deformed and show signs of rickets. Perhaps also owing to malnutrition or, more likely, to the fact that the lake water contains a high proportion of natron and other minerals, they also suffer from bad teeth and gums. They are a friendly and generous people and a stranger is always welcomed with a gift of fresh fish. Their fishing is mostly carried on by means of nets, which they make out of doum-palm fibre, the only fibre that does not rot in the alkaline water; while the giant Nile perch, which runs up to 200 pounds and over, and crocodile and hippo, are harpooned from rafts made from three palm logs lashed roughly together. These unwieldy craft are poled along in the shallows and never venture far out for fear of the violent winds which often sweep the lake and sometimes attain a velocity of over ninety miles an hour. Indeed it is the wind which makes life thoroughly uncomfortable for any traveller in this region. It is impossible to pitch a tent, food is either blown out of the plate before one can eat it, or so covered with grit as to be inedible. Sleep is almost impossible because of the tearing gusts which fill eyes, nose and ears with sand and almost lift up the bed. Yet, in spite of these torments, the lake has real beauty in its quieter moments, and exercises a fascination difficult to describe, which makes one want to return again and again.

The first ten days took us along its shore. The country around was grim: lava and more lava, only the consistency of the lava differed. Sometimes it was cinder-fine dust, at others sharp-edged so that our feet became sore from slipping and sliding over the uneven ground. In certain places there was deep sand, and as we waded along each step was an effort. Or again, we had to make our way across coarse grit or pebbles and at all times the hot wind blew, sapping our energy and making us feel dizzy. There was little vegetation, only a few thorny meagre plants which pricked, and razor-edged grass, which cut the skin.

To keep Elsa's paws in good condition, I had often to grease them, an act which she seemed to understand and to like. During the midday rest, I usually lay on my camp bed so as to be able to relax in more comfort than the hard pebbles provided. Elsa saw the point of this, adopted my idea and joined me. Soon I could consider myself fortunate if she left me a small corner, and sometimes I was unlucky and had to sit on the ground while she stretched herself full-length on the bed. But as a rule we curled up together on the bed, I hoping that it might not break beneath our combined weight. During our long marches Nuru always carried drinking water and a bowl for Elsa; she had her evening meal towards nine o'clock and afterwards slept heavily, tied up near my bed.

One evening we lost our way and were guided by Very lights to the camp, which we reached late at night. Elsa seemed exhausted, so I left her unchained to recover; but although she looked sleepy she suddenly rushed at full speed to the thorn enclosure in which the donkeys spent the night, and crashed through the fence in real feline style. Braying, panic and pande-monium ensued and before we could intervene, all the donkeys had bolted into the darkness. Luckily, we soon caught Elsa and I gave her a good hiding. She seemed to understand that she deserved it and, as far as she could, showed that she was sorry. I felt guilty at having underestimated her natural instinct and the tremendous temptation that a nice-smelling donkey herd must be to her, especially at an hour when the hunting spirit is most alive in wild animals.

Luckily only one poor donkey had received scratches and these were not serious. I dressed them and they soon healed, but this episode was a warning to me never to leave her unguarded.

Fish were plentiful and, as a rule, George and Julian were able to keep the camp supplied with delicious fish called giant *tilapia*, a *spécialité* unique to Lake Rudolf. These they caught either by rod or line, or by stunning them with a rifle bullet. The Game Scouts seemed to prefer the ugly-looking catfish which lay in the shallows and which they were able to kill with sticks and stones. Elsa was always ready to join in the fun and sometimes she would retrieve a catfish, soon to drop it and wrinkle up her nose in disgust. One day we saw Nuru, who always carried a shotgun, lifting it up by the barrel and clubbing a catfish with it. He did this with such force that the stock split through in many places, broke and projected at right angles to the barrel. Nuru was so delighted with his catfish that he was quite oblivious to the damage he had done. When George pointed it out to him, he replied calmly, 'Oh, Mungo [God] will help you to get another gun.' Elsa, however, took her revenge, for she ran off with Nuru's sandals which he had left on the shore, and galloped away with them; it was a funny sight to watch the two trying to outwit each other. In the end, the sandals were in poor shape when their owner got them back.

Before we reached Alia Bay some hundred miles to the north it was necessary to cross the long Longondoti range. In several places the hills fall straight into the lake, so the donkeys with their bulky loads had to make a detour inland, while the lion party struggled across the rocks and kept to the shore. At one point we looked like being defeated by a difficult corner, for here Elsa, to wade round the point, had the choice of either jumping down a fifteen-foot cliff, covered with a slippery deposit on which it was impossible for her to get any grip, to land in the shallow water below, or scrambling down an equally steep rock to land in the foaming waters which crashed against its foot. The water was in fact only about her own depth, but the foam made it look very dangerous and she did not know what to do. She tried every ledge of the rock, padding desperately on her small platform, till bravely she jumped into the lashing waves and finally, coaxed by us, soon reached dry ground. It was touching to see how delighted and proud she was of her achievement and also at having pleased us.

For most of the way we had to drink and to cook with brackish lake water which, although harmless and so soft that it is beautiful for bathing and does not need soap for washing, has a disagreeable taste and tainted all our food. So it was indeed a pleasant surprise to find a little spring of fresh water at the foot of the hills called Moiti.

The route we took along the western foot of these hills had, so far as we knew, never before been travelled by a European; the few who had visited this region in the past had kept well to the east. Nine days out of Loyongalane, we camped at the northern end of the hills. As usual, we had sent a party of Game Scouts ahead to spy out the country and keep a lookout for poachers. Early in the afternoon they returned and reported seeing a large body of men in canoes. The only tribe on the lake which possesses proper dugout canoes is the Galubba, a turbulent people, well supplied with rifles, who constantly carry out raids from across the Ethiopian border into our territory, looting and murdering. The band which the Scouts had seen might be either a raiding party, or a poaching and fishing expedition. In any case, they had no right to be there. Elsa and I remained in camp, with four Game Scouts armed with rifles to protect us, while the rest of the party went off to reconnoitre.

When they had reached the top of a ridge which overlooked the bay, they saw three canoes with twelve men on board, close in shore, paddling in the direction of our camp. However, they at once spotted our party, so that by the time George and the other men had reached the water's edge the canoes were a good 200 yards out, making for a small island and paddling madly. They did not appear to have firearms, though, of course, they might have had rifles concealed in the canoes. Looking through glasses, George saw a body of at least forty men on the island and several canoes drawn up on its shore. He watched the canoes reach the beach and an obviously excited group gather round them. Then – since without a boat there was nothing much that they could do – the party returned to camp. We packed up at once and moved to the bay below, as close as possible to the island. That night, extra sentries were posted and every man slept with his rifle, loaded, beside him. When dawn broke, we saw that the island was deserted. Evidently the Galubba had not liked the look of us and had decided to get away during the hours of darkness, in spite of a heavy gale which had blown up during the night. To make sure that they really had gone, George sent patrols along the shore. Soon after sun-up we saw a multitude of vultures and marabous descending upon the island; this led us to suppose that the Galubba had been on a poaching and fishing expedition and had no doubt killed several hippo, on the remains of which the vultures and storks had come to feast.

At about eleven in the morning two canoes suddenly issued out of a dense belt of reeds, to the south of the camp, and made for open water. To discourage them, George put a few bullets across their bows, which sent them back into the reeds in a hurry. He then sent some Scouts to try to make contact with the Galubba and persuade them to come ashore. But, although the Scouts managed to get within hailing distance, the poachers would not respond and retreated farther into the swamp. Throughout the day, we could see their heads bobbing above the reeds to inspect us. We estimated that there were four canoes in the reeds, probably stragglers from the main body. Since it was impossible to reach them, George thought the next best thing was to encourage them to make for home so, as soon as it was dark, he fired tracer bullets and a few Very lights at intervals over the swamp.

By now our supplies were running low and it was time to turn back. As it turned out, the first part of the safari had been luxury compared to the second because we had had plenty of water from the lake. Now, instead of retracing our steps, we decided to take an inland route. Goite, our Turkana guide, did not seem very sure of the way and, what was worse, was not certain whether we should find water when needed. For the region was dependent on waterholes, which at this dry season were few and far between. George, however, calculated that we should never be more than a long day's march from the lake so, if pressed for water, could make for it. We missed the cooling breeze off the lake, and there were times when I felt nearly dehydrated by the heat. The country here was even more desolate than the one we had passed through on our outward march. There was nothing but lava, so, understandably, there was little game and no population. Luckily we had bought sheep at Loyongalane and, though Elsa's living larder was rapidly dwindling away, it was sufficient to solve her feeding problem. But all of us lost most of our surplus weight during this time. Our march back was rapid, because the donkeys were now carrying less weight and, much of the route being waterless, we had to do longer marches.

After eighteen days we got back to Loyongalane and spent three days there, refitting, mending saddlery, etc., in preparation for the second part of our safari, the ascent of Mount Kulal. This mountain which lies twenty miles east of the lake rises out of the surrounding desert to about 7,500 feet, it catches all the moisture from the monsoon on its upper levels and has developed rich forest on its summit. It is a narrow volcano, twenty-eight miles long, with a crater in the centre about four miles wide. This crater is split in half and divides the mountain into a southern and northern portion. There is a theory that, after the volcano became extinct, an earthquake broke Kulal into deep crevasses, and cracked the awe-inspiring fissure through the crater. Its smooth walls are split like the peel of an orange when it is cut. These deep ridges fall 3,000 feet from the crater's lip. At the bottom, invisible from the top, is a gorge called Il Sigata which leads into the heart of the mountain. Its sheer walls tower hundreds of feet high and the opening is in places so narrow that the sky above is only visible through a slit. We tried to explore the gorge, entering from the only accessible opening, which lies towards the eastern foot of Kulal, but we were defeated, after a few hours, by huge rocks and deep waterpools which blocked the way.

To cover the mountain thoroughly it was necessary to go up one half, down again to the bottom and then up the second part.

The object of the safari was to find out whether the game on the mountain was holding its own, or decreasing as a result of poaching, by comparing the present situation with that found by George, when twelve years previously he had last visited the area. In particular, we wanted to investigate the state of the greater kudu.

Kulal does not look impressive from below: a long stretching mountain, with broad ridges leading to its summit. As we were to discover, these ridges became so narrow that the approaches for pack animals are very limited.

The first day's march, over thickly strewn lava boulders, was extremely arduous for laden animals. Later the ascent up knife-edged ridges was, in many places, very difficult to negotiate and we found it necessary to off-load the donkeys and manhandle the loads.

On the second night we were two-thirds of the way up the mountain and camped in a precipitous valley choked with lava boulders, near a little spring which provided just sufficient water for one animal at a time. It was very late before the last donkey had its much needed drink. This was one of the few waterholes on Kulal and so it was naturally a vital centre for the Samburu tribesmen who bring their livestock up to Kulal in the dry season.

It must have been difficult for Elsa, to meet these large herds of camels, cattle, goats and sheep around this and other waterholes; but she was intelligent and good-natured and, apparently realizing what the situation was, she put up with the tantalizing smell of these animals which often passed within a few feet of her. On these occasions we put her on the chain but she made no attempt to attack and only wanted to get away from the dust and the noise.

The route up Kulal was steep and the climate became arctic as we reached the higher slopes. We walked over saddles, crossed deep ravines and struggled along precipices. Here the bush was lower and then it changed into beautiful alpine flora.

Next morning we reached the top of Kulal; it was a relief to be walking on more or less even ground. Camp was pitched in a beautiful little glade, close to a rather muddy spring, fouled by the cattle of the Samburu tribesmen. Their astonishment was great at finding a nearly fully grown lion in our camp.

In the dense forest belt near the top on most mornings there was heavy mist, so we made a blazing cedar-log fire to keep us warm. At night it was so cold that I kept Elsa in my small tent, made her a nest of lichen and covered her with my warmest blanket. Most of my night was usually spent replacing it as it fell off continually and Elsa would begin to shiver. When I did this, she always licked my arm. She never made any attempt to tear the tent and get out; on the contrary she remained in it long after her usual waking hour, snuggling in her nest, where she was warm and cosy, whereas outside there was a blasting gale and wet mist. But as soon as the sun had cleared the fog away, she came to life and enjoyed the invigorating mountain air. Indeed she loved the place, for the ground was soft and cool, the forest gave thick shade and there were plenty of buffalo droppings to roll in.

Because of the shade and altitude, walking during the heat of the day was no effort in this region, and she was able to explore the mountain with us. She watched the eagles circling high in the air and was annoyed by the crows who followed her and dived low to tease her, and on one occasion woke a buffalo out of his sleep and chased him. She had excellent scent, hearing and eyesight and never lost herself in the thick undergrowth. One afternoon we were following the advance party, which had gone well ahead through the forest, and Elsa was ambushing us in a playful way from behind every bush, when suddenly, from the direction in which she had just disappeared, we heard a panic-stricken bray. A moment later a donkey broke through the wood with Elsa clinging to it and mauling it. Fortunately the forest was so thick that they could not go very fast, so we quickly reached the struggling pair and gave Elsa the beating we thought she deserved; she had never done anything of this sort before, and I was very much alarmed, for I had prided myself on the fact that she always obeyed my call instead of chasing an animal unduly. But again I could only blame myself for not putting Elsa on the lead.

One day we stood on the lip of the crater which divides the mountain and looked across to the northern part which was not more than four miles distant, though we knew that it would take us a full two days' march to get there. Nonchalantly Elsa balanced herself on the edge of the two thousand foot precipice, a sight which nearly sent me into hysterics. But animals seem to have no fear of heights. The following day we descended and the safari reached the mouth of the great Il Sigata gorge; there we made camp.

During the day thousands of camels, goats and sheep herded by tall, good-looking Rendile tribesmen, passed by on their way to water four miles up the gorge. They were followed by women leading strings of camels tied nose to tail loaded with water containers. These held about six gallons each and were made of closely woven fibre. We walked up the cleft, or rather, literally *into* the mountain. The floor of the gorge is a dry watercourse which, for about five miles, rises gently between towering walls which climb sharply on each side; when one penetrates still farther these walls attain some 1,500 feet in height and are sheer precipice. In places the gorge is so narrow that two laden camels cannot pass abreast and the cliffs overhang, shutting out the sky. We went far beyond the watering place of the stock, where the trickle of water becomes a sizable brook, with many rockbound pools of clear water. Finally we were halted by a sheer fall of thirty feet. Herbert, who is a mountaineer, managed to get up it only to find another high fall beyond.

The Il Sigata used to be a favourite place for poachers since it was easy to lie in wait for animals going to water. In fact, once an animal had entered the trap it was doomed, since there was no way out except that which led past the waiting hunters.

From Il Sigata it was a day and a half's march to the top of the northern massif, which we found to be more thickly inhabited by the Samburu and their livestock than the southern part. So Elsa's liberty had here to be curtailed.

We saw little game. Buffalo, of which there used to be a lot, had not, we were told, visited the northern end of the mountain for the last six years. There were also no greater kudu to be seen, though we observed the spoor of a few. George considered that this absence of game was probably due to the great number of

Samburu stock which were eating up the grazing and rapidly denuding the mountain.

Owing to sharp broken lava, the descent to Loyongalane was a most exhausting struggle and not even the superb view of Lake Rudolf far below, reflecting the setting sun in its lead-coloured surface against deep indigo hills and an orange-yellow sky, could compensate us for our tumbles, which grew more and more frequent.

Elsa kept looking back at the mountain and cool forest and started to run towards them, so we had to put her on the chain. Towards nightfall we lost our way in the dark. Elsa lay down every few yards, making it very plain that she had had enough. Although she was nearly full-grown, she still liked to suck my thumb when she felt nervous, and there was a lot of thumb-sucking that night. At last some tracer bullets, fired by the advance party, guided us to the camp. When we staggered in after our nightmare march, Elsa refused food and only wanted to be near me. I also could not eat from exhaustion and could well imagine the effort it had cost Elsa to carry on. She, of course, could not know why we were doing such a senseless thing as to struggle across sharp lava at night, and it was only her affection for us and her trust that kept her going. In spite of the hardships she had endured on this safari, in the course of which she had walked well over 300 miles, the bond between us had only been strengthened. As long as she was with us and knew herself to be loved and secure, she was happy. It was very touching to watch her trying to control the strong forces within her and to adapt herself to our way of life in order to please us. Her good-natured temperament was certainly due in part to her character, but part too may have come from the fact that neither force nor frustration was ever used to adapt her to our way of life. For we tried by kindness alone to help her to overcome the differences that lie between our two worlds.

In natural life, as long as he finds food, a lion does not wander over great distances, and certainly Elsa had seen more of the world than she would have done living with a pride. Yet she knew her home, and whenever we returned from safari she would go straight back to her habits and usual routine.

5. Elsa and Wild Lions

Elsa has charming manners; no matter for how short a time we have been separated, she will greet us ceremoniously, walking from one to the other, rubbing her head against us while miaowing in a low moan. Invariably, I come first, then George, followed by Nuru, and whoever happens to be near is afterwards greeted in the same way. She knows at once who likes her and reacts affectionately. She tolerates justifiably nervous guests, but those who are really scared have a hard time. Not that she has ever done them any harm but she delights in thoroughly terrifying them.

Since she was a tiny cub she has known just how to use her weight. By now it had become much more effective. Whenever she wanted to stop us, she flung herself with all her force at our feet, pressing her body against our shins and thus knocking us over.

Soon after our return from Lake Rudolf when we took her out for her evening walks she began to display a growing restlessness. Sometimes she refused to return with us, and she spent the night out in the bush. Usually we succeeded in getting her back by going to fetch her in the Land Rover. In fact, she soon decided that it was a waste of energy to walk home when a car had been specially brought to fetch her. So she would jump on to the canvas roof and loll at her ease, and from this vantage point she could watch out for game as we drove along. This was a very satisfactory arrangement from her point of view but, unfortunately, the manufacturers had not designed the roof as a couch for a lioness. As a result the supports began to give way under the strain and we found Elsa gradually subsiding on top of us. So George had to rig up extra supports and reinforce the canvas.

When she was not with us, Nuru was still always in charge of Elsa; one day we wanted to film him with her and told him that he should wear something rather smarter than his usual tattered shirt and trousers. In a few minutes he reappeared in a startling, close-fitting cream-coloured jacket, with braid and frogging down the front, which he had bought for his wedding. We thought that he looked just like a professional lion tamer in it. Elsa took one look at him and made at once for the bush; from there she peeped out from behind a shrub until she had established his identity. Then she came up to him and gave him a smack as though to say, 'What the devil do you mean by giving me such a fright?'

Nuru and Elsa had many adventures together; for instance, one day Nuru told us that while they were resting under a bush a leopard approached them down wind. Elsa watched eagerly and, although tense with excitement, kept still and controlled herself, except for her tail, until the leopard was nearly on top of her. Then suddenly the animal noticed the switching tail and bolted like lightning, nearly running over Nuru in its flight.

Elsa was now twenty-three months old and her voice broke to a deep growl. A month later she seemed to be in season again and placed her jets on many bushes, no doubt as an invitation to a mate. Normally she followed us on our walks wherever we went, but now for two days she had seemed determined to cross the valley. On this particular afternoon, she led us in *her* direction, and we soon found the fresh pugmarks of a lion. At dark, she refused to return. As we were near a car track, we went back to get the Land Rover, and George set off in it while I stayed at home in case she took a short cut back. When he reached the place where we had left her, George shouted to her for some time, but there was no response – only the hills echoed his calls . . . He drove on for another mile, calling at intervals. Then, hoping that Elsa had already come home, he returned. I told him I had waited for two long hours, but there was still no sign of her, so he left again and some time after he had gone I heard a shot. Until he came back I was very anxious, and then most upset by what he had to tell me.

He had driven out and called for a good half-hour, but Elsa had not shown up. Then he had stopped the car in an opening in the bush, wondering where to look next. Suddenly, some 200 yards behind the car there had been a great uproar of lions quarrelling. Then, the next moment a lioness flashed by with another in hot pursuit. As they shot past, George seized his rifle and put a bullet under the second animal, assuming, probably rightly, that she was a jealous lioness, bent on Elsa's destruction. Then he jumped into the car and gave chase. He drove along a narrow lane between dense thornbush, flashing a spotlight from side to side, until he was brought up short by a lion and two lionesses, who only very reluctantly moved out of his way, giving vent to loud roars.

Now he had come to fetch me; we drove back to the scene, but though we called desperately for Elsa – called and called – no familiar sound came in answer. But presently, as if in derision, the lion chorus started up a few hundred yards away. We drove towards them until we could see the glint of three pairs of eyes. There was nothing more to be done. So, with heavy hearts, we turned for home. Would Elsa be killed by a jealous lioness? In her present condition, she might easily have mated with the lion and it was a question of whether his lioness would tolerate a rival.

However, to our great relief, we had not gone more than a mile along the track when we came upon Elsa, sniffing at a bush. She utterly ignored us. We tried to persuade her to join us but she remained where we had found her, gazing wistfully into the bush in the direction in which the lions had last been heard. Presently they started calling again, and approached. Thirty yards behind us was a dry river bed, and here the pride stopped, growling vigorously.

It was now well after midnight. Elsa sat in the moonlight between the lions and us; both parties called her to their side. Who was going to win the contest? Suddenly Elsa moved towards the lions and I shouted, 'Elsa, *no*, don't go there, you'll get killed.' She sat down again, looking at us and looking back at her own kind, undecided what to do. For an hour the situation did not alter, then George fired two shots over the lions; this had the effect of sending them off in silence. Then, as Elsa had still not made up her mind, we drove slowly back, hoping that she might follow us; and so she did. Very reluctantly, she walked parallel with the car, looking back many times, till finally she hopped on to the roof and we brought her back to safety. When we arrived home she was very thirsty and exhausted and drank without stopping.

What had happened during the five hours which Elsa had spent with the lions? Would a wild pride accept her in spite of the human smell which she carried? Would a male ignore a female in season? Why had she returned with us instead of joining her own kind? Was it because she was frightened of the fierce lioness? These were some of the questions we asked ourselves. The fact remained that she had come to no harm as a result of this experience.

But after this adventure the call of the wild evidently grew stronger and stronger. Often she did not return with us at dark and we spent many evenings looking for her. In the dry season water was our main hold on her, for this she could only get at the house.

Rocks were her favourite places, and she always chose the top of a cliff or some other safe position as her lookout. Once, in spite of hearing a leopard 'coughing' close by, we had to leave her on such a rock. Next morning she returned with several bleeding scratches and we wondered whether the leopard was responsible for them.

Another time, after sunset, she followed the laughing cries of a hyena; soon these increased to hysterical shrieks to which Elsa replied by loud growls. George rushed to see what was happening and was just in time to shoot one or two hyenas which were closing in on Elsa. After this she pulled her 'kill' into a bush, dragging it between her front legs as she had often done with a groundsheet when she was a cub. But, although she was now two years old, her teeth could not yet penetrate the skin of a hyena, and she did not know what to do with her quarry.

At this age giraffes still remained her favourite friends. She would stalk them, using every stratagem of her kind, but invariably they would spot her before she got too close; this was mainly because Elsa seemed unable to control her tail. Her body would freeze without so much as the twitch of an ear, but the conspicuous black tassel on her tail would never keep still. Once the giraffes had spotted her, there would be a competition to see who would be the boldest among them. One by one in a half-circle, they would edge forward, giving vent to low, long-drawn snorts, until Elsa could contain herself no longer and would make a rush and put the herd to flight. On two occasions she had made a sustained chase after a huge old bull; only after they had gone about a mile the giraffe, either winded or fed up with being chased, turned at bay. Elsa then circled him closely, keeping just out of reach of the mighty pounding forelegs, a blow from which could easily have smashed her skull.

She seemed to come into season every two and a half months. We had been told that the most obvious indication of this condition was a loud purring; although she had by now been twice in season we had never noticed anything of the kind, but each time she had a peculiar smell and sprayed her invitation jets on the bushes.

Soon after her adventure with the lions, Nuru reported that, when in the morning he tried to follow her, Elsa had growled at him repeatedly. Obviously she wished him to remain behind, while she walked determinedly into the hills. So, in spite of the increasing heat, she had trotted off quickly until he lost her tracks in the rocks. In the afternoon, we followed her spoor, but soon lost it and could only call to her from the foot of the cliffs. A reply came, a strange growl, unlike Elsa's voice but undoubtedly that of a lion. Soon afterwards we saw her struggling downhill, over the boulders, calling in her familiar way. When she reached us she flung herself exhausted on to the ground, panting and very excited. We had brought water with us and she could not have enough of it. Now we noticed several bleeding claw marks on her hind legs, shoulders and neck and also two bleeding perforations on her forehead, which were definitely made by teeth and not by claws.*

Although normally she had no personal smell, she now certainly had a very strong one, much stronger than her present seasonal smell. As soon as she had recovered a little, she greeted us in her customary manner, as well as purring at each of us in turn in a most startling way, as though to say, 'Listen to what I have learned.'

*Is it a coincidence that when two years later I visited the Rome Zoo on my way to London, I saw a couple of lions mating and as the last gesture of the siring act, the male bit the lioness on the forehead? Soon afterwards I saw the same action take place in the same circumstances in the London Zoo.

When she had assured herself of our admiration, she threw herself on the ground again and fell fast asleep for two hours. She had obviously just been with a lion when we had interfered by calling to her.

Two days later she spent a whole day and night away, and when we followed her spoor we found hers in the company of a lioness; both having laid up several times together.

From this time onwards, Elsa spent more and more nights away. We tried to induce her to come home by driving near to her favourite places and calling to her. Occasionally she came, more often she did not. Sometimes she was away, without food or water, for two or three days. Water was still some hold over her, but soon the rains were due and we realized that when they came we should lose all control of her. This raised a problem which we had to solve; it was one which was made more urgent by the fact that our long overseas leave was due in May. Elsa was now twenty-seven months old, almost full grown. We had always known that we could not keep her free indefinitely at Isiolo. Our original idea had been to send her to join her sisters at the Rotterdam Zoo, and we had even made the necessary arrangements in case an emergency should arise. But now she had taken her future into her own paws and her latest developments were decisive in altering our plans for her. Because we had been so fortunate in bringing her up in her natural environment and because she seemed so much at home in the bush and was accepted by wild animals, we felt that she might well prove to be the exception to the rule that a pet will be killed by its own kind because of its human smell and ignorance of bush life. To release Elsa back to the wild would be an experiment well worth trying.

We intended to spend two or three weeks with her, then, if all went well, we would take our long leave; this one is supposed to spend outside Kenya, in order to have a change of climate.

Next we had to consider where to release Elsa? Unfortunately

Isiolo was far too populated for us to let her go wild there. But we knew of an area which for most of the year was devoid of inhabitants and livestock but had an abundance of game, especially lion.

We received permission to take Elsa to this place; as the rains were expected any day, we had no time to lose, if she were to reach her possible future home before they began.

In order to get to this area we should have to travel 340 miles, crossing the highlands on our way and also the great rift valley, going through relatively thickly populated country where there were many European farms. Because we feared that Elsa might be embarrassed by gaping crowds and inquisitive Africans at every halt, and also to avoid the heat of the day, we decided to travel by night. We settled to start about seven in the evening, but Elsa had other ideas. Before setting off we took her out for her usual walk to her favourite rocks, across the valley from our house. There I photographed her for the last time in her home. She is genuinely camera-shy and always hates being filmed or sketched. As soon as she sees one of those awful shiny boxes focused on her she invariably turns her head, or covers it with a paw, or just walks away. On this last day at Isiolo she had to endure a lot from our Leica and plainly got thoroughly fed up with it. So finally she took her revenge. When, for a moment, I left the camera unguarded, she leapt up, sprang upon it and galloped away with it over the rocks, she shook it most provokingly between her teeth, or chewed at it, holding it firmly between her paws. Finally we recovered it, and miraculously it was not badly damaged.

By then, it was time to get back to the house and start off on the long journey, but just then Elsa sat herself on a rock and gazed across the valley in the contemplative manner of her kind and nothing would move her. Obviously she had no intention of walking back and expected the car to be brought for her. All hope of making an early start was gone. George went home, fetched the car and came back to the foot of the hills where we had left Elsa, but she was no longer there and had apparently gone for her evening stroll. He called to her, but there was no response. Not until eleven at night did she reappear, jump on to the roof of the Land Rover and consent to be driven home.

6. The First Release

It was after midnight when we had at last secured Elsa in her travelling crate and started off. In the hope of making the trip easier for her I gave her a tranquillizer; we had been told by the vet that the drug was harmless and that the effect would last about eight hours. To give Elsa all the moral support I could, I travelled with her in the open lorry. During the night we passed through country that is 8,000 feet above sea level, and the cold was icy. Owing to the effect of the tranquillizer Elsa was only semi-conscious, yet even in this state every few minutes she stretched her paws out through the bars of the crate, to assure herself that I was still there. It took us seventeen hours to reach our destination. The effect of the tranquillizer did not wear off until an hour after we had arrived. During these eighteen hours Elsa became very cold, her breathing was slow and for a time I feared that she was going to die. Luckily she recovered, but this experience showed us that one should be very careful with drugs where lions are concerned, for they are far more sensitive to them than other animals and individually they react differently. We had had previous experience of this when we had powdered all three cubs with an insecticide – one took it well, one became sick, and Elsa was very ill with convulsions.

It was late in the afternoon by the time we reached our destination; there we were met by a friend who is the Game Warden of this district. We pitched camp on a superb site at the base of a 1,000-foot escarpment overlooking a vast plain of open bush country, through which a belt of dark vegetation marks the course of a river. As we were at an altitude of 5,000 feet, the air was fresh and brisk. Immediately in front of our camp lay open grassland sloping towards the plain, on which herds of Thomson's gazelle, topi, wildebeeste, Burchell's zebra, roan antelope, kongoni, and a few buffalo were grazing. It was a game paradise. While the tents were being pitched we took Elsa for a stroll and she rushed at the herds, not knowing which to follow, for in every direction there were animals running. As if to shake off the effects of the ghastly journey, Elsa lost herself among these new playmates, who were rather astonished to find such a strange lion in their midst; one who rushed foolishly to and fro without any apparent purpose. Soon, however, Elsa had had enough and trotted back to camp and her dinner.

Our plan was this: we would spend the first week taking Elsa, perched on the roof of the Land Rover, round the new country, thus getting her used to it and to the animals, many of which belonged to species which do not live in the Northern Frontier and she had therefore never seen. During the second week we intended to leave her overnight, while she was active in the bush, and to visit and feed her in the mornings when she was sleepy. Afterwards we would reduce her meals, in the hope that this would encourage her to kill on her own, or to join a wild lion.

On the morning after our arrival we started our programme. First we took off her collar, as the symbol of liberation. Elsa hopped on to the roof of the Land Rover and we went off. After only a few hundred yards we saw a lioness walking parallel to us downhill; she passed close to many antelope who took no notice of her, realizing no doubt from her determined steady stride that, at the moment, she was not interested in killing. We drove closer to the lioness. Elsa displayed much excitement, jumped off her seat and, making low moaning noises, cautiously followed this new friend. But as soon as the lioness stopped and turned round, her courage failed her and she raced back as fast as she could to the safety of the car. The lioness continued her purposeful walk, and we soon detected six cubs waiting for her on a small anthill in tall grass.

We drove on and surprised a hyena chewing a bone. Elsa jumped off and chased the startled animal, who had only time to grasp her bone and lumber away. In spite of her ungainliness, she made good her escape but lost her bone in the process.

Later we passed through herd after herd of different antelope, whose curiosity seemed to be aroused by the sight of a Land Rover with a lion on it and allowed us, provided that we remained in the car and did not talk, to approach within a few yards of them. All the time Elsa watched carefully, but did not attempt to leave the car unless she spotted an animal off guard, grazing with its back towards her, or fighting; then she would get down quietly and creep forward with her belly close to the ground, taking advantage of every bit of cover, and thus advance towards her victim. But as soon as the animal showed any suspicion, she either froze to immobility or, if the situation seemed better handled in another way, she pretended to be uninterested, licked her paws, yawned, or even rolled on her back until the animal was reassured. Then she would at once start stalking again. But however cunning she was, she never got close enough to kill.

The little Thomson's gazelles provoked Elsa, very unfairly, relying on the unwritten law of the bush that a superior creature will not attack a smaller one, except for food. They are the real urchins of the plain, most inquisitive and always busy with their tails. Now they challenged her, teased her and simply asked to be chased; but Elsa only looked bored, ignored them and, with dignity, put them in their place.

Buffalo and rhino were quite another matter. They *had* to be chased. One day, from the car, we watched a buffalo cantering across the plain. Perhaps his curiosity was aroused by seeing a lion on the Land Rover. Quickly Elsa jumped to the ground and, using the cover of a bush, set out to stalk him. The buffalo had the same idea and also used this cover but starting from the opposite direction. We waited, and watched, until we saw them nearly collide. Then it was the buffalo who bolted, with Elsa bravely following him.

On another occasion, from her seat on the Land Rover she saw two buffaloes asleep in a bush. Off she went; bellows, crashing, and a wild commotion followed, then the buffaloes broke through the thicket and galloped away in different directions.

Rhino too were most inviting; one day we came upon one standing fast asleep with its head buried in a bush. Elsa stalked him very carefully and succeeded in nearly rubbing noses with him. Then the poor beast had an abrupt awakening, gave a startled snort and, looking bewildered, spun round on himself and dashed into a nearby swamp. There he churned up the water and gave Elsa a shower-bath; she splashed on after him; outlined against high sprays of water, the pair disappeared from our sight, and it was a long time before Elsa returned, wet but proud.

She loved climbing trees, and sometimes when we had looked in vain for her in the high grass we found her swaying in the crown of a tree. More than once she had difficulty in getting down again. Once, after trying various possibilities, and making the branch she was on bend alarmingly under her weight, we saw her tail dangling through the foliage, followed by her struggling hind legs, till finally she fell on to the grass well over twenty feet below. She was most embarrassed at having lost her dignity before an audience, for, while she always enjoyed making us laugh when she meant to do so, she hated being laughed at when the joke was against her. Now she walked quickly away from us and we gave her time to regain her self-respect. When we looked for her later on, we found her holding court with six hyenas. These sinister creatures sat in a circle around her, and I felt rather nervous for her. But as though to offset her earlier clumsiness in the tree she now showed us that she was very superior to the hyenas who bored her. She yawned, stretched herself and, ignoring the hyenas, walked up to us. The hyenas hobbled off, looking over their shoulders, perhaps puzzled by the appearance of Elsa's strange friends.

One morning we followed circling vultures and soon found a lion on a zebra kill. He was tearing at the meat and paid no attention to us. Elsa stepped cautiously from the car, miaowing at him and then, though she did not get any encouragement, advanced carefully towards him. At last the lion looked up and straight at Elsa. He seemed to say, 'Don't you know lion etiquette? How dare you, woman, interfere with the lord while he is having his meal? You are allowed to kill for me, but afterwards you have to wait till I have had my lion's share, then you may finish up the remains.' Evidently poor Elsa did not like this expression and returned as fast as she could to the safety of the car. The lord continued feeding and we watched him for a long time, hoping that Elsa might regain her courage; but nothing would induce her to leave her safe position.

Next morning we had better luck. We saw a topi standing, like a sentry, on an anthill, looking intently in one direction. We followed his glance and discovered a young lion resting in the high grass, sunning himself. He was a magnificent young male with a beautiful blond mane, and Elsa seemed attracted by him. Just the right husband for her, we thought. We drove to within thirty yards of him. The lion looked mildly surprised when he saw his prospective bride sitting on the top of a car, but responded in a friendly manner. Elsa, apparently overcome by coyness, made low moans but would not come off the roof. So we drove a little distance away and persuaded her to get down, then, suddenly, we left her and drove round to the other side of the lion: this meant that she would have to pass him in order to reach us. After much painful hesitation, she plucked up enough courage to walk towards the lion. When she was about ten paces away from him, she lay down with her ears back and her tail swishing. The lion got up and went towards her with, I am sure, the friendliest intentions, but at the last moment Elsa panicked and rushed back to the car.

We drove away with her and, strangely enough, right into a pride of two lions and one lioness on a kill.

This was luck indeed. They must have killed very recently for they were so intent upon their meal that however much Elsa talked to them they paid not the slightest attention to her. Finally they left the kill, their bulging stomachs swinging from side to side. Elsa lost no time in inspecting the remains of the carcase, her first contact with a real kill. Nothing could have served our purpose better than this meal, provided by lions and full of their fresh scent. After Elsa had had her fair share, we dragged the kill back to the handsome young lion who had seemed so friendly. We hoped that if Elsa provided him with a meal he would have a favourable opinion of her. Then we left her and the kill near to him and drove away. After a few hours we set out to see what had happened but met Elsa already half-way back to the camp. However, since this lion had shown an interest in her, we took her back to him during the afternoon. We found him still in the same place. Elsa talked to him from her couch as though they were old friends, but had plainly no intention of leaving the car.

To induce her to quit her seat, we drove behind a bush and I got out but was nearly knocked over by a hyena who dashed out of his cool retreat, in which we then found a newly killed baby zebra, no doubt provided by the blond lion. It was Elsa's feeding time, so regardless of the consequences, she jumped out of the car on to the carcase. We took this opportunity to drive away as fast as we could and left her alone for her night's adventure. Early next morning, anxious to know the outcome of the experiment, we set off to visit her, hoping to find the happy pair. What we found was poor Elsa, waiting at the spot at which we had left her, but minus the lion and minus the kill. She was overjoyed to see us, desperate to stay with us, and sucked my thumbs frantically to make sure that everything was all right between us. I was very unhappy that I had hurt her feelings without being able to explain to her that all we had done was intended to be for her good. When she had calmed down and even felt safe enough in our company to fall asleep, we decided, rather sadly, that we must break faith with her again and we sneaked away.

Till now we had always given her her meat already cut up, so that she should not associate her food with living animals. Now we needed to reverse our system, so during her midday sleep we drove sixty miles to shoot a small buck for her. We had to go this distance because no one was allowed to shoot game near the camp. We brought her a complete buck wondering if she would know how to open it, since she had had no mother to teach her the proper way of doing it. We soon saw that by instinct she knew exactly what to do; she started at the inner part of the hind legs, where the skin is softest, then tore out the guts, and after enjoying these delicacies, buried the stomach contents and covered up the blood spoor, as all proper lions do. Then she gnawed the meat off the bones with her molars and rasped it away with her rough tongue.

Once we knew that she could do this it was time for us to let her do her own killing. The plain was covered with isolated bush clusters, ideal hideouts for any animal. All the lions had to do, when they wanted a meal, was to wait under cover until an antelope approached down wind, rush out and get their dinner.

We now left Elsa alone for two or three days at a time, hoping that hunger would make her kill. But when we came back we always found her waiting for us and hungry. It was heart-breaking having to stick to our programme, when obviously all she wanted was to be with us and sure of our affection. This she showed very clearly by sucking my thumbs and holding on to us with her paws. All the same we knew that for her good we must persevere.

By now we realized that it was going to take us much longer to release her to nature than we had expected; we therefore asked the government if we could use our long leave in the country for the purpose of carrying out this experiment and, very kindly, they consented. After receiving this permission we felt much relieved since we knew that we should now have the time required for our task.

We increased the number of days on which Elsa was left on her own and we reinforced the thorn fences round our tents, so that they were strong enough to keep any lion out. This we did specifically to prevent Elsa from visiting us when she was hungry.

One morning, when she was with us, we located a lion, who seemed placid and in a good mood: she stepped off the car and we tactfully left the pair alone. That evening while sitting in our thorn-protected tent, we suddenly heard Elsa's miaow and before we could stop her, she crept through the thorns and settled down with us. She was bleeding from claw marks and had walked eight miles back, obviously preferring our company to that of the lion.

The next time we took her a longer distance away from camp. As we drove we saw two eland bulls, each weighing about

1,500 lb, engaged in a fight. Elsa promptly jumped off the car and stalked them. At first, they were so engaged in their fight that they did not notice her, but when they became aware of her presence she narrowly missed a savage kick from one of them. They broke off the fight and Elsa chased them a short distance and finally came back very proud of herself.

Soon afterwards we met two young lions sitting on the grass in the open. They looked to us ideal companions for Elsa, but by now she was very suspicious of our tricks and would not leave the car, although she talked very agitatedly to them; as we had no means of dropping her off we had to miss this opportunity and went on until we met two Thomson's gazelle fighting; this sight caused Elsa to jump off and we drove quickly away, leaving her to learn more about wild life.

It was nearly a week before we returned. We found her waiting, and very hungry. She was full of affection; we had deceived her so often, broken faith with her, done so much to destroy her trust in us, yet she remained loyal. We dropped some meat which we had brought with us and she immediately started to eat it. Suddenly we heard unmistakable growls and soon we saw two lions trotting fast towards us. They were obviously on the hunt and probably they had scented the meat; they approached very quickly. Poor Elsa took in the situation and bolted as hurriedly as she could, leaving her precious meal. At once a little jackal appeared which up till now must have been hiding in the grass; he lost no time in taking his chance and began to take bite after bite at Elsa's meat, knowing that his luck was not going to last long. This proved true for one of the lions advanced steadily upon him, uttering threatening growls. But meat was meat and the little jackal was not to be easily frightened away; he held on to his possession and took as many bites as he could until the lion was practically on top of him. Even then, with unbelievable pluck he tried to save his meal. But size prevailed over courage and the lion was the winner. Elsa watched this scene from a distance and saw her first meal, after so many days, being taken away from her. In the circumstances it seemed hard that the two lions took no interest in anything but their food and completely ignored her. To compensate her for her disappointment we took her away.

While we were in camp we had some human visitors. The first party came to look at game. George asked them in and was just about to explain that we had a tame lioness in camp, when Elsa, having heard the car, came bounding in, full of curiosity and friendliness. They looked a little startled, to say the least of it, but took it very well.

Later a Swiss couple, having heard that we had a lion cub, came to see it. I think they had visions of something small which could be picked up and cuddled, but seeing the 300-odd pound Elsa on the roof of the Land Rover made them pause, and it was a little time before we could persuade them to get out of their car and join us at lunch. Elsa was courtesy itself, welcomed the strangers, and only once swept the table clear with her tail. After this, they could not have enough of her and had themselves photographed with her at every angle.

We had been in camp for four weeks and although Elsa had spent most of the last fortnight in the bush, she had not yet started killing for herself. By now, the rains had begun and every afternoon there were heavy showers. The conditions in this region were very different to those at Isiolo; for one thing it was much colder, for another while the ground at Isiolo is sandy and dries within a few hours, here there was black cotton soil which turns into a morass after rain; moreover, it is covered with waist-high grass which prevents it drying for weeks on end. At home Elsa had enjoyed the rains and had been invigorated by them, but here she was very miserable.

One night very heavy rain fell without stopping; at least five inches came down before daybreak and the country was flooded. In the morning we waded out often knee-deep in mud, and we met Elsa already halfway back to the camp. She looked so unhappy and wanted so desperately to stay with us that we took her home. That evening we suddenly heard a terrified galloping come past our camp followed by a stillness. What drama was happening outside? Next arose the hysterical chuckles of hyena mingled with the high-pitched yells of jackal, but these were soon silenced by the growls of at least three lion. We realized that they must have killed just outside the camp. What a chance for Elsa. But while we listened, fascinated, to the grandiose chorus of shrill, piercing staccato noises interspersed with deep guttural rumblings, she rubbed her head against us and showed how glad she was to be inside the thorn fence in our company.

After a few days the rain decreased and we renewed our efforts to turn Elsa into a wild lioness. But she had become so suspicious of being deserted again that we had great difficulty in inducing her to follow us into the plains.

She did, however, in the end accompany us and we met two lionesses who came hurriedly towards the car, but Elsa bolted from them and seemed more nervous than ever.

It was evident that in this place she was scared of lions, so we decided not to go on trying to force her to make friends with them, but to wait till she came into season again, then perhaps she would choose her own mate by mutual attraction.

Meanwhile we would concentrate our efforts on training her to kill her food and thus to become independent of us. Also, once she could kill, she would be a more suitable partner for a lion, should she decide to join one. The plains were still under water and most of the game had concentrated on the few bits of slightly higher ground which were drier. Elsa loved one little hillock which was studded with rocks, and we therefore chose this place as her experimental headquarters. It was unfortunately only eight miles from our camp; it would have been better if we could have moved off to a greater distance but, under the existing weather conditions, this was not practicable.

We left Elsa for a week on her hillock but, when we returned, she looked so unhappy that it needed all my willpower to harden myself sufficiently to carry on with her education. We sat with her during the midday lull until she dozed off with her head on my lap. Suddenly, in the bush, just behind us, there was a frightening crash and a rhino appeared. We both jumped up like lightning, and while I ran behind a tree, Elsa gallantly charged the intruder and drove it away. Most unfairly, during her absence we deserted her again.

Late that afternoon the atmosphere became heavy with moisture and the setting sun was spectacularly reflected against dark red curtains of cloud hanging out of a grey sky pierced by fragments of parallel rainbows. This kaleidoscope of luminous colour changed rapidly into threatening dark clouds loaded with rain which finally towered above us in one black mass. All was in suspense waiting for the firmament to burst.

Then a few heavy drops fell like lead to the ground and now, as if two giant hands had torn the heavens apart, a deluge descended with such torrential force that soon our camp was in the middle of a running stream. For hours the flood continued. I imagined poor Elsa alone in this icy night, drenched, shivering and miserable; thunder and lightning added to my nightmare. Next morning we waded the eight miles to the ridge where we had left her. As usual, she was waiting for us, overjoyed to see us and greeted us each in turn by rubbing her head and body against us repeatedly, uttering her moaning noise. But today, there was no doubt that she was miserable, indeed she was nearly crying. We decided that, though it would interrupt her education, we could not leave her out in such weather. Unlike the local lions used to this climate, she came from semi-desert country and could not quickly adapt herself to very different conditions. Now she was pleased to walk back with us splashing in her familiar Isiolo way through the swamp and showing how happy she was.

Next day she was ill. When she moved she was in great pain, her glands were swollen and she had a temperature. We made her a bed of grass in the annexe to George's tent and there she lay, panting, listless and pathetic. I treated her with M and B, the only drug which I thought might help. She wanted me to be near her all the time, which, of course, I was.

The rains had now set in, even a car with a four-wheel drive could not plough through to the nearest place at which blood slides could be tested, so we sent a runner the hundred-odd miles with various samples. The reply, when it came, stated that Elsa was infected with hookworm and tapeworm from both of which she had previously suffered and which we knew how to treat. But neither of these troubles could account for her swollen glands or her temperature. We believed that she had also become infected by some tick-borne virus. If this proved true it would suggest that an animal, immune to diseases in its own environment, when transferred to another, does not carry the same immunity to local strains, and might be one explanation for the often puzzling distribution of animals found in East Africa.

Elsa became so ill that for a time we did not think that she would recover. However, after a week the fever became intermittent, every three or four days her temperature would rise and then go back again to normal. She was rapidly losing her beautiful golden colour, her coat was dull, like cotton wool, and she developed many white hairs on her back. Her face became ash grey. She had difficulty in dragging herself from the tent into the sparse sunshine; the only hopeful sign was her appetite. We gave her as much meat and milk as she wanted although both had to be fetched from a long distance. We also succeeded in spite of the transport difficulties arising from the weather in corresponding regularly with the Veterinary Laboratory in Nairobi, but as no sign of a parasite was found in the samples we provided we had to treat her more or less by guesswork.

We dosed her for hookworm and for Rickettsia, a tick-borne parasite, which had been suggested as a possible cause for her illness, but as it was impossible to insert a hypodermic needle into a gland in order to obtain the fluid from which her illness might have been diagnosed, all we could do was to keep her as quiet as possible and give her the affection she needed. She was very gentle and responsive to all we did for her and often hugged me with her paws when I rested my head on her shoulders.

During her illness, because she lived so intimately with us, Elsa became more dependent on us and tamer than ever. Most of the day, she lay across the entrance to our thorn-fence enclosure, in a strategic position, which enabled her to watch everything that went on inside the camp and outside on the plain as well. At meal times she preferred to have the boys step over her as they brought in our food than to move from her place. The staff laughingly competed at running the gauntlet while balancing full soup plates, getting spanked by Elsa in a friendly way as they passed over her.

She slept in the tent with George but was free to come and go as she pleased. Late one night, he was awakened by her low calls and heard her trying to get out of the back of the tent. He sat up and saw a shape in the doorway of the tent. Thinking that Elsa could not have got around so quickly he switched on his torch and saw a wild lioness blinking in the glare. He shouted at her and she went off. No doubt she had scented Elsa and, reassured by the lion noises coming from inside the tent, had decided to investigate.

It was now five weeks since Elsa's illness had started, and her condition had only improved slightly. It was plain that the climate in this region was against her, also that she might not be immune from local infections such as ticks and tsetse, which vary according to localities. Besides this she was different in appearance from the local lions – much darker in colour, with a longer nose, bigger ears and generally much larger. In every way she belonged to the semi-desert and not to the highlands.* Finally, being in a game reserve meant that not only did George have to go twenty miles by car to get outside the reserve to shoot meat for her, but also that he could not take her hunting with him and thereby give her the opportunity of being in at the kill and getting the feel of pulling down a live animal – an experience which, in her wild state, she would have gained from her mother. It was evident therefore that after having camped here for three months we must try to choose a better home for her.

It was not easy to find an area which had a suitable climate, permanent water, enough game to supply her with food, and no tribesmen or hunting parties; moreover, it needed to be accessible by car. Eventually we discovered such a paradise and received the government's permission to release a lion there. As soon as the rains ceased we decided to go there.

Camp was struck, and everything loaded into the cars, except Elsa. She chose that very day to come into season and had disappeared into the bush. We had waited for two and a half months for just this to happen, but we knew now that we could not allow her to go wild in this area. During the day there was no sign of her. We hunted for her everywhere, in the Land Rover and on foot, but without success; finally we became very worried in case she might have been killed by a wild lioness. However,

*There are two types of lion in Kenya:
1. *Felix massaica* – buff-coloured with a yellow mane.
2. *Felix leo somaliensis* – smaller with larger ears, more pronounced spots and a longer tail. Elsa belongs to the *somaliensis* type.

there was nothing to do but wait for her return. For two days and nights she kept away, except for one short visit during which she rushed up to us, rubbed her head against our knees and dashed off again, only to come back a few minutes later, indulge in some more rubbings, then make off a second time and as quickly return, as though to tell us: 'I am very happy, but please understand I *must* go. I just came to tell you not to worry.' Then she was off again.* When she finally returned, for good, she was badly scratched and bleeding from several claw marks and was very irritable when I tried to dress her wounds. It needed much patience to make her jump into the truck.

Thus ended the first three months of our experiment. We had failed this time owing to her illness but felt confident that given time and patience we would succeed.

7. The Second Release

Now we had before us a journey of about 440 miles. On some trips everything seems to go wrong, and this was one of them. After only twelve miles, one of the front bearings went on George's car. I drove to the nearest Administrative Post, which was ninety miles away, to get a new one sent out. I had to spend

---

*We often wondered why Elsa never produced cubs as a result of being with a lion while she was in season. Later I learned from a zoo authority that during the four relevant days the male sires the female at least six to eight times a day and that it is thought that it is only on the fourth day that the siring becomes effective. If this is so, it is obvious that Elsa never had sufficient opportunity, as the jealous lioness, holding guard over her male, would not be likely to tolerate too frequent love-making with a newcomer to the pride.

the night there with poor Elsa locked up in the back of my car. Meanwhile, when the bearing reached George he found that he had no spanner large enough to fit, but by using a hammer and a cold chisel he finally managed to get it fixed by the evening, and joined me. During that night and the following morning we had six punctures; finally at nine in the evening, when we were still twelve miles short of our destination, my car began to make the most alarming noise. So we stopped and put up our camp beds in the open. We were all completely exhausted after fifty-two hours of continuous driving. Elsa had behaved splendidly and had never made a protest; now she just flung herself down beside us and went to sleep. Next morning, we thought that we might have great difficulty in persuading her to re-enter the car, particularly as she had already gone off to lie up for the day in the dense reeds growing by a little stream near our camp. Crossing the stream was going to be difficult, so we decided to get the cars across first, and then collect Elsa.

The Land Rover went through without trouble, but my car got stuck and had to be towed out. We then re-crossed the stream on foot to try and persuade Elsa to leave her shady retreat and follow us back to the cars. She came at once and jumped in my car, as though she knew that the journey was not yet at an end and wished to co-operate. We started off along a rough track through thick bush. Even now our troubles were not over; and after a few miles a rear spring in my car broke, so it was late in the afternoon when we reached Elsa's new home.

It was truly a corner of Africa where 'the foxes say good night to each other'. To reach an ideal camp site, George and the boys cut a new track, through thick bush; it took them four days. Our final camp was on a beautiful river lined by walls of doum-palms, acacias and fig trees, interwoven with creepers. The water rushed foaming and bubbling through rapids, passed between islands covered with reeds, and in the farther reaches calmed into many rock-bound pools of cool clear water, deep enough to hold many fish. It was a fisherman's paradise and George could not wait to set out his rod.

The country was quite different from the region we had left. It was much hotter; there were no great herds of game grazing peacefully on grassy plains; only thornbush, with visibility reduced to a few yards – a hunter's nightmare. But it was only thirty-five miles from Elsa's birthplace and was the type of country that was natural to her.

When we left the lush tropical greenery, which was confined to the river banks, we felt the intense heat of the sun hitting us like a hot wave. We were within a short distance of the equator; our altimeter read 1,600 feet. The dense dry thornbush was only penetrable by a network of game paths; these were also useful in warning us of elephant, rhino and buffalo whose spoor and droppings left no doubt that the paths were in daily use. About 200 yards from the camp there was a salt lick and many impressions of rhino horns and elephant tusks in the salt told us that they were frequent visitors to it; also nearly every tree of any size had its bark polished or worn off by elephants rubbing their bodies against it. Because of this Elsa found it difficult to do her daily claw exercises, as there were few trees left with any rough bark. Only the baobabs; their giant purple-grey shapes towering over the low thornbush were untouched, for their smooth trunks were of no use to animals.

The great attraction of the place was a huge ridge of reddish rock with cliffs and caves, in whose shadows we saw hyrax dashing about. It was an ideal lion's home, with a splendid lookout. From its top, we watched giraffe, waterbuck, lesser kudu, gerenuk and bushbuck moving towards the river which was their life artery in this otherwise waterless semi-desert country.

Either as a result of our Rickettsia treatment or owing to the change in climate, Elsa's condition improved daily, so we were able to re-start her education. Every morning, as soon as it got light, we took Elsa for a walk, and did so again in the afternoon. These walks, which took us along the numerous game paths and sandy watercourses, were full of interest. Elsa loved them; she sniffed and followed the spoor of animals which had been there during the previous night, rolled in elephant and rhino droppings and chased warthog and dik-dik. We, too, were on the alert, taking note of animal tracks, their freshness and direction, which way the wind was blowing, and kept ears and eyes open for tell-tale sounds and sights. This was necessary because otherwise one was apt to run unexpectedly into rhino, buffalo or elephant, and it is these surprise meetings at close quarters which can lead to trouble.

Here, unlike the first place to which we had taken her, Elsa was able to go out hunting with George. We both hate killing animals, but now we had to make some sacrifices to Elsa's education, and the knowledge that in her natural state she would have been killing them on her own account appeased our qualms. The sooner she learned to do it properly, the better for all concerned. For the present she must stalk her quarry, then, if she were not able to kill, George would bring the animal down with a bullet and leave her to give the *coup de grâce*. After this she would be left to protect her kill against vultures, hyenas and lions, and in this way would meet these animals in natural circumstances.

We heard several lion close to the camp and often saw their pugmarks.

One evening Elsa did not come back from her favourite lookout on top of the rocks. It was a splendid place where she found the breeze cool, where no tsetse fly molested her and from which she could watch the animals below. But as we had only been a short time in the area, we were worried at her absence and went out to look for her. By then it was well after dark, the bush was alive with dangerous animals, and we found creeping through the dense scrub nerve-racking. There was no sign of Elsa, so, defeated, we returned.

At dawn we resumed our search, and soon found her pugmarks mixed up with those of a large lion; the spoors led down to the river and reappeared on the far side. Here there were outcrops of rock, and we thought that perhaps the lion had his domain there and had taken Elsa to his lay-up.

About lunch-time a wild chatter started up among the baboons near the camp; we hoped that this might herald Elsa's return and, sure enough, soon she came, swimming across the river. She greeted us, rubbing her head against us in turn and talking to us excitedly about her adventures. We were glad not to find any scratches on her. Since it was only a fortnight since she had been badly treated by a lion when we were still at our former camp, we hoped that the fact that her new escapade had been voluntary was a good augury for her release.

One morning a waterbuck offered an excellent opportunity for initiating Elsa into killing. George shot it, but before it fell Elsa jumped at its throat and hung on like a bulldog until in a few minutes the animal died of suffocation. It was her first experience of killing a large animal of about her own weight. We now saw that she knew the vital spot by instinct and also the way of effecting a quick death, in fact she had made use of a lion's normal method of killing a prey, which is not as some people imagine by breaking its neck. She first ate the tail, and this, as we were to discover, became her normal practice; then she opened the animal between the hind legs, ate the guts and carefully buried the stomach, covering up all traces of blood. Might this be a way of deceiving the vultures? Then she seized the buck by the neck, and straddling it between her forepaws, dragged it into a strategically well-chosen spot, in this case a shady thicket some fifty yards away. We left her there to guard her kill by day from vultures, and, after dark, from hyena. One frequently hears stories of lion carrying their victims away by swinging them across their backs. Neither George nor I have ever seen a lion act in this way; though it is true that they will carry a small animal such as a dog or a hare in their mouths. We have always seen them drag anything larger in the way which Elsa used on this and all other occasions.

About teatime we went back to visit her, and brought her water. Although she loved her afternoon walk with us, this time she made no attempt to leave her kill. When it became dark she did not return, but about three a.m. we were awakened by a heavy cloudburst and soon after this she appeared and spent the rest of the night in camp.

Early in the morning we all went out to see what had happened to her kill. Of course it had disappeared, and the ground was patterned with lion and hyena spoor. Nearby, we heard some lion grunts; these made us wonder whether it was the rain or the lions which had made Elsa leave her kill during the night.

Although Elsa's health had greatly improved, she was still far from her usual self and preferred to spend most of her day in camp. In order to break this habit and to make her lie up in the cool shade of the river, George took her out fishing with him. She would watch intently for the slightest ripple in the water and as soon as he hooked a fish she plunged into the river to give the wriggling creature the *coup de grâce* and retrieve it. Sometimes we had great difficulty in removing the hook before she dashed off to camp with the fish; once there, she usually placed the fish on George's bed, as if to say: 'This cold, strange kill is yours', and then she would return to await the next catch. This new game was great fun, but we needed to find another device to attract her away from the camp.

Close to the river stood a magnificent tree, its branches nearly sweeping the water. Under its green canopy, protected by its cool shade and subdued light from the glaring sun, I felt as though I were under a dome. Here, concealed by the low branches, I watched many wild creatures, lesser kudu and bush-buck, which came to the river to drink, a hammer-headed stork also came to quench his thirst and there were baboons; they provided the real fun. Sitting there with Elsa close to me, I felt as though I were on the doorstep of paradise; man and beast in trusting harmony; the slow-flowing river adding to the idyll. I thought that this place would make a stimulating 'studio' for me to paint or write in, so we nailed some chop-boxes across a wooden frame and improvised a table and bench, and soon I began to work there, leaning against the broad trunk of the tree.

Standing on her hind legs, Elsa inspected my paintbox and typewriter suspiciously; and resting both her front paws on the unfortunate tools, she licked my face and wanted to be assured of my affection before I was allowed to start work. Then she settled down at my feet and I began, full of inspiration; but I had not reckoned with our audience. As soon as I tried to concentrate I heard the inquiring bark of a baboon peeping through the foliage; then the bush on the opposite bank became alive with inquisitive watching faces. Soon, intrigued by Elsa, they came more and more into the open, swinging recklessly from tree to tree, screaming and barking, sliding backwards down the trunks or hopping and swaying like shadows in the treetops, until one little chap fell with a splash into the river. At once, an old baboon came to its rescue, and clutching the wet, struggling creature, raced off with it to safety. At this, all the baboons in the world seemed to have got loose and the screeching was deafen-ing. Elsa, who could tolerate the noise no longer, plunged into the river and swam across, accompanied by the hilarious shrieks of the baboons. As soon as she had reached firm ground she jumped at the nearest of the little tormentors. He swung tantalizingly low but nimbly avoided a spanking by hopping to a higher branch, from which place of safety he pulled faces and shook the branch at Elsa. The others joined in the game, and the more infuriated Elsa became, the more they enjoyed teasing her – they sat just out of her reach, scratching their posteriors, pretending to be utterly unaware of the raging lioness just below. The scene was so funny that in spite of Elsa's humiliation I opened my ciné camera and filmed it. This was too much for her; as soon as she saw me focusing the hated box on her, she splashed back through the river and, before I had time to secure the camera, she leapt on me and we both rolled over in the sand with the precious Bolex. Everything was wet; the baboons applauded our performance enthusiastically, and I fear that in the eyes of our audience both Elsa and I lost face very considerably.

After this the baboons looked every day for Elsa, and both sides got to know each other very well. As she tolerated their provocations and took to ignoring them, they grew bolder and bolder. Often they squatted for their daily drinks at the edge of the rapids, separated by only a few yards of water from her. One would keep sentry duty while the others sat on their haunches and, bending low, slowly drank their fill.

They were not the only cheeky small animals who annoyed Elsa. For instance, once when we had brought back a buck a bush monitor appeared. These harmless large lizards, which are about three to five feet long and four to six inches wide, have forked tongues, they live in rivers and eat fish, but also enjoy meat. A superstition is that they give warning of the approach of crocodiles; in fact, they do eat the eggs of crocodiles and so act as one of nature's controls. Now, this one endeavoured to snatch a few bites from Elsa's meal. She tried to catch him, but he was much too quick for her. So she covered the kill safely out of his reach, and thus prevented him from stealing another scrap of her carcase. This behaviour was in contrast to her attitude towards us. She liked me to hold her food for her while she ate it and would allow George and Nuru to handle her 'kill'. We were her 'pride' and she was quite prepared to share everything with us, but she had no intention of sharing with a monitor. In fact, she also differentiated between myself, George, Nuru and the rest of our staff; she would, for instance, allow any of us to take her meat out of the tent, but she did not allow the boys or the cook to do so.

Our idyll would have been perfect if Elsa had not been a carnivore which had to be trained to kill. Our next victim was a gerenuk. After Elsa had done her share in the killing we left her, some miles away from our camp, in charge of the carcase. On our way home we saw a lion walking in her direction. Had he already scented the kill? When, in the afternoon, we went to visit Elsa, she as well as the kill had gone, but plenty of big lion spoor told us what had happened. We followed her pugmarks for over two miles; they led towards her favourite rock, on which, with our field glasses, we eventually detected her. She had been clever enough to choose the only spot where she felt strategically safe from lion and could also be seen by us from a distance.

One night we were awakened by snorts and commotion coming from the direction of the salt lick. Before we were properly awake, Elsa rushed out of the tent to protect her 'den'. There followed more snorts and commotions, which gradually faded away. Evidently Elsa had done her stuff; soon she returned panting, flung herself down next to George's bed and, putting one paw on him, seemed to say, 'Now all is safe again. It was only a rhino.'

She did the same thing a few nights later with a herd of elephant. Their startled screams coming from behind the camp were enough to send her into action, and fortunately she succeeded in chasing the giants away. Their trumpeting was terrifying. I am always scared of elephant – they are the only big game which really do frighten me. Now I could not help thinking how easily the situation might have been reversed. The elephants might have chased Elsa, and she would of course have come back to us for protection. George laughed at my fears, but I felt far from confident in always trusting to luck.

Every day a buffalo approached our camp until one morning he became a victim: George shot him. Although he was dead long before Elsa arrived, she went wild with excitement – indeed, she got far more worked up over this carcase than we had ever seen her before at a kill. She pounced madly on the dead buffalo, attacking from every side and turning somersaults across the body. But however uncontrolled her movements seemed to be, she took good care to keep out of reach of the deadly horns. Finally she tapped the buffalo on the nose with her paw to make sure that he was dead.

George's main purpose in shooting such a big beast had been to attract wild lion to the kill. We hoped that if they came, Elsa could join in the feast and make friends with them. In order to control whatever might happen, we decided to drag the carcase close to the camp and then leave Elsa in charge of it. Meanwhile we went off to fetch the car. When we returned the trees around were weighed down with vultures and marabou storks, but Elsa was keeping them at bay, sitting out in the hot sun next to her kill. She was plainly much relieved when we, her 'pride', took over and made it possible for her to retire to a shady bush. But as soon as the boys started to cut open the inch-thick skin of the buffalo, she could not resist it and rushed up to join in. While they were slicing open the stomach, she helped, tore out guts between the busy knives, and chewed them with delight under the very hands of the butchering boys. She sucked the intestines into her mouth like spaghetti, at the same time pressing with her teeth so that the unwanted contents were ejected like toothpaste from a tube. Good-naturedly she watched the carcase being fastened to a chain and attached to the car. Then while the poor Land Rover jerked across uneven ground towing the heavy buffalo, she rode – as usual – on the canvas roof, adding another 300 lb to the load.

After the kill had been secured with a chain to a tree close to camp, Elsa guarded it jealously during the whole of the following day and night. Judging by the never-ending chorus of high-pitched chuckles from hyena, she was kept very busy after dark but next morning when we returned she was still protecting the carcase. Only then did she leave it, making it very plain that it was now *our* turn to be on guard while she trotted away to the river. We covered the kill with thorns as a protection from vultures and so saved it for another night's 'defence' lesson.

Elsa joined us on our usual afternoon's walk, her swaying belly full of buffalo meat. After a short time through the bush she spotted a hyena making its way slowly towards the kill. Immediately she froze, her left front paw suspended in the air. Then, with the utmost caution, she lowered herself to a crouching position, blending among the straw-coloured grass till she was almost invisible. Tense with controlled excitement, she watched the hyena hobbling peacefully along, quite unaware that it had an audience. When it came to within a few yards, Elsa rushed forward and gave it a well-aimed smack. With a yell the animal rolled over and lay on its back emitting howls and long-drawn moans. Elsa looked at us, and jerked her head in her characteristic way towards her victim, as though saying: 'What shall we do next?' As she did not get any encouragement from us, she started licking her paws and appeared utterly bored by the miserable creature in front of her. Gradually the hyena pulled itself together and eventually, still whining protests, sneaked away.

Elsa's trust in us was shown on other occasions.

Late one afternoon we had left her in charge of a buck which she and George had killed a long distance from the camp. Knowing that she would not remain with it alone during the night so far away from us, we collected a car to bring it nearer to camp. But on our return, Elsa and the kill had gone. Soon, however, she appeared through the bush and led us to the hide-out to which she had dragged it during our absence. Although she was very pleased to see us, she would not allow us to pull the kill to the car, and all the tricks I tried to make her leave it failed: she was not going to be fooled. Finally we manoeuvred the car in front of the carcase, and I pointed first to the car and then to the buck, then to the car and again to the buck, trying to make her see that we wanted to help her. She must have understood, for suddenly she got up, rubbed her head against my knees and pulled her kill from under the thornbush towards the car. Finally she tried to lift it by the head into the Land Rover; soon realizing that she could not do this from outside, she then leapt into the car, and from there, gripping the head, pulled with all her strength while we lifted the hindquarters. When the buck was safely inside, Elsa sat on it panting, while George drove on. However, she found that bumping through the bush was not at all comfortable in her cramped position, so she jumped out again and on to the roof, bending her head frequently to see if all was well inside and the kill still there.

When we arrived at the camp we had to face the problem of getting the buck out of the car, but now Elsa treated us as her allies and let us do most of the pulling. Everyone was helping except myself, so Elsa walked up to me and gave me an encouraging spank, as though to say, 'What about you helping too?'

Although we had left the kill fairly near the camp, we soon heard her dragging it along with the intention, no doubt, of bringing it inside our tent. We quickly closed the thorn fence, locking her out with her smelly buck. Poor Elsa, it was much safer inside the tent; now she would have to spend the whole night protecting it. The best thing she could do was to place it against the outside of the thorn fence and this she did. As a result, the hyenas came so close and made so much noise that sleep was impossible. Finally Elsa must have got tired of chasing the creatures away, for we heard her dragging the buck towards the river and then splashing through the water with it. This defeated the hyenas and they left. Did she know that they would not follow her through water?

Next morning we found her spoor and the marks left by dragging the kill. They led across the river but then, it seemed, she had not wanted to be separated from us and so she had dragged it back to our side. Here she had placed it in impenetrable bush, right at the water's edge, so that no animal could get at it unless they approached from the river. We now found her resting with the buck, and she made it obvious that she was very much hurt that we had locked her out; it took us a long time to win back her confidence and to be forgiven.

Although Elsa had no mother to teach her, she knew by instinct how far she could go with wild animals. Many times on our walks through the bush we watched her, sniffing the air and then stalking determinedly in one direction until we heard the crashing of big bodies breaking through the woods. On several occasions she detected rhino and chased them away from us; in fact she was an excellent watchdog.

Several herds of buffalo had made their home on a nearby ridge and Elsa never missed an opportunity of stirring these heavy animals into commotion. More than once she surprised them fast asleep, dodged round them, hopping nimbly out of range of their horns, and she always stood her ground until the buffaloes departed.

One morning we walked in a dry river bed and read the 'news' about last night's visitors in the sand. Two lion and plenty of elephant were of major importance. The sun was getting hot and we were all tired after a three-hour walk. The wind was against us and, coming carelessly round a bend, we nearly collided with a herd of elephant. Luckily Elsa was trotting a short distance behind us, so we had time to jump on to the high bank, while the elephants climbed up the other side and took three tiny calves into safety, and one old bull kept in the rear, ready to charge should there be any nonsense. Elsa came sleepily along, then, seeing the bull, sat down. We watched, wondering what would happen. Both sides looked at each other for what seemed to us an endless time. Finally, it was the elephant who gave in and joined his herd, while Elsa rolled on her back, getting rid of some tsetse flies.

On our way home George shot a waterbuck which was standing in the river. Badly hit, it dashed across to the opposite side, followed by Elsa who splashed unbelievably fast through the deep water. When we arrived at the other bank we found her amongst the river bush, panting, on top of the dead buck. She was very excited and did not allow us to touch her kill. So we decided to return home and leave her to guard it. As soon as we started wading back through the water, she began to follow us, but seemed torn between conflicting impulses: she did not want to be left on the wrong side of the river with her kill, on the other hand she did not want to lose it. Eventually she returned reluctantly to it, but soon made another attempt to cross, only to turn back again but undecidedly. However, by the time we had reached the opposite bank Elsa had made up her mind.

Now we saw her dragging the buck into the water. What was she up to? Surely she could not bring this heavy animal across alone? But Elsa was not going to be defeated. She held the carcase in her mouth and swam with it through the deep water, her head often submerged to get a better grip. She hauled and tugged, pushed and pulled, and when the buck got stuck, pounced on it to get it floating again. Often both disappeared from view and only Elsa's tail or one leg of the buck told us of the struggle that was going on at the bottom of the river. We watched fascinated. After half an hour of strenuous effort, she trailed her quarry proudly through the shallow water near to us. By now she was really exhausted, but her task was not finished yet. After tugging the buck into a little sheltered bay where the current could not carry it away, she looked for a safe hiding place. The bank here was a solid network of sharp-edged, thorn-hooked doum-palm seedlings, which overhung the steep walls that lined the river; even Elsa could not penetrate this thicket.

We left her with her kill and went back to camp to collect some bush knives and ropes and to have our overdue breakfast. When we returned, we cut a passage through the doum-palm under-growth to the water's edge and, while Elsa watched the men suspiciously, I slipped a rope noose over the buck's head. Now all was ready to haul it up the steep bank. At the first tug Elsa growled and flattened her ears warningly – obviously she thought that her kill was going to be taken away from her. But as soon as she saw me join in the pulling, she relaxed, and climbed up the bank. Our combined efforts landed the buck ten feet above the river where the boys had cut a well-protected shady shelter for Elsa and her kill. Now she realized what we had done for her and it was touching to see her going from one to another of us, rubbing her head and thanking everyone in turn with a low moan.

On two occasions I watched her walk unconcernedly through a broad stream of black soldier ants, scattering their organized columns in all directions with her large paws. Although these fierce ants usually bite at anything which disturbs their migra-tion, for some reason they did not take their revenge on Elsa.

One day we were very tired and I was walking along absentmindedly behind Elsa. Suddenly she gave a terrific grunt, reared up on her hind legs and leaped back. We were passing a tree which forked about five feet above the ground and now coiled up in it I saw a red cobra, erecting its hood towards us. Thanks to Elsa, nothing happened, but to pass a cobra at such close range might have been serious. It was the first time I had seen one in a tree. Even Elsa was impressed, and during the next few days she made a careful detour whenever we came near to that tree.

At this time it was very hot and Elsa spent much of her time in the river. Often she stood half-submerged in the cool water; although we often saw crocodiles, they never seemed to worry her. Whenever George shot a guinea fowl near the river, Elsa retrieved it from the water and used its rescue as an excuse for prolonged splashings with the bird in her mouth; she enjoyed the game just as much as we loved watching her.

She had now completely recovered and was perfectly fit. She was very conservative in her habits and except for slight variations our routine was the same every day: an early morning walk, followed by her midday slumber close to me by our tree on the river bank. This lasted until teatime, then came our afternoon stroll. On our return she found her meal waiting for her; she usually carried it on to the roof of the Land Rover, where she remained until the lights were put out and everybody went to bed. Then she joined George in his tent, sleeping next to his bed on the ground, a paw always in touch with him.

One afternoon Elsa refused to come for a walk. When we returned after dark she had disappeared and did not return until early next morning. Later we found large lion pugmarks close to camp, and when she came back I again noticed the peculiar smell which was typical of her being in season. Her manners were another indication of this condition. Although she was very friendly, the real affection was missing. Soon after breakfast she was off again and kept away all day. After dark we heard her hopping on to the Land Rover and I went out at once to play with her. But she was aloof and very restless, jumped down, and vanished into the dark. During the night I heard her splashing in the river, to the accompaniment of agitated noises coming from alarmed baboons; this lasted until early morning. Then Elsa returned for a quick visit to the camp, tolerated George's pattings, purred at him and went off again. It was obvious that she was in love.

We knew now by experience that this period lasted about four days. Unlike the conditions in our former camp, everything here was favourable to giving her an opportunity to go back to her natural life. The right moment seemed to have come, so we decided to withdraw tactfully for one week and leave her alone – we hoped in the company of a mate. We had to act quickly in order to avoid her seeing our departure.

While we were packing, Elsa returned. We therefore arranged that while I looked after her George would break camp, drive the loaded cars a distance of about one mile, and send a message to me to join him when everything was ready.

I took Elsa away from the camp to our tree. Would this be the last time we should see it together? She knew something was wrong; and though I tried to keep to our normal routine and had taken the typewriter along and made the familiar tickings to appease her suspicions, she was not reassured, nor could I type properly for my mind was too upset. Although we had prepared ourselves for this release and hoped it might give Elsa a happier future than she would have living in captivity, it was a different matter when it came to making the break, and actually to cut through our affection and leave her, possibly never to see her again. Elsa must have felt my emotion for she rubbed her silky head against me.

The river flowed slowly in front of us, as it had flowed yesterday and it would flow tomorrow. A hornbill called, some dry leaves fell off the tree and were carried away by the water. Elsa was part of this life. She belonged to nature and not to man. We were 'man' and we loved her and she had been brought up to love us. Would she be able to forget all that had been familiar to her until this morning? Would she go and hunt when she was hungry? Or would she wait trustfully for our return, knowing that up to now we had never let her down? I had just given her a kiss to reassure her of my affection and to give her a feeling of security, but was it a kiss of betrayal? How could she know that it needed all the strength of my love for her to leave her now and give her back to nature – to let her learn to live alone until she might find her pride – her real pride?

Nuru came, and called me away. He had brought some meat along and Elsa followed him trustfully into the reeds and started to eat – then we stole away.

8. The Final Test

We drove ten miles to another river, smaller but much deeper than the one we had left; here we intended to spend a week. Late in the afternoon George and I strolled along the bank; we walked quietly, our thoughts with Elsa. I realized acutely how much I had become dependent on her; how much I had for nearly three years lived the life of a lioness, shared her feelings, interests and reactions. We had lived so intimately together that being alone seemed unbearable. I felt desperately lonely with no Elsa walking at my side, rubbing her head against me and letting me feel her soft skin and warm body. There was of course the hope of seeing her again in one week's time. How much that meant to me.

The sun was sinking, and its warm light was reflected on the shiny fronds of the doum-palms, tinting their tops with a golden glow.

Again I thought of Elsa – what a beautiful world she had been born into. Whatever losing her might mean to me, we must now try our utmost to give her back to this life and save her from a captive existence, in which she would be deprived of all that nature intended for her. Although, up to now, there was no record of a hand-reared lion being successfully liberated, we still hoped that Elsa would be able to adapt herself to wild life, to a life to which she had always been so close.

At last, the week of anxiety ended and we went back to see how Elsa had stood up to the test.

When we arrived at our former camp we looked at once for her pugmarks; there was no sign of them. I began to call. Soon afterwards we heard her familiar 'hnk-hnk' and saw her coming from the river trotting as fast as she could. Her welcome showed us that she had missed us as much as we had missed her and her rubbings and miaowings touched us deeply. We had brought her a buck, but she hardly glanced at it and continued her greetings. As soon as the great rejoicings were over I looked at her stomach: it was full. She must have eaten recently; this took a great load off my mind for it meant that she was now safe. She had proved that she could fend for herself and be independent of us, at least so far as food was concerned.

While our tents were being pitched, I took her to the river and there we rested together. I was happy now and could relax, feeling that Elsa's future was assured. She must have felt the same, for she laid her big soft paw on me and dozed off. I was awakened by her raising her head and looking at a bushbuck, whose reddish shape appeared through the foliage on the opposite bank. Elsa watched without interest while the antelope stepped slowly along, unaware of our presence. However happy

Elsa might be at the moment I knew that her lack of interest in the buck was partly due to her full belly. What had she eaten? Some little vervet monkeys were watching us silently through the trees, but where were our noisy friends, the usually ever present baboons? Later on, my fears about her first kill were confirmed for we found tufts of baboon hair close to the drinking place, where they had so often teased Elsa.

Now that our minds were at ease regarding Elsa's future, we decided to enjoy her company for another short period and wait till an opportunity occurred of making the final break, in some way which would not be too painful. We took up our life where we had left it off. Although Elsa seldom let us out of her sight, we thought it a good omen that she continued to follow her hunting instinct and sometimes, when we were on our walks, deserted us for an hour.

The country had become very dry and often the sky was lit up by grass fires. The short rains were due in the next two or three weeks and the parched ground was thirsty for the life-giving food. Tsetse flies were very active and poor Elsa found them most irritating, particularly just after sunrise and again before sunset. She would rush frantically through the low bush to brush them off or would fling her itching body on to the ground, her normally sleek coat standing on end.

To make her more independent of our camp life, we took her out for the whole day and after an early morning walk of two or three hours, settled down in a shady place along the river. We picnicked and I took out my sketchbook. Elsa soon dozed off and I often used her as a pillow when I read or slept. George spent most of the time fishing and usually produced our lunch straight from the river. Elsa had to have the fish first, but after mouthing it for a short time she would pull a grimace of disgust and showed no further interest in the rest of George's catch. Nuru and the gun bearer proved to be

The cubs, soon after their arrival with the author, and Pati-Pati, who accepted them as desirable companions.

Above: Stalking practice
– from the earliest age
they knew by instinct
how to do it properly.

Left: The tyre game.

Elsa after her sisters had left for Rotterdam – it was heartbreaking to see her searching for them.

Left and above: By the Indian Ocean – at first she was nervous of the rush and roar of the waves, but very soon she became quite water crazy.

Sharing my camp bed at Lake Rudolf.

Elsa resting in a tree to
catch the breeze.

Elsa's daily claw-
strengthening exercises.

Elsa with Nuru Makedde and Ibrahim.

We found Elsa waiting and very hungry after the second release.

Elsa with the author.

Elsa preferred the Land Rover roof for short rides.

Elsa's favourite lookout – she found the breeze cool, no tsetse fly molested her and she could watch the animals below.

Hollow baobab trees always attracted Elsa.

Reunion after my return from England – she used her 300 lb to bowl me over.

excellent chefs and roasted our meal as soon as it had been caught.

Once we surprised a crocodile sunning itself on a rock; startled, it plunged into a narrow pool which was cut off by rapids at either end. The water was so clear and shallow that we could see the bottom, but we could see no sign of the 'croc' and we wondered where it could have got to. We settled down to our meal; Elsa relaxed on the water's edge and I leant against her. Soon George got up to go on with his fishing; but first, to make sure that the croc was not still in the pool, he prodded along the bottom with a long stick; suddenly it was wrenched from his hand and a six foot croc, which had been hiding in the sand, slithered over the rapids and disappeared into another pool. It had bitten off the end of the tough stick. As Elsa had not noticed this incident, and as we did not wish to encourage her to hunt crocodile, we moved away.

Shortly afterwards, a warthog came along for his noonday drink. Elsa stalked him carefully, then, helped by a bullet from George's rifle, seized the pig by the throat and suffocated it. The encounter took place at a little distance from the river and, as I thought it would be more comfortable for Elsa to guard her kill in the shade by the water, I pointed to the pig and then to the river, several times, saying, '*Maji*, Elsa, *maji*, Elsa.' She was familiar with the word *maji*, which I used when I wanted Nuru to fill her water bowl. Now it seemed that she perfectly understood this Swahili word for water, for she dragged her pig to the river. She played with the carcase in the water for nearly two hours, splashing and diving with it, and thoroughly enjoying herself until she was quite exhausted. Finally she pulled the pig on to the opposite bank and disappeared with it into a thicket; there she guarded it until it was time for us to return to camp, then she seemed determined not to be left behind, for as soon as we got up to go, she dragged the kill back to our side. We cut it up before her and, having distributed the meat between Nuru and the gun bearer, set off with Elsa trotting good-naturedly behind us.

From then on, every time Elsa made a kill near the river, she went to great pains to drag it down to the water and repeated the game she had had with the warthog. We were at a loss to account for this strange behaviour: perhaps she had accepted '*Maji*, Elsa' as a good rule and as part of her education.

These daily excursions brought all of us much closer together and even Nuru and the gun bearer felt so much at ease in Elsa's presence that they did not bother to get up when she strolled over to them for a nose-rubbing or sat on them, in her playful way. Nor did they mind sharing the back of the Land Rover with her and when she dumped her 300 lb between their bony legs, they only laughed and petted her, while she licked their knees with her rough tongue.

Once, when we were resting on the river bank with Elsa lying asleep between us, George noticed two black faces peering at us out of the undergrowth on the opposite bank. They were a couple of poachers armed with bows and poisoned arrows, who had chosen this spot to lie up and ambush game coming down to the water to drink.

Immediately he gave the alarm and dashed across the river closely followed by Nuru and the gun bearer; Elsa, suddenly alerted and always ready for a bit of fun, joined in the chase. The poachers made good their escape, but I would give a lot to hear the tale they had to tell when they got back to their village about how 'bwana game' (George's native name) was now employing lions to hunt poachers.

Early one morning when we were out on our pre-breakfast walk, Elsa took the lead and with great determination headed in a set direction, towards a point at which we had heard much trumpeting of elephant during the night.

Suddenly she stopped sniffing the wind and, with her head stretched out, went off at a fast trot, leaving us behind. A few moments later, in the far distance, we heard the faint call of a lion. She stayed away all that day. Late in the evening we heard her call a long way off mingled with that of another lion. During the night hyena were much in evidence and kept us awake with their inane laughter. At dawn, we followed Elsa's spoor and soon found it leading away from camp and mixed up with the pugmarks of the other lion. The next day we found her spoor alone; on the fourth day of her absence, we tracked her across the river. We searched for her all that day until we found ourselves unexpectedly in the middle of a herd of elephant; then there was nothing to do but to run for it. Early on the fifth morning Elsa returned very hungry and ate until her belly was near to bursting point. After that, she retired to my camp bed and made it clear that she was not to be disturbed. Later I noticed two deep bites and several smaller claw marks on the curve of her hind legs; these I dressed as best I could. She responded affectionately, sucking my thumbs and holding me close. In the afternoon, she did not want to go for a walk and sat on the roof of the Land Rover until dark, then she disappeared into the night. Some two hours later we heard a lion's roar in the distance and Elsa's immediate reply. At first, the sound came from near the camp but gradually her voice faded away in the direction of the lion.

The following morning, we decided that this was an opportune moment to leave her alone for another few days and moved camp so as not to handicap her association with the wild lion, who might take exception to our presence. We knew now that she was quite capable of looking after herself, which made this parting less painful than the first one, but I was worried about her bites, which looked as though they might turn septic.

After a week we returned to our camping place and interrupted Elsa while she was stalking two waterbuck. It was early in the afternoon and very hot; poor thing, she must have been very hungry to be hunting so late in the day. She gave us a touching welcome and gorged herself on the meat we had brought her. I noticed a new bite on her elbow and her old wounds were badly in need of dressing. For the next three days she made up for her period of starvation.

By now, Elsa's fame had spread far and wide and a party of American sportsmen paid us a visit specially to film her. She entertained them royally and did everything she could to please them. She climbed a tree, played in the river, hugged me, joined us for tea and behaved in such a docile manner that none of our guests could believe that she was a full-grown lioness, who shortly before they arrived had been equally at ease in the company of wild lions.

That night, we heard a lion call and Elsa promptly vanished into the darkness and was away for two days. During this time she returned for one brief visit to George's tent. She was most affectionate and nearly broke his camp bed by sitting on top of him, as he lay asleep. After a short meal, she went off again. In the morning we followed her spoor which led us to a rocky ridge near the camp. After climbing to the top and looking unsuccessfully for her in all her favourite lying-up places, we nearly fell over her in a clump of thick bush. Obviously she had kept quiet in the hope that we should not see her. Yet, in spite of her obvious wish to be alone, she gave us her usual affectionate greeting and pretended to be very pleased to see us. We respected her feelings, and tactfully left her alone. Late that evening we heard the roar of a lion and the howling of his retinue of hyena up river. Soon Elsa's voice sounded close to camp. Perhaps by now she had learned to keep away from her lord and master while he was at his kill and was waiting until he had his fill before making a closer acquaintance with him. Later she returned to George's tent for a few moments, put her paw affectionately round him and moaned softly, as if to say to him: 'You know that I love you, but I have a friend outside to whom I simply *must* go; I hope you will understand,' then she was off again. Early next morning, we found the pugmarks of a big lion close to camp; obviously he had waited while Elsa went to George's tent to explain the situation. She kept away for three days, returning each evening for a few minutes just to show us her affection but going off again without touching the meat which was ready for her. When she returned after such escapades she always seemed more affectionate than ever, as though she wished to make up for having neglected us.

The rains had started and as usual they stimulated Elsa's energy and playfulness. She just had to ambush us from any suitable cover. As among our pride I was her favourite 'lioness' she honoured me with most of her attentions, and so I was the one who usually found myself on the ground with Elsa's soft, but heavy, body on top of me, holding me down until George released me. Although I knew it was only affection that singled me out for these privileges, I had to stop this practice as I was quite unable to get her off me without help. Soon she understood by the tone of my voice that the game was not popular and it was touching to see how she tried to control her pent-up energy so that, even when she was making a flying leap, she would control it at the last moment and reach me in a dignified manner.

After the first downpour of rain the dry, grey thornbush changed within a few days into a garden of Eden. Every grain of sand seemed to give way to a seed bursting up from beneath. We walked along tracks of luxuriant sap-green growth; each bush a giant bouquet of white, pink or yellow blossom. But, however pleasing this transformation was to our senses, it only added to the anxieties of our walks, for now visibility was reduced to a few feet. There were rain pools everywhere and each was a concentration of freshly marked game tracks. Elsa took full advantage of these bush newsreels and would often leave us to go hunting. Sometimes, we watched her stalking waterbuck, which she drove towards us, at others, followed her tracks while she was in pursuit of bushbuck; when doing this she would cleverly cut in a straight line across their winding tracks. However, as in these days she was well fed and had a full stomach, she regarded such hunts more as a pastime than as serious work.

One morning, we were walking quietly along the river, intending to spend the day out; Elsa was with us, full of energy, and, judging by the twitching of her tail, was having a wonderful time. After walking for two hours we were looking for a place to have breakfast when, suddenly, I saw her stop abruptly, her ears cocked and her body tense with excitement. The next moment she was off, jumping noiselessly down the rocks which flank the river at this point; then she disappeared into the thick undergrowth below. Here the river is divided by several islets, each an impenetrable thicket of bush, fallen trees and debris. We had stopped to wait for the outcome of her stalk, when we heard, as I thought, the unmistakable sound of elephant trumpeting. Deep vibrations shook the air and I was convinced that there was more than one elephant in the thicket below. George disagreed, saying that the noise was made by a buffalo. I had heard countless buffalo making their various expressive bellows but none had ever made such a typical elephant sound. We waited for at least five minutes, hoping that Elsa would get bored with her big friends as, after a short time, she usually did. Then came a deep rumbling sound and before I realized what was happening George leapt down the rocks, saying that Elsa was in trouble. I followed, as fast as I could, but was brought to a halt by a fresh outburst of violent bellowings just ahead. I felt most uneasy as I penetrated the thick bush, imagining that at any moment the massive shape of an enraged elephant would break through and squash everything in its path. Instinctively the men and myself stopped and called to George not to go on, but nothing would deter him and he disappeared behind the green walls of creepers and trees. Now we heard an ear-splitting scream followed by urgent shouts from George: 'Come, quick, quick!' My heart turned to lead – an accident must have happened. As I stumbled as fast as I could through the thicket, terrible scenes flashed through my mind. But soon, thank God, I saw George's sunburnt back through the foliage; he was standing upright, so all must be well.

Again he repeated his summons to hurry. When I finally broke through the bush to the river bank, what I saw was Elsa dripping wet, sitting on top of a bull buffalo in the middle of the rapids. I could not believe my eyes; here was a buffalo helplessly forced down with his head half submerged, while Elsa tore away at its thick skin and attacked from every angle. We could only guess at what had happened since, ten minutes earlier, I first heard my 'elephant noise'. Elsa must have disturbed the buffalo, an old bull past his prime, as we later discovered, while he was resting close to the water, and chased him towards the river. Then in his attempt to cross, he must have fallen on the slippery rock of the rapids; and Elsa had taken advantage of his predicament, jumped on him and held his head under water until he was half drowned and too exhausted to get up. After this she had attacked him at his most vulnerable spot, between the hind legs, and was doing so when we arrived.

George waited until Elsa gave him a chance to end the unfortunate animal's agony with a merciful bullet. As soon as this *coup de grâce* had been delivered, we saw Nuru wade, waist deep, into the foaming rapids. He could not resist the chance of gorging himself on this mountain of meat, but, as he was a Mohammedan, he would not be able to eat the buffalo unless he had cut its throat before it died. There was no time to lose, so there he was venturing between the hidden, slippery rocks towards the kill. From her position on top of the buffalo Elsa watched his every movement with tense excitement. Although she had known Nuru since she was a tiny cub and had allowed him every sort of familiarity, she was now highly suspicious and, with flattened ears and threatening growls, defended her buffalo even against her nanny. She looked really dangerous; but Nuru, driven by gluttonous visions, paid no heed to her warnings. It was a ludicrous sight to see his fragile skinny figure staggering fearlessly towards the fiercely growling lioness, perched on the top of a dying and kicking buffalo; as he advanced he waved his first finger at her, calling out, 'No, No.'

Incredible as it may seem, Elsa obeyed him and, sitting quietly on top of the buffalo, allowed him to cut its throat.

The next problem was to get the dead beast out of the river. We had to drag it through the rapids between the slippery rocks. To achieve moving 1,200 lb in such circumstances with an excited lioness guarding it, was no easy task.

But Elsa, intelligent as she is, soon realized what was required, and by seizing him by the root of the tail, while three men pulled at the head and legs, literally helped to get the buffalo out. Combined with much laughter at Elsa's efforts, their joint strength succeeded in hauling out the carcase, which was then cut up. Here again, Elsa was most helpful. Each time one of the big, heavy legs was severed from the body, she at once dragged it into the shade of a bush, thus saving the boys the task of doing so later on. Luckily we were able to bring the Land Rover to within a mile of the scene and managed to get most of the meat to camp.

Elsa was exhausted: she must have swallowed quantities of water during her battle with the great beast and she had spent at least two hours up to her neck in the fast current of a river. But, tired as she was, she would not leave her kill until she knew that it was safe and that all had been cut up; only when all was finished did she retire to the shade of a bush.

When I joined her a few moments later, she licked my arm, embraced me with her paw and hugged me to her wet body. We relaxed after the morning's excitement. I felt very touched by her gentleness and the care with which she treated my skin and avoided scratching me with claws that only a few minutes ago had been so deadly to the thick skin of a powerful buffalo.

Even for a wild lion, it would have been a remarkable achievement to kill a buffalo bull single-handed, let alone for Elsa, who had only recently learned the art of hunting from her very inferior foster parents. Although the river had been a good ally to her, it had needed considerable intelligence on her part to take advantage of it and I felt very proud of her.

Late in the afternoon on our way back to camp, we came upon a giraffe drinking on the opposite bank of the river. Forgetting her weariness, Elsa stalked it; she crossed the river, most carefully, downwind and out of view of her quarry, and, avoiding making the least splash, she disappeared into the riverine bush. The giraffe, unaware of any danger, splayed its forelegs as far as possible, and bent its long neck down to the water to drink. We held our breath, expecting that at any moment Elsa would leap out of the bush and attack, but, to our great relief, the giraffe heard, or sensed, Elsa's presence in the nick of time and with a swift movement turned and galloped away. It was lucky for the giraffe that Elsa was so full of buffalo meat. Her adventures for the day were not yet at an end and as her motto seemed to be 'the bigger the better', it only remained for an elephant to appear, ambling slowly along the game path towards us. While we hurriedly retreated in order to make a detour round him, Elsa sat quietly in the middle of the path and waited until the mighty animal was nearly upon her, then sprang nimbly aside, causing him to turn and make off at high speed. After this she quietly followed us back to camp, flung herself down on George's bed and quickly went to sleep. Not a bad record for one day.

Not long afterwards we were walking together along the shady river bank when we noticed basin-shaped circular depressions of mud about three feet in diameter, in a shallow lagoon. George told me they were the breeding-places of *tilapia*, a fish we had not so far seen in the river. While we investigated these mud hollows Elsa sniffed with great interest at a bush and wrinkled up her nose, a thing she often did when scenting a lion. Now we saw fresh pugmarks nearby and Elsa, who was purring distinctly, followed the spoor and disappeared. She kept away all night and the following day. When, in the afternoon, we looked for her, we detected her through field glasses outlined on her favourite rock. She must have seen us, for we heard her calling, but she made no attempt to move from her position. Thinking she might be near wild lions, we did not want to interfere, and returned home. After everyone had gone to bed, George heard the agonized cries of an animal in pain, and after a short time Elsa appeared in the tent and threw herself down next to his bed. She patted him several times with her paws as though she wanted to tell him something. Then after a few minutes she left again and was absent all night and the following day.

While we were having our dinner next evening, she walked into the tent, rubbed her head affectionately against me and then went out and spent the night away. In the morning we tracked her spoor over a long distance; it led far away. That evening she failed to come back; she had now kept away for three days, except for brief visits during which she had shown us her affection. Might this be her touching way of telling us that she had found her pride and, while she still loved us, was trying to loosen our ties?

During the night we were awakened by the most alarming

lion growls mixed with the laughing of hyenas. We listened, expecting Elsa to come in at any moment, but morning dawned and she did not return. As soon as it became light, we went in the direction from which the growls had come, but stopped after a few hundred yards, startled by an unmistakable lion grunt coming from the river below us. At the same time we saw an antelope and some vervet monkeys racing in flight through the bush. Creeping cautiously through thick undergrowth down to the river, we found the fresh pugmarks of at least two or three lions in the sand; they led across the river. Wading through, we followed the still wet spoor up the opposite bank when I noticed, not fifty yards away, through the dense bush the shape of a lion. While I strained my eyes to see if it was Elsa, George called to her. She walked away from us. When George repeated his call she only trotted faster along the game path until we saw the black tuft on the end of her tail swish for the last time through the bush.

We looked at each other. Had she found her destiny? She must have heard us; by following the lions she had decided her future. Did this mean that our hopes for her to return to her natural life had been fulfilled? Had we succeeded in letting her part from us without hurting her?

We returned to camp alone, and very sad. Should we leave her now, and so close a very important chapter of our lives? George suggested that we should wait a few more days to make sure that Elsa had been accepted by the pride.

I went to my studio by the river and continued to write the story of Elsa, who had been with us until this morning. I was sad to be alone, but tried to make myself happy by imagining that at this very moment Elsa was rubbing her soft skin against another lion's skin and resting with him in the shade, as she had often rested here with me.

9. Postscripts

To us it seemed impossible, after more than three years of such close companionship, that we should lose all touch with Elsa, so long as she was willing to keep in touch with us.

As George, in the course of his duties, is constantly travelling, we have endeavoured to pay a visit to the area where Elsa lives, at intervals of about three weeks. On arrival in camp we always fire a shot or two, or let off a thunderflash, and on nearly every occasion she has come running into camp within a few hours, giving us a great welcome and showing more affection than ever. Once it was fifteen hours before she came, and once thirty hours, when she must have been very far off and sensed our arrival in some mysterious way. During our three days' stay she never lets us out of her sight and is touchingly glad to be with us.

When the time comes for us to leave, George goes about ten miles away and shoots a buck or a warthog as a farewell gift to Elsa while the tents are being struck and loaded up. In the meantime, I sit with her in my studio under the big tree and try to divert her mind. As soon as the buck arrives she has a good feed, though we usually find her fat and well. She obviously learned long ago to make her own kills and is quite independent of us for food. While she is eating, the loaded cars are taken about a mile away and, as she becomes drowsy after her meal, we sneak away.

For some time before the final parting she becomes noticeably aloof and turns her face away from us; although she wants desperately to be with us, yet, when she realizes we are going, she makes it easier in this touching, dignified and controlled way. As this happens every time, it can hardly be coincidence.

A short time later I went to England to arrange for the publication of Elsa's book. During the months I have spent in London, George has written me accounts of all his visits to Elsa and her story is carried on by his letters. They prove not only her continued ability to combine the life of a wild lioness with her old relationship with us, but also that this relationship continues to be one of absolute equality quite different from that between a dog and his master.

Isolo, 5 March, 1959

I was able to get off to see Elsa on the evening of the 25th. Fifteen minutes after my arrival, she appeared from across the river. She must have heard the diesel lorry. She was looking fit, but thin and hungry. As usual, she made a great fuss of me before going to her meat. She was nothing like as thin as on the first occasion, and in a couple of days had put on flesh and looked as fit as ever. Obviously she was much puzzled that you were not there and went several times into your boma, and looked inside the lorry, calling. However, she soon settled down into the usual routine, except that she absolutely refused to leave the camp for a walk. She would go to the studio in the morning and spend the whole day there with me. When I brought her the second buck on Sunday morning, she would not let anyone go near it and was quite fierce. But as soon as I went down to the studio she dragged the buck along, deposited it by my seat, and did not mind my cutting it up. In the afternoon when I went back to my tent, she picked up the buck and brought it along to the tent. The next afternoon I said, 'Elsa, time to go home.' She waited until I picked up the remains of the buck and then solemnly walked ahead to the tent. The white spots on her back had disappeared. Her friend the monitor was still there, waiting to steal what he could. Now, she seems to accept him and pays no attention when he comes to the meat. Still no sign of her contacting lions.

I left Elsa on Tuesday. I took particular care to keep her down at the studio while the camp was being packed up. But as soon as she heard the diesel go off, she knew at once that I was going to leave her and adopted the same aloof manner and would not look at me. I intend to go and see her again on the 14th.

Isiolo, 19 March, 1959

I went again to visit Elsa on the 14th. Got away about 10.15 a.m. I arrived about 6.30 p.m. – there was no sign of Elsa, no spoor. I let off three thunderflashes during the course of the night, and a Very light. Next morning at dawn I set off to look for her. Went as far as the large water pool along the track where Elsa ambushed the elephant. The pool was dry and no spoor of Elsa. I let off another thunderflash and returned along the top of the ridge to the car track, and then back to camp along the sand lugga* behind the camp. Still no signs. Got into camp about 9.15 a.m. A quarter of an hour later she suddenly appeared from across the river, looking very fit with plenty of flesh on her bones. She must have killed at least once since I left her eleven days before. She gave me a tremendous welcome. She had some scars, probably caused in the struggle with her last kill, but they were superficial and had hardly penetrated the skin. She settled down straight away to her usual routine. She was rather full of beans and twice knocked me over, once into a thornbush! She condescended to go out once for a short walk down the river, but spent most of the days with me in the studio.

Still no signs of her being in contact with wild lions. I did

*Dry river bed.

not hear any on this trip. The country is very dry, which probably makes it easier for Elsa to hunt, as everything has to come to the river to drink and visibility is better. As I had only the mountain tent with me, it was a bit crowded at night with Elsa in it as well, but she behaved very well and never once wetted the groundsheet! As usual she would wake me up several times at night by 'rubbing noses' and sitting on me. There was no trouble in leaving her, which I did on Wednesday. In fact, I think she is becoming more independent and does not mind being left alone. I really have no patience with people who maintain that an animal's life and actions are governed by pure instinct and conditioned reflexes. Nothing except reasoning powers can explain the careful strategy used by a pride of lions in hunting, and the many examples we have had from Elsa of intelligent and thought-out behaviour.

Isiolo, 4 April, 1959

I reached camp about 8 p.m. Let off the usual thunderflashes and a Very light. But there was no sign of Elsa and she did not appear during the night. Early next morning I went to the track where we shot the guinea fowl, and found the remains of a recent camp there. I then carried out a wide half-circle on the far side of the river, hoping to find her spoor, but saw no traces. By the time I got back to camp I was almost fearing that she had been shot.

I arranged with Ken Smith to follow me, as he was very keen to see Elsa again. He was in camp when I got in and told me that he had seen Elsa on top of the big rock. He had called to her but she seemed nervous and would not come down. I went along with him and as soon as I called and Elsa recognized my voice, she came tearing down the rock and gave me a terrific welcome, and she was just as friendly to Ken. She looked the picture of health, her stomach bulging. She must have killed the previous night. Ken put his bed in your boma and Elsa did not worry him at all during the night. We even went out for a walk all together and spent the day in the studio, Elsa asleep on my bed and Ken on his, although she did sit on him once out of pure friendliness.

Thursday evening, Ken having left the previous day, I took Elsa up to the rock. As I was thinking of returning to camp, a leopard started to grunt just below. Promptly Elsa went off to stalk it, but I think it must have heard me and gone off. I left her on Friday morning with a fat warthog to keep her happy. Promptly she took it into the river and had a tremendous game with it. Elsa is now in quite perfect condition, no bones showing at all.

Isiolo, 14 April, 1959

I had intended going to see Elsa yesterday, but I had to go and chase more elephants out of gardens. However, whatever happens I am setting off tomorrow. I can't tell you how much I always look forward to seeing her and her never-failing loving welcome. If only she could find herself a mate, I would feel much happier about her. It must be very lonely for her. She must at times feel very frustrated, but it never seems to make any difference to her good nature and friendliness. What is touching is that she always knows when I am leaving her, yet accepts the fact and makes no attempt to interfere or to follow. In her dignified way she seems to know that it is unavoidable.

Isiolo, 27 April, 1959

I set off to see Elsa on the afternoon of the 15th. Arrived about 8 p.m., nearly having run into two rhino round a corner. Passed them a few feet off the track. I let off the usual thunderflashes and Very lights, but there was no sign of Elsa that night. Next morning I went to the rock and set off more flashes. No spoor to be seen anywhere. She did not turn up during the day or night. There was very heavy rain during the night with fantastic lightning and thunder and the river came down in flood. Next morning I walked to the 'buffalo ridge' and down into the sand lugga, which had also been in flood, in fact, I had to leave it because of the quicksands. In one place I suddenly plunged up to my waist in sand and had quite a job getting out. I then followed the game path down a ridge to near the junction of the lugga with the river. Rather farther than we went before. Had lunch on the river bank and then crossed over with the water waist deep, and red with mud. Of course the rain had washed out any spoor there might have been but, anyway, I followed the river back to camp.

At one place I saw an object in the water which I thought was the body of some dead animal. I went closer and was about to throw a stone at it when suddenly a head emerged and it was a hippo. Shortly afterwards there was a tremendous snorting, grunting and squealing in the bush alongside the path – a couple of rhino making love! Reached camp about 5 p.m. – still no sign of Elsa! I was really very worried, as she had never before taken so long to appear. Forty-eight hours after I arrived, at about 8.30 p.m., I heard her low call across the river and a few moments later she came racing into camp, the picture of health and terribly pleased to see me. There was nothing to suggest that she might have been with other lions. She was hungry and finished off most of the hind-quarters of the rather smelly *granti* I had shot on my way down. Next morning, I went and got her a pig, which she much enjoyed. In fact she ate so much that she would not move out of camp.

On Sunday morning as we were in the studio – Elsa in deep sleep behind – I saw an eight foot croc come out of the water on to the rocks opposite. I crawled to the edge of the river and took a ciné shot and crept away to get my rifle from camp. Finally shot it through the neck. It never moved off the rocks. I sent Makedde over to tie a rope round its neck and then pulled it across. Elsa watched the proceedings with much interest, but still hadn't spotted the croc – not until it was close into the bank. She approached it very carefully, just like the buffalo, put out a paw and tapped it on the nose cautiously, and then, satisfied it was dead, seized hold of it and brought it on to the bank, making a frightful grimace of disgust. She made no attempt to eat it, preferring the pig which by now was very high.

I left Elsa on Monday morning; met a huge bull buffalo on one of the rain pools. The next morning went to hunt the big lion which we did not get the time Elsa's mother was shot. He has been giving a lot of trouble and eaten twelve of Roba's cattle during the last few weeks. Spent four nights sitting up over kills and part of the days looking along the rocky hills for his spoor. All I found was the spoor of a lioness with two cubs of about three or four months old – doubtless cousins or step-sisters of Elsa! Anyway I am not sorry the old lion did not turn up. I do not think he would be suitable for trapping, and taking to Elsa.

Isiolo, 12 May 1959

Well, I left on Sunday, 3rd May, and made camp about 12.30 a.m. on the 5th. There were no signs of Elsa, and the river was in high flood, higher than we ever saw it. Naturally any spoor there might have been was washed out by the rain. Let off thunderflashes and Very lights in the evening. Next morning still no Elsa. Went and shot a gerenuk for Elsa, as the *granti* I had brought for her was stinking. Elsa did not turn up that day, nor the next two. I could not help feeling worried, although the most likely reason was that she had gone off with wild lions. I sent Makedde and Asman to make enquiries at the African settlements, but nothing had been heard or seen of any lions. So on Saturday morning with a heavy heart I started to pack up (I had been away a week already).

Suddenly there was a great uproar from the baboons across the river and in came Elsa dripping wet, looking as fit as ever. Her stomach was empty but she was not hungry as she turned up her nose at the gerenuk, for which I don't blame her as it was stinking. She was the same old Elsa, full of affection and so pleased to see me. There was no indication that she had been with other lions, nor since you left has there been any sign of her being in season, but of course she may have been, in between visits. After she had settled down, I went off and got her a fresh gerenuk. At night she brought it into the little mountain tent. As you can imagine there was not much room for myself, Elsa and the buck! However, as the buck was fresh I did not mind much, in spite of the blood and muck all over me and the tent.

Elsa has now been on her own for nearly six months. She is just as competent to look after herself as any wild lion and obviously goes off on long safaris, yet her friendliness and affection have not altered in the least degree and she is just the same as when you left. She is a wild lioness in every respect except one. And that is her extraordinary friendliness towards Europeans. I feel sure that she looks on us as some kind of lion, not to be feared and to be treated with ordinary casual friendliness. There is now no question of Elsa waiting and pining for my return. She is always very pleased to see me and obviously does not like to see me leave her, but if I were to stay away for good, I do not think it would upset her life very much.

Isiolo, 20 May, 1959

There is nothing more I can tell you about Elsa. I put every detail in my letters. You know when she is full of meat she will not go far from camp and just spends the days with me under the studio trees. Unless something unusual happens, it is the same routine as before you went away. Elsa is certainly more independent and goes farther afield and no longer has to rely on me for food. She is perhaps a little more suspicious of strange Africans and will not let Nuru or Makedde come too near when she is with her meat. When it comes to moving the meat, either from the tent to the studio in the morning or from the studio to the tent in the evening, I have to carry it with Elsa marching behind. Even in the little mountain tent, Elsa brings the meat into it and I just have to put up with it, or if it is too smelly, move my bed outside! Obviously she knows that when the meat is put near me it is quite safe. I feel sure that when she has cubs she will bring them along and deposit them with me to look after. When that happens I do not think it will be possible to have anyone near, apart from us. The staff will have to be left behind.

I look forward to seeing Elsa again. She was rather pathetic when I left her the last time. I tried to sneak away unseen, but when I looked back she was standing on the edge of the salt lick watching me go away. She never made any attempt to follow. I felt like a thief stealing away.

Isiolo, 3 July, 1959

I have been to see Elsa again. A quarter of an hour after getting to camp, she appeared, and gave me the usual welcome. She looked fit but was very hungry, and during the night ate nearly half the Grant's gazelle I had brought her. Early next morning she dragged the remains into the bush below camp and stayed there the whole day, paying me a few visits at the studio just to make sure I was still there. On Tuesday morning, having finished her meat, she followed me down river for half a mile. Suddenly she became very interested in the far bank, and had obviously scented something. Presently she very cautiously went upstream along the bank and crossed the river. I hid myself opposite the place she seemed so interested in and waited. I could neither see nor hear anything. Suddenly, there was a commotion and a male waterbuck burst out of the bush into the river and came straight towards me, with Elsa close on its heels. Seeing me, it tried to turn, but Elsa was on it and brought it down. There was a tremendous struggle in the water. Elsa quickly changed her grip and clamped on to its throat. Then, when its struggles had become feeble, she got it by the muzzle, enveloping the whole of the forepart of its face in her jaws, obviously with the idea of cutting off its breathing. At length, I could not stand the sight any longer and gave it a merciful bullet. The buck must have weighed a good 400 lb. With a tremendous effort Elsa dragged it halfway up the almost sheer bank, then seemed defeated. I tried to help her but could not move it. I left her and went back to camp to get Nuru and Makedde with ropes. When we returned, the buck was high and dry on top of the bank! Elsa's strength is incredible – imagine what she could do with a mere human if she wanted? It just shows how forbearing and gentle she is with us. I left her on the 2nd, with much difficulty. She knew I was leaving, and for a long time watched me intently and would not let me out of her sight. Finally, after two hours she fell asleep and I was able to steal away.

Prepare yourself for a tremendous welcome! In fact, I think it would be best if you did not show yourself until after she has greeted me and settled down a little.

*

On my return to Kenya, George pointed out that our old Land Rover was falling to pieces. I was sorry to part with it, dented and scratched though it was by Elsa's claws. However, we bought a new model and wondered how Elsa would react to it.

George had arranged his local leave to coincide with my return and soon we were on our way to Elsa. When we arrived at her camp on 12th July, it was already getting dark. About twenty minutes later, while we were putting up my tent, we heard the well-known barking of baboons coming from the river; these always heralded Elsa's arrival.

George suggested that I should get into the truck until Elsa had used up a little of her energy in greeting him, as he was afraid that in her excitement at seeing me after such a long parting she might not be able to control her great strength and might do me some injury.

Rather reluctantly I followed his advice and watched her welcome him, but after a few minutes I got out. Suddenly she saw me, and, as though it were the most natural thing in the world, walked quietly over from George and started rubbing her face against my knees and miaowing in her usual way. Then, with claws well tucked in, she used her 300 lb to bowl me over, after which she played in her usual friendly way without any fuss or excitement. She has filled out and grown enormously and I was glad to see that her stomach was full; owing to this it was a long time before she showed any interest in the Grant's gazelle which George had brought. To our surprise, later, she jumped on to the roof of our new, shiny Land Rover with the same matter-of-factness with which she had greeted me, though it looked so very different from the old battered vehicle she was used to.

For the night we decided that I would put my camp bed into my truck, in case Elsa might feel inclined to share it with me. This proved a wise precaution, for soon after the lamps were turned out she crept determinedly through the thorn fence which surrounded my boma and, standing on her hind legs, looked into the truck, and satisfied herself that I was there. However, after this she settled down next to the car till the early morning; then I heard her dragging the Grant's gazelle carcase down to the river bank, where she guarded it until George got up and called for breakfast. Then she reappeared and was about to make a flying leap towards me; but when I called, 'No, Elsa, no,' she controlled herself and walked up quietly, and, while we ate, sat with one paw touching me. Then she returned to her neglected kill.

For the next six days Elsa shared our camp routine and our morning and evening walks. One day we watched her stalk a waterbuck while he was drinking on the other side of the river. She 'froze' rigid in a most uncomfortable attitude till he gave her a chance to move swiftly down wind, then, crossing the river without the slightest splash, disappeared in the bush. When she returned she rubbed her head against us as if to tell us about the obvious failure of her hunt. On another occasion we surprised a large bird of prey on the body of a freshly killed dik-dik; when it left its victim we offered this little antelope to Elsa but she refused it, wrinkling up her nose in her usual grimace at anything she does not like. Another time we picnicked down river for a day's fishing and I sat making sketches of her. As soon as I started eating my sandwiches she insisted on getting her share and tried with her big paws to snatch them from my mouth.

At other moments she was not so gentle and we had to be on the alert to avoid her playful ambushes, for she has become so strong now that the impact of her heavy body is certainly no mutual pleasure.

One morning she had a wonderful game in the river with a stick which George had thrown to her. She retrieved it, leapt in cabrioles around it, splashing all the water she could whip up with her tail, dropped the stick again only to have an excuse to dive for it and bring it proudly to the surface. While George was filming her near the water's edge, she pretended not to notice him but cunningly manoeuvred herself closer and closer; then she suddenly dropped the stick and leapt on the poor fellow as if to say, 'That's for you, you photographer.' When George tried to get his revenge, she hopped away and with unbelievable swiftness climbed a sloping tree trunk out of everyone's reach. There she sat, licking her paws, looking utterly innocent.

After this performance Elsa paid us only short visits for the next two days and became very detached. On the 23rd she did not come for our morning walk, but in the late afternoon we observed her outlined on the rock near camp and could hardly believe our eyes when we saw a whole troop of baboons within twenty yards, apparently quite unconcerned. Very reluctantly she answered our call and joined us at the foot of the rock, but soon afterwards walked away as fast as she could into the bush. We followed until it was dark. Later she came back to us and put up with my patting her but was obviously restless and uneasy and wanted to go off. All that night and the next day she was away, only coming once for a quick meal. The following day while we were talking after supper she suddenly appeared dripping wet from having crossed the river. She greeted George and me affectionately but while eating her dinner she constantly stopped to listen to something outside. By morning she was gone. This strange behaviour puzzled us. She showed no sign of being in season and we began to wonder whether we had outstayed our welcome. This was far the longest we had spent with her since her release.

Next evening again at dinner time Elsa suddenly appeared out of the darkness and with one swish of her tail swept everything off the table; after embracing us with rather excessive affection she went off into the night, though she returned for a brief moment as if to apologize.

Next morning the explanation for her strange behaviour was

written plain in the pugmarks of a large lion. In the afternoon we saw, through our field glasses, a lot of vultures circling and went to investigate; we found the spoors of many hyenas and jackals and the pugmarks of a lion. These led towards the river where the lion had no doubt drunk and had left a large pool of blood-soaked sand. But there was no sign of Elsa's tracks and no kill to account either for the vultures or for the blood. We spent six hours searching the surrounding area but had to return to camp without Elsa. That evening she came in very hungry and spent the night with us, but was gone by dawn.

On the 29th we saw her on the high rock ridge and after a few minutes' calling she joined us, purring repeatedly and affection-ately, but soon returned to her rock. Now we saw that she was in season, which explained her recent behaviour. When we visited her again in the afternoon, although she replied to our calls, she would not come down and we had to climb up the rock. When it was getting dark, she got up and as if saying goodbye to us rubbed her head against me, George and the gun bearer and then walked slowly towards her lie-up. Only once did she look back at us. Next day I saw her through my field glasses resting on her rock. If she could have spoken she could hardly have told us more convincingly that she wanted to be left alone. However much affection we gave her, it was plain she needed the company of her own kind.

We decided to break camp. As our two cars passed below her rock, she appeared on the skyline and watched us driving away.

Our next visit to Elsa was between 18 and 23 August. She was as usual most affectionate while she was with us, but out of these five days she spent two alone in the bush and, although we did not see the spoor of a lion, she seemed to prefer solitude to sharing our life. It was of course best for her that she should become independent of our ties.

On 29 August George was obliged to go to Elsa's area for

game control and arrived at 6 p.m. at her camp to spend the night there. He fired off two thunderflashes to attract her attention. At about 8 p.m. he heard a lion down river and let off another thunderflash. The lion continued to call throughout the night, but there was no sign of Elsa. Next morning George found the pugmarks of a young lion or lioness close to camp. He had to leave immediately afterwards but returned at 4 p.m. An hour later Elsa came across the river, looking very fit and full of affection. Although she was not hungry, she ate a little of the buck which George had brought her and then dragged the carcase into the tent. Soon after dark a lion began to call. Much to George's surprise, she completely ignored the invitation which continued throughout most of the night.

Early next morning she made a hearty meal and then without any show of hurry disappeared in the direction from which the lion had called. Shortly afterwards George heard her voice and saw her sitting on a big rock and heard her making deep grunts. As soon as she spotted him, she came down and met him but, although pleased to see him, made it obvious that she wanted to be alone and after a brief head-rubbing disappeared into the bush. Guessing the direction she had taken, George followed and found her running tracks heading for the river. Presently he saw her sitting on a rock almost hidden by a bush. He watched her for some time. First she miaowed, then with a startled 'whuff-whuff' dashed down the rock and streaked past George into the bush. Next moment a young lion appeared, evidently in hot pursuit and not sensing George came straight towards him. When the lion was less than twenty yards away George thought it time to act and waved his arms and shouted. Startled, the beast spun round and made off the way he had come. A few seconds later Elsa reappeared, squatted nervously close to George for a few moments and then followed the lion. George withdrew and moved camp.

Two days later he had to revisit the same area. A few hundred yards before reaching Elsa's camp one of the men in the car saw her under a bush close to the track, apparently hiding: most unusual behaviour, for normally she would rush out to meet the car and greet everyone. Thinking the man might have mistaken a wild lioness for Elsa, George turned the car and drove back. There she was sitting under the bush. At first she made no movement; then, realizing that she had been caught out, she came forward and was courtesy itself, making a great fuss of George and pretending to be as pleased as ever at seeing him, and she condescended to eat some of the meat he had brought her. While she was eating, George walked up the track to look for spoor. He found her pugmarks together with those of another lion. Then he saw the lion himself peeping at him from behind a bush. It appeared to be the same one which he had seen with Elsa a few days earlier. Presently there was an uproar from a troop of baboons by the river, which heralded the approach of the lion. Hearing this Elsa hurriedly finished her meal and went off to find her lord and master.

George went on and pitched camp and left the remainder of the meat in the tent for Elsa, before going on to do his work. On his return to camp the meat was still untouched and Elsa did not appear during the night.

At last Elsa had found her mate and perhaps our hopes would be fulfilled and one day she would walk into camp followed by a litter of strapping cubs.

PART TWO

10. Elsa Mates with a Wild Lion

It was between 29 August and 4 September 1959 that George saw Elsa and her lion courting. Quickly he made a calculation – 108 days' gestation – this meant that cubs might arrive between 15 and 21 December.

When on his return to Isiolo he told me what he had seen I could hardly wait to start off for camp, for I was afraid that Elsa might now follow her mate into a world beyond our reach.

But when we arrived she was there waiting for us by the big rock close to the car track.

She was very affectionate and also very hungry.

As our tents were being pitched her lion started calling and during the night he circled round the camp, while she remained with George eating heartily and quite uninterested in her mate's appeal. At dawn we heard the lion still calling but from much farther away.

For two days she remained in camp eating so enormously that she was too sleepy to move till the afternoon when she went out fishing with George.

During the third night she ate so much that we were quite worried about her; yet in the morning, in spite of her bulging belly, she trotted into the bush with us and first stalked two jackals and then a flock of guinea fowl. Of course, each time she closed in on them they flew off, whereupon she sat down and licked her paws. I was walking ahead but stopped dead at the sight of a ratel; this animal, also known as a honey badger, is rarely seen. It had its back turned towards me and was so absorbed digging for grubs in the rotten wood of a fallen tree that it was quite unaware of Elsa's approach. She saw it and crept forward cautiously till she was practically on top of it.

Only when their heads nearly bumped together did the ratel take in the situation; then hissing and scratching he attacked her with such courage and so savagely that she retreated.

Using every advantage that the ground offered the ratel made a fighting retreat, charging often, and eventually disappeared none the worse for its adventure.

Elsa returned defeated and rather bewildered; plainly she was too well fed to hunt except for sport and there was no fun to be had with such a raging playmate.

This incident made us sure that we had been right in suspecting a ratel when, in the early days of Elsa's release, we had found deep bites and gashes on the lower part of her body. For no other small animal is so fearless and bold.

On our walk home Elsa, full of high spirits and affection, rolled me over several times in the sand, while I listened to the trumpeting of elephants which were much too close for my liking.

That night she slept in front of my tent, but just before dawn her lion started calling and she went off in his direction.

Their calls were easy to distinguish; Elsa has a very deep guttural voice, but after her initial roar only gives two or three whuffing grunts, whereas her lion's voice is less deep and after his roar he always gives at least ten or twelve grunts.

During Elsa's absence we broke camp and left for Isiolo hoping that she was in the company of her mate; we were away for about three weeks.

We returned to the camp on 10 October. An hour after we got back we saw her swimming across the river to greet us, but instead of the exuberant welcome she usually gave us, she walked slowly up to me. She did not seem to be hungry and was exceptionally gentle and quiet.

Patting her, I noticed that her skin had become extremely soft and her coat unusually glossy. I saw, too, that four of her five nipples were very large.

She was pregnant. There was no doubt about it. She must have conceived a month ago.

It is widely believed that a pregnant lioness who is handicapped in hunting by her condition is helped by one or two other lionesses who act as 'aunts'. They are also supposed to assist in looking after the new-born cubs, for the male is not of much practical use on such occasions and, indeed, is often not allowed near the young lions for some weeks.

Since poor Elsa had no aunts, it would be our job to replace them. George and I talked over plans to help to feed her and avoid any risk of her injuring herself during her pregnancy.

I was to stay in camp as much as I could and, at the nearest Game Scout Post, some twenty-five miles away, we would establish a herd of goats from which I could collect a few in my truck at regular intervals.

Nuru would remain with me to help Elsa and Makedde would guard us with his rifle, Ibrahim could drive and I would keep one boy, the Toto (the word Toto means child in Swahili), to act as personal servant.

George would visit us as often as his work allowed.

As though she had understood our conversation, Elsa hopped on to my camp bed as soon as it was made ready and looked as if she thought it the only suitable place for someone in her condition.

From now on she took possession of it, and when next morning, as I did not feel well, I had it carried down to the studio, she came to share it with me. This was uncomfortable, so after a time I tipped it over and rolled her off. This indignity caused her to retire, offended, into the river reeds till the late afternoon when it was time for our walk.

When I called her she stared at me intently, advanced determinedly up to my bed, stepped on to it, squatted, lifted her tail and did something she had never before done in so unsuitable a place.

Then with a very self-satisfied expression she jumped down and took the lead on our walk.

Apparently, now that she had had her revenge everything was again all right between us.

I observed that her movements were very slow and that even the noise of elephants close by only made her cock her ears. That night she rested in George's tent, unresponsive to the call of a lion who seemed to be very near the camp.

As in the early morning the lion was still calling, we took Elsa for a walk in his direction. There, to our surprise, we found the spoor of two lions.

When she began to show an interest in these pugmarks we left her and returned home. She did not come back that night, so we were surprised to hear a lion grunting extremely close to the camp. (Indeed, in the morning his pugmarks proved that he had been within ten yards of our tent.) The next day Elsa again stayed away. Hoping to make the lions kindly disposed towards her, George shot a buck and left it as a farewell gift; then we returned to Isiolo and spent a fortnight there. I then decided to go back to see how Elsa was.

It was dark when we reached camp, but she appeared within a few moments. She was extremely thin, very hungry and had deep, bleeding gashes and bites on her neck, and also the claw marks of a lion on her back.

While she gnawed at the meat we had brought and I dressed her wounds she responded by licking me and rubbing her head against mine.

During the night we heard her dragging the carcase down to the river and splashing across with it, and later we heard her returning. Shortly afterwards some baboons gave an alarm and were answered by a lion across the river. Elsa replied from our side with soft moans. Very early in the morning she tried to force her way through the wicket door of the thorn enclosure which surrounds my tent. She pushed her head half-through but then got stuck. Her attempt to free herself caused the door to give way and she finally entered wearing the gate round her neck like a collar. I freed her at once but she seemed restless and in need of reassurance, for she sucked my thumb frantically. Though she was hungry she made no attempt to recover or to guard her 'kill' as she usually does. All she did was to listen intently when any sound came from the direction of the carcase. We were puzzled by this odd behaviour, so George went to investigate what had happened to the kill. He discovered that Elsa had taken it across the river, but the spoor he found on the far side suggested that another lioness had then dragged it about four hundred yards, eaten part of it and afterwards taken the remains towards some nearby rocks. Assuming that this lioness had cubs concealed in the rocks, George did not go on with his search. He observed, however, that beside the spoor of the strange lioness were the pugmarks of a lion – and that they were not those of Elsa's husband. The evidence suggested that this lion had not touched the meat but had followed the lioness at some distance, and left the kill to her.

Does this mean that though lions are not of much use to a lioness who is in cub or nursing and therefore handicapped for hunting, they do make sacrifices for their mate? Had Elsa, though she was hungry, suffering from still unhealed wounds and herself in need of an aunt on account of her pregnancy, gone to the help of a nursing lioness? This was something we could only wonder about.

She was now rather heavy and all exercise had become an effort to her.

When she came with me to the studio she often lay on the table. I was puzzled about this, for though the table is perhaps a cooler place it was certainly a lot harder than my bed, or the soft sand below. During the following days Elsa shared her time between her mate and me. On our last night in camp Elsa made a terrific meal of goat and then, very heavy in the belly, went to join her lion who had been calling for her for many hours. Her absence gave us an excellent opportunity to leave for Isiolo.

In the second week of November we went back to the camp. When we got near Elsa's lie-up we found the spoor of many sheep and goats and the camp site itself patterned with hoof marks. I trembled to think what might have happened to her should she have killed one of the goats which had been grazing so provokingly in what she regarded as her private domain. Later our fears were increased by finding the body of a crocodile close to the river; it had been speared quite recently. George sent a patrol of Game Scouts to deal with the poachers while he and I went out to look for Elsa.

For some hours we walked through the bush, calling to her and at intervals shooting into the air, but there was no response. After dark a lion began to call from the direction of the Big Rock, but we listened in vain for Elsa's voice.

We had run out of thunderflashes so when it became dark all we could do to let her know that we were there was to turn on the penetrating howl of the air-raid siren, a relic of Mau-Mau days. In the past it had often brought her into camp.

It was answered by the lion; we sounded it again and again he replied, and this strange conversation went on until it was interrupted by Elsa's arrival. She knocked us all over; as her body was wet we realized that she must have swum across the river and had come from the opposite direction to that from which the lion was calling.

She seemed very fit and was not hungry. She left at dawn but returned at teatime when we were setting out for our walk. We climbed up the Big Rock and sat there watching the sun sink like a fireball behind the indigo hills.

At first Elsa blended into the warm reddish colour of the rock as if she were part of it, then she was silhouetted against the fading sky in which a full moon was rising. It seemed as though we were all on a giant ship, anchored in a purple-grey sea of bush, out of which a few islands of granite outcrop rose. It was so vast a view, so utterly peaceful and timeless, that I felt as though I were on a magic ship gliding away from reality into a world where man-created values crumble to nothing. Instinctively I stretched my hand towards Elsa who sat close to me; she belonged to this world and only through her were we allowed to glance into a paradise which we had lost. I imagined Elsa in the future playing with her happy little cubs on this rock, cubs whose father was a wild lion: and at this very moment he might be waiting nearby. She rolled on her back and hugged me close to her. Carefully I laid my hand below her ribs to feel whether any life were moving within her, but she pushed it away making me feel as though I had committed an indiscretion. Certainly her nipples were already very large.

Soon we had to return to camp, to the safety of our thorn enclosure, and the lamps and rifles with which we armed ourselves against those dark hours in which Elsa's real life began.

This was the moment at which we parted, each to return to our own world.

When we got back we found that there were a number of Boran poachers in camp who had been rounded up by the Game Scouts. As a Senior Game Warden, one of George's most important tasks is to put down poaching for it threatens the survival of wild life in the reserves.

Elsa kept away during the night and the following day. This worried us as we would rather have had her under our eyes while so many tribesmen and their flocks were around. In the after-noon we went to look for her. As I came near to the rock, I called out to warn her of our approach but got no reply. It was only when we had climbed on to the saddle where we had sat on the previous evening that we suddenly heard an alarming growl, followed by crashes and the sound of wood breaking inside the big cleft below us. We rushed as fast as we could to the top of the nearest rock, then we heard Elsa's voice very close and saw her lion making away swiftly through the bush.

Elsa looked up at us, paused and silently rushed after her mate. Both disappeared in a direction in which we knew there were some Boran with their stock.

We waited until it was nearly dark and then called Elsa. To our surprise she came trotting out of the bush, returned to camp with us and spent the night there, going off only in the early morning.

George went back to Isiolo with the prisoners but left some Game Scouts in camp.

The bush was full of sheep and goats which had straggled away from the flocks and several newly born lambs were bleating piteously. With the help of the Scouts I found them and returned them to their mothers.

The evening was lit by lightning, a sure sign that the rains would start soon. Never had I greeted the first downpour with such a sense of relief. For this drenching meant that the Boran would return to their pastures and temptation and danger would be removed from Elsa's path.

Fortunately, as she did not like the crowd of Game Scouts who now shared our camp, she spent these last dangerous days on the far side of the river where there were neither Boran nor flocks.

Daily now the parched ground was soaked by showers. The transformation which always results from the onset of the rains is something which cannot be imagined by anyone who has not actually witnessed it.

A few days before we had been surrounded by a grey, dry, crackling bush, in which long white thorns provided the only variation in colour. Now, on every side there was lush tropical vegetation decked with myriad multi-coloured flowers, and the air was heavy with their scent.

When George returned he brought a zebra for Elsa. This was a special treat. As soon as she heard the vibrations of the car she appeared, spotted the kill and tried to pull the carcase out of the Land Rover. Then, finding it too heavy for her, she walked over to where the boys were standing and jerking her head at the zebra made it plain that she needed help. They hauled the heavy animal a short distance amid much laughter and then waited for Elsa to start her meal. To our astonishment, although zebra was her favourite meat she did not eat but stood by the river roaring in her loudest voice.

We presumed that she was inviting her mate to join in the feast. This would have been good lion manners, for according to the recorded habit of prides, whilst the females do most of the killing, they then have to wait to satisfy their hunger until the lion has had his fill.

The next morning, 22 November, she swam across the heavily flooded river, came up to the zebra and roared repeatedly in the direction of the rocky range which is on our side of the river.

I saw that she had a deep gash across one of her front paws, but she refused to have it dressed, and after she had eaten as much as she could, she went off towards the rocks.

That night it rained for eight hours, and the river turned into a torrent which it would have been very dangerous for Elsa to cross even though she is a powerful swimmer. I was therefore very pleased to see her in the morning returning from the Big Rock.

Her knee was very swollen and she allowed me to attend to her cut paw.

I noticed that she had great difficulty in producing her excrement and when I inspected the faeces I was surprised to see a rolled-up piece of zebra skin which when unfolded was as large as a soup plate. The hair had been digested but the hide was half an inch thick. I marvelled at the capacity of wild animals to rid themselves of such objects without suffering any internal injury.

For several days she divided her time between us and her lion.

When George returned from a patrol he brought Elsa a goat. Usually she dragged her kill into his tent, presumably to avoid the trouble of having to guard it, but this time she left it lying beside the car in a spot which could not be seen from the tent. During the night her mate came and had a good feed; we wondered whether this was what she had intended.

Next evening we took the precaution of placing some meat at a certain distance from the camp, for we did not want to encourage him to come too close.

Soon after dark we heard him dragging it away and in the morning Elsa joined him.

We were now faced with a problem. We wanted to help Elsa, who was increasingly handicapped by her pregnancy, by providing her with regular food, but we did not wish to interfere with her relations with her mate by our continued presence in the camp. He had a good right to resent this, but did he in fact object to us? On the whole, we thought that he did not, and I think we were justified in our opinion for, during the next six months, though we did not see him, we often heard his characteristic ten or twelve whuffing grunts and recognized his spoor, which proved that he remained Elsa's constant companion.

Though he still kept out of our sight, he had become bolder and bolder, but an extraordinary kind of truce seemed to have been established between us. He had come to know our routine as intimately as we had come to know his habits. He shared Elsa's company with us and we thought that in return he could fairly expect an occasional meal as compensation.

In view of his attitude we stilled our qualms of conscience and stayed on.

One afternoon walking with Elsa through the bush we came upon a large boulder with a crack in it. She sniffed cautiously, pulled a grimace and did not seem anxious to go closer to it. Next we heard a hissing and, expecting a snake to appear, George held our shotgun ready; but what emerged from the crack was the broad head of a monitor lizard who soon wriggled out into the open. He was an enormous size, about five feet long and nearly a foot broad and he had blown himself up to his fullest capacity. He extended his neck, moved his long forked tongue rapidly and lashed out with his tail so violently that Elsa thought it wise to retreat.

Sitting at a safe distance, I admired his courage; although he had no means of defence except his threatening appearance and thrashing tail, which he used like a crocodile, he chose to come out and face the danger, rather than find himself trapped in the crack.

For a few days we saw little of Elsa but as we often heard her lion roaring and frequently saw his pugmarks we did not worry.

George unfortunately had to leave but I stayed on and Elsa spent three days in camp with me in spite of the continual calling of her mate.

One evening she looked towards the river, stiffened and then rushed into the bush. A tremendous barking of baboons ensued, till it was silenced by her roars. Soon she was answered by her lion – he must have been only about fifty yards away. His voice seemed to shake the earth and increased in strength. From the other side Elsa roared back. Sitting between them, I became a little anxious in case the loving pair should decide to come into my tent, for I had no meal to offer them. However, in time they appeared to have roared themselves hoarse. Their whuffings died away and no further sound came from the bush except for the buzzing of insects. Luckily on the following evening George returned with a goat for Elsa.

11. The Birth of the Cubs

It was now nearly mid-December and we believed that the cubs might arrive at any moment.

Elsa was so heavy that every movement seemed to require an effort; if she had been living a normal life she would certainly have taken exercise, so I did my best to make her go for walks with me, but she kept close to the tents. We wondered what place she would choose for her delivery and even thought that since she had always considered our tent as her safest 'den' the cubs might be born in it.

We therefore prepared a feeding bottle and laid in some tinned milk and some glucose, and I read all the books and pamphlets I could find on animal births and possible complications.

Since I had no experience of midwifery I felt very nervous and also asked advice of a veterinary surgeon. In order to judge how far Elsa was advanced in her pregnancy I pressed my hand gently against her abdomen just below her ribs. I could not feel any movement and wondered whether we had been mistaken about the date at which she had been mated.

The river was now in flood and George and I decided to walk three miles downstream to look at some cataracts which are very impressive when the water is high. Elsa watched our departure from the top of the Land Rover. She made no attempt to join us and looked sleepy. The bush we had to go through was very thick and as we walked I wished she were with us to warn us of the approach of buffalo and elephant, for droppings proved that they must be close by.

The cataracts were a magnificent sight, the foaming water cascading through the gorges, thundering across the rocks and then flooding out into deep whirlpools.

On our way back, as soon as I was out of earshot of the cataracts, I heard Elsa's familiar 'hnk-hnk' and soon saw her trotting along the path as quickly as she could to join us. She was covered in tsetse flies, but she greeted us most affectionately before she flung herself on the ground, and tried to rid herself of the flies by rolling.

I was very touched that she had made the effort to join us, the more so that though her lion had roared desperately for her during the whole of the previous night and had gone on doing so until nine in the morning, she had made no attempt to join him.

This was very gratifying but it also reminded us of our fear that her lion might get tired of sharing her with us. It had taken us a very long time to find a mate for her; it would be unforgivable if our interference now caused him to leave her. We wanted her cubs to grow up as wild lions and to do this they needed their father.

We decided to go away for three days. It was of course a risk, for the cubs might be born during this time and Elsa might need us, but we thought the danger that her lion might desert her the greater of the two evils – so we left.

We returned on 16 December and found a very hungry Elsa waiting for us. For two days she remained in camp; possibly frequent thunderstorms made her reluctant to leave its shelter. She did, however, to our surprise, take a few short walks, always to the Big Rock, but returned quickly. She ate unbelievably and we felt that she was stocking up a reserve for the days that lay ahead.

On the night of 18 December she crept in the dark through the thorn fence which surrounded my tent and spent the night close to my bed. This was something which she had very rarely done, and I took it as a sign that she felt that her time was near.

The next day when George and I went for a walk Elsa followed us, but she had to sit down at intervals panting and was plainly in great discomfort. When we saw this we turned back and walked very slowly. Suddenly to our astonishment she turned off into the bush in the direction of the Big Rock.

She did not return during that night, but in the morning we heard her calling in a very weak voice. We thought this meant that she had had her cubs and went out to trace her spoor. These led us close to the rock but the grass was so high that we lost track of her. The rock range is about a mile long and though we searched for a long time we could not discover where she was.

We set out again in the afternoon and eventually we spotted her through our field glasses. She was standing on the Big Rock and from her silhouette we saw that she was still pregnant.

We climbed up and found her lying close to a large boulder which stood at the top of a wide cleft in the rock; near to it there was some grass and a small tree provided shade. This place had always been one of Elsa's favourite 'lookouts' and we felt that it would make an ideal nursery, since inside the cleft was a rainproof and well-protected cave.

We left her to take the initiative and presently she came slowly towards us, walking very carefully and obviously in pain. She greeted us very affectionately, but I noticed that blood was trickling from her vagina, a sure sign that her labour had started.

In spite of this she went over to Makedde and the Toto, who had remained behind, and rubbed her head against their legs before she sat down.

When I came near her she got up and moved to the edge of the rock, and remained there with her head turned away from us. It seemed to me that she chose this precipitous position to make sure that no one could follow her. At intervals she came back and rubbed her head very gently against mine and then walked determinedly back to the boulder making it plain that she wished to be left alone.

We went a short distance away and for half an hour watched her through our field glasses. She rolled from side to side, licked her vagina and moaned repeatedly. Suddenly she rose, went very carefully down the steep rock face and disappeared into the thick bush at its base.

Since there was nothing we could do to help her, we went back to camp. After dark we heard her lion calling; there was no reply.

I lay awake most of the night thinking about her and when, towards morning, it started to rain my anxiety increased and I could hardly bear to wait till it was light to go out and try to discover what had happened.

Very early, George and I set out; first we followed the spoor of Elsa's lion. He had been close to the camp, had dragged off the very smelly carcase of the goat which Elsa had not touched for three days, and had eaten it in the bush. Then he had walked to the rock near to the place where we had seen Elsa disappear.

We wondered what we should do next. We did not want our curiosity to bring any risk to the cubs and we were aware that captive lionesses who have been disturbed soon after giving birth to cubs have been known to kill their young. We also thought that her lion might be very near, so we decided to stop our search; instead George went off and shot a large waterbuck to provide Elsa and her mate with plenty of food.

I, in the meantime, climbed the Big Rock and waited for an hour, listening for any sound which might give us a clue to Elsa's whereabouts. I strained my ears but all was still; finally I could bear the suspense no longer and called. There was no answer. Was Elsa dead?

Hoping that the lion's spoor might lead us to her we took up his tracks where we had left them and traced them till they reached a dry watercourse near the rock. There we left his meal thinking that if he came for it this might help us to find Elsa.

During the night we heard him roaring in the distance and were therefore surprised next morning to find his pugmarks close to the camp. He had not taken the meat we had put out close to the camp but had gone to the kill we had left for him near the rock. This he had dragged for at least half a mile through most difficult terrain, across ravines, rocky outcrops and dense bush. We had no wish to disturb him at his meal, so we set about looking for Elsa, but found no trace of her. After returning to the camp for breakfast we went out again and suddenly, through our field glasses, saw a great flock of vultures perched on the trees which grew around the spot where we thought that the lion had made his meal.

Assuming that he had finished by now, we approached the place and as we came near to it found every bush and tree loaded with birds of prey. Each was staring at the dry watercourse and there was the carcase lying out in the hot sun. Since the meat was in the open and yet the vultures did not leave their perches we concluded that the lion was guarding his kill. As far as we could see he had not touched it, so we thought that Elsa too might be close by and that her gallant mate had dragged the 400-pound burden this long distance for her benefit. We felt it would be unwise to continue our search and went back to camp for lunch after which we set out again.

When we saw that the vultures were still on the trees, we circled the place down wind and approached it very cautiously from the high ground.

George, Makedde and I had just passed a very thick bush

which overhung a deep crack in the ground when I suddenly had a strange uncomfortable feeling. I stopped and looking back, saw the Toto, who was close behind me, staring intently at the bush. Next there was a terrifying growl and the sound of snapping branches; a second later all was quiet again – the lion had gone. We had passed within six feet of him. I think that my sense of uneasiness must have been due to the fact that he had been watching our movements with great intensity. When the Toto stooped to see what was in the bush he couldn't stand it and went off. They had actually looked straight into each other's eyes and the Toto had seen his big body disappearing into the deep crack. Feeling we had been very lucky, we went home and left three lots of meat in different places before night fell.

As soon as it was light we went to inspect the deposits; all of them had been taken by hyenas.

By the river we found the spoor of Elsa's mate, but there was no sign of her pugmarks. All the little rain pools had dried up long ago and the river was the only place where she could quench her thirst; the absence of any trace of her was very worrying. Eventually we found, close to the spot where three days before we had last seen her, a few pugmarks which could have been hers, though this was not certain. Full of hope, we made a thorough search along the base of the Big Rock, but in vain.

Since the vultures had now gone we were left with no clue to her whereabouts.

Again we put out meat close to the rock and near to the camp. In the morning we found that Elsa's lion had dragged some of it to the studio and eaten it there, while the rest had been disposed of by hyenas.

It was now four days since we had seen Elsa and six since she had eaten anything, unless she had shared the waterbuck with her mate.

We believed that she had given birth to the cubs on the night of 20 December and we did not think that it could be a coincidence that her lion, who had not been about for days, had reappeared on that night and remained close to the rock ever since; which was most unusual.

On Christmas Eve George went to get a goat while I continued the fruitless search and called to Elsa without getting any answer.

It was with a heavy heart that I prepared our little Christmas tree. In the past I had always improvised one; sometimes I took a small candelabra euphorbia, from whose symmetrical branches I hung tinsel chains and into whose fleshy fibre I stuck candles; sometimes I used an aloe with its wide-spreading sprays of flowers, sometimes a seedling of the thorny balanitis tree, which is very ornamental and has splendid spikes on which to hang decorations. When I could find nothing else I filled a dish with sand, stuck candles into it and decorated it with whatever plants I could pick in our semi-desert surroundings.

But tonight I had a real little tree complete with glittering tinsel branches, sparkling decorations and candles. I placed it on a table outside the tents which I had covered with flowers and greenery. Then I collected the presents which I had brought for George, Makedde, Nuru, Ibrahim, the Toto and the cook and the sealed envelopes containing money for the boys on which I had painted a Christmas tree branch. There were also packets of cigarettes and dates and tins of milk for them.

I changed quickly into a frock and by then it was dark enough to light the candles. I called the men, who came dressed up for the occasion, grinning but a little shy, for never before had they seen a Christmas tree of this kind.

I must admit to having been myself deeply moved when I saw the little silver tree sparkling in the vast darkness of the surrounding bush, bringing the message of the birth of Christ.

On Christmas Eve I always feel like a small child. To break the tension, I told the men about the European custom of celebrating Christmas Eve with a tree. After I had given them their presents, we all gave three cheers for 'Elsa – Elsa, Elsa'. The sound seemed to hang on the air and I felt a lump rise in my throat – was she alive? Quickly I told the cook to bring in the plum pudding which we had brought from Isiolo and then to pour brandy over it and light it. But no bluish flame arose, for our Christmas pudding was a soggy mass which had a distinct smell of Worcester sauce. Certainly the cook had never before been in charge of such a ritual; he had paid no attention to my instructions and had remained fixed in his belief that George so loved his Lea and Perrins, that it must be appropriate to souse even the plum pudding with it.

We were not, however, the only ones to be disappointed in our Christmas dinner. We had hung a goat carcase out of the reach of predators, which we would lower if Elsa appeared. After we had gone to bed we heard her lion grunting and growling by the tree and performing all sorts of acrobatics. He went on for a long time and then retired exhausted.

Early on Christmas morning we went in search of Elsa. We followed the lion's spoor across the river, and again screened the bush all round the spot to which he had dragged the waterbuck. After hours of fruitless tracking we came back for breakfast. During the morning George shot at an aggressive cobra which we found close to the camp.

Later we set out once more for the rocky range; something seemed to tell us that if Elsa were still alive that was where she was. We wriggled through dense bush and I crept hopefully into every crevice trying to prevent myself from expecting to find Elsa dead but hidden from the vultures by the impenetrable thorn thickets.

When we were all tired out we sat down to rest in the shade of an overhanging rock and discussed every possible fate which might have overtaken Elsa. We were very depressed and even Nuru and Makedde spoke in subdued voices.

We tried to cheer ourselves up by quoting cases of bitches who would not leave their litter for the first five or six days because they had to keep them warm, feed them and massage their bellies to help their digestive functions to start working. Indeed, we had expected Elsa to have a rather similar reaction, but this did not account for the absence of any trace of her. Also, bitches do occasionally go and visit their masters even during this first period after their delivery and as Elsa had shown more attachment to us than to her mate up to the time at which her labour began, it seemed improbable and ominous that the fact of giving birth to cubs should have caused her to go completely wild.

At midday we returned to camp and began a very gloomy and silent Christmas meal.

Suddenly there was swift movement and before I could take in what was happening Elsa was between us sweeping everything off the table, knocking us to the ground, sitting on us and overwhelming us with joy and affection.

While this was going on the boys appeared and Elsa gave them too a full share of her greetings.

Her figure was normal again, she looked superbly fit but her teats were very small and apparently dry; round each was a dark-red circle some two inches wide. Cautiously I squeezed a teat; it produced no milk. We gave her some meat which she immediately ate. Meanwhile, we discussed many questions. Why had she come to visit us during the hottest part of the day, a time when normally she would never move? Could it be that she had chosen it deliberately because it was the safest time to leave the cubs since few predators would be on the prowl in such heat; or, had she heard the shot which George had fired at the cobra and had she taken it as a signal to her? Why were her teats small and dry? Had she just suckled the cubs? But this would not seem to explain why her milk glands which had been so big during her pregnancy had now shrunk to their normal size. Had the cubs died? And whatever had happened, why had she waited for five days before coming to us for food?

After she had had a good meal and drunk some water she rubbed her head affectionately against us, walked about thirty yards down the river, lay down and had a doze. We left her alone, so that she should feel at ease. When I looked for her at teatime she had gone.

We followed her spoor for a short way; it led towards the rock range, but we soon lost it and returned none the wiser about her cubs. However, now that we were reassured about Elsa our morale was restored.

During the night we heard her lion calling from the other side of the river, but she did not answer him.

Next day we began to worry about the cubs. If they were alive was their mother able to suckle them from those dry teats? We tried to comfort ourselves by saying that the red rings round them were probably due to blood vessels being broken by suckling, but we were very anxious because we had been warned by zoo authorities that hand-reared lionesses often produced abnormal cubs which do not live, and indeed one of Elsa's sisters had suffered such a misfortune. We felt we just must know about the cubs and rescue them if necessary. So the next morning we searched for five hours, but we did not find so much as a dropping or a crushed leaf, let alone any spoor to show where Elsa's nursery was.

We carried on equally unsuccessfully in the afternoon. While plodding through the bush George nearly stepped on an exceptionally large puff adder and was lucky to be able to shoot it just before it could strike.

Half an hour later we heard Ibrahim popping off a gun, a signal that Elsa had arrived in camp.

Obviously she had responded to the shot with which George had dispatched the puff adder.

She was most affectionate to us when we got back, but we were alarmed to observe that her teats were still small and dry. Ibrahim, however, assured us that when she had arrived they and her milk glands had been enormous, hanging low and swinging from side to side.

He also told us that her behaviour had been very unusual. When he fetched the gun from the kitchen which was in the direction from which she had come she dashed angrily at him. Possibly she thought he was going to her cubs. Later when he went to the studio to collect her meat which was hanging there in the shade, she had prevented him from touching her kill. After this she had settled on the Land Rover and it was then that Ibrahim noticed that her teats and glands had shrunk to their normal size. She had, he said, 'tucked them up', and he told us that camels and cattle can withhold their milk by retracting their teats. If then their owner insists on getting milk he is obliged to tie the animal to a tree and apply several tourniquets; these have the effect of raising the pressure of the blood in the muscles until it reaches a point when they automatically relax and it becomes possible to start milking. We wondered whether such a reaction explained the peculiar state of Elsa's teats. Was it not possible that a lioness might be capable of a similar reaction and would contract her teats when hunting? Certainly if she could not do this she would be greatly handicapped by her heavy undercarriage, and besides this her teats might be injured by the thorny bush.

While we were asking ourselves these questions Elsa, having eaten enormously, had settled down and showed no intention of returning to her cubs.

This alarmed me because it was getting dark and the worst moment to leave them alone.

We tried to induce her to return to them by walking along the path down which she had come. She followed us reluctantly, listening alertly in the direction of the rock, but soon returned to camp. We wondered whether she might be afraid that we would follow her and find her cubs. Meanwhile she went back to her meal and it was only after she had methodically cleaned up every scrap of it that, much to our relief, she disappeared into the dark. Very likely she had waited till there was no light to make sure we could not follow her.

We were now convinced that she was looking after her cubs. But after the warnings we had had from the zoo experts we could not be happy until we had seen for ourselves that they were normal.

We made one more unsuccessful search before our return to Isiolo where we spent the last three days of December. On our way back to camp we nearly collided with two rhino and then met a small herd of elephant. We had no choice but to rush at them, hoping we should make it, but the big bull of the herd took umbrage and chased us for quite a long way. I did not enjoy this as elephants are the only wild animals which really frighten me.

We hooted several times before we reached camp to let Elsa know we were arriving and found her waiting for us on top of a large boulder at the point at which the track passes the end of the Big Rock.

She hopped in among the boys at the back of the Land Rover, then she went to the trailer in which there was a dead goat. I had rarely seen her so hungry.

I noticed at once that her teats were still small and dry; I squeezed them but no milk came. We thought this a bad sign and after she had spent seven hours in camp, eating and hopping on and off the Land Rover, we began to be afraid that she no longer had any cubs to look after. She only left us at two in the morning.

Very early we set out and followed her spoor which led towards the Big Rock. Close to it was what seemed to us an ideal home for a lioness and her family. Very large boulders gave complete shelter and they were surrounded by bush that was almost impenetrable. We made straight for the topmost boulder and from it tried to look down into the centre of the 'den'. We saw no pugmarks but there were signs that some animal had used it as a lie-up.

Nearby we observed some old blood spoor. This was very close to the place where we had seen Elsa in labour, so we thought that she had perhaps given birth to the cubs there. On the other hand, we had been within three feet of it on one of our previous searches and it seemed almost impossible that Elsa should have been there hiding her cubs and not made us aware of her presence.

As though to prove that we were wrong in thinking this, after we had called loudly for half an hour, she suddenly appeared out of a cluster of bush only twenty yards away. She seemed rather shocked at seeing us, stared and kept silent and very still as though hoping we would not come nearer.

Perhaps we were so close to her nursery that she thought it better to appear and so prevent us from finding it. After a few moments, she walked up to us and was very affectionate to George, myself, Makedde and the Toto, but never uttered a sound. To my relief I saw that her teats were twice their normal length and that the hair around them was still wet from suckling.

Soon she went slowly back towards the bush and stood, for about five minutes, with her back turned towards us listening intently for any sound from the thicket. Then she sat down, still with her back turned to us. It was as though she wanted to say to us: 'Here my private world begins and you must not trespass.'

It was a dignified demonstration and no words could have conveyed her wishes more clearly.

We sneaked away as quietly as we could, making a detour in order to climb to the top of the Big Rock. From it we looked down and saw her sitting just as we had left her.

Obviously she had got our scent, knew just what we were doing and did not intend to let us discover her lie-up.

This made me realize how unaware we had been, in spite of our intimacy with Elsa, of the reactions of wild animals. It amused me to remember how we had prepared ourselves against the possibility of the cubs being born in our tent and how we had flattered ourselves that Elsa regarded it as the place in which she felt safest. Although the spoor we had recently found had all led towards the lower rock, we thought it possible that the cubs had been born in the boulder hideout and that later Elsa had moved them about thirty yards to where they now were.

If this were the case she had probably made the move after the rains stopped – for while the boulder lie-up was rainproof, the new one was not, though otherwise it was an ideal nursery.

We decided that we must respect Elsa's wishes and not try to see the cubs until she brought them to us, which we felt sure she would do one day. I determined to stay on in camp in order to provide her with food so that she would have no need to leave her family unguarded for long periods while she went out hunting for them. We also decided to take her meals to her, so as to reduce the time during which she had to desert the cubs.

We put our plan into immediate operation and that afternoon went by car close to her lie-up. We knew that Elsa would associate the vibrations of the engine with us and with food.

As we neared the place where we had last seen her we started to call out – *maji, chakula, nyama* – Swahili words, meaning water, food, meat, with which Elsa was familiar.

Soon she came, was as affectionate as usual and ate a lot. While she had her head in a basin, which we had sunk in the ground to keep it steady, and was busy drinking, we went off. She looked round when she heard the engine start but made no move to follow us.

Next morning we took her day's rations but she failed to turn up, nor was she there when we went again in the afternoon. During the night a strange lion came to within fifteen yards of our tent and removed the remains.

After breakfast we followed his spoor which led to the Big Rock and pugmarks there showed that another lion had been with him. We hoped that Elsa was enjoying their company and that perhaps they were helping her with her housekeeping.

We went down to the river to see whether she had left any spoor there. She had not, but soon afterwards George, who was going to fetch another goat, met her near her rock. She was very thirsty, the aluminium drinking basin had gone and we wondered whether the other lions had stolen it. On his return George fed her and from her appetite he thought it unlikely that the lions had provided her with any of the food they had stolen.

Later in the day George went off to Isiolo. Elsa stayed in camp with me till the late afternoon, then I saw her sneak into the bush upstream and followed her. Obviously she did not wish to be observed, for when she caught my scent, she pretended to sharpen her claws on a tree. Then as soon as I turned my back on her, she jumped at me and knocked me over, as though to say, 'That's for spying on me!' Now it was my turn to pretend that I had only come to bring more meat to her. She accepted my excuse, followed me and began eating again. After this nothing would induce her to return to the cubs until long after night had fallen and I was reading in my tent and she felt certain that I would not be likely to follow her.

During the following days I went on taking food to the spot near to which we believed the cubs to be. Whenever I met Elsa on these occasions, she took great pains to conceal the whereabouts of her lie-up, often doubling back on her tracks, no doubt to puzzle me.

One afternoon when I was passing the Big Rock I saw a very strange animal standing on it. In the dim light it looked like a cross between a hyena and a small lion. When it saw me it sneaked off with the gait of a cat. It had obviously spotted the cubs and I was much alarmed. Later when I brought up some food, Elsa came at once when I called her; she seemed unusually alert and was rather fierce to the Toto. I left her still eating on the roof of my truck. It was there that we placed the meat in the evening to keep it out of the reach of predators, few of which would be likely to risk jumping on to this unknown object, even if they were capable of doing so. I did not know what to do for the best. If I continued to leave food close to Elsa's nursery, would it not attract predators? Alternatively, if I kept the meat in camp and Elsa had to desert her cubs to come and fetch it, might they not be killed while she was absent? Faced with these two unsatisfactory choices, I decided, on balance, to go on providing food near to her lie-up. When I did so on the following evening, I heard the growls of several lions close to me and Elsa appeared to be both very nervous and very thirsty.

After this I made up my mind that in spite of her disapproval I had better find out how many cubs there were and whether they were all right. I might then be able to help in an emergency. On 11 January I did an unpardonable thing. I left a Game Scout (Makedde was ill) with the rifle on the road below and, accompanied by the Toto, whom Elsa knew well, I climbed the rock face calling repeatedly to warn her of our approach. She did not answer. I told the Toto to take off his sandals so as not to make any noise.

When we had reached the top we stood on the edge of the cliff and raked the bush below with our field glasses. Immediately under us was the place from which Elsa had emerged that first time, when we had surprised her and she had stood on guard.

Now, there was no sign of her, but the place looked like a well-used nursery and was ideal for the purpose.

Although I was concentrating very hard on my examination of the bush below us I suddenly had a strange feeling, dropped my field glasses, turned and saw Elsa creeping up behind the Toto. I had just time to shout a warning to him before she knocked him down. She had crept up the rock behind us quite silently and the Toto only missed toppling over the cliff by a hair's breadth and that mainly because his feet were bare which gave him the chance of getting a grip on the rock.

Next Elsa walked over to me and knocked me over in a friendly way, but it was very obvious that she was expressing annoyance at finding us so close to her cubs.

After this demonstration, she walked slowly along the crest of the rock, from time to time looking back over her shoulder to make sure that we were following her. Silently she led us to the far end of the ridge. There we climbed down into the bush. As soon as we were on level ground she rushed ahead, repeatedly turning her head back to confirm that we were coming.

In this way, she took us back to the road, but she made a wide detour, presumably to avoid passing near the cubs. I interpreted her complete silence as a wish not to alarm them or to prevent them from emerging and following us.

When we walk together I usually pat Elsa occasionally and she likes it, but today she would not allow me to touch her and made it clear that I was in disgrace. Even when she was eating her dinner on the roof of the car back in camp, whenever I came near her she turned away from me.

She did not go to the cubs until it was dark.

Now George came up from Isiolo and we changed guard. Elsa had made me feel that I could do no more spying on her;

George had not had the same experience, so he had fewer inhibitions. My curiosity was immense and I felt that it would be a happy compromise if he did 'the wrong thing' and I were to profit by his misdeed.

12. We See the Cubs

One afternoon, while I was at our home in Isiolo a hundred miles away, George crept very quietly up Elsa's Big Rock and peered over the top.

Below he saw her suckling two cubs and as her head was hidden by an overhanging rock, he felt sure that she had not seen him. Having seen the family, George went back to camp and collected a carcase.

We had brought a number of goats into camp so as to supply Elsa with food and thus prevent her from having to desert the cubs while she went hunting for them, and in doing so risk their being killed by predators.

After depositing the food nearby, George waited to see what would happen. Elsa did not come to fetch the meat. This made him feel guilty. The meat we had put near to where we imagined her to be had always been eaten. Did the fact that on this day she refused to go near the kill indicate that she was aware that George had spied on her? When, during the following day, she failed to come to camp, George feared that this might be the case. However, at nightfall she arrived and was so ravenously hungry that she even condescended to eat a dik-dik, which she usually despises. It was all he had been able to find for her, and I did not return from Isiolo till a few days later, having picked up a new supply of goats *en route*.

How thrilled I was upon arrival to hear the good news!

George left for Isiolo the next day and I took on the task of supplying Elsa with the vast quantity of food she needed while suckling the cubs.

I noticed very soon that while she was as affectionate as ever to me, even allowing me to hold bones while she gnawed at them, and equally affectionate to George when he was there, she had become much more reserved in her attitude towards Africans, and even her old friends Nuru and Makedde who had known her since she was a cub were not allowed to be as familiar with her as they had been before the arrival of her family.

One day Elsa caused me a lot of anxiety by arriving in camp soon after lunch and showing no sign of returning to her family after she had had her meal. When it got dark I tried to induce her to go back to them by walking in their direction accompanied by the Toto.

She began by following us but after some time turned into the bush, went forward a hundred yards and then sat down with her back towards us blocking our way.

Nothing would budge her, so we took the hint and retired hoping that once we were out of sight she would rejoin her cubs.

On the following day she again showed that she was determined to conceal the whereabouts of the cubs. The Toto and I were taking an afternoon stroll past the Big Rock, walking very quietly. Suddenly Elsa appeared, rubbed her head against my knees and then led us silently away from the Big Rock, where the cubs were, towards a collection of small rocks which we call the Zom rocks.

She crept in and out of crevices, passed between narrow clefts, and seemed to enjoy making us struggle through the most awkward places. If we fell behind she waited for us, often jerking her head as though to show that she expected us to follow her. Finally I sat down, partly to show that I knew I was being fooled.

After this Elsa left the Zom rocks and led us through thorny thickets and boulders, farther and farther away from her lie-up.

At times she sniffed long and portentously at promising places and seemed to be teasing us by trying to make us think that she was taking us to the cubs. Later we passed a place where she was in the habit of ambushing me. I was tired and not prepared to be knocked down, so I made a detour. When she realized this, she emerged from her hideout looking very dignified but obviously disappointed at being cheated of her fun.

The brief sight George had had of the two suckling cubs had not given him time to discover whether they were normal or not and of course he could not tell whether there might be others hidden from his view. So on the afternoon of 14 January, when Elsa was in camp feeding, he crept off to the Zom rocks, while I kept her company.

For two days she had been constantly in this area, so we supposed that she had changed the place of the nursery.

George climbed up to the top of the centre rock and inside a cleft saw three cubs; two were asleep, but the third was chewing at some sansevieria; it looked up at him but as its eyes were still blurred and bluish he did not think that it could focus well enough to see him.

He took four photographs but did not expect to get good prints for the cleft in which the cubs lay was rather dark. While he was doing this the two cubs who had been sleeping woke up and crawled about. It seemed to him that they were perfectly healthy.

When he came back to camp and told me the excellent news Elsa was still there and quite unsuspicious.

At dusk we drove her near to the Zom rocks. But only after we had tactfully walked away and she was reassured by hearing our voices fading into the distance did she jump off the Land Rover and, presumably, rejoin the cubs.

George now went back to Isiolo. The morning after he had left I heard Elsa's mate calling from the other side of the river but I listened in vain for her reply. In the afternoon, however, she roared very loudly quite near to the camp and went on doing so until I joined her. She seemed overjoyed at seeing me and came back to camp with me, but ate very little and went off when it became dark.

During the next two days she did not turn up, but her mate called to her repeatedly during both nights. On the third day, while I was having breakfast, I heard a terrific roaring coming from the direction of the river. I rushed down to it and saw Elsa standing in the water making as much noise as she could.

She looked very exhausted and soon turned back and disappeared into the bush on the opposite bank. I was puzzled by her odd behaviour. At teatime she came into camp for a hurried meal and then disappeared. On the following day she did not come, but that night I was woken up by the sound of a large animal thumping at my truck. It stood just outside my thorn enclosure. At night we used it as a goats' stable to protect them from predators. Evidently a lion was trying to get at the goats. I did not think it could be Elsa for she usually gave a characteristic low moan, so I suspected her mate.

I listened intently but, believing that a wild lion was close, I did not make a sound. However, when the banging and rattling increased to such a pitch that I feared the car might be destroyed I flashed a torch. The only result was still heavier thumping.

Suddenly I heard Elsa's mate calling from across the river; this proved it must be she who was attacking the truck. She was plainly furious, but it was dark and I did not want to call the boys to let me out of my enclosure, particularly as I feared that her battering might induce her mate to come to help her. All I could do was to shout. 'Elsa! No – No!' I had little hope of being obeyed and was very surprised when she at once stopped her attack and soon left the camp.

On the following afternoon – it was 2 February – while I was writing in the studio the Toto came running to tell me that Elsa was calling in a very strange voice from the other side of the river. I went upstream following the sound, till I broke through the undergrowth at a place close to camp, where in the dry season there is a fairly wide sandbank on our side and on the other a dry watercourse which drops abruptly into the river.

Suddenly I stopped, unable to believe my eyes.

There was Elsa standing on the sandbank within a few yards of me, one cub close to her, a second cub emerging from the water shaking itself dry and the third one still on the far bank, pacing to and fro and calling piteously. Elsa looked fixedly at me, her expression a mixture of pride and embarrassment.

I remained absolutely still while she gave a gentle moan to her young, that sounded like 'm – hm, m-hm'; then she walked up to the landing cub, licked it affectionately and turned back to the river to go to the youngster who was stranded on the far bank. The two cubs who had come across with her followed her immediately, swimming bravely through the deep water, and soon the family were reunited.

Near to where they landed a fig tree grows out of some rocks, whose grey roots grip the stone like a net; Elsa rested in the shade, her golden coat showing up vividly against the dark green foliage and the silver-grey boulders. At first the cubs hid, but soon their curiosity got the better of their shyness. They began by peeping cautiously at me through the undergrowth and then came out into the open and stared inquisitively.

Elsa 'm – hm, m-hm''d which reassured them and when they were quite at their ease they began to climb on to their mother's back and tried to catch her switching tail. Rolling affectionately over her, exploring the rocks and squeezing their fat little tummies under the roots of the fig tree, they forgot all about me.

After a while Elsa rose and went to the water's edge intending to enter the river again; one cub was close to her and plainly meant to follow her.

Unfortunately, at this moment the Toto, whom I had sent back to fetch Elsa's food, arrived with it. Immediately she flattened her ears and remained immobile until the boy had dropped the meat and gone away. Then she swam quickly across followed by one cub, which, though it kept close to her, seemed to be unafraid of the water. When Elsa settled down to her meal, the plucky little fellow turned back and started to swim over on its own to join, or perhaps to help, the other two cubs.

As soon as Elsa saw it swimming out of its depth, she plunged into the river, caught up with it, grabbed its head in her mouth and ducked it so thoroughly that I was quite worried about the little chap.

When she had given it a lesson not to be too venturesome, she retrieved it and brought it, dangling out of her mouth, to our bank.

By this time a second cub plucked up courage and swam across, its tiny head just visible above the rippling water, but the third staying on the far bank looking frightened.

Elsa came up to me and began rolling on her back and showing her affection for me; it seemed that she wanted to prove to her cubs that I was part of the pride and could be trusted.

Reassured, the two cubs crept cautiously closer and closer, their large expressive eyes watching Elsa's every movement and mine, till they were within three feet of me. I found it difficult to restrain an impulse to lean forward and touch them, but I remembered the warning a zoologist had given me: never touch cubs unless they take the initiative, and this three-foot limit seemed to be an invisible boundary which they felt that they must not cross.

While all this was happening the third cub kept up a pathetic miaowing from the far bank, appealing for help.

Elsa watched it for a time, then she walked to the water's edge, at the point at which the river is narrowest. With the two brave cubs cuddling beside her she called to the timid one to join them. But its only response was to pace nervously up and down; it was too frightened to try to cross.

When Elsa saw it so distressed she went to its rescue accompanied by the two bold ones who seemed to enjoy swimming.

Soon they were all on the opposite side again where they had a wonderful time climbing up the steep bank of a sand lugga, which runs into the river, rolling down it, landing on each other's backs and balancing on the trunk of a fallen doum-palm.

Elsa licked them affectionately, talked to them in her soft moaning voice, never let them out of her sight and whenever one ventured too far off for her liking, went after the explorer and brought it back.

I watched them for about an hour and then called Elsa who replied in her usual voice, which was quite different from the one she used when talking to the cubs.

She came down to the water's edge, waited till all her family were at her feet and started to swim across. This time all three cubs came with her.

As soon as they had landed she licked each one in turn and then, instead of charging up to me as she usually does when coming out of the river, she walked up slowly, rubbed herself gently against me, rolled in the sand, licked my face and finally hugged me. I was very much moved by her obvious wish to show her cubs that we were friends. They reached us from a distance, interested, but puzzled and determined to stay out of reach.

Next Elsa and the cubs went to the carcase, which she started eating, while the youngsters licked the skin and tore at it, somersaulted over it and became very excited. It was probably their first encounter with a kill.

The evidence suggested that they were six weeks and two days old. They were in excellent condition and though they still had a bluish film over their eyes they could see perfectly. Their coats had fewer spots than Elsa's or her sisters', and were also much less thick than theirs had been at the same age, but far finer and more shiny. I could not tell their sex, but I noticed immediately that the cub with the lightest coat was much livelier and more inquisitive than the other two and especially devoted to its mother. It always cuddled close up to her, if possible under her chin, and embraced her with its little paws. Elsa was very gentle and patient with her family and allowed them to crawl all over her and chew her ears and tail.

Gradually she moved closer to me and seemed to be inviting me to join in their game. But when I wriggled my fingers in the sand the cubs, though they cocked their round foxy faces, kept their distance.

When it got dark Elsa listened attentively and then took the cubs some yards into the bush. A few moments later I heard the sound of suckling.

I returned to camp and when I arrived it was wonderful to find Elsa and the cubs waiting for me about ten yards from the tent.

I patted her and she licked my hand. Then I called the Toto and together we brought the remains of the carcase up from the river. Elsa watched us and it seemed to me that she was pleased that we were relieving her of the task of pulling the heavy load. But, when we came within twenty yards of her, she suddenly rushed at us with flattened ears. I told the boy to drop the meat and remain still and I began to drag it near to the cubs. When she saw that I was handling the kill alone, Elsa was reassured and as soon as I deposited it she started eating. After watching her for a while, I went to my tent and was surprised to see her following me. She flung herself on the ground and called to the cubs to come and join me. But they remained outside miaowing; soon she went back to them and so did I.

We all sat together on the grass, Elsa leaning against me while she suckled her family.

Suddenly two of the cubs started quarrelling over a teat. Elsa reacted by rolling into a position which gave them better access. In doing so she came to rest against me and hugged me with one paw, including me in her family.

The evening was very peaceful, the moon rose slowly and the doum-palms were silhouetted against the light; there was not a sound except for the suckling of the cubs.

So many people had warned me that after Elsa's cubs had been born she would probably turn into a fierce and dangerous mother defending her young, yet here she was trusting and as affectionate as ever, and wanting me to share her happiness. I felt very humble.

13. The Cubs Meet Friends

When I woke up next morning there was no sign of Elsa or the cubs, and as it had rained during the night all spoor had been washed away.

About teatime she turned up alone, very hungry; I held her meat while she chewed it so as to keep her attention and meanwhile told the Toto to follow her fresh pugmarks to get a clue to the present whereabouts of the cubs.

When he returned Elsa hopped on to the roof of my car, and

from this platform she watched the two of us walking back along her tracks into the bush.

I did this deliberately to induce her to return to the cubs. When she realized where we were going she promptly followed us, and, taking the lead, trotted quickly along her pugmarks; several times she waited till, panting, we caught up with her. I wondered whether at last she meant to take us to her lie-up. When we reached the 'Whuffing Rock', so named because it was there that we had once surprised her with her mate and had been startled by their alarming whuffing, she stopped, listened, climbed swiftly halfway up the slope, hesitated until I had caught up with her and then rushed ahead till she had reached the saddle of the rock from which the big cleft breaks off on the far side. There, much out of breath, I joined her. I was about to pat her when she flattened her ears, and with an angry snarl gave me a heavy clout. Since it was plain that I was not wanted, I retreated. When I had gone halfway down the face of the rock I looked back and saw Elsa playing with one cub, while another was emerging from the cleft.

I was puzzled at the sudden change in her behaviour, but I respected her wishes and left her and her family alone. I joined the Toto who had waited in the bush just below and we watched Elsa through our field glasses. As soon as she saw that we were at a safe distance she relaxed and the cubs came out and began playing with her.

One cub was certainly much more attached to her than the others; it often sat between her front paws and rubbed its head against her chin, while the two others busily investigated their surroundings.

George returned on 4 February and was delighted to hear the good news of the cubs; in the afternoon we walked towards the Whuffing Rock hoping that he too might see them.

On our way we heard the agitated barking of baboons. We

thought it very likely that Elsa's presence was the cause of the commotion, so, as we approached the river, we called out to her. She appeared immediately, but though she was very friendly she was obviously upset and rushed nervously backwards and forwards between us and the bush, which grew along the river's edge. She seemed to be doing her best to prevent us from reaching the water.

We assumed that her cubs were there and were surprised that she should try to prevent George from seeing them. In the end she led us back to the camp by a wide detour.

Two days later we saw her near the Whuffing Rock. As we were walking towards it we talked rather loudly to give her notice of our approach. She emerged from the thick undergrowth at the mouth of the cleft and stood very still, gazing at us. After a few moments she sat down facing us – we were still some two hundred yards away – and made it very plain that we were not to come any nearer. Several times she turned her head towards the cleft and listened attentively, but apart from this she remained in her 'guarding' position.

We now realized that she made a difference between bringing the cubs to see us and our visiting them.

Two weeks passed before she brought the cubs to camp to introduce them to George. This was not entirely her fault for during this time we were obliged to go to Isiolo for a couple of days and while we were away she and the cubs had arrived at the camp one morning looking for us, but had only found the boys.

Makedde told us that he had gone to meet her and she had rubbed her head against his legs and one plucky cub had boldly walked up to within a short distance of him.

However, when he squatted and tried to pat it, it had snarled and run off to join the others who were hiding some distance away. They had stayed in camp till lunchtime and then left. Elsa returned alone during the afternoon asking for meat, but the goat carcase was by then very high and she left in disgust after dark.

I arrived about an hour after she had gone. Makedde was delighted with the plucky cub; he said he was sure it was a male and told me he had given it a name, which was, he said, very popular with the Meru tribe. It sounded like Jespah. I asked him and the other boys where the name came from. They said it was out of the Bible, but as each boy pronounced it slightly differently it was difficult for me to trace it. The nearest phonetic association I could find was Japhtah, which means 'God sets free'. If that were the origin of the little cub's name it could not be more appropriate. Later, when we knew that the family consisted of two lions and a lioness, we called Jespah's brother, who was very timid, Gopa, for in Swahili this means timid, and his sister we named Little Elsa.

The next day Elsa arrived in the afternoon; she was extremely pleased to see me and very hungry. After a while I went for a walk hoping that in my absence she would return to her cubs, and when I came back she had gone.

The following morning it was drizzling. I woke up to hear Elsa's typical cub moan coming from across the river; I jumped out of bed and was just in time to see her crossing the river with her cubs, Jespah close to her and the other two some way behind.

She walked slowly up to me, licked me and sat down next to me. Then she called repeatedly to the cubs. Jespah ventured fairly near to me, but the others kept their distance. I collected some meat which Elsa promptly dragged into a nearby bush; she and the cubs spent the next two hours eating it, while I sat on a sandbank watching them.

While they ate Elsa talked continuously to the cubs in a series of low moans. They often suckled, but also chewed at the meat. Elsa did not regurgitate any meat for them, though considering the vast amount that she had eaten lately when she came alone to the camp it seemed likely that she might have regurgitated some of the meat later in the day for the benefit of the cubs. But this is speculation. We never saw her doing it.

The cubs were now about nine weeks old and for the first time I was able to confirm Makedde's belief that Jespah was a lion.

After a while I went off to have breakfast and soon afterwards saw Elsa leading the cubs in a wide circle to the car track. I followed slowly hoping to take some photographs but she stopped suddenly broadside across the road and flattened her ears. I accepted the reproof and went back, turned to have a last look at them and saw the cubs bouncing along behind their mother going in the direction of the Big Rock. By now they were lively walkers, chasing and prodding one another as they tried to keep pace with Elsa. In spite of their high spirits they were most obedient to her call, and were also already well trained in cleanliness and always stepped off the path when they were producing their excrements.

During the next few days Elsa often came alone to visit us. She was always affectionate but some of her habits had altered since she had given birth to the cubs. She now very seldom ambushed us, was less playful, more dignified.

I wondered how she placed her cubs when she came out on these long visits. Did she instruct them not to move till she returned? Did she hide them in a very safe spot?

When, on 19 February, George came 'on duty', I returned to Isiolo to meet Lord William Percy and his wife and bring them to see Elsa's family.

In general we discouraged visitors, but we made an exception for these old friends who had known Elsa since she was a cub and had always shown the greatest interest in her development.

On our arrival in camp, George greeted us with the news that he had seen the cubs. That morning he woke up while it was still dark and heard quick, short lapping sounds, as well as long laps, coming from the direction of Elsa's water bowl. He looked out and saw the cubs dimly outlined around the bowl; a few minutes later they all went off.

He said that just at that moment in which he had first heard the vibrations of our car, Elsa had been about to cross to our side of the river with her cubs, but when she had become aware of a car approaching she had retired into the bush.

Soon she emerged but seemed nervous and disinclined to enter the water. To induce her to join us I called to her and placed a carcase close to the river.

She made no move till I had gone back to join our friends, then she swam quickly across, seized the goat and rushed back with it to the cubs. Once across she dragged it on to a grassy patch, where the whole family set to and had a good meal; we watched them through our field glasses.

After it had grown dark we heard fearful growls and by the light of our torches saw Elsa defending her kill from a crocodile, which, when it observed us, disappeared quickly into the water.

In the morning an examination of the spoor showed that in the end the croc had been successful in stealing the carcase. We were impressed by the fact that Elsa always seemed to know just how far she could go with these reptiles. She had never shown any fear of them, although we knew that in this river there were many crocodiles measuring twelve feet or more. She had her favourite crossings and avoided the places where the river was very deep, and besides taking this precaution there can be no doubt that she had some means of sensing the presence of crocs. How this worked we could not guess. We had our own method of discovering the presence of crocs; we knew that they invariably respond to a certain sound, which can roughly be represented by 'imn, imn, imn', and we often took advantage of our knowledge.

If we suspected the presence of crocodiles we would keep

ourselves hidden from the river and repeat 'imn, imn, imn'; then if there were any crocs within 400 yards, they would come to the water's edge as though drawn by a magnet. Often we went on until we saw many ugly periscopic nostrils sticking out above the water. If we moved, and our noises then came from a different place, they would follow them.

George had learned this trick from African fishermen on Lake Baringo which is infested by crocs.

Next day, Lady William started sketching Elsa. This was something Elsa usually disliked, but today she seemed to have no objection. All the same, I kept close by in case she might suddenly take a dislike to serving as a model. However, as she appeared quite indifferent to what was going on, after a while I went away. As soon as my back was turned she rushed like lightning at the artist and embraced her playfully. As Elsa weighs about three hundred pounds I admired the calm way in which Lady William accepted the demonstration.

At teatime the next day we saw Elsa and the cubs on the opposite side of the river, but when she spotted us she moved her family a short distance downstream, then they crossed the river. We quickly fetched some meat which Elsa promptly collected and then took into the bush to her cubs who were out of sight.

Later, they all got thirsty and came to the water's edge to drink. I was glad that our guests should have this splendid view of them drinking close together, their heads stretched forward between the pointed elbows of their front legs, which were bent. At first they just lapped noisily, then they plunged into the shallow water and began to play. They were certainly not water-shy, as cats are said to be.

How lucky these little cubs were to be living in such a lovely and exciting place. The rocky range on which they were born started on our side of the river, crossed it and circled for several miles on the other side. It was broken up by cracks and caves in which hyrax and other small animals had made their homes; around it on all sides stretched the bush, which was full of spoor and of the scent of wild animals, and then there was the river, with its rock and sandbanks on which turtles, looking like giant pebbles, basked in the morning sun.

In other places the river is bordered by fig trees, acacias and phœnix palms from which lianas and tendrils dangle and twist their way into the thick undergrowth and thereby provide impenetrable hideouts for many animals.

Here live the graceful vervet monkeys, the clowning baboons, the turquoise-coloured agamas, all kinds of lizards, some with bright orange heads, others with vivid blue tails, and also our friend the monitor. Bushbuck, lesser kudu and waterbuck come here to drink and the flattened, trampled ground shows that rhino and buffalo also visit it. Of all the inhabitants of the bush the most fascinating to us are the many coloured birds which throng the bush: the orioles, the brilliant kingfishers, the iridescent sunbirds, the fish eagle and the palm-nut vulture, black and white and very large, the hornbills whose rhythmic croaking rises to a crescendo and only drops to rise again.

After our friends had gone to bed, George and I returned to see Elsa. We found her standing at the water's edge facing a crocodile, whose head rose out of the water about four feet away.

We did not want to frighten the cubs by firing a shot, so I tempted Elsa to leave the place by offering her a treat of which she was very fond; it consists of brains, marrow, calcium and cod-liver oil. I began giving it to her when she was pregnant and she found it irresistible.

Now she followed the bowl in which I carried it and came with the cubs to sit in front of our tent, facing the bright lamplight.

The cubs were unperturbed by the glare; perhaps they thought it was some new kind of moon. .

After I had gone to bed, George turned out 'the moon' and

sat for a while in the dark. The cubs came within touching distance of him, then, having had a drink for the road, they all trotted off towards the Big Rock, from which immediately afterwards he heard Elsa's mate calling.

Later George went to collect the remains of the carcase, but found it had already been pulled into the water by a crocodile. He shot at the thief and rescued the meat.

Early one morning Elsa visited the camp before anyone was up. I heard her and followed her. She was already in the water when I called to her, but she came back at once, settled with me on a sandbank and began to miaow at the cubs, encouraging them to come near us. They approached within three yards but obviously did not wish to be handled, and as the last thing I wanted was that they should become tame, I was very pleased about this.

Elsa seemed puzzled that they should still be scared of me, but in the end she gave up her attempt to make us fraternize, took her family across the river and disappeared into the bush.

At ten o'clock she returned alone, sniffed restlessly in the river bush and then trotted, scenting, along the road she had taken in the morning.

After we had lost sight of her we heard her growling fiercely. She returned along the track still sniffing anxiously and finally roared at full strength towards the rock, after which she rushed into the river and disappeared into the bush on the far side. We did not know to what to attribute her strange behaviour, but thought perhaps she might have lost a cub.

When at lunchtime Ibrahim brought in three tribesmen who said they were looking for a goat which had strayed, but carried bows and poisoned arrows, we felt sure that we had been right: no doubt their arrival had startled the little ones and they had bolted.

Elsa did not bring the cubs into camp again for a couple of

days. That morning we had taken our friends to see the magnificent falls of the Tana River, which few Europeans visit because they are so inaccessible.

On our return we found Elsa and the cubs in camp and while we had our sundowners they enjoyed their dinner. We were silent for we knew how sensitive the cubs were to the sound of talking. They did not mind the chatter of the boys, far away in the kitchen, but if we were near them and said a word to each other, even in a low voice, they sneaked away. As for the clicking of a camera shutter – it gave them the jitters.

They were ten weeks old and Elsa had begun to wean them. Whenever she thought they had had enough milk she either sat on her teats or jumped on to the roof of the Land Rover. So if the cubs did not want to starve they had to eat meat. They tore the intestines of the kills out of their mother's mouth and sucked them in like spaghetti, through closed teeth, pressing out the unwanted contents, just as she did.

That evening one cub was determined to get some more milk and persistently pushed its way under Elsa's belly until she became really angry, gave it a good spank and jumped on to the car.

The little ones resented this very much; they stood on their hind legs resting their forepaws against the car, miaowing up at their mother, but she sat and licked her paws, as though she were quite unaware of the whimpering cubs below.

When they had recovered from their disappointment they bounced off, cheerfully making explorations which took them out of her sight. Elsa became extremely alert if they did not come when she called them, and if they did not reappear quickly she hopped off the car and fetched them back to safety.

The next two evenings Elsa came to the camp with her family. She was exuberantly affectionate and swept the table clear of our sundowners. On the third evening she brought the cubs with her and behaved in the same way. We were rather surprised to observe that the cubs were not in the least startled when our supper landed on the ground with a noisy clatter.

They now seemed quite at home in our presence, so it astonished us that on the two following evenings Elsa left them at an open salt lick about a hundred yards away, and we were also puzzled to know how she trained them to stay put while she enjoyed a good meal in full view of them.

During all that night it poured without stopping. On such occasions Elsa always takes refuge in George's tent, and now, in she came, calling to the cubs to follow her. But they remained outside apparently enjoying the deluge and soon their poor mother felt it her duty to go out and join them.

The following day I went off to Isiolo with our friends. George stayed on in camp. We knew that, now the rains had started in earnest, transport would soon become very difficult, so we had to make our plans accordingly.

14. The Cubs in Camp

When I came back to camp two days later to relieve George, I found that I had to be careful about letting any of the boys come near Elsa when she had the cubs with her. If even Makedde approached them she flattened her ears and looked at him through half-closed eyes which had a cold, murderous expression. Me, she trusted completely and gave proof of it by sometimes leaving the cubs in my charge when she went to the river to drink.

For several nights we had terrific thunderstorms and the lightning and the crashes came so close together that I was quite frightened. The water poured down as though it were flowing through a pipe.

As George's tent was empty, Elsa and the cubs could very well have sheltered in it, but the youngsters' inbred fear of man was so great that they preferred to soak outside. This trait was the most obvious sign of their wild blood and it was something we were determined to encourage, even at the expense of a wetting and even in defiance of Elsa's wish to make them into friends of ours. Often she seemed to be playing a sort of 'catch as catch can' with them, circling nearer and nearer to the tent in which I was sitting, as though she wanted to bring them into it without their becoming aware of what was happening.

Twice she dashed into the tent and peeping over my shoulder called to them. But whatever she did they never overstepped their self-imposed frontier.

It seemed that our rearing of their mother in domesticity had in no way impaired the instinct which all wild animals possess and which warns them against approaching an unknown danger. Moreover, Elsa herself had shown by concealing her cubs from us for five or six weeks, that her own instinct for protecting her young was still alive.

Now, she was plainly disappointed that her efforts to make one pride of us were proving unsuccessful, partly owing to the cubs' fear of man and partly owing to what she must have taken as heartless lack of co-operation on our part. She seemed very puzzled, but had no intention of giving up her plan. One evening she entered my tent, deliberately lay down behind me and then called softly to the cubs inviting them to suckle her. By doing this she tried not only to make the cubs come into the tent but also to force them to pass close to me. No doubt they would have been pleased if I had retired behind their mother and she would have been pleased if I had done something to encourage them, but I remained where I was and kept still. To have moved would have defeated Elsa's intention and to have encouraged them would have been against our determination not to tame them. I was sorry because I longed to help the cubs and felt distressed when Elsa looked at me for a long time with a disappointed expression in her eyes and then went out to join her children. Of course she could not understand that my lack of response was due to our wish to preserve the cubs' wild instinct. She plainly thought me unfeeling, whereas I was suppressing all my feelings for the good of her family.

The cubs were worried about our relationship for the opposite reason and became anxious every evening when Elsa, persecuted by tsetse flies, flung herself in front of me, asking me to dispose of these pests.

When I started squashing the flies and in the process slapping Elsa, the cubs were very upset. Jespah in particular would come close and crouch, ready to spring should his mother be in need of protection. No doubt they found it odd that she should seem grateful for my slappings.

On one occasion when Elsa, Jespah and Little Elsa were drinking in front of the tent Gopa was too nervous to come to the water bowl. Seeing this, Elsa went to him with great deliberation and cuffed him several times, after which he plucked up enough courage to join the others.

Jespah's character was quite different – he was rather too brave. One afternoon after they had all fed and when their bellies were near bursting point Elsa started off towards the rock. By then it was nearly dark. Two cubs followed obediently but Jespah went on gorging. Elsa called twice to him, but he merely listened for a moment and then went on feeding. Finally, his mother came back, and it was in no uncertain manner that she walked up to her son. Jespah realized that he was in for trouble, so gobbling the meat and with large bits of it hanging out of either side of his mouth, trotted after her.

At this time I had to go for a few days to Isiolo while George came to look after the camp.

By now Elsa had won the hearts of thousands of people and became famous over night. It was gratifying but we feared she might have to share the fate of all celebrities – lack of privacy.

People from all over the world wrote saying they would like to come and see her. After all the trouble we had taken to keep her and the cubs wild we could not agree to Elsa and her family being turned into a tourist attraction. We could, of course, appeal to her admirers, to sportsmen and to our friends not to invade her privacy, but we had no legal means of keeping people out and we were very worried in case some visitor should, in our absence, provoke Elsa and accidentally cause trouble.

The way in which the cubs were developing into true wild lions exceeded our hopes, but their father was a great disappointment to us.

No doubt we were partly to blame, for we had interfered with his relationship with his family – but certainly he was of no help as a provider of food for them; on the contrary, he often stole their meat. Moreover, he caused us a lot of trouble. One evening he made a determined attempt to get at a goat which was inside my truck, and another time when Elsa and the cubs were eating outside our tent she suddenly scented him, became very nervous, sniffed repeatedly towards the bush, cut her meal short and hurriedly removed the cubs.

George went out with a torch to find out what the trouble was; he had not gone three yards when he was startled by a fierce growl and saw the cubs' father hiding in a bush just in front of him. He retreated rapidly and luckily so did the lion.

The next day another menace appeared. Makedde reported that an enormous crocodile was sleeping at the place where Elsa usually crossed the river. George took a rifle and went to the spot. The croc was still there, and huge it was, for after he had shot it he measured it – it was twelve feet two inches, a record for that river.

If Elsa had been attacked by such a monster she would not have stood a chance.

When I returned to camp I took Nuru with me, he had only just returned to us; he had been home for six months because he had suffered from an internal illness. Now he was well again, but he blamed Elsa for his sickness. This surprised me as he had always been very devoted to her, but it seemed that the onset of his malady had coincided with the time at which we had engaged him to look after Elsa and her two sisters. Because of this he was convinced that she had cast the evil eye on him.

It was to dispel this belief that I was now taking him to the camp with me. As we waited in the drizzling rain, I told him about the cubs and he seemed very interested.

During the night the river fell, so we were able to reach camp in the early hours of the morning. Elsa, attracted by vibrations of the car, gave us a welcome which, in our exhausted state, we found almost too boisterous.

In the afternoon, hoping to be able to show Nuru the cubs, we all walked in their direction. Suddenly we heard Elsa talking to them in the bush just ahead of us.

Soon she came bouncing out and after greeting us made a great fuss of Nuru. Indeed, she was so overwhelmingly happy to see her old friend again after such a long absence, that he was very much touched; he began to pat her and discarded all his superstitious fear of her evil eye. After this reunion he became even more devoted to her than he had been before his illness. She did not, however, show him her cubs on this occasion and only brought them into camp after dark.

Unlike their mother, they had never had any man-made toys to play with, but they wrestled in the bright lamplight and were never at a loss to find a stick to fight for. At other times they played hide-and-seek and ambushes. Often they would get locked in a clinch, the victim struggling on his back with all four paws in the air. Elsa usually joined in their games; in spite of her great weight, she sprang and hopped about as though she were herself a cub.

We had provided two water bowls for them, a strong aluminium basin and an old steel helmet mounted on a piece of wood, which Elsa had used since her youth. This was the more popular of the two with the cubs. They often tipped it over and were alarmed at the clatter it made when it fell. Then recovering from their fright they faced the shiny moving object with cocked heads and finally began to prod it cautiously. We took flashlight photographs of these games.

We had more difficulty in taking pictures of them at play during daylight, because they were then less active. Our best chance was in the late afternoon, when they went to a favourite playground near to a doum-palm which had fallen at the edge of the riverbank, some two hundred yards from the camp. This place afforded all amenities: it overlooked a wide-open space, it had thick bush close by into which they could disappear if any danger threatened, it was near to a salt lick, and also to the river, should they want a drink. Besides this I often placed a carcase nearby.

George and I used to hide in the bush and take films of the family climbing up and down the fallen trunk, teasing their mother who was always there to guard them.

They knew we were near but this did not disturb them; if, however, an African appeared, even in the distance, the game stopped at once and the cubs disappeared into the bush, while Elsa faced the intruder with flattened ears and a threatening expression.

On 2 April George went back to Isiolo but I stayed on in camp.

As the days passed I observed that the cubs were getting more and more shy even of me. Now they preferred to sneak through the grass in a wide circle to reach their meat, rather than follow their mother in a straight line, because this involved coming very close to me.

To prevent predators from stealing the meat during the night I started dragging the carcase from the doum-palm near to my tent, to which I attached it by a chain.

It was often a heavy load and Elsa used to watch me, apparently content that I had taken on the laborious task of protecting her meat.

Jespah was much less happy when he saw me handling the kill. After several half-hearted attacks he sometimes charged me in a proper fashion, first crouching low and then rushing forward at full speed. Elsa came instantly to my rescue: she not only placed herself between her son and me, but gave him a sound and deliberate cuff. Afterwards she sat with me in the tent for a long time, totally ignoring Jespah, who rested outside looking bewildered. He lay by the helmet bowl, his head against it, occasionally lapping lazily.

Touched as I was by Elsa's reaction, I also understood that Jespah should be disconcerted by his mother's disapproval of his instinctive reaction and I was most anxious not to arouse his jealousy.

He was still too small to do very much harm but we both recognized that it was essential to establish a friendly truce with the cubs while they were still dependent upon us for food and before they had grown big enough to be dangerous. It was a difficult problem because while we did not want them to be hostile, neither did we want them to become tame. Recently Elsa herself seemed to have become aware of our difficulty and to be making her contribution to solving it. While she spanked Jespah if in his attempts to protect her he attacked me, she also dealt firmly with me if she thought I was getting too familiar with her children. For instance, several times when I came close to them while they were at play, she looked at me through half-closed eyes, walked slowly but purposefully up to me, and gripped me round the knees in a friendly but determined manner, which indicated very plainly that her grip would become much firmer if I did not take the hint and retire.

15. The Personality of the Cubs

One morning I was woken up by the arrival of a Land Rover bearing a message which told me to expect the arrival of two English journalists, Godfrey Winn and Donald Wise.

This worried me as Elsa's reactions were unpredictable when she had the cubs with her – she had lately even objected to Nuru's presence. I sent the driver back with the message begging George to halt the party ten miles away from the camp and suggested that I should meet them there.

Having taken these precautions I was rather surprised when the party nevertheless turned up, and I was trying to argue our guests into retiring when I heard Elsa's 'mhn, mhn'. Probably she had been attracted by the vibration of the engine; anyway, there she was and the cubs with her. In the circumstances all I could do was to make the best of the situation.

I took our guests to the studio to have tea while George tied a carcase to the fallen doum-palm trunk, so that we could watch Elsa and the cubs eating. I told Mr Winn that I had no wish to monopolize Elsa and her family but was anxious that the lions should live a wild life, which entailed preserving their privacy.

We spent a pleasant evening together, dining beside the tent.

After a while Elsa jumped up on to the Land Rover which was standing not very far away from us.

On the following evening we tied up a carcase near our tent. Elsa soon came for her meal and did all she could to induce the cubs to join her. She pranced round and did her best to cajole them and tried by every means to break down their fear, but not even Jespah ventured into the lamplight. That evening we heard their father calling and by the next morning they had all gone.

When, on 8 April, George left for Isiolo I stayed on. One night Elsa turned up her nose at the meat I offered her; afterwards the boys told me that the goat had been ill; so her instinct had evidently warned her that the meat was infected. The cubs also would not touch it. As a rule, they were remarkably greedy, ate enormously and insisted on being suckled by Elsa as well as eating meat.

Elsa spent that evening resting her head against my shoulder and 'mhn-mhning' to the cubs, a very sonorous sound, although it came through closed lips; fruitlessly, she tried to make them come to me.

I was always touched by the way in which she discriminated when she played with me or with them. With the cubs she was often rather rough, pulling their skin, biting them affectionately or holding their heads down so that they should not interfere with her meal; it would have been most painful if she had treated me in the same way, but she was always gentle when we played together. I attributed this partly to the fact that when I stroke her, I always do so very gently, talking to her at the same time in a low, calm voice, to which she responds quietly. I am sure that if I treated her roughly, it would provoke her to demonstrate her superior strength.

That night, after I had gone to bed, I heard Elsa's mate calling, but instead of going to him, she tried to creep through the thorn fence into my boma. I called out, 'No, Elsa, no,' and she stopped at once. She then settled her cubs by the wicker gate and there they spent the night.

The next day she did not appear till after dark and then only brought two cubs with her. Jespah was missing. Elsa settled down to her meal with Gopa and Little Elsa. I was anxious about Jespah but in the dark I could not go and look for him, so I tried to induce his mother to do so, by imitating his high-pitched 'tciang-tciang' at the same time pointing to the bush. After a while, she went off. The two cubs did not seem to be worried by her absence and went on eating for at least five minutes before they made up their minds to follow her. A little later the three of them returned, but there was still no sign of Jespah. I repeated my tactics and Elsa made another search but again returned without him; a third time I induced her to go to find him but this proved equally unsuccessful.

I then discovered that Elsa had a large thorn stuck deeply into her tail. It must have been very painful, and when I tried to pull it out she became irritable. Luckily, I did eventually manage to extract it, then she licked the wound and afterwards my hand, by way of thanking me. By this time Jespah had been missing for one hour.

Suddenly and without any prompting from me she and the two cubs walked purposefully off into the bush and soon I heard Jespah's familiar 'tciangs'.

Presently he appeared with the others, nibbled at some meat and came to lie within five feet of me. I was thankful to see him safely back as the hour he had chosen to go off on his own was the most dangerous so far as predators are concerned, and he was still much too young to tackle even a hyena let alone a lion. I suspected that he had been at the diseased carcase which his mother had refused to touch and which I had ordered to be thrown away at a good distance from the camp.

To provide him with something harmless on which to spend

his energy I got an old inner tube and wriggled it near him. He attacked it at once and soon his brother and sister joined in the new game. They fought and pulled until there was nothing left but shreds of rubber.

That night it rained. In the morning I was much surprised to see not only Elsa's pugmarks, but those of a cub inside George's empty tent. It was the first time that one had entered the self-imposed forbidden area.

On the following night Elsa, observing that the boys had forgotten to place thorn branches in front of the entrance to my enclosure, pushed the wicker gate aside, entered the tent and promptly lay down on my bed. Wrapped up in the torn mosquito netting she looked so content that I saw myself having to spend the night sitting in the open.

Jespah followed his mother into the tent and stood on his hind legs examining the bed, but fortunately decided against trying it out. The other cubs stayed outside.

We spent most of the evening trying to lure Elsa out of my tent – it was a difficult task since we dared not open the door in case all the cubs were to rush in and join their mother. What we intended was that Elsa should crawl out through the wickerwork door. For some time our hopes of success were pretty dim, then I began to make 'tcianging' noises round the camp and to flash my torch, pretending that the cubs were lost and that I was looking for them. This soon caused both Elsa and Jespah to rush out. She came through the door; how he got out I do not know. I now had my tent to myself but was unable to sleep because Elsa noisily attacked my truck. However, as on a previous occasion, to my surprise, she stopped when I shouted, 'No, Elsa, no,' to her. I could not understand why she went for the goats' truck, for if she were hungry there was still some meat down by the river.

The cubs were about sixteen weeks old and by now the family should have been guarding its kill. Had Elsa become so lazy that she expected us not only to provide her with food but also to relieve her of the task of protecting it?

Were we ruining her wild instincts and should we leave her? The moment did not seem a propitious one for deserting her, because we had recently found the footprints of two strange Africans very near the camp. No doubt they had been reconnoitring our whereabouts, for the drought was again with us and probably they intended to bring their stock into the game reserves to graze, though this was illegal. In the circumstances, I felt I must go on providing the family with food; if not, Elsa would surely kill some trespassing goat. I comforted myself with the thought that very soon the rains would come, the tribesmen would go away and by the next dry season Elsa would have the cubs well on the run to hunt with her.

Meanwhile, I was immensely interested in observing their development. Already they stretched their tendons; they stood on their hind legs and dug their claws into the rough bark of certain trees – preferably acacias – in so doing they exposed the pink bases of their claws. When they had finished this exercise, the bark showed deep gashes.

I noticed a curious fact about Elsa's faeces, which I had previously often examined for parasites. Before she gave birth to the cubs I had always found them riddled with tapeworm and roundworm, and although I had been told that the presence of tapeworm in a lion's intestines is beneficial (and indeed in the post-mortems we made of any lion George had been asked to shoot, we always found quantities of them), I had nevertheless dosed Elsa from time to time to keep her clear of worms. But since she had had her family I never found a trace of a worm in her faeces nor were there any in those of the cubs. Only after they were nine and a half months old did I find tapeworms in all their droppings again.

Another change related to cleanliness. In the past she had

often wetted the groundsheet inside the tent and even some-times the canvas roof of the Land Rover, but since she had become a mother she never permitted herself such bad manners and made the cubs walk off the path whenever they needed to relieve themselves.

None of them showed any sign of the 'ridge back' which is so characteristic of lions. It is a patch about one foot long and two or three inches wide down the middle of the spine on which the hair grows in the opposite direction to the rest of the coat. Elsa and her sister, the Big One, grew their ridge backs very early, but Lustica, the third sister, never developed one.

The cubs were very easily distinguishable. Jespah was much the lightest in colour, his body was perfectly proportioned and he had a very pointed nose and eyes so acutely slanted that they gave a slightly Mongolian cast to his sensitive face. His character was not only the most nonchalant, daring and inquisitive, but also the most affectionate. When he was not cuddling up against his mother and clasping her with his paws he demonstrated his affection to his brother and sister.

When Elsa ate I often saw him pretending to eat too, but in fact only rubbing himself against her. He followed her every-where like a shadow. His timid brother Gopa was also most attractive; he had very dark markings on his forehead but his eyes, instead of being bright and open like Jespah's, were rather clouded and squinted a little. He was bigger and more heavily built than his brother and so pot-bellied that at one time I even feared he might have a rupture. Though he was by no means stupid, he took a long time to make up his mind and, unlike Jespah, was not venturesome; indeed, he always stayed behind till he was satisfied that all was safe.

Little Elsa fitted her name, for she was a replica of her mother at the same age. She had the same expression, the same markings, the same slender build. Her behaviour, too, was so strikingly like

Elsa's that we could only hope that she would develop the same lovable character.

She knew of course that for the moment she was at a disadvantage compared to her two stronger brothers, but she used cunning to restore the balance. Though all the cubs were well disciplined and obeyed Elsa instantly on all important occasions, when playing they showed no fear of her and were only occasionally intimidated by the cuffs she gave them when they became too cheeky.

One evening when the whole family were lying in front of the tent, I started to light the Tilley pressure lamp. Suddenly it burst into flames and I had only time to throw it on to the ground outside the tent before it flared up so alarmingly that I ran for Ibrahim to help me put it out. We collected some old rags to beat it with but by the time we returned it had gone out. During all this commotion the cubs lay very close, quietly watching the strange behaviour of their 'moon'. Elsa also came up to investigate the blaze and I had to shout, 'No, Elsa,' in my most commanding voice to prevent her from singeing her whiskers. She and the cubs then settled outside my tent for the night.

Before I went to sleep I heard what sounded to me like the love-making of a pair of rhinos. These bulky beasts utter the most unexpectedly meek sounds when mating. Another possibility was that the noises came from a pair of buffalo. But whatever it was I was glad that my rifle was near to my bed in case of an emergency. However, nothing more happened and I went to sleep, to be woken up next morning by the sound of crockery clattering on to the ground. The next moment the Toto rushed into the tent minus the teatray. Breathlessly, he told me that as he was carrying my early morning tea into the tent he had been nearly knocked down by a buffalo. He had only just managed to reach the gate of my enclosure ahead of the beast and to close it in his face. It made me smile to think that a light wicker gate should have given the poor fellow a sense of security when pursued by a charging buffalo.

By the time the cubs were eighteen weeks old Elsa seemed to have become resigned to the fact that their relationship with us would never be the same as ours with her.

Indeed, they were growing more shy every day and preferred to eat outside the area lit by our camp, except for Jespah, who, as he followed his mother everywhere, often came with her into the 'danger zone'. Elsa now often placed herself between us and the cubs in a defensive position.

As they were in excellent condition we thought that we should risk leaving them to hunt with Elsa, anyway for a few days. Their father had been about lately and as the family had only come into camp for short feeding visits, we assumed that they were spending most of their time with him.

While the boys were breaking camp I went to the studio, and sitting on the ground, with my back against a tree, started reading a huge bundle of letters from readers of *Born Free*. They had come up with the Land Rover which had arrived to transport our belongings. I was worrying about how I should find time to answer them all, as I wanted to, when suddenly I was squashed by Elsa. As I struggled to free myself from beneath her three hundred pounds the letters were scattered all round the place and, when I had got on to my feet again and begun to collect them, Elsa bounced on to me every time I bent down to pick one up and we rolled together on the ground. The cubs thought this splendid fun and dashed round after the fluttering paper. I thought that Elsa's admirers would have enjoyed seeing how much their letters were appreciated. In the end, I am glad to say that I recovered every one of them; I sent for Elsa's dinner and this diverted her attention and that of the cubs.

By this time the boys had finished packing and the loaded cars were waiting some distance away.

In spite of the loud noise of the cataracts Elsa at once heard the vibrations of the engine. She listened alertly and then looked up at me, her pupils widely dilated, so that her eyes seemed almost black. I had a strong impression that as on previous occasions she realized we were about to desert her and her expression seemed to say: 'What do you mean by leaving me and my cubs without food?' Then she abandoned her half-eaten meal, moved slowly down the sandy lugga with her children and disappeared.

16. Elsa Meets Her Publisher

After a five-day absence we returned on 28 April to camp; ten minutes later Elsa arrived alone. She was in excellent condition and delighted to see us, but made away with the carcase we had brought for her before we had time to tie it up for the night.

She did not reappear for twenty-four hours, then she came alone, ate enormously and by the morning was gone.

The absence of the cubs worried us, the more so because Elsa's teats were heavy with milk, but to our relief the next afternoon we found the whole family playing in a dry riverbed. They followed us back to the camp. Soon afterwards a thunderstorm broke out; Elsa at once joined us in our tent; but the cubs sat outside, at intervals shaking the water off their coats. No one looks his best when drenched and cold, but the cubs certainly looked most endearing, if rather pathetic: their ears and paws seemed twice their normal size against their soaking bodies. As soon as the worst of the downpour was over Elsa joined them and they had an energetic game together, perhaps to warm themselves. After this they settled down to their dinner and tore at the meat so fiercely that beneath their coats which now were dry and fluffy we could see the play of their well-developed muscles. At the end of their meal we, for the first time, saw them bury the uneaten part of the kill. They scratched sand over the little pile most carefully until nothing of it could be seen. Perhaps their mother had taught them to do this during the five days in which they had lived totally wild. After everything had been neatly cleaned up the cubs settled round Elsa and she suckled them for a long time.

As this visit of ours was intended to be a short one, we were anxious to take some photographs but Elsa defeated all our efforts by spending most of her time away from camp. We also wanted to feed her up before another absence, so early one morning we called to her from the foot of the Big Rock. She came down with Jespah at her heels. The other two kept at a little distance. For a time they followed us along the car track, the cubs gambolling and wrestling and Elsa often pausing to wait for them. It was a glorious morning, the air still brisk and the beautiful clouds which usually pattern the Kenya sky on even the brightest days had not yet had time to form. Full of *joie de vivre* the cubs bustled along, knocking each other over, until Elsa turned into the bush, probably intending to take a short cut to the camp. Little Elsa and Gopa chased after her, but Jespah stayed on the track. It seemed that he felt in charge of his pride and we were certainly not included; he was making sure that we were not following. He paid no attention to his mother's call, and advanced towards us in a most determined fashion, sometimes crouching low and then making a short rush forward. When he was quite close he stopped, looked at us and rolled his head from side to side. He appeared embarrassed and as though he did not know what he should do next. Meanwhile, Elsa returned to fetch her disobedient son, who, having stepped nimbly aside to avoid a vigorous cuff, trotted off after his brother and sister.

We spent a happy day in the studio where the family gorged on a carcase. When they could eat no more, the cubs rolled on their backs and with paws in the air dozed off. I leant against Elsa's stern and Jespah rested under her shin. As soon as the cubs recovered from their siesta they explored the low branches which overhang the rapids halfway across the river. They seemed to have no fear of heights or of the rushing water below and turned with the greatest ease on even the thinnest boughs.

When it was nearly dark I began to drag the remains of the meat back to camp. While I was doing this Jespah charged at me twice, but Elsa gave him such a disapproving look that he stopped and sneaked away.

In the afternoon of a day on which George had to go off on patrol, I made another attempt to get some photographs. I took the Toto with me to help carry the camera and found the family, all very sleepy, in what we call 'the kitchen lugga', a sandy part of a dry riverbed. When I had spotted them I told the Toto to return to camp. It was very hot, but the sky was overcast and there were some dark rain clouds. I placed the cameras in position and Elsa came up and rolled between the tripods, but without upsetting them. The cubs appeared and were much intrigued by the shining objects and anxious to investigate the bags which I had hung out of their reach. Soon it began to drizzle, but, as it was the kind of shower that never lasts long, I slipped plastic bags over the cameras and did not bother to move them.

Suddenly I saw Elsa standing rigid and looking through half-closed eyes in the direction I had come from.

Then with flattened ears she rushed into the bush like a streak of lightning. I heard a yell from the Toto and dashed after her shouting, 'No, Elsa, no.' Luckily, I was in time to control her. I called to the Toto to make his way back to the camp very slowly and quietly, so as to give Elsa no incentive to chase him. I realized that seeing the rain, he had decided, against my orders, to come back and help me move the heavy cameras. He narrowly missed being very ill-rewarded for his kindness.

As soon as he was out of sight I succeeded in calming Elsa, by stroking her and telling her over and over again in a reassuring voice that it was only the Toto, Toto, Toto, whom she knew so well. Then I packed up the equipment and started back to the camp. It was not an easy return. Elsa remained very suspicious; she kept rushing ahead of me to make sure that all was safe. As a result I often found myself between her and the cubs and this they did not like. Jespah kept charging me. Eventually I managed to lead the party, which was my intention, for I did not want Elsa to be the first to arrive in camp. I was handicapped because in order to see what was going on behind me I was obliged to walk backwards, carrying my heavy load and constantly talking to Elsa in a casual, reassuring tone of voice, hoping to get her into a peaceful frame of mind before we reached home.

When I was within earshot of the boys I shouted to them to provide a carcase, and I kept Elsa back until it was in position. As a result our return went off peacefully.

After George came back we made another photographic expedition. We went close to the rock where in the morning we had seen Elsa but though we called to her she did not appear. Only after the light had become too weak for filming did she suddenly emerge silently from a bush only ten yards away from us.

She seemed very composed; perhaps she had spent all the afternoon there watching us. She rubbed her head against our knees but made no sound. We knew she kept silent when she did not wish the cubs to follow her. As quietly as she had appeared she vanished into the bush. Later we saw the pugmarks of her lion and concluded that they must be together.

The next afternoon I saw Elsa through my field glasses near

to the spot where she had disappeared on the previous afternoon. She was on the ridge outlined against the sky, watching intently a little gap between some rocks. Though she saw me, she paid no attention to me. I remained there till it was nearly dark, and during all that time she never moved, and seemed to be on guard. Then suddenly her attention became fixed in the direction of the track; probably she heard the sound of George's car returning from patrol.

Soon it appeared, stopped and I got into it and began talking to George. In the back I observed some guinea fowl which he had shot, and looked forward to a pleasant change from the tinned food on which we had been living.

But with a rush Elsa had leapt between us and was among the birds. Feathers began to fly in all directions as she jumped about making frantic efforts to pluck the birds. It looked as though nothing would be left of them, so George picked up a guinea fowl and threw it to the cubs. Immediately Elsa rushed after it and we took the opportunity to start up the engine and move off. Seeing this, Elsa bounded on to the roof of the Land Rover and insisted on being driven home. We hoped that after we had gone a few hundred yards her motherly instinct would make her return to the cubs, but she felt far from motherly and we had to bang from the inside on the canvas roof until we made her quite uncomfortable before she decided to jump off and rejoin her bewildered family.

Later they all came to camp and had great fun with the guinea fowl. We were amused to observe how very cunning Little Elsa had become. She allowed her brothers to pull out the prickly quills of the feathers and then when the bird had been nicely plucked took the first opportunity of grabbing it.

After this she defended it with snarls, growls and scratchings, her ears flattened and with such a forbidding expression that the boys thought it wiser to go off and pluck another bird.

Sometimes the fights between the cubs over food were quite rough, but they never sulked afterwards or showed any resentment. We were surprised that they preferred guinea fowl to goat meat. When she was a cub Elsa had regarded a dead guinea fowl merely as a toy and seldom considered eating it.

The family spent that night close to the camp and in the morning we thought we knew why, for father's pugmarks were all around the place and we assumed that he had intended to share their meal. Elsa had obviously not been agreeable to this plan for she had dragged the carcase into a thicket between our tents and the river, where it was unlikely that he would care to come.

She remained with her cubs in this stronghold for the next twenty-four hours, and only left it when she heard George returning from patrol in his Land Rover. He had brought some more guinea fowl and the fun and feast of the night before were repeated.

At dusk I went for a stroll and was surprised to see the pugmarks of Elsa's lion superimposed on the tyre tracks of George's car which had just returned. Father must have been around very recently. When I got back I found Elsa listening very attentively and soon afterwards she moved the cubs and the carcase into her stronghold. A few moments later we heard the lion 'whuffing' close by; he went on all night.

The next morning we had to return to Isiolo for eight days. Though Elsa must certainly have heard the familiar noises of breaking camp, she never emerged from her thorny fortress.

On our return to Isiolo we were thrilled to hear that a call from London had come through three times in the last few days and was now booked for the next morning.

To speak to someone in England, 4,000 miles away over the telephone is very exciting when one is in a remote outpost. Now we heard Billy Collins accepting our invitation to come out and meet Elsa.

We chartered a plane to bring him from Nairobi to the nearest place at which an aeroplane can land and then, two days beforehand, we set off. We were determined to find Elsa and try to keep her and the cubs near to the camp so that she should be there to meet her publisher.

We arrived in camp early. George fired a shot to notify Elsa of the fact, and soon we heard her 'hnk-hnk' but she did not turn up. As her voice came from the direction of the studio, I went to it and saw her and the cubs by the river drinking. She glanced at me and went on lapping, as though she were not in the least surprised to see me after eight days' absence.

But later she came up and licked me, and Jespah settled himself about a foot away; then she sprang on to the table and lay stretched at full length on it. Jespah stood on his hind legs and rubbed noses with her. Though they ate a little of the meat I had brought them, they did not seem hungry. However, when George tried to rescue the remains of the carcase, Elsa pulled it gently away from him and took it into a thicket. During the evening we heard Elsa's mate calling and around midnight George woke up to find her sitting on his bed and licking him, while the cubs sat outside the tent watching her. Next morning I went with Ibrahim to meet Billy Collins.

At lunchtime we arrived in the little Somali village where we expected the aeroplane to land, and I told the Africans to keep the airstrip free of livestock, as a plane might arrive at any moment.

This airfield was originally made for locust control; only a few bushes needed to be cleared to bring it into existence. It is now seldom used and, as the local herds often cross it, blends so well into the surroundings that it is difficult to find from the air.

About teatime we heard the vibrations of an engine, but it was a long time before the circling aircraft landed. Then the airstrip was suddenly covered by the entire village population, chattering excitedly. The colourful turbaned Mohammedans, clad in loose-falling garments, watched Billy Collins and the pilot clamber out from the small cabin. Billy had only arrived three hours earlier at Nairobi after a night flight in a Comet. I thought it very sporting of him to venture immediately afterwards on this rather different flight in a four-seater, bumping through notorious airpockets round the massive Mount Kenya and searching for the small airstrip in the vast sandy plains of the Northern Frontier.

Expecting Billy to be tired after his long flight from London and also feeling not too happy about the possibility of meeting elephants in the dark, I suggested camping there for the night, but after a discussion with Ibrahim and the Game Scout we decided to drive on.

When we reached the outpost where Elsa's goat deposit is stationed the man in charge gave me a note for George, asking urgently for his presence next day at the nearest administration post as witness in a game case. After two more hours of brushing and winding our car through thick bush, we arrived at camp, ready for a reviving drink, but before George had time to pour it out we heard the familiar 'hnk-hnk' and a few moments later Elsa came rushing along, followed by her cubs. She welcomed us in her usual friendly manner and after a few cautious sniffs also rubbed her head against Billy, while the cubs watched from a short distance. Then she took the meat and dragged it out of the lamplight into the dark near my tent, where she settled with her children for their meal. While this went on we had our supper. We had made a special thorn enclosure next to George's tent for Billy's tent and after introducing him to his home, barricaded his wicker gate from outside with thorns and left him to a well-deserved night's sleep.

Elsa remained outside my tent enclosure and I heard her softly talking to her cubs, until I fell asleep. At dawn I was woken by noises from Billy's tent and recognized his voice and George's: evidently they were trying to persuade Elsa to leave Billy's bed. As soon as it got light she had squeezed herself through the densely woven wicker gate and hopped on to Billy's bed, caressing him affectionately through the torn mosquito net and holding him prisoner under her heavy body. Billy kept admirably calm considering that it was his first experience of waking up with a fully grown lioness resting on him. Even when Elsa nibbled him slightly in his arm, her way of showing her affection, he did nothing but talk quietly to her.

Soon she lost interest and followed George out of the enclosure where she romped round the tents with her cubs. Afterwards the family disappeared towards the Big Rock and later George left to attend the court.

When he returned at teatime he told us that he had just passed a herd of elephant close to camp, so we finished our tea quickly and drove along the track to film them, but when we came to the Big Rock we noticed Elsa on its top posing magnificently against the sky. We forgot about the elephants and walked to the base of the rock, hoping to film Elsa and her cubs. As she repeatedly listened to some sound coming from behind a large boulder nearby it seemed likely that they were close. Elsa watched our every step, but never moved, however coaxingly we called to her. She kept aloof, and the cubs did not appear. We waited for a considerable time but as nothing happened we decided to try our luck with the elephants.

As soon as we had returned to the car Elsa stood up and called her cubs; as if to tease us, all of them now posed splendidly. We had been waiting for over one hour for just this. However, as Elsa had made it so clear that she was in no mood to be filmed, we drove on to the spot where George had met the elephants, but we found nothing but their footmarks and we returned to Elsa.

By the time we reached the rock the light was too weak for

photographing, so we just watched the family through our field glasses. The cubs chased and ambushed each other round the boulders while Elsa kept her eyes fixed on us. Finally, we called her and she came down at once, rushed through the bush and, after greeting us all affectionately, landed with a heavy thud on the roof of the Land Rover. While we patted her paws which dangled over the windscreen, she watched the cubs which were still playing on the rock quite unconcerned at her departure. Though Elsa seemed to enjoy our attentions, she never took her eyes off her children until they finally scrambled down the rock. Then she jumped off the car and disappeared into the bush to meet them.

We took this opportunity to drive home and prepare a carcase for the family. As soon as it was ready they arrived and began to tear at the meat, while we had our sundowners a few feet away. All that evening we watched the lions who seemed to have accepted Billy as a friend.

Before daybreak I was again woken up by noises coming from his tent, into which Elsa had once more found her way to say good morning. After some coaxing from George, who had come to his rescue, she left. George then reinforced the thorns outside the wicker gate with such a bulk that he felt sure Elsa would not be able to penetrate this barricade, so he went to bed again. But Elsa was not going to be defeated by a few thorns and so after a short time Billy found himself again being embraced by her and squashed under her weight. While he struggled to free himself from the entangling mosquito net George came to his rescue, but this time he took much longer to remove the thorns outside the gate, and by the time he got inside Elsa had managed to clasp her paws around Billy's neck and held his cheekbones between her teeth. We had often watched her doing this to her cubs; it was a sign of affection, but the effect on Billy must have been very different.

I was very much alarmed at Elsa's unusual behaviour. She had never done anything like this to a visitor and I could only interpret it as a sign of affection; if she had not done it in play she could have acted in a very different way. In spite of my remaining with Billy she forced herself a third time through the wicker gate before either George who was outside or I who was inside could stop her. Billy was standing up this time and, being tall and strong, braced himself against Elsa's weight when she stood on her hind legs, resting her front paws on his shoulders, and nibbled at his ear. As soon as she released him I gave her such a beating that she sulkily left the tent and in a rather embarrassed way spent her affection on Jespah, rolling with him in the grass, biting and clasping him exactly as she had done Billy. Finally, the whole family gambolled off towards the rocks. I do not know who was more shaken – poor Billy or myself. All we could think was that this extraordinary reaction of Elsa to Billy was her way of accepting him into the family, for only to her cubs and to us had she ever shown her affection in this way. But we did not want to risk a repetition of her demonstrations towards our friend, so we decided to break his visit short and leave camp immediately after breakfast.

After a few miles we saw two elephants some thirty yards off the road. They tested our scent with raised trunks, made a few undecided, swaying motions and moved away. Ibrahim then walked along the track to see if all was safe for we were handicapped in our driving by the heavily loaded trailer which made any quick reversing in an emergency impossible. His reconnoitre saved us from driving straight into a single bull elephant who had remained on the road. We gave him time to move away, but he took much longer than we needed to take photographs before he disappeared into the bush. After that we continued without further excitement, if one discounts two punctures which landed us in a ditch. About two hours before reaching

Isiolo the car stopped with an abrupt jerk. The trailer had lost one wheel and jammed its axle into the ground. There was nothing to do but leave our escorting Game Scout in charge of the wreck and send the lorry to tow it home. When we finally arrived at Isiolo it was well past midnight.

17. The Camp Is Burned

At the beginning of June, after ten days' absence, we returned to camp and, just before sunset, reached a place about six miles short of it. We saw that every tree and bush was loaded with birds of prey, and drove slowly towards them. Then suddenly we found ourselves surrounded by elephant who had closed in on us from every direction. It must have been the herd, numbering some thirty or forty head, which had been in the neighbourhood for the past weeks. They had a large number of very young calves with them whose worried mothers came close to the car with raised trunks and fanning ears, shaking their heads angrily at us. It was a tricky situation and it was not improved by the arrival of my truck, which, driven by Ibrahim, was following close behind us. George at once jumped on to the roof of the Land Rover and stood there, rifle in hand. We waited for what seemed an endless time, then some of the elephants started to cross the car track about twenty yards from us.

It was a magnificent sight. The giants moved in single file, jerking their massive heads disapprovingly in our direction; to protect their young they kept them closely wedged between their bulky bodies.

After making infuriated protests, most of the herd moved away, leaving small groups still undecided in the bush. We waited for them to follow and eventually all but two went off; these stood their ground and seemed to have no intention of budging.

George wanted to see the kill which had attracted the birds and since the light was failing he decided to walk, with Makedde, between the two remaining groups of elephant. Meanwhile, Ibrahim and I stood on the roof of the car and kept a close watch on the beasts, so that we could warn George of their movements. He found a freshly killed waterbuck and lion spoor around it. Very little had been eaten, so plainly the lion had been interrupted by the arrival of the elephants.

When he returned the light was failing rapidly and the elephants still blocked our way. We could not drive round them, so we decided to make a dash for it and drove both cars past them successfully.

We wondered whether it might have been Elsa who had killed the waterbuck, but it was far from her usual hunting ground, and, besides, for her to tackle a beast with such formidable horns and heavier than herself (the buck must have weighed about 400 pounds), while protecting her cubs, would have been a very dangerous enterprise, and we felt sure she would not have done such a thing unless she was very hungry indeed.

The day after our return to camp we saw Elsa and her cubs on the Big Rock. As soon as she spotted us she rushed down and ended by throwing the whole of her weight against George who was squashed by her affection, then she bowled me over, while the puzzled cubs craned their heads above the high grass to see what was going on.

When we got back to camp we provided a meal for them over which they competed with such growls, snarls and spankings that we thought they must be very hungry. Little Elsa had the best of it and eventually went off with her loot, leaving her brothers still so hungry that we felt obliged to produce another carcase for them.

Later, while we were resting, Jespah, with surprising boldness, started chewing at my sandals and poking at my toes. As his claws and teeth were already well developed I quickly tucked my feet under me. He seemed most disappointed, so I stretched my hand slowly towards him in a friendly gesture. He watched it attentively, then looked at me and walked off.

That evening Elsa took up her usual position on the roof of the Land Rover, but the cubs instead of romping about flung themselves on the ground and never stirred. As it was the hour at which they were usually most energetic, we were surprised. During the night I heard Elsa talking to them in a low moan and also heard suckling noises. They must indeed have been hungry to need to be suckled after consuming two goats in twenty-four hours.

In the morning they had gone. We followed their spoor and it led straight to the waterbuck kill. So it must have been Elsa who two days earlier after a long stalk had tackled this formidable beast. It was hard luck on her that the arrival of the elephants had prevented her and the cubs from having a good meal out of her kill.

Now we understood why they had all been both so hungry and so exhausted when they came into camp.

We collected the fine horns of the waterbuck and hung them in the studio, a proud record of the cubs' first big hunt with their mother. They were now five and a half months old.

One evening when Elsa and her cubs were walking back with us, she and Jespah got in front of us while Gopa and Little Elsa stayed behind. This worried Jespah very much; he rushed to and fro trying to marshal his pride, until his mother stood still, between us and him, and allowed us to pass her, thus reuniting the family. Afterwards she rubbed our knees affectionately as though to thank us for having taken the hint. That night a boiled guinea fowl disappeared from the kitchen. The cubs' father was the thief for we found his spoor by the kitchen tent.

The next morning I woke up to hear Elsa moaning to the cubs in a nearby thicket. Since their birth we had never used the wireless when they were in camp so as not to frighten them. But today George turned on the morning news. Elsa appeared at once, looked at the instrument, roared at it at full strength and went on doing so until we turned it off. Then she went back to the cubs. After a while George tuned in again, whereupon Elsa rushed back and repeated her roars until he switched off.

I patted her and spoke reassuringly to her in a low voice, but she was not satisfied till she had made a thorough search inside the tent. Then she went to her family. I had often been asked how Elsa reacted to different sounds and had flattered myself that I knew how to answer these questions, but this reaction of hers was unexpected; before her release, when she was living with us, we had listened daily to the wireless, and though when we first tuned in she had always been startled, as indeed she usually was if I played the piano, as soon as she realized where the sounds came from she paid no attention to them. She differentiated between the engine of a car and of a plane. However loud the noise of the plane might be she ignored it, but the faintest vibration from a car engine alerted her, often before we heard it. I had tried singing to her to test her reactions, but whatever the melody I never observed any response. On the other hand, when occasionally I imitated the cubs' call in order to make her search for them she reacted at once as I intended she should, but if I did this for fun she paid no attention.

As a wild animal she could of course recognize various animal sounds and interpret the mood of the approaching beast. She could also sense our mood by the intonation of our voices. I think I am right in saying that she preferred a low voice in human beings to a high-pitched one, even where shrillness was not due to agitation.

*

On 7 June we went back to Isiolo for nine days and on our return Elsa came into camp half an hour after we had fired a thunder-flash. The cubs were with her. She gave us a great welcome, but I noticed that she had wounds on her head and chin and a deep gash on her right ankle which was very swollen. This must have been painful for she was not keen on moving more than was necessary and she refused to let me dress her cuts. The whole family were very hungry and it took two goat carcases to satisfy them.

Next morning we followed their spoor to see where they had laid up the night before we arrived. We knew it was on the far side of the river which she always preferred, though to us the two sides seemed identical. We were worried by her choice because we knew that the far bank was frequented by poachers and while, on her own, Elsa could not have been in any danger from them, with three cubs the situation was very different.

We had chosen the area in which we had released her because on either side of the river tsetse flies were very active in a belt a few miles wide. The bite of this species of tsetse is harmless to man and to most wild animals, but fatal to livestock, so we had good hopes that no tempting goats would come within Elsa's reach. She was very conservative in her habits, and though every two or three days she changed her lie-up she only moved around a very confined area, and this added to our reassurance.

Lately we had had plenty of evidence that neighbouring tribesmen were trespassing, so we felt it would be a good thing if we could identify the lie-up she was now most frequently using as this might enable us to come to her help if an emergency arose. We followed her spoor, which led us from the river, along a dry watercourse to a rocky outcrop about half a mile away from the camp, to what we called the Cave Rock. This contained a fine rainproof cavity with several 'platforms', ideal resting places from which to survey the surrounding bush. Besides these amenities there were some suitable trees for the cubs to climb, growing nearby. This seemed to be Elsa's present lie-up.

When we got back to camp she and the cubs were waiting for us; she was nervous, but was very affectionate with me, allowing me to use her as a pillow; she also hugged me with her paws. Jespah, who had been watching us, apparently did not approve for after his mother had left he crouched and then started to charge me. He did this three times and though he swerved at the last moment, pretending to be more interested in elephant droppings, his flattened ears and angry snarls left me in no doubt about his jealousy. But it was significant that for his attack he chose a moment when his mother could not observe it. To placate him I gave him some titbits and then tied an inner tube to a ten-foot-long rope which I jerked about. While a tug-of-war was going on we suddenly heard the rumblings of elephant, which seemed to be having a game of their own in the studio.

On 20 June the cubs were six months old; to celebrate their first half year George shot a guinea fowl. Little Elsa, of course, took possession of it and disappeared into the bush. Her indignant brothers went after her but returned defeated and tumbling down a sandy bank landed on their mother. She was lying on her back, her four paws straight up in the air. She caught the cubs and held their heads in her mouth. They struggled to free themselves and then pinched Mum's tail. After a splendid game together, Elsa got up and walked up to me in a dignified manner and embraced me gently as though to show that I was not to be left out in the cold. Jespah looked bewildered. What could he make of this? Here was his mother making such a fuss of me, so I couldn't be bad, but all the same I was so different from them. Whenever I turned my back on him, he stalked me, but each time I turned and faced him he stopped and rolled his head from side to side, as though he did not know what to do next. Then he seemed to find the solution: he would go off; he walked straight into the river evidently intending to cross to the other bank. Elsa rushed after him. I shouted, 'No, no,' but without effect and the rest of the family quickly followed them. Young as he was Jespah had now taken on the leadership of the pride and was accepted by the family.

When they returned Elsa dozed off with her head on my lap. This was too much for Jespah. He crept up and began to scratch my shins with his sharp claws. I could not move my legs because of the weight of Elsa's head resting on them, so in an effort to stop him I stretched my hand slowly towards him. In a flash he bit it and made a wound at the base of my forefinger. It was lucky that I always carry sulphanilamide powder with me so I was able to disinfect it at once. All this happened within a few inches of Elsa's face but she diplomatically ignored the incident and closed her eyes sleepily.

After this we all returned to camp and Jespah seemed so friendly that I began to wonder whether when he bit me it was only in play. Certainly, between himself and his mother, biting was a proof of affection.

By now we were, however, beginning to worry about his relationship to us. We had done our best to respect the cubs' natural instincts and not to do anything to prevent them from being wild lions, but inevitably this had resulted in our having no control over them. Little Elsa and her timid brother were as shy as ever and never provoked a situation which required chastisement. But Jespah had a very different character, and I could not push his sharp, scratching claws back by saying, 'No, no,' as I used to do when Elsa was a cub and so taught her to retract her claws when playing with us. On the other hand, I did not want to use a stick. Elsa might resent it if I did and indeed she might cease to trust me. Our only hope seemed to lie in establishing a friendly relationship with Jespah, but for the moment his variable reactions made a truce more possible than a friendship.

After five days in camp we returned to Isiolo and, when we reached home, found that in a short time it was going to be necessary for George to go to the north for a three-week safari. We did not wish to desert Elsa for so long, and as in the absence of George and his Land Rover, I should not be left with enough transport to go backwards and forwards between Isiolo and the camp, I decided that I would spend these three weeks in the bush, even if it upset the cubs' wild life.

Before setting off I had two weeks by myself at Isiolo after which I planned to meet George in the first week of July at the camp. He would then be returning from patrol and on his way to Isiolo to get ready for the safari to the north.

As I approached the camp I was worried because I did not see George and drove on filled with foreboding which was increased when, as I drew nearer, the air became so full of smoke that my lungs were stinging.

When we arrived I could hardly believe my eyes. The thorn bushes were in ashes and smouldering tree trunks added to the grilling heat. The two acacia trees which provided shade and were the home of many birds were scorched. In the charred and blackened scene the green canvas of the tents stood out in sharp contrast. I was much relieved when I found George inside one of them eating his lunch.

He had plenty to tell me. When he had arrived, two days earlier, he had found the camp burning and seen the footprints of twelve poachers. Not only had they set fire to the trees and the thorn enclosure but they had also destroyed everything they could find. They had even uprooted the little vegetable garden that Ibrahim had planted.

George had been very worried about Elsa and had fired several thunderflashes between seven and ten p.m. without

Elsa bringing the cubs over the river. The third cub kept up a pathetic miaowing from the far bank.

Once over, they climbed on her back and played with her tail.

Above and right:
Claw exercises.

Right: Elsa meets her publisher, Billy Collins.

Below: Elephant at a watering hole.

Crossing the river with the cubs.

Elsa still suckled the cubs at nine months.

Above: Elsa and Jespah.

Right: The family together at the burnt camp site.

Left: Little Elsa.

Below: Siesta!

Buffalo.

The cubs' first Christmas. Jespah sat down and watched the candles burn lower and lower.

One year old.

getting any response. Then at eleven she and the cubs had suddenly appeared, all ravenously hungry. Within two hours they had eaten an entire goat. Elsa had been most affectionate and had several times come to lie on George's bed during the night: he noticed that she had several wounds. She left at dawn; soon afterwards he followed her spoor and eventually saw her sitting on the Whuffing Rock.

Then he went off to try and discover where she had come from on the previous evening. Her spoor which led down from the river was mixed up with the footprints of the poachers. He wondered whether they had been hunting Elsa and the cubs.

After lunch he sent three Game Scouts to search for the camp burners. They returned with six of the culprits. He kept them busy rebuilding the camp, which was no agreeable task, considering the amount of thorny bush which they were obliged to cut for our enclosures.

Elsa and her cubs who had spent the night in camp left soon after daybreak. Half an hour later George heard roars coming from the direction of the Big Rock, which was the way they had gone, so he assumed it must be Elsa; he was therefore much astonished to hear her voice coming from across the river soon afterwards. Then she appeared wet and without the cubs and seemed very agitated: she had several bleeding marks on her hindquarters.

In a few minutes she left hurriedly, rushing towards the Big Rock calling loudly. George felt sure that she must recently have had an encounter with an enemy for her wounds were not made by a quarry; also, her nervous state suggested that she knew that whatever beast had threatened her was still in the neighbourhood. George now thought that the roars he had first taken for Elsa's were probably those of some fierce lion who had attacked her and that while the two were fighting the cubs had scattered and after the battle Elsa had escaped across the river. Now he followed Elsa in search of her family. Together they climbed up the Big Rock. When they got to its top Elsa called in a very worried tone of voice.

At one moment she became interested in some dense bush and remained beside it. As George saw no sign of the cubs in the thicket, he went on searching, but fruitlessly. Later he found Elsa at the base of the Whuffing Rock, still calling desperately for her children. Together they crept along the ridge, looking into all possible hideouts. They found the spoor of a large lion and of a lioness and Elsa seemed most upset. During the morning she had insisted on taking the lead, but now she was content to follow George.

After they had reached the end of the rock, near to the place where the cubs were born, Elsa sniffed very persistently into a cleft. Suddenly George saw one cub peeping over the top of the rock above them and soon another appeared; they were Little Elsa and Gopa. Jespah was missing.

When they saw their mother they rushed down and rubbed noses with her and finally went off with her towards the kitchen lugga. All this had taken place just before I had arrived and as soon as he had finished his lunch George intended to look for Jespah. Naturally I went with him.

About an hour later Elsa appeared at the foot of the Big Rock and gave me a most heartening welcome. As I was brushing off the tsetse flies from her coat and dressing her wounds, the two little cubs peeped at me from a distance of about sixty yards and then ran off. When I began to rub the M and B powder into Elsa's injuries I found that not only had she gashes on her hindquarters but very nasty tears on her chest and chin.

While all this was going on the cubs remained in the bush and Elsa paid no attention to them. To encourage them to come to their mother we retired behind some rocks and after a while they rushed to her.

As soon as they were safely settled on the top of the ridge, George went off to search for Jespah by the Zom rocks, while I investigated the foot of the range. Looking back at Elsa I noticed that she was pulling a grimace and scenting in the direction of the thicket which George said had interested her so much in the morning, but when I called to her she did not budge. The ground was covered with fresh lion spoor, so I understood why she was frightened. However, after George returned, she and the two cubs joined us below the rock.

Now she trotted ahead of us towards the interesting thicket. Just after she had passed it I suddenly saw that not two, but three cubs were scampering behind Elsa, in the most casual manner. Jespah's reappearance after a day's absence seemed to be taken by the family as the most natural thing in the world. We, however, were greatly relieved and followed them to the river where they stopped for a long drink, while we went ahead to prepare a carcase for them in camp. When finally we were able to sit down and enjoy our dinner we discussed Elsa's curious behaviour. Why had she not persevered in the search for Jespah? Had she known all the time that he was hiding in the thicket? But was this likely? Why should he have remained alone for twelve hours only a very short distance from the camp, the river and the rocks where the rest of his family were; and why had he not answered his mother's call and ours?

Had the strange lions still been near the rocks, this would have explained Elsa's fears and Jespah's, but had this been the case it was unlikely that the other two cubs would have chosen to take refuge there.

After dinner George had to start back for Isiolo to prepare for his three weeks' safari. I was not very happy to see him go at this late hour, when all the wild animals were on the move.

Soon after he had left the lions began to roar from the Big Rock and kept on calling for most of the night. Elsa when she heard them at once moved herself and the cubs as near as possible to my enclosure and stayed there till dawn.

One afternoon I called to Elsa, who was on the far bank. She appeared at once and was preparing to swim across with the cubs, when suddenly they all froze and stared intently into the water. Then Elsa took the cubs higher up the river and they appeared opposite the kitchen lugga. Here the water is very shallow in the dry season. In spite of this they did not cross for an hour, nor did the cubs indulge in their usual splashing and ducking games. This was reassuring for it showed their prudence, but it was characteristic of their variable reactions that next day when I called Elsa from the same place at the same time, they all swam across at once, and without the slightest hesitation. Then I noticed that Elsa had a wound the size of a shilling in her tongue, and a very deep gash across the centre which was bleeding. This did not prevent her from licking the cubs, which surprised me.

When it was getting dark we were all sitting near to the river. Suddenly Elsa and the cubs looked at the water, stiffened and pulled grimaces and three or four yards away I saw a croc. I knew that he must have been a big fellow for his head was about a foot long.

I fetched my rifle and killed him. Although the cubs were less than three feet from me, the shot did not upset them. Elsa afterwards came and rubbed her head against my knee as though to thank me.

Nearly every afternoon she brought her cubs to the sandbank. Among its attractions were fresh buffalo droppings and sometimes elephant balls as well; in these they rolled to their great satisfaction. The cubs also played on the fallen palm logs. There was no question, when they fell off as they frequently did, of their landing on their feet, like the proverbial cat; on the contrary they fell clumsily on to the grass like a dropped parcel and seemed most surprised at their abrupt descent.

It was about this time that Jespah became more friendly. Now he sometimes licked me and once even stood on his hind legs to embrace me. Elsa took great care not to show too much affection to me in the presence of the cubs, but when we were alone was as devoted as usual. Her trust in me was as complete as ever and she even allowed me to take her meat from her paws and move it to a more suitable spot when I thought this necessary. She also permitted me to handle the cubs' meat. For instance, in the evening, when I wanted to remove a partly eaten carcase from the riverbank so that the crocs should not finish it off, she never interfered, even if I was obliged to drag it over her, and, still more remarkable, even when the cubs were hanging on to it and defending it.

At dusk the cubs were always full of energy and played tricks on their mother which made it hard for her to retain her dignity. Jespah, for instance, discovered that when he stood on his hind legs and clasped her tail she could not easily free herself. In this fashion they would walk round in circles, Jespah behaving like a clown until Elsa had had enough of it and sat down on top of him. He seemed to be delighted by her way of putting an end to the game and would lick and hug his mother until she escaped into our tent.

But it was not long before the tent ceased to provide her with an asylum, for he followed her into it, giving a quick look round and then sweeping everything he could reach to the ground. During the night I often heard him busily engaged in sorting through the food boxes and the beer crate; the clattering bottles provided him with endless entertainment. One morning the boys found fragments of my precious rubber cushion in the river; but I really could not blame Jespah for this as I had stupidly forgotten to remove it from my chair the evening before. He became quite at home in the tent, but his brother and sister were less venturesome. They always stayed outside.

18. Elsa's Fight

One morning Makedde observed vultures circling and, going to the spot about a mile downstream, found the remains of a rhino which had been killed by poisoned arrows the day before while drinking.

The poachers had left plenty of footprints and had erected machans on trees close to the drinking place.

On the night of 8 July there was quite a concert, Elsa's lion 'whuffing', a leopard coughing and hyenas howling. The next evening while I was taking tsetse flies off Elsa as she sat in my tent with her head on my lap, I was startled by a great roar from her lion. Like a flash she dashed off in the direction of the kitchen lugga. The cubs rushed after her but soon returned and sat looking bewildered outside the tent. Later, Elsa came back and stayed in camp until the lion ceased to call. As soon as she had gone, I heard the cracking of bones and realized that the hyenas were feeding.

The following evening she brought the cubs with her. After I had gone to bed she set off three times to cross the river, but as I did not see why I should be obliged to provide free meals for any predator who happened to be in the neighbourhood, I called her back each time and insisted that she should guard the remains. She obeyed and only made a final departure just before daybreak, when the carcase needed no more protection.

For three days she arrived in camp long after dark, and on the fourth (15 July) brought only two cubs; Jespah was missing. I was very worried, so after waiting for some time, I began repeating his name over and over again, till Elsa decided to go upstream and look for him, taking the two cubs with her.

For over an hour I heard her calling, till the sound gradually receded into the distance.

Then suddenly there were savage lion growls, accompanied by the terrified shrieks of baboons. As it was dark I could not go to see what was happening and awaited the outcome feeling miserable, for I was sure that Elsa was being attacked by lions.

She came back after a while, her head and shoulders covered with bleeding scratches and the root of her right ear bitten through. There was a gap in the flesh into which one could stick two fingers. This was much the worst injury she had ever suffered. Little Elsa and Gopa came back with her and sat a short distance away looking very frightened. I tried to put sulphanila-mide into Elsa's wounds but she was far too irritable to let me come near her, nor was she interested in the meat which I brought her. I placed the carcase halfway between myself and the cubs. They pounced on it, dragged it into the dark and I soon heard them tearing at it.

I sat a long time with Elsa; she held her head on one side and the blood dripped from her wound. Eventually she rose, called the cubs and waded across the river.

I could hardly wait till it was light to go and look for Jespah. Next morning, following Elsa's spoor, Makedde, Nuru and I went to the Cave Rock and were much relieved to find the family reunited. I was happy to know that Jespah was safe and that I could now concentrate on treating his mother. The wound in her ear was still bleeding profusely, and at intervals she shook her head to drain the cavity. Owing to its position she could not lick the wound, but scratched constantly to keep off the flies; none of this was likely to improve the cleanliness of the wounds.

All the cubs seemed very subdued though Jespah licked his mother affectionately.

The boys stayed out of sight while I tried to put M and B into the injury, but Elsa was not co-operative and each time I approached her head she moved away, apparently with considerable effort. Suddenly I was startled to hear voices. I thought they were probably those of poachers. I had to think quickly. Was it best to stay put? Probably not, for Elsa did not seem to want our company and might well go off with the cubs and fall into the poachers' hands. I went back to camp, hoping that as she must be hungry she would follow.

We made a detour on our return journey, so as to inspect the previous night's battlefield. We found it on a sandbank in the middle of the river, about half a mile from the camp. There were plenty of lion pugmarks mixed up with baboon spoor, but though we could distinguish the imprints of one male lion we could not be sure whether he had been alone or not.

I waited anxiously till the late afternoon for Elsa and her family to arrive. I then managed to introduce some M and B tablets into the meat which she took from my hand. I thought that if I could get fifteen tablets down her daily, there was a good chance that her wound would not go septic. Her ear drooped, suggesting that the muscles had been injured and she constantly shook her head to get rid of the oozing liquid.

Jespah, who had been the cause of the encounter, was very friendly. He licked me and several times tilted his head looking straight at me for a long time.

There is a belief that the members of the cat tribe can never look one in the face for any length of time; this is not true of Elsa and her sisters or of her cubs. Indeed, I have found that they convey their feelings by the varying expressions of their eyes, far more explicitly than we do in words.

After Elsa had settled down for the night a lion began calling. This seemed to alarm her and she shortly afterwards went off with the cubs.

I was glad when they all returned during the following afternoon; Jespah occasionally poked his nose into my back, in a friendly fashion, but apparently Elsa did not approve for she placed herself between him and me.

Towards evening Nuru herded the goats towards the truck. This was the first time I saw the cubs take any interest in them. We had, of course, been careful to avoid any contact between the cubs and living goats and they had never before reacted to their bleating.

During the night I heard two lions grunting as they cracked the bones of a carcase which was lying in front of George's tent. They spent a long time over their meal and only went off at dawn when the boys began talking in the kitchen. Then they crossed the river accompanied by the barking of baboons, to which they replied by loud 'whuffings'. We found the spoor of a large lion and of a lioness.

Elsa kept away for some days. I thought her absence was explained by the presence of this pair who had remained nearby, and who the following night grunted round the goat truck.

The boys and I made several searches for Elsa, but these were unsuccessful; while so occupied, we put up a rhino and a few buffalo.

After Elsa had been absent for four days I became very anxious, for her wound must be a very big handicap to her in hunting, and I was afraid also that the poachers might do her some harm. When on the evening of 20 July I saw vultures circling, my heart sank. We went to investigate but all we found was more evidence of the poachers. They had made hides near to every drinking place, on both sides of the river. We also found the ashes of recent fires and charred animal bones.

Three hours later I returned to camp to be told by two Game Scouts whom the warden had just sent to catch the poachers that they had seen Elsa and the cubs under a bush on the opposite side of the river, about a mile inland.

She was lying in the shade and the cubs were asleep. She had seen the men approach but had not moved. This sounded odd, unless she were so ill that she did not care if even strangers were close by.

Makedde suggested that we should take some meat to her, but not enough to satisfy her hunger, and so tempt her to come back to camp. As we approached her lie-up I signalled to the men to stay behind and called to her.

She emerged, walking slowly, her head bent low to one side. I was surprised and alarmed that she should have settled in such an exposed place where she could easily be seen by poachers. I noticed that her ear had gone septic and was discharging pus; she was obviously in great pain and when she shook her head, as she did very often, it sounded as if her ear were full of liquid. Besides this, both she and Little Elsa were covered with blow-flies. I was able to rid Elsa of hers, but the cub was far too wild to let me help her. Meanwhile, she and her brothers fought over the section of carcase we had brought them and soon there was nothing left for Elsa but polished bones. She looked on resignedly and certainly gave the lie to the well-established legend that lionesses gorge themselves and let their cubs go hungry. Jespah thanked me for his meal by licking my hand with his rough tongue. I tried to induce Elsa to come back to camp by calling, *maji*, *chakula*, *myama*, but as she did not move, went home without her.

As I had taken a lot of photographs I went to the camp to get another film; then I heard the cubs arrive on the opposite bank and took a short cut down to the river. Suddenly Elsa broke out of a bush and knocked me over. She obviously was suspicious that I had returned from a different direction, and feared for her cubs. She had been nervous all the afternoon and was plainly in pain for whenever the cubs accidentally touched her ear she snarled and cuffed them irritably. Jespah seemed aware of her state and constantly licked her.

That night after I had gone to bed – Elsa and the cubs had left the vicinity soon after – I heard a leopard cough and a lion roar. I got up and called to the boys to open my thorn enclosure so that I could go out and put the remains of the meat into my car. I did not wish to encourage all the predators in the neighbourhood to share Elsa's food supply and in doing so drive her away.

As soon as her ear had healed and she could hunt, I was determined to leave her. By now I had been three weeks alone in camp and George was overdue. I wished he would return soon for when his tent was occupied the predators never came near the meat which was tied up close to it. In his absence wild lions prowled round the camp every night and although Makedde and Ibrahim could have used their rifles if an emergency arose, I was nervous about the safety of the boys.

At last George arrived and was greeted by the roars of a strange lion. Hearing that Elsa had not been seen for several days, he decided to go and look for her, and he was also determined to try to scare off the strange lion and his fierce lioness who had so often injured Elsa. We knew her and her mate quite well by now, at least by voice, and we were also familiar with their spoor. They ranged along the river for about ten miles. Of course they shared the country with other lions besides Elsa, but she was the only one who kept permanently to the vicinity of the camp. The fierce lioness had lived in this region long before Elsa but we did not know what she had done to displease this disagreeable beast. We were pretty sure that she had not competed for the attention of her mate, but had kept strictly to her own young lion. Perhaps Elsa had interfered with her hunting or her territorial claims, or perhaps the creature was just bad-tempered. Anyway, we were sure now that she had chased Elsa and the cubs over the river and towards the poachers and that she and her mate had, for several days, taken over the Big Rock.

Tracking on the far side of the river we eventually found the cubs' pugmarks leading into a large group of rocks which we called the Border Rocks, as they were at the boundary of Elsa's territory, but by then it was too dark to do anything except go home. When we returned next morning we found the fresh spoor of a lion and a lioness superimposed upon the cubs' imprints. We were full of hope until we saw that the spoor led so far away that it was unlikely to have been made by Elsa. On our way home we observed a drop-spear trap close to the river. It was suspended from a tree which overhung the game path.

The drop-spear trap is a deadly device consisting of a log about one foot in diameter and two feet in length; to the cross section which faces the ground is attached a poisoned harpoon. When the log is released it falls upon the animal passing below and its weight is sufficient to ensure that the harpoon penetrates the thickest hide.

Next day we searched upstream on the far side of the river. Here, too, there were plenty of lion pugmarks – including those of a lioness with three cubs. They led us five miles from camp to a part of the bush which, so far as we knew, Elsa had never visited. As we approached a baobab tree, we heard the sound of startled animals bolting and the Toto caught a glimpse of the hindquarters of a lion and of three cubs which could have been Elsa's. They were gone in a flash and though we called and called there was no response.

George and I followed their tracks for some way, but we were puzzled; if they were Elsa's family why had they rushed away from us? On the other hand, was it likely that there was another lioness about with three cubs of around the same size as Elsa's? On our way back we found fresh spoor of a lion leading in the direction we had just come from.

Next morning we returned to this place and within 500 yards saw some very recent spoor of a lion, a lioness and cubs. This led us up a dry watercourse, then towards some rocks, but before reaching them, the pride had abruptly turned back, run fast to the river and crossed it.

The pugmarks on the far bank were still wet. It was plain that having heard us the pride had bolted. All we could be sure of was that they had scattered and run very fast.

After two more hours' tracking we found that the pride had reassembled in a sandy watercourse. We kept very quiet till we heard the agitated barking of baboons and simultaneously the roar of a lion. He was very close to us.

His voice was familiar to us for we had often heard it at night. He sounded hoarse and the boys used to say that he must have malaria.

George proceeded to stalk him and we came so close that I was nearly deafened by his next roar. Suddenly I caught sight of his hindquarters only thirty yards away and the boys actually saw his head and mane.

It is most unusual for lion to roar at eleven in the morning. This one was evidently calling to a lioness, whom presently we heard replying from the direction of the barking baboons. Hoping it might be Elsa, we bypassed the hoarse lion and had a good look round, but saw nothing.

Finally, tired and thirsty, we sat down and made tea. Here we discussed the two possible explanations of Elsa's disappearance. Rather than stay in camp and risk being mauled by the ill-tempered lioness, she might have decided to share the hazards of the hoarse lion's life, whose spoor might have been the one we found the previous day. That was an optimistic solution to the mystery; a pessimistic alternative was that Elsa had died of her septic ear and that the cubs had been adopted by a pair of wild lions.

On our way back we saw flocks of vultures around the kitchen lugga and the boys went ahead to inspect the kill.

I hung back dreading to learn what they had discovered, but

soon they shouted that they had found the carcase of a lesser kudu, which had probably been killed during the night by wild dogs.

We spent the next two days covering the boundaries of Elsa's territory, partly on foot and partly by car.

George left in the last week of July and I continued to look for Elsa, and the next morning, walking with Makedde along the car track towards the Big Rock, traced the spoor of a single lion who had evidently come towards the camp; I also saw the imprints of pointed shoes, which Makedde recognized as identical with those which he had recently seen near a poacher's hideout. Both spoors were superimposed on the tyre marks of George's car.

Plainly the poachers were keeping an eye on our movements, and no doubt, having heard George's car go off, had next morning come to reconnoitre. How disappointed they must have been to discover that I was still in residence.

It was now over a fortnight since the fierce lioness had attacked Elsa and except for the occasion when the Game Scout had found her in the bush, she had not been seen, nor had there been any trace of the cubs.

Feeling miserable, I asked Makedde whether he loved Elsa. He looked startled but replied warmly: 'Where is she that I could love her?' This made me even more depressed. Makedde, watching me, scolded more angrily: 'You have nothing but death in your mind, you think of death, you speak of death and you behave as though there were no Mungo [God] who looks after everything. Can't you trust him to look after Elsa?'

Encouraged, I got up and went on with the search; but two days passed without bringing any result.

On the evening of the sixteenth day since Elsa and the cubs had disappeared, after lighting the lamps I poured myself a drink and sat in the dark straining my ears for any hopeful sound. Then, suddenly, there was a swift movement, and I was nearly knocked off my chair by Elsa's affectionate greeting. She looked thin but fit and the wound in her ear was healing from the outside, though the centre was still septic. Plainly she was very hungry for when the boys came towards us with the carcase I had asked for, she rushed at them. I yelled, 'No, Elsa, no.' She stopped, obediently returned to me and controlled herself until the meat had been attached to a chain in front of the tent, then she pounced on it and ate voraciously. She seemed to be in a great hurry, gorged herself on half the goat and then withdrew out of the lamplight and cunningly moved farther away till she finally disappeared in the direction of the studio.

I was immensely relieved to know that she was well, but where were the cubs? Her visit had only lasted half an hour and I waited long into the night hoping that she might return with them to finish off the goat. As this did not happen, I eventually carried the remains into my car to save them from being eaten by predators, and went to bed.

At dawn on 1 August I was woken by the miaowing of the cubs and saw them crawling close to my thorn enclosure. I called to the boys to bring the meat and joined Elsa who was watching her youngsters fighting over the meat.

It was soon obvious that what remained of Elsa's last night's supper was not going to satisfy four hungry lions, so I ordered Makedde to kill another goat and managed to keep Elsa quiet while this was going on. Her self-control was astonishing, and only when the men dropped the carcase within ten yards of her did she get up and drag it into the bush near the river.

Little Elsa and Gopa followed her, but Jespah was far too busy crunching bones to pay any heed to what was going on and only after he had been on his own for some time did he decide to join the family, and straddling what was left of the old kill he took it down to the river.

I sat under a gardenia bush close by waiting my chance to

introduce some medicine into Elsa's meat, to help her septic ear heal. I was relieved, but puzzled, not to see a single new scratch on her or the cubs, though they must have hunted during all these days when they were absent from camp.

The cubs growled, snarled and cuffed at each other for the best bits of meat. Living in the bush had certainly made them become more wild, for now they were constantly on the alert for suspicious sounds and nearly panicked when some baboons barked.

The two little cubs were shyer than ever and were frightened if I made the least movement, but, to my surprise, Jespah came up to me, tilted his head on one side with a questioning look, licked my arm and plainly wished to remain friends.

The sun was high, it was getting hot, and so when the cubs had eaten all they could they had a splendid game in the shallows, ducking, wrestling, splashing and churning up the water till at last they collapsed in the shade on a rock, where Elsa joined them.

As I watched them dozing contentedly with their paws dangling over the boulder I humbly remembered Makedde's reprimand for my lack of faith – a happier family one could not wish to see.

In order to try to discover what they had been up to during their long absence I had asked him to follow the spoor which Elsa had made when she had arrived in camp.

Meanwhile, I dressed her wound while she was too sleepy to object to the treatment. When it got dark I went to the tents to hear Makedde's report.

He told me he had traced her to the limit of her territory and that there, on some rocky outcrops, he had found not only her pugmarks and those of the cubs, but also the spoor of at least one lion, if not two.

This probably explained how she and the cubs had been fed and also accounted for her strange behaviour when she was surprised by the Game Scout and us, for her reactions were typical of a lioness in season.

It may seem odd that this solution had not occurred to us but as Elsa was still suckling her cubs we had not expected her to be interested in a mate. We had accepted the general belief that wild lionesses only produce cubs every third year, because in the interval they are teaching the young of the last litter to hunt and become independent. Could Elsa have returned more quickly than we expected to breeding condition because of the food we had supplied? Certainly at seven and a half months the cubs could have survived on a meat diet and obviously she could not know that we were only staying on so as to treat her wounds and help her to get fit and able to teach her cubs hunting.

19. Dangers of the Bush

At about nine that evening Elsa and the cubs came from the river and settled themselves in front of my tent and demanded their supper. As the remains of the meat were still by the gardenia bush I called to Makedde and the Toto and asked them to come and help me drag it in. I collected a pressure lamp and we went down the narrow path which we had cut through the dense bush from the camp to the river.

Makedde, armed with a stick and a hurricane lamp, went ahead, the Toto followed close behind, and carrying my bright lamp I brought up the rear. Silently we walked a few yards down the path. Then there was a terrific crash, out went Makedde's lamp and a second later mine was smashed as a monstrous black mass hit me and knocked me over.

The next thing I knew was that Elsa was licking me. As soon

as I could collect myself I sat up and called to the boys. A feeble groan came from the Toto who was lying close to me holding his head, then he got up shakily, stammering, 'Buffalo, buffalo.' At this moment we heard Makedde's voice coming from the direction of the kitchen; he was yelling that he was all right. As we pulled ourselves together the Toto told me that he had seen Makedde suddenly jump to the side of the path and hit out with his stick at a buffalo. The next moment the Toto had been knocked over and then I had been overrun. What had happened when Elsa and the buffalo met face to face none of us will ever know. Luckily the Toto had no worse injury than a bump on his head, caused by falling against a fallen palm trunk. I felt blood running down my arms and thighs and was in some pain, but I wanted to get home before examining my wounds. This incident certainly belied the popular belief that a lion however tame becomes savage at the scent or taste of blood.

Elsa, who had obviously come to protect us from the buffalo, seemed to realize that we were hurt and was most gentle and affectionate.

I had no doubt as to the identity of the buffalo, since for several weeks past we had seen the spoor of a bull buffalo, going from the studio through the river bush to the sandbank, where a triangular line of impressions marked his drinking place. After quenching his thirst he usually continued upstream.

He had never come out for his drink till well after midnight.

This evening he must have been unusually thirsty and arrived very early. Probably Elsa had heard him on the move and that was why she had brought the cubs into the camp at nine. When he saw us come down to the river with our lamps the buffalo had evidently been frightened and rushed up the nearest path to safety, only to find us blocking his way.

I received several kicks which left their marks on my thighs and I could only feel very thankful that they had not landed on more vulnerable parts of my anatomy.

Elsa came back with us to camp where we found the cubs waiting for her; how she had prevented them from following her puzzled me.

I was worried about Makedde and went at once to the kitchen to see what condition he was in. There I found him, unhurt and having a splendid time, recounting to his awestruck friends his single-handed combat with the buffalo. I am afraid his heroic stature was slightly diminished by the appearance of my bleeding legs, but the main thing was that we were all safe.

I spent a very uncomfortable night, for as well as my painful wounds all my glands began to swell and it was difficult to find a position in which I could relax, or to breathe without increasing the discomfort of my aching ribs.

The next afternoon Elsa took great care to drag her kill a long way upstream and to straddle it across the river and then up a bank which was so steep it was unlikely that any beast would come after it. I wondered whether this unusual behaviour was due to her having been as frightened by the buffalo as I had been.

By the beginning of August Elsa had become increasingly co-operative, but her son Jespah did not follow her example; every day he became more obstreperous. For instance, Elsa never interfered with our flock of goats, but Jespah now took much too much interest in them.

One evening when Nuru was herding them towards my truck, he made a beeline for them, rushed through the kitchen, passed within a few inches of the devout Ibrahim, who was kneeling on his mat absorbed in his evening prayers, dodged between the water containers and round the open fire and arrived at the truck just as the goats were about to enter it.

There was no doubt as to his intentions, so I ran and grabbed a stick, and holding it in front of him shouted, 'No, no,' in my most commanding voice.

Jespah looked puzzled, sniffed the stick and began spanking it playfully, which gave Nuru time to lift the goats into the truck. Then Jespah walked back with me to Elsa who had been watching the game. Often she helped me to control him, either by adding a cuffing to my 'noes' or by placing herself between the two of us. But I wondered how long it would be before, even with her support, my commands and my sticks failed to have any effect. Jespah was so full of life, and curiosity and fun; he was a grand little wild lion, and a very fast-growing one too, and it was high time that we left him and his brother and sister to live a natural life. While I was thinking this, he was chasing after the other cubs, and in doing so tipped the water bowl over Elsa giving her a drenching. He got a clout for his pains and then she squashed him under her heavy, dripping body. It was a funny sight and we laughed but this was tactless and offended Elsa, who, after giving us a disapproving look, walked off followed by her two well-behaved cubs. Later she jumped on the roof of my Land Rover and I went to make friends again and apologize.

The moon was full and in the sky the stars sparkled brilliantly, and Elsa, her great eyes nearly black owing to her widely dilated pupils, looked down at me with a serious expression as though saying: 'You spoilt my lesson.' For a long time I remained with her, stroking her soft silky head.

Presently we heard the whinnying and grunts of two love-making rhinos coming from the salt lick. Elsa glanced alertly towards the cubs, but when she saw that they were entirely absorbed in their meal, she decided to pay no attention to the love-sick pair and presently we heard them crossing the river. George had rejoined me and had brought an anti-poaching team; one that operates throughout the Northern Frontier. The first thing he now wanted them to do was to find some man belonging to the tribe on the far side of the river, who, for a suitable reward, would supply information about the poachers. As soon as the team was established we had every intention of leaving Elsa and her family to look after themselves. Her wounds were more or less healed and we wanted the lions to lead a natural life. But when the Scouts returned we found that we had to change our plans. They brought in some prisoners and an informer told George that the poachers had determined to kill Elsa with poisoned arrows as soon as we left the camp. He also said that after burning the camp three of the culprits had climbed Elsa's big rock to hunt hyrax, but had given up when one of them got bitten by a snake.

We realized that as the drought increased, so would the poachers' activities, and however efficient the anti-poaching team might be, it would be impossible for them to prevent Elsa, if unfed by us, from hunting farther afield and risking an encounter with the tribesmen.

Obviously, if we stayed on, the cubs' education in wild life would be delayed and they would probably get spoilt, but it was better to face this than risk a tragedy.

One evening the tsetse flies were particularly active and Elsa and her two sons rolled on their backs inside my tent trying to squash their tormentors. In doing so they knocked down two camp beds which were propped up against the wall. Elsa lay down on one of them and Jespah on the other, while Gopa had to be content with the groundsheet. The sight of two lions lolling in bed, while far from our ideal picture of Elsa's family returned to a wild life, was comic enough. Only Little Elsa stayed outside: she was as wild as ever and nothing would induce her to enter the tent, so she at least appeased my conscience.

One afternoon when we were on the riverbank with Elsa and her cubs, I had a good chance of examining her wounds, and I found that although I had given her plenty of sulphanilamide they had not yet healed. I took the opportunity also to examine her teeth and saw that two of her canines were broken.

The hookworm infection she had suffered from as a cub had left a groove round the edge of her teeth and the breaks had occurred along these indentations. These broken teeth would, I thought, hamper her when hunting even though her claws were her main weapons.

When it got dark we went back to the tents; all that evening Elsa was alert and restless and eventually she and the cubs disappeared into the bush.

About midnight I was woken up by the roaring of several lions. This was followed by the frightening noise of a fight and after a pause, another fight and later a third. Finally, I heard the whimpering of a lion who had obviously got hurt in the battle and I could only hope it was not Elsa. Next there was the sound of an animal crossing the river and then all was quiet.

At dawn, we got up and went out to track the spoors left by our quarrelsome visitors. We recognized those of the fierce lioness and her mate. Evidently Elsa had challenged them when they neared the camp. For six hours we followed her pugmarks which led across the river to the Border Rocks; they joined up with those of the cubs.

All day we searched fruitlessly and at sunset fired a shot. After some time we heard Elsa calling from very far away, and eventually she appeared, followed by Jespah.

She was limping badly, but seemed to wish to get to us as fast as she could hobble, though she stopped once or twice and looked back, to see whether the other two cubs were coming. Both she and Jespah when they joined us showed how pleased they were by rubbing themselves against our legs. I then saw that Elsa had a deep gash in one of her front paws, which was bleeding and obviously causing her a lot of pain. The only way of helping her was to get her home and dress the wound.

The camp was far off, it was getting dark and judging by the many buffalo and rhino spoors we had seen, it was essential not to get benighted. Everything indicated that we should hurry, but in spite of George's impatient shouts urging us to make haste we had often to stop and wait for the little ones whose pace was rather slow. Jespah acted like a sheep dog running between George and the rearguard trying to keep us all together.

For once, the tsetse flies were a help. Elsa was covered with them and so kept up with me in the hope that I would brush them off her back. Jespah, too, was attacked by them and, for the first time, pushed his silky body against my legs asking me to deliver him too from this plague. It was all against my principles to touch him, but it was difficult to resist brushing off the flies.

Elsa often stopped to spray her jets against a bush. Was she in love again?

We were all completely exhausted when we got back. Elsa refused to eat, but sat on the Land Rover watching the cubs tearing at the meat, at intervals looking with great concentration into the darkness. It was barely nine when she left the camp with her family and about midnight we heard a lion calling from the Big Rock.

During the next days she came into camp every afternoon and I dressed her wounds.

When she was better, she and the cubs came along the river with us on a croc hunt. Then we had another example of the way in which she could apparently order the cubs to stay put and be implicitly obeyed.

She scented a buck and stalked it unsuccessfully; meanwhile the cubs remained as still as though they had been frozen to the ground and there was never a question of their interfering with her hunt, though later they were lively enough splashing in the water and climbing trees. This they achieved by hooking their claws into the bark and pulling themselves up; sometimes they got as high as ten feet above the ground.

Another of Elsa's instinctive reactions showed up on this occasion. The cubs were playing within one hundred yards of a crocodile who lived in a deep pool but she plainly regarded this croc as harmless. Perhaps she knew that he was replete, for she was quite unconcerned by his proximity though, as a rule, the slightest ripple on the water would cause her to become suspicious. We had always observed that she differentiated between harmless games, such as a tug-of-war between George and Jespah over a carcase, and one that might become dangerous, or frightening, as when George threw a stick into the river. Then she would immediately place herself between the cubs and the water – either to prevent them from jumping into it or if they were alarmed perhaps to reassure them that the thing they saw was only a piece of floating wood and not the snout of a crocodile.

On 12 August I went to Nairobi for six days and returned on 18 August. While we were having a belated supper, we heard two lions roaring. From the noise we gathered that they were approaching the camp rapidly from upstream. Elsa rushed off in their direction leaving the cubs behind; she returned after about three-quarters of an hour, but by then the cubs had gone, so she began to look for them all round the camp and seemed very nervous.

Suddenly we were startled by the most deafening roar which seemed to come from just behind the kitchen and George, looking in that direction, saw the torchlight reflected in the shining eyes of a lion.

Standing close to our tent Elsa roared back defiantly until, luckily, the cubs arrived. She took them off at once and soon we heard them hurriedly crossing the river.

After this all was quiet and we went to bed. But about

1.30 a.m. George was woken by a noise near his tent and flashing his torch saw a strange lioness sitting some thirty yards away. She got up slowly and he put a shot over her to speed her on her way, but this had no effect except to start another lion roaring.

For half an hour roars, growls and grunts succeeded each other, then the lions moved on.

Next evening Elsa came in very late and settled near the tents while Jespah, who was in one of his energetic moods, amused himself upsetting everything within reach; the tables were swished clear of bottles, plates and cutlery, the rifles were pulled out of their stands and the haversacks full of ammunition carried away, and cardboard containers were first proudly paraded in front of the other cubs and then torn to shreds. In the morning we found the family still in camp, a most unusual occurrence. The boys kept well inside the kitchen fence waiting for them to go, then, as they showed no intention of leaving, George walked up to Elsa, whereupon she knocked him down. After this George released me from my thorn enclosure and I tried my luck. I approached Elsa, calling to her, but as she looked at me through half-closed eyes, I kept on my guard while she came slowly towards me, and I was justified, for when she was within ten yards of me she charged at full speed, knocked me down, sat on me and then proceeded to lick me.

She was extremely friendly, so this, it seemed, was no more than her idea of a morning game. But she knew quite well that the knocking down trick was not popular with us and this was the first time since the birth of the cubs that she had indulged in it.

Later she took the cubs to a place below the studio, and in the afternoon we joined them there. Jespah was very much interested in George's rifle and tried his best to snatch it away from him, but soon he realized that it was impossible to do this so long as its owner was on his guard; after this discovery it was amusing to see how he tried to distract George's attention by pretending to chase his brother and sister. When George's suspicions were allayed and he put the rifle down to pick up his camera, Jespah pounced on it and straddled it. A real tug-of-war followed, which Elsa watched attentively. Finally, she came to George's rescue by sitting on her son and thereby forcing him to release his hold on the gun. She continued to sit on the cub for such a long time that I got worried about him. When she finally released him, though he looked longingly at the rifle and crouched near it, he was very subdued and left it alone. Nevertheless, for a while Elsa remained suspicious of his good behaviour and at intervals placed herself between him and the gun.

Finally, she rolled on her back with her paws in the air and moaned softly. The cubs responded at once and began suckling. Elsa looked utterly happy, but I could not help wondering how the cubs avoided hurting her with their sharp teeth. It was a most idyllic scene and just at that moment a paradise flycatcher flew over us trailing its white tail feathers like a long train behind it. The cubs were eight months old that day and she had every reason to be proud of them.

When they dozed off, their round bellies filled to bursting point, Elsa got up, arched her back, gave a long yawn, came over to me, licked me, sat beside me and rested her paw on my shoulder for some time, then she put her head on my lap and went to sleep. While she and the two small lions slept, Little Elsa kept guard over the family and twice unsuccessfully stalked a waterbuck.

When we were in bed we heard sounds of crunching, which went on until morning; evidently the family were spending the night in camp, finishing up the carcase. During the following day, they stayed very close to the tents. That evening we heard the cubs' father calling and thought it was because he was nearby that Elsa had preferred not to go far afield. For three more days she never left us.

20. Cubs and Cameras

There was truly a Garden of Eden atmosphere about life around the precincts of the camp, for the animals who shared this territory with us had got so used to our presence that they often came very close without showing alarm. Even the fish had become friendly and when they saw us swam towards us.

As I am typing these words a troop of some fifty baboons are pacing along the bank opposite me. In the middle of them are three bushbuck, a ram, a doe and their fawn. They seem to have joined the troop for safety and are not in the least concerned when a baboon brushes past them.

No scene could be more peaceful or further removed from the generally accepted picture of baboons tearing small animals to pieces. I thought that, if it were not threatened by the poachers, wild life here would be ideal, for even the fierce lioness is much less of a danger to Elsa than these men. In any case, she is a natural part of bush life; so are feuds between lions.

It was encouraging to know that Elsa now went out to meet her enemy. We had first noticed this during the third week of August, the night when Elsa and the cubs were eating their supper in front of the tent. Suddenly she growled and went off, and only returned an hour later. During that night I heard two lions approaching camp, and soon afterwards a fearful quarrel broke out. Towards dawn I heard Elsa moving the cubs in the direction of the Big Rock. In the afternoon we met her in the bush on her way to camp, her head, especially near her wounded ear, covered with bleeding bites.

After she reached home I got out the remains of their last night's supper; there was not much left. Elsa wouldn't touch it but the cubs ate ravenously. When a new carcase was brought by the boys she, too, began to eat. I wondered why, if she was so hungry, she had refrained from touching the first course I had provided. Could it have been that she saw that there was not enough to go round and wanted the cubs to have a chance of filling their bellies before she took her share?

That evening Ibrahim arrived with a new lion-proof Land Rover I had recently ordered. He also brought the mail, and I settled down to read an article about Elsa in the *Illustrated London News*. She was described as a world-famous animal. This was gratifying, but at the moment poor Elsa was tilting her head in great pain.

When she joined us in the studio next day she was still very distressed, not that this prevented her from disciplining Jespah with a series of well-aimed clouts when, intrigued by the clatter of my typewriter, he teased me.

Poor Jespah, he still had a lot to learn, not about the wild life which is his, but about the strange world which is ours and which he showed so great a wish to investigate. One night, for instance, I heard him apparently very busy in George's tent. How busy I only discovered next morning when I noticed that my field glasses were missing. Eventually, I found bits of their leather case in the bush below the tent. They bore the imprint of Jespah's milk teeth. Close by lay the glasses, and luckily, by some miracle, the lenses were intact. Yes, there was no doubt that Jespah could be a nuisance but he was irresistible and one couldn't be cross with him for long.

At eight months he had now lost his baby fluff but his coat was as soft as a rabbit's. He had begun to imitate his mother and to wish to be treated by us as she was. Sometimes he would come and lie under my hand, evidently expecting to be patted and, though it was against my principles, I occasionally did so. He often wanted to play with me, but though his intentions were entirely friendly I never felt sure that he might not bite or scratch me as he would his own family. He was not like Elsa who controlled her strength on such occasions, for he was much closer to a wild lion.

We were both very interested in observing the different relationships which Elsa's cubs were developing towards us. Jespah, prompted by an insatiable curiosity, had overcome his earlier inhibitions, mixed with us and was most friendly but allowed no familiarities.

Little Elsa was truly wild, snarled if we came close and then sneaked away. Though she was less boisterous than her brothers, she had a quiet and efficient way of getting what she wanted. Once I watched Jespah trying to drag a freshly killed goat into a bush. He pulled and tugged and somersaulted across it – but nothing would move the carcase. Then Gopa came to his aid and between the two they tried their best – but finally gave up exhausted and sat panting next to it. Now Little Elsa, who had watched their exertions, came along and pulling hard, straddled the heavy load into a safe place where she was joined at once by her panting brothers.

Gopa quite often made use of the tent when the tsetse were most active, and it was on these occasions that I noticed how jealous he was. For instance, if I sat near Elsa he would look long and scrutinizingly into my eyes with an expression of disapproval and made it extremely plain that she was his mum and that he would prefer me to leave her alone. One evening I was sitting at the entrance of the tent while he was in the annexe at the far end and Elsa lay between us watching both of us. When Gopa started chewing at the tent canvas, I said as firmly as I could, 'No, no'; to my surprise, he snarled at me, but stopped chewing. A little later he took up the canvas again and, though my 'No' was answered with another snarl, he again stopped.

So far, all the cubs responded when we said 'No' although we had never enforced our prohibition with a stick or anything else which could frighten them.

After a peaceful day and night around the camp, Elsa and her cubs left early one morning and crossed the river, so I was surprised when shortly afterwards Makedde reported having found the spoor of a lioness which last night had come from upstream as far as the kitchen and returned the same way. Was this the fierce lioness? Though Elsa had shown no sign of alarm, she kept away for one and a half days and when she did return it was after dark. She kept the cubs hidden at some distance and dragged the meat away quickly, keeping out of view with the cubs all the time. Next morning all of them had crossed the river. A few nights later while the family were still in camp, we heard, towards dawn, two lions approaching from upstream. Elsa at once took her children away and I saw them in the dim light rushing towards the studio. Soon afterwards Elsa returned alone and trotted determinedly in the direction of the lions. Neither I nor the boys heard a sound, though we listened intently, until after half an hour Elsa came back and called her cubs. There was no reply and she rushed round desperately calling and calling. As soon as I had disentangled myself from my thorn enclosure, I joined her in her search, but she only snarled at me and, sniffing along the road, disappeared in the direction of the Big Rock. A little later we heard lots of 'whuffings' coming from this direction, but assuming that the two lions were close, we did not follow Elsa until the afternoon, when all was quiet. On the road we found not only Elsa's pugmarks, but also those of another lioness, both leading to the rock.

Elsa did not come to camp that night, but two hours after George returned from Isiolo the next afternoon, Elsa arrived with her cubs, all fit but very nervous. She inspected the bush round the camp several times and left long before daylight.

At the beginning of September we heard that Sir Julian

Huxley was soon coming on a mission sponsored by UNESCO to investigate the problem of the conservation of wild life in East Africa. When he wrote asking us if we could show him parts of the Northern Frontier Province we were very pleased as this would give us the opportunity of acquainting him with the local problems, and the lack of means for dealing with them.

We believed that Sir Julian's visit would be a great encouragement to all those interested in the preservation of wild life. We also knew that he wished to see Elsa. We limited her visitors to those who had good and sufficient reasons for seeing her and, as Sir Julian clearly had these, we were glad that he should spare time to do so.

Between 7 and 9 September we showed Sir Julian something of the North Frontier District, and late one afternoon we arrived in Elsa's domain.

We fired the usual signal shots and twenty minutes later were delighted to hear the barking of baboons which usually heralded the arrival of Elsa and the cubs. In her enthusiastic welcome she nearly knocked me down and then hopped on to the top of the Land Rover. Meanwhile, the cubs were busy dragging the carcase we had provided for them into a safe place. For half an hour we watched them and then left. Elsa had a very puzzled expression when she saw the cars going off after such a short time.

During my next visit to Elsa George arrived bringing a lorry as well as his car, and, attracted by the noise of the engines, Elsa and the cubs soon turned up. George told me that next morning David Attenborough and Jeff Mulligan were arriving from London and that we were to collect them at the nearest airstrip. For some time we had been corresponding with David Attenborough about making a film of Elsa and her cubs for the BBC.

We had had previous suggestions for filming her but these we had refused fearing that the arrival of a large film unit might upset her. The coming of only two people was much less worrying, but even they would need constant protection. We hoped to provide for their safety at night by making one sleep in my lion-proof Land Rover which was driven into a large thorn enclosure; our other guest's sleeping quarters were to be a tent rigged up on a lorry which also stood in the enclosure. Another tent would serve as dressing room, bathroom, laboratory and equipment store.

Soon after we had gone to bed we heard a lion roaring upstream and observed that Elsa at once left the camp. Next morning, 13 September, George called me early to his tent and there I saw Elsa, in a terrible state, her head, chest, shoulders and paws covered with deep bleeding gashes. She appeared to be very weak and when I knelt beside her to examine her wounds, she only looked at me. We were very much surprised for we had not heard any growls during the night and were quite unaware that a fight had taken place. When I began to try to dress her wounds Elsa struggled to her feet and slowly dragged herself towards the river, obviously in great pain. I went at once to mix some M and B tablets with her food hoping to counter the risk of sepsis in this way, since any external treatment was obviously going to hurt and irritate her. When everything was ready I spent twenty minutes looking for her but could find no trace of her. Then I had to start off to meet our guests, leaving George to search for the missing cubs. It was the worst moment to have visitors – let alone film producers – and I feared that they might have no chance of doing any work. I greeted them with this depressing news and soon realized that we had been more than lucky in finding two such animal lovers as David and Jeff.

We arrived in camp at lunchtime and found George who had just returned from a fruitless search for the cubs. While our guests settled in I went to look for Elsa and found her under a thick bush near the studio. She was breathing very fast and lay quite still as I swished the flies off her wounds. I went back to camp to get water and to mix the M and B tablets with her meat. When David saw my preparations he offered to help, and walked with me to the studio carrying the basin of water. I made him put it down a short distance from Elsa and then I took over.

Poor Elsa, I had never before seen her in so much pain. She made no effort to raise her head and it was only when I lifted it that she began to drink; then she lapped for a long time. After that she ate the meat but made it very plain that she did not want company, so we left her.

Since there was nothing more we could do for Elsa, George and I set out to look for the cubs on the other side of the river. We walked shouting all the names by which we address Elsa and also calling Jespah. Finally, behind a bush, we caught sight of one cub, but as we approached it bolted. In order not to frighten it further we decided to go home and hope that the cubs would make their own way back to their mother. Jespah was the first to do so; about six in the evening he crossed the river and rushed up to Elsa, then we heard another cub miaowing from the far bank. Elsa heard it too, and dragged herself to the riverbank and began calling to it. It was Gopa and when he saw his mother he swam across. I provided some meat which the little lions devoured, but Elsa would not touch it. While Jespah and Gopa were eating we took our guests for a stroll along the river and were much surprised on our return to find Elsa on the roof of the Land Rover which was parked in front of our tents. We had our drinks and our supper within a few yards of her but she took no notice of us. We remained anxious about Little Elsa until some time after we had gone to bed George spotted her coming into the camp.

Soon after midnight the family moved off and a little later we heard the roars of the fierce lioness. During the following day

Elsa kept away, and we knew why, for George saw the fierce lioness on the Big Rock. That night we again heard her roaring. We were very worried about Elsa, so, as soon as it was light, George went upriver to try to find her, while I went in the opposite direction accompanied by Makedde, Nuru and a Game Scout; we carried water with us in case we found her. We picked up Elsa's spoor half a mile beyond the Border Rock, which was farther than we had ever known her to go. She reconnoitred the neighbourhood to see whether all was safe and then the cubs appeared. They were terribly thirsty. I could not pour the water out quickly enough and I had some difficulty in avoiding getting scratched and in preventing the plastic water bowl from being torn out of my hands.

When we started for home and rejoined the boys who had stayed behind, both Elsa and Jespah sniffed very suspiciously at the Game Scout. He followed my advice and stood absolutely rigid but his face betrayed less ease than his action suggested. As soon as it was possible I sent him ahead back to camp with Makedde.

Elsa's wounds had improved but still needed dressing. It took a lot of coaxing to get the family to follow us and we made our way slowly back to camp. Nuru stayed with me as gun bearer, but when I thought we were nearly home I told him to go on and warn David of our coming, so that he would be able to film the lions crossing the river. After he had gone I felt a little uneasy and then became really worried for I found that I had miscalculated the distance and had lost myself in the bush. By then it was midday and very hot and the lions stopped under every bush to pant in the shade. I knew that the best thing to do was to find the nearest lugga and follow it, for it must lead to the river from which I would be able to get my bearings. Fairly soon I came upon a narrow lugga and walked along between its steep banks. Elsa followed me and the cubs scampered along some way behind her. I had turned a bend when I suddenly found myself standing face to face with a rhino. There was no question of 'jumping nimbly aside and allowing the charging beast to pass' as one is supposed to do in such encounters, so I turned and ran back along my tracks just as fast as I could with the snorting creature puffing behind me. At last I saw a little gap in the bank and before I knew I had done it, I was up it and running into the bush. At this moment the rhino must have seen Elsa for it swerved abruptly, turned round and crashed up the opposite side. Elsa stood very still watching the pair of us. This was very lucky for me and I was extremely glad that she had not followed her usual habit of chasing any rhino she saw.

A few moments later I was greatly relieved to see Nuru coming towards me. I was going to thank him for running to my rescue, but before I had time to speak he told me that he, too, had met a rhino and been chased by it and that this was what had brought him to where I was. We had a good laugh over our frights and then, keeping close together, we went back to the camp.

We found it deserted, for when Makedde had come in and told them that I had found Elsa, George, David and Jeff had set out to help me. I sent a scout after them to tell them that we had all reached home safely. Meanwhile, Elsa and the cubs had a game in the river and got nice and cool after their long hot walk. Then they retired with a carcase into the bush and remained there till about midnight when they crossed over to the other side of the river.

Assuming that there would be no opportunity of filming the lions till late the next day we spent the morning photographing hyrax on the rocks. We returned hot and exhausted to a belated lunch and then went down to the studio, where camp beds had been put out for us so that we could enjoy a siesta. The beds were set out in a row; mine was on the outside, David's in the middle and George's beyond his. Jeff was some way off loading the cameras. Soon I fell asleep but woke up very suddenly to find a wet Elsa sitting on top of me, licking me affectionately and keeping me a prisoner under her immense weight; simultaneously David took a leap over George and went to join Jeff. Between them they quickly got the cameras working. Elsa made a bound on to George, greeted him affectionately and then walked in a most dignified manner up to the tents and settled herself inside one of them. She completely ignored the presence of our guests and behaved in the same way later in the evening when we were having our drinks. She had been inside a tent with Jespah and coming out passed within six inches of Jeff's feet, but did not take the slightest notice of him; so far as she was concerned he might not have been there.

Next morning we followed her spoor and found her halfway up the Whuffing Rock sleeping. As we did not wish to disturb her, we went home and only came back after tea. This time we took with us a sufficient number of cameras to take films from every angle.

We were very lucky for she and the cubs could not have been more obliging and posed beautifully on the saddle of the rock. Finally, Elsa came down and this time she greeted all of us, including David and Jeff, by rubbing her head gently against our knees. She stayed with us until it got dark and we went back to camp, but the cubs, possibly made nervous by the presence of strangers, stayed on the rock.

Although Elsa had not seemed upset by being filmed I wondered whether she would come for her evening meal. Lately if even one of her favourite boys was visible she had kept away from the camp. I need not have worried; just as I was going to explain to our guests that she might very well not turn up I was nearly knocked over by her stormy greeting. The fact that she appeared confirmed my impression that while she had become much more nervous of Africans she did not seem in the least suspicious of Europeans.

I mixed a dish of her favourite meat with some cod-liver oil and was taking it to her when Jespah ambushed me and licked the dish.

While this was happening Jeff was testing the sound recorder and happened to run through some recordings of the fierce lioness roaring. Jespah cocked his ears and tilted his head sideways as he listened attentively to the hated voice. Then he left his titbits and rushed to warn his mother of the danger.

On the following afternoon we again filmed Elsa on the rock and had further proof of her friendliness towards David and Jeff: this time she brought the cubs to play with us. I was most interested to observe that Jespah reacted just as Elsa used to when she was a cub; he knew at once whether someone liked him, felt a bit nervous of him or was really frightened, and treated him accordingly. David, I am sorry to say, he singled out for stalking and ambushing, and most of his time was spent trying to dodge Jespah. It was a great pity it was too dark to get a film of this game.

On their last evening our guests said goodbye to Elsa while she was sitting on the Land Rover; they shook her paw and I felt that she had become more to them than a mere film attraction. I was most grateful to both David and Jeff for all the tact and kindness they had shown while making their film.

21. Elsa Educates the Cubs

On the afternoon of 21 September, George and I and the Toto met the family in the bush. Elsa greeted us as usual and Jespah licked both of us, but when he went on to lick the Toto Elsa stepped disapprovingly between the two of them. This confirmed that her attitude had altered for she had become as fond of the Toto by now as she was of Nuru and Makedde; since the birth of the cubs she had objected when they approached Africans or vice versa. Now, obviously, the ban had been extended to the Toto.

The next afternoon we saw the family playing in the river. While the cubs splashed about and fought over floating sticks Elsa placed herself near to the Toto in a position from which she could keep an eye on all of us.

As we walked home Jespah became very much interested in the Toto's rifle and persistently stalked and ambushed him. Elsa came to the rescue several times and sat on her son long enough to allow the Toto to get well ahead unmolested.

That evening the tsetse flies were particularly annoying and Elsa flung herself on the ground inside my tent miaowing for help in getting rid of them. I came in to perform my task but Jespah and Gopa had already rushed up to their mother and were rolling round squashing the flies. When I approached Elsa they snarled at me and when I began to deal with the tsetse she began licking the cubs no doubt to quiet their jealousy. Usually, I was allowed to do this for her, and any help was gratefully accepted. I was therefore surprised when next morning while I was watching the cubs enjoying a game with their mother Elsa spanked me twice and even jumped at me.

During the night she only came into camp for a quick visit after we had gone to bed, and did not appear again till the following evening when she arrived with the cubs, but was very aloof, collected her meat, dragged it out of my sight and left soon afterwards.

When I returned the next evening from a walk on which I had found many fresh elephant spoors I saw Jespah busily reducing my only topee to pulp. This was a bore as I needed it when I went out in the hot sun. Elsa, perhaps to make up for her son's naughtiness, was particularly affectionate. We sat for a long time together near the river watching a kingfisher. It seemed to have no fear of either of us and came very close.

It was about this time that I began to notice how very jealous Gopa was growing, not only of me but also of his brother. When Jespah played with their mother he would push his way between the two of them and when Elsa came close to me he crouched and snarled until she went over to him.

After George went away I slept in the Land Rover close to which the carcase was chained at night; by doing so I hoped to preserve it from chance predators.

One night I was woken up by the sound of breaking trees and the trumpeting of elephant. They were down by the river, between the studio and the tents, but gradually moved nearer which worried me, for I could not think what I should do if they came up to the tents. Elsa sat with her cubs by my 'sleeper' facing the noise and perhaps harbouring similar misgivings. We all listened intently. Suddenly I saw a huge shape moving along the top of the bank; it stopped and stood still for what seemed an endless time, then it vanished into the darkness. Elsa and the cubs kept as quiet as I did and remained in their 'guarding' position until the sound of crashing had ceased. Then I thought I saw her go off.

Soon afterwards my torchlight was reflected in a pair of green eyes which gradually came closer. Assuming it was a prowling predator, I got out of the car intending to cover the carcase with thorns, but before I had dragged one big branch into position Elsa bounced on me. I climbed back into my bedroom, then when she and the cubs seemed to have finished their meal and gone away, I came out again for I was determined not to give a free meal to the jackals. Once more Elsa jumped on me and defended her kill. We spent the rest of the night watching each other. She won the game but probably at the cost of eating a lot more than she wanted.

By October both Billy Collins and I felt that it would be useful to meet and discuss the plans for the sequel to *Born Free*.

I went to Nairobi to fetch him; we reached the camp at supper time and found the lion family in front of the tents eating. I was a little apprehensive, but Elsa welcomed us both in the most friendly fashion and then returned to her dinner. We spent the rest of the evening within a few yards of her but she paid no attention to us.

The next day was very hot indeed and the bush was depressingly dry, so that even the studio, which is usually cool, was oppressive when we went there in the morning and started our work. Although we were much distracted by baboons, antelopes and various birds, we achieved a lot and it was not till after tea that we went to look for Elsa. We did not find her on our way out, but as we were returning to camp along a little game path I suddenly felt her and Jespah rubbing themselves against my legs.

Elsa treated Billy just as she did us, but Jespah was greatly intrigued by his white socks and tennis shoes. Crouching low and hiding behind every available tuft he prepared to ambush him, but we intervened, so eventually he became disgusted at being thwarted and went off and joined the other cubs. Elsa spent the evening on the roof of the Land Rover.

Next morning she woke me up by licking me through my torn mosquito net. How had she got into my tent? I was worried in case she might also have tried to visit Billy, and shouted to him. He replied that Elsa had only just left him. At this moment the Toto arrived with my morning tea. Seeing him, Elsa stepped slowly off my bed and moved to the wicker gate of the thorn enclosure. There she waited until the Toto pushed it aside for her, then she walked out sedately, collected the cubs and they trotted off towards the big rocks.

I dressed quickly and went with some apprehension to find out how Billy had fared. He told me that Elsa had squeezed her way through the wicker gate of his enclosure which we had barricaded with thorn and then jumped on to the Land Rover. Only when she realized that she couldn't get at him had she gone off to visit me.

She had never paid the slightest attention to David Attenborough or to Jeff who had slept in the same position. The only people whose beds she insisted on sharing were George's and mine.

In the afternoon we visited the family which we found on the Whuffing Rock. As soon as Elsa and Jespah spotted us they came down and gave us a great welcome. Makedde was with us and Elsa greeted him too, but by stepping briskly between them she pointedly prevented Jespah from rubbing his head against Makedde's legs. Gopa and Little Elsa stayed on the rock, but after we had walked some hundred yards into the bush Elsa called them and they came down, but kept out of our sight. Only when we reached the river did they appear, and then they behaved very quietly, sitting in the water to cool themselves while watching us attentively. Jespah later joined Elsa and was very affectionate but on our way home his antics delayed us till we became benighted. Although Billy had discarded his white socks he still fascinated Jespah who sat himself squarely in front of his feet, looking up at him with the most cheeky expression and making all progress impossible. Billy tried to make a series of detours to avoid him but in vain for the next moment Jespah was always at his feet. Elsa intervened once or twice and rolled her son over, but this only encouraged him to be more mischievous. George had gone ahead but suddenly felt himself clasped from behind by two paws and nearly tumbled over. Jespah certainly had a good evening's fun! It was only when we reached camp and he settled to his dinner that we were left in peace.

The 12 October was the last day which Billy was to spend in camp, so we made a determined effort to find the family; we failed but on our return we found Elsa and Jespah in camp. Billy patted Elsa as she lay on the Land Rover and stroked her head, something which as a rule she only allows me to do.

During the second week of October, George returned to camp and for several days life went on uneventfully until one night the fierce lioness and her mate announced their arrival by impressive roarings from the Big Rock. Elsa took the hint and at once moved her family across the river.

Early next morning George saw the fierce lioness standing on the Big Rock clearly outlined against the sky. She allowed him to come within four hundred yards of her and then made off.

Elsa came in for a quick meal that evening but did not reappear for forty-eight hours. During this time we changed guard. Worried by Elsa's absence, I went out to look for her but could find no pugmarks. Next morning we found her spoor and those of the cubs all over the camp, and I thought it very strange that they had made no sound to indicate their presence. Following the pugmarks found them mixed up with the imprints of rhino and elephant.

That evening the family turned up, but Elsa was in a queer mood; she showed no interest in me or in Gopa or Little Elsa and was entirely absorbed in Jespah. I felt really sorry for Gopa who tried very hard to attract her attention, rolling invitingly on his back with outstretched paws whenever his mother passed close to him, with no result except that she stepped over him to join Jespah.

About 8.30 p.m. two lions started roaring; all the family listened intently, but only Elsa and Jespah trotted quickly towards the studio; Gopa and Little Elsa after going a short way with them came back to finish their meal. They went on gorging until there was a frightening roaring so close that they

246

rushed at full speed after their mother who by now had crossed the river.

I brought the remains of their meal into safety, which was as well, for the lion duet went on all through the night. The following afternoon when the light was already fading Makedde and I saw the lioness climbing up the Big Rock and then sitting on top of it – undoubtedly this was the fierce lioness. I got out my field glasses and had my first good look at her. She was much darker and heavier than Elsa and rather ugly. I observed that she was staring at us and from the top of the rock she kept up a constant roaring. There was no question of sleep during that night and Elsa naturally kept away.

In the morning we tracked the fierce lioness's pugmarks and those of her mate; they had gone upstream back to the area in which we believed they usually lived. Elsa no doubt knew this for that night she brought the family into camp for their dinner. She now paid little attention to me until the cubs had settled down to their meal, then she was as affectionate as ever. This was plainly a new stratagem she had devised so as not to arouse their jealousy.

The air was oppressive and lightning streaked the horizon at frequent intervals; soon after I had gone to bed a strong wind started blowing, the trees creaked and the canvas of the tent flapped; then the first drops of rain fell and it was not long before I seemed to be under a waterspout. The downpour continued throughout the night. We had not expected this deluge and had not hammered our tent pegs in; as a result the poles collapsed and I spent my time trying to raise them sufficiently to keep some shelter over my head, while a river seemed to run round my feet.

When I emerged I saw that George's tent had also collapsed and from inside it I heard Elsa moaning in a low voice. Soon she appeared with Jespah and Gopa, rather bedraggled but dry. But even this downpour had not induced Little Elsa to seek shelter and when I caught sight of her outside the thorn fence I saw that she was drenched.

I began to sort out our soaked belongings and remove them to the cars to save them from the lions, and in this I was 'helped' by Jespah who had great fun defending each box I wanted to move. When I had finished my work Elsa, Jespah, Gopa and I crowded into my tent and Little Elsa consented to come inside the flaps but no farther; at least she had some protection there.

The rain continued for four days.

Elsa's home though in semi-desert country benefits from a nearby mountain range from which several small streams run into the arid region. The one nearest to the camp now rose higher than I had ever seen it. A roaring, red torrent thundered over its banks and flooded the studio up to the level of the table, depositing a great deal of debris including a doum-palm which had been uprooted. I was exceedingly glad that Elsa and the cubs were on our side of the river and that we had sufficient food for them.

Within three days the scorched parched surroundings of the camp had become green and the dry brittle bush had turned into luxurious vegetation. But it seemed as though it had exhausted its strength in putting out such a profusion of many-coloured flowers, for within three or four days the ground was carpeted with many-coloured petals.

The animals of the bush reacted instantly to the change from the barrenness of the drought to the rich abundance which succeeded it.

After a week when the rains stopped I observed many baby animals: some small brightly coloured monitors were sunning themselves along the river but dived into the foaming waters when I approached them. Two tiny turtles, no larger than a shilling piece, were swimming near the studio. They were perfect miniature replicas of the adult turtles, about the size of a large soup plate, which I had often watched on the rocks opposite. But the queerest nursery of all I discovered one morning when I was walking down the river. Close to one of Elsa's favourite crossing places is a deep pool, where I observed what seemed to be gigantic tadpoles; they kept in a vertical position by paddling energetically. When I looked at them closely I saw that they were baby crocs, though they must have measured no more than seven inches and could not have been more than two or three days old.

George had reached camp as soon as the condition of the ground made it possible for him to travel, and had brought five Game Scouts with him. They were to provide a permanent patrol and put down poaching. It was necessary that they should live some distance away from Elsa and from our camp, and so George now began supervising the establishment of their post and cutting a motor track to it.

In two weeks' time we hoped that this work would be well advanced, then we would start deserting Elsa for increasingly long periods so as to compel the cubs to go hunting with her and assume their true wild life. Our unexpectedly prolonged stay in the bush had caused them to get a little too used to camp life, and, though we had no control over them, Jespah was now on quite intimate terms with us; but apart from this their wild instincts were intact and certainly Gopa and Little Elsa only put up with us because they saw that their mother insisted that we were friends.

We wondered whether she communicated her wish that they should not hurt us, which they were now well equipped to do, or whether they simply followed her example. Jespah in particular, when he was playing with us or when he was jealous, could have done a lot of damage if he had not controlled himself, but he always did so and even when he was in a temper gave us good warning of the fact.

Gopa was less friendly but so long as we left him alone did nothing to provoke an incident.

Little Elsa remained shy, though she now seemed less nervous of us than she used to be. We were surprised that none of the cubs ever attempted to follow Elsa on to the roof of the Land Rover, though they often gazed up at their mother with disappointed expressions, when she was resting on the canvas to escape their teasing. Judging by their ability to climb trees they could very easily have jumped on to the bonnet and then taken another leap on to the roof, and indeed Elsa had done this at a younger age, but for some reason they seemed to regard the Land Rover as out of bounds.

During George's absence Jespah and Gopa used his tent as a sort of 'den'. As a result on his return he found it rather crowded at night. I was a little worried; George prefers to sleep on a low hounsfield bed and with Elsa, Jespah and Gopa around it I wondered whether one night there might not be trouble, but they behaved remarkably well. Whenever Jespah tried to play with his toes, George's authoritative 'no' made him stop at once.

The extent to which they felt at home was illustrated when one night Elsa rolled round and tipped over George's bed, throwing him on top of Jespah. No commotion followed and Gopa who was sleeping near George's head did not even move.

A day later when we were returning to camp we found the family except for Jespah gorging on a carcase. It was not long before we discovered the missing cub behind the tents enjoying a roast guinea fowl which he had stolen off the table, but he had such a mischievous expression that we could do nothing but laugh at the little rascal. We were surprised, however, that he preferred cooked meat to fresh. Next day we had a further surprise when we came across the family in the bush and found the cubs being suckled. They were now ten and a half months old, and I do not think that they could have got much milk as Elsa's teats seemed to be empty.

Although they were still being suckled we now noticed the first signs of adolescence in Jespah and Gopa; they had grown fine fluff round their faces and necks, and if they looked a bit unshaven their appearance was certainly very endearing. Elsa greeted us warmly and while she was doing so, Jespah pushed himself between us and demanded to be patted too. Elsa watched us and then licked her son approvingly.

We walked back to camp together. In front of it were the remains of last evening's meal, but Elsa refused even to sniff at it and demanded a new kill. Later a leopard grunted from the other side of the river, and this caused her to rush off leaving the cubs – after about fifteen minutes they followed her. We were very glad to see that Elsa now took the initiative and was prepared to defend her territory.

That night a lion roared and when we later traced his pugmarks they led to the Big Rock; evidently something had given the cubs a fright, for on 24 November, when Elsa swam over, they refused to follow her and she had to go back twice to encourage them before they, too, swam across. Once landed they had a great game, Elsa rolling Jespah round and round like a bundle, which he loved, and poor Gopa jumping clumsily between them asking to be noticed; when I came close to photograph them Gopa growled at me, whereupon Jespah gave him such a clout that he looked quite stupefied by his punishment. It was all done in fun, but it showed up the different characters of the brothers. But as always when they settled down to their dinner all jealousy was forgotten.

George had shot a guinea fowl and I brought it out hidden behind my back because I wanted to give it to Little Elsa. I waited for a moment in which only she was looking up and then showed it to her. She took in the situation at once and while continuing to eat with her brothers watched me carefully as I walked a little distance away. I waited until Jespah and Gopa were concentrating upon the meat and when only Little Elsa saw what I was doing, dropped the bird behind a bush. Then, when she alone was watching me, I kept on pointing from her to the guinea fowl until suddenly she rushed like a streak of lightning, seized the bird and took it into a thicket where she could eat it unmolested by the others.

Next day we saw the family sitting on the rocky platform on the opposite side of the river to the studio, below which there is a deep pool which was at one time inhabited by a large crocodile. The cubs seemed nervous and only Elsa swam across. We had brought a carcase with us, she grabbed it, and crossed the river with it, but this time avoided the pool and swam higher upstream where the bank was much steeper but where we had never seen crocs.

The family were not apparently hungry, for they did not eat but indulged in a game of tree climbing; the cubs balanced on the sloping branches which overhung the river and seemed intent on tripping one another up and throwing their adversary into the water. Finally, Elsa joined them; she seemed to us to be giving them a demonstration of how to turn on a branch and how to go from one branch to another.

When it grew dark the meat was still untouched and as we neither wished to lose it nor to provoke a fight between Elsa and some chance predator George determined to recover it.

The first thing was to get the family over to our side, otherwise they would object to the removal of their kill. While George went up the river out of their sight and began to wade across, I swung a guinea fowl temptingly in the air. This did the trick and brought the lions over to join me. Unfortunately, when George reached the carcase Elsa observed this, swam hurriedly back and defended it. It took a lot of coaxing on his part to let her allow him to float the kill over, and even then she swam beside him with a very suspicious expression on her face. While this was going on the cubs rushed up and down the bank, obviously most upset but making no attempt to join Elsa. I was surprised for usually they showed no fear of the river and by now it was quite fordable. However, later that day they redeemed their reputation: shortly after dark, when we heard sounds which indicated that a rhino was at the salt lick, Elsa dashed after it and the cubs with her and judging by the snortings that followed the rhino must have made a very rapid retreat.

Brave the cubs certainly were to tackle such a great and fierce beast.

Jespah in his playful moods liked acting the clown. One day when he was being especially lively, teasing everybody and asking for a game, I placed a round wooden tea tray in a branch that hangs over the river to see what he would do about it. He climbed up and tried to grip the inch-thick rim between his teeth, using one paw to steady it as it swayed. When he got a sufficiently good grip to carry it horizontally he came down very cautiously, pausing several times to make sure that we were watching him. Finally, he reached the ground and then paraded round with his trophy, until Little Elsa and Gopa chased him and put an end to his performance.

George's leave was coming to an end and this appeared to be the right time for us to go. The poachers seemed to have left; Elsa was now able to defend her territory and the cubs had become powerful young lions, and it was time that they should hunt with their mother and live their natural life; also as they were growing increasingly jealous we considered that it would be unfair to provoke them by our affection for their mother into doing something which might be harmful.

We decided to space our absences. On the first occasion we had intended to leave for only six days, but in fact, because of very heavy rains, it was nine before I could return.

Elsa did not turn up in answer to the shots we fired, nor were there any signs of spoor around the camp, but these might well have been washed away by the flooding of the river. After a while, I walked towards the Big Rock and came upon Elsa trotting along with the cubs; they were panting and had probably come a long way in answer to my signal. They were delighted to see me and Jespah struggled to get between Elsa and myself so as to receive his share of the welcome. Gopa and Little Elsa, however, kept their distance. All were in excellent condition and as fat as they had been when we left.

I had brought a carcase, but though Elsa settled down to it the cubs were in no hurry to eat and played about for some time before joining her. When she had had her fill she came over to me and was very affectionate and as the cubs were too busy eating to notice this there were no demonstrations of jealousy, which seemed to be what their mother had intended.

How anxious Elsa was to prevent rows or ill-feeling was clearly shown next day. I had given the cubs a guinea fowl and was watching them fighting over it. Gopa growled most alarmingly at Jespah, Little Elsa and myself. Hearing this, Elsa instantly rushed up to see what was going on, but as soon as she had satisfied herself that nothing serious had provoked Gopa, she returned to the roof of the Land Rover.

A few minutes later, while the cubs were still eating, I went up to her; she snarled at me and spanked me twice. I retired immediately, surprised, as I did not think I had deserved such treatment. Soon afterwards Elsa jumped off the car and rubbed herself affectionately against me, obviously wishing to make up for her bad behaviour. I stroked her and she settled down beside me, keeping one paw against me. When the cubs joined us she rolled on to the other side and I ceased to exist for her.

She constantly showed how anxious she was for the cubs to be friends with us. One evening, after having gorged himself on the meat we had provided, Jespah came into the tent. He was too full to play and rolled on to his back because his bulging belly was more comfortable in that position. He looked at me plainly demanding to be patted. As he was in a docile mood I felt comparatively safe from his swiping paws and sharp claws, so I stroked his silky fur. He closed his eyes and made a sucking noise, a sure sign of contentment. Elsa, who had been watching us from the roof of the car, joined us and licked both Jespah and me, showing how glad she was to see us on such good terms.

This happy scene was abruptly ended by Gopa who sneaked up and sat on top of Elsa, with a most possessive expression which left me in no doubt that I was not wanted. So I withdrew.

Fond as Elsa was of her children she never failed to discipline them when they were doing something of which she knew we disapproved, even when they were acting only in accordance with their natural instincts.

We usually kept the goats locked up inside my truck at night, but for a short time we were obliged to secure them inside a strong thorn enclosure because the truck had to go away for repairs. During this time, Jespah on one occasion besieged the boma so persistently that we were worried for the safety of the goats. All the tricks we invented to divert his attention failed to produce any effect. Then Elsa came to our aid. She pranced round her son trying to entice him away, but he paid no attention to her; then she spanked him repeatedly. He spanked back. It was amusing to watch the two outwitting each other. Finally, Jespah forgot all about the goats and followed Elsa into the tent where their dinner was waiting for them.

But when he had finished his meal Jespah, having been cheated of his fun with the goats, looked for other amusement.

He found a tin of milk which he rolled across the ground-sheet of the tent until it was covered with a sticky mess. Then he took George's pillow, but the feathers tickled him, so he looked for another toy and, before I could stop him, seized a needle case which I was using and raced out into the dark with it. I was terrified that it would open under the pressure of his jaws and that he might swallow its contents, so I grabbed our supper, a roast guinea fowl, and ran after him. Luckily, the sight of the bird proved too much for him; he dropped the case, scattering the needles, pins, razor blades and scissors over the grass. We carefully collected them so they should not prove a danger to the cubs.

22. A New Year Begins

It was now time for us to go back to Isiolo and leave the cubs to a spell of wild life.

On 3 December I called on the District Commissioner in whose area Elsa's home lies. He warned me that it might become necessary to remove Elsa from her home, as the tribesmen blamed her for the stricter supervision of poaching due to our presence and used the recent killing of a woman by a tame lion in Tanganyika to stimulate ill-feeling against Elsa.

Four days later a rumour reached us that two tribesmen had been mauled by a lion fourteen miles from Elsa's camp. George left at once to investigate. He reached camp too late to pursue his enquiries. That evening Elsa and the cubs played happily round the tent; though they ate greedily they were in excellent condition, which was satisfactory as they had been left to themselves for seven days. As daylight broke George went to the

Game Scout Post; no one had heard of any tribesman being mauled by a lion. So he sent the Scouts to the scene of the alleged accident and returned to camp.

In order to keep the lions near to the tents he gave them a carcase which they dragged into a bush close by. They stayed there until the evening.

When, a day later, I arrived at the camp it was dark and the men were too tired to unload the truck and put the goats I had brought into it for the night. We therefore secured them in a thorn enclosure.

Although, as we had two cars, our arrival was noisy and Elsa must have heard us, she did not come to welcome me. This was the first time she had failed to do so.

After I had gone to bed I heard the cubs attacking the goats' boma. The sounds of breaking wood, growling lions and stampeding animals bleating, left no doubt as to what was happening. We rushed out but not before Elsa, Gopa and Little Elsa had each of them killed a goat. Jespah was holding one down with his paw which George was able to rescue unhurt.

It took us two hours to round up the bolting, panic-stricken survivors of the herd and secure them in the truck, while hyenas, attracted by the noise, circled round.

Elsa took her kill across the river. George who followed her saw a large crocodile making for Elsa and shot at but missed it. He spent until 2 a.m. sitting close to Elsa to see if it would reappear, but it did not. The cubs were very much upset at finding themselves and their kills separated from Elsa by the river; after half an hour of anxious miaowing they joined their mother without having started to eat the goats they had killed.

In the afternoon, the Game Scouts returned; they had not got any confirmation of the rumour that tribesmen had been mauled by lions, but they had collected plenty of evidence to show that, influenced by poachers and political agitators, the tribesmen were becoming increasingly hostile to Elsa. We realized that her life was in danger and discussed what we should do.

We had spent six months in camp, much longer than we had originally planned, in order to protect Elsa and her cubs from poachers and by doing so had inevitably interfered with their natural life. If now we stayed on the cubs would become so tame that they would have little chance of adapting themselves in the future to the life of the bush.

Besides this, if we went on camping in the reserve we should only aggravate the antagonism of the tribesmen. Since we could not, in the circumstances, leave Elsa and the cubs alone, the only solution we could think of was to look for a new home for them and move them as soon as possible.

Finding a suitable place for Elsa's release had proved very difficult; to find one for her and the cubs was likely to be still more difficult. We knew that by now, with their mother's help in teaching them to hunt and protecting them from natural foes, they were capable of living the life of the bush; but where would they be safe, not only from wild animals but also from man, who now proved to be their most dangerous enemy?

Leaving me in charge of the camp, George returned next morning to Isiolo hoping to find a solution to this problem.

In the afternoon I walked with Nuru to the Whuffing Rock where we had spotted Elsa. She came down at once to greet us, but when I started to climb up the saddle to join the sleeping cubs, she prevented me from doing so by sitting squarely across my path, and only after we were on our way home did she call her children. Through my field glasses I saw Jespah and Gopa climb down, but Little Elsa remained on top like a sentry.

When it was dark the family arrived in camp and after eating their dinner, Elsa and her sons played happily in the tent until they dozed off in a close embrace. I sketched them, while

Little Elsa watched us from outside the tent. In the night a lion called and for the next three days he kept close to the camp. During this time Elsa stayed in the immediate vicinity. It was only after the lion had left the neighbourhood that she ventured to take the cubs to the Big Rock and then by teatime she returned as though to ensure an early dinner undisturbed by the possible appearance of another lion.

I usually met the family on their way to camp and was often touched by Jespah's behaviour. When Elsa and I greeted each other he didn't want to be left out, but I think he knew that I was scared of his claws, for he would place himself with his rear towards me and keep absolutely still as though to assure me that like this I would be quite safe from accidental scratches while I patted him. From then on he always adopted this attitude when he wanted to be stroked.

December 20 was the cubs' first birthday. The river had risen so much that we couldn't cross it to look for them, so when about teatime the family turned up, wet but well, I was very happy.

As a birthday treat I had a guinea fowl, which I cut up into four portions so that each should have a share. After gobbling these titbits Elsa hopped on to the Land Rover while the cubs tore at some meat we had prepared for them.

As all the lions were happily occupied I called to Makedde to escort me for a walk. As soon as we set out Elsa jumped off the car and followed us; then Jespah, seeing his mother disappear, stopped his meal and ran after us, and we had not gone far before I saw Gopa and Little Elsa parallel to us chasing each other through the bush.

As we came to the place where the track comes nearest to the Big Rock, the lions sat down and rolled in the sand. I waited for a little while and watched the setting sun turn the rock to bright red; then since Elsa looked settled, I walked back, expecting the family to spend the evening on the rock. I was surprised when she followed me. She kept close so that I could help with the tsetse flies, and Jespah trotted next to us like a well-trained child. Gopa and Little Elsa took their time; they scampered about a long way behind us and we often had to stop to wait for them.

Elsa seemed to have come along just to join me in my walk; this was the first time she had done so since the cubs were born. I thought it a charming way of celebrating their birthday.

When we arrived in camp Elsa flung herself on the ground inside my tent and was joined by her sons who nuzzled and embraced their mother with their paws. I sketched them until Elsa retired to the roof of the Land Rover and the cubs started to eat their dinner. When I was sure that the cubs would not observe me I went over to Elsa and stroked her and she responded very affectionately. I wanted to thank her for having shared her children with us during their first year and having shared her anxieties during the period which is so full of dangers for any young animals. But, after some time, as though to remind me that in spite of our friendship we belonged to two different worlds, a lion suddenly started roaring and after listening intently Elsa left.

Next morning we found the spoor of a lioness upstream, but no trace of Elsa. She did not turn up that day or during the following night. On the second night we heard two lions roaring and understood why she had not come to camp. I was, there-fore, astonished to see her next morning about 9 a.m. on the Whuffing Rock, roaring as hard as she could. I called to her but she paid no attention and went on roaring for an hour. To whom was she calling at this unusual time of day?

She brought her cubs in for dinner that night but when a lion started roaring she left at once, crossing the river.

Elsa and the cubs spent the night of 23 December in camp and after breakfast when I strolled along the road to read in the sand the report on last night's visitors, she and the cubs followed

me. I called to Makedde and we all walked along together for
about two miles.

Jespah was particularly friendly, brushing against me, and
even standing quite still while I removed a tick which was close
to one of his eyes. We observed two jackals basking in the sun; on
earlier walks I had seen them in the same place and they had
never shown any fear at our approach. Now, although we were
only some thirty yards from them, they did not move and it was
only after Elsa made a short rush at them that they sneaked away,
and the moment she turned back they peeped around the
bushes, seemingly quite unalarmed.

We went on until we came to a rain pool where the lions had
a drink. By now the sun was getting hot and it would not have
surprised me had Elsa decided to spend the day in this place, but
good-naturedly she turned back when we did and trotted slowly
home with us.

I could not help feeling as though we were all taking our
Sunday family walk. Though in fact this was the morning of
Christmas Eve, and Elsa could have no knowledge of special
days, by a strange coincidence she had chosen a day I felt the
need to commemorate by coming for a walk with me and
bringing her family with her.

When we reached the place where we had seen the jackals we
found them still there and as the lions were too lazy for a game,
the jackals did not even bother to get up as we passed.

Elsa and the cubs were feeling the increasing heat very much
and often stopped under the shade of a tree to rest, yet when
we came near the Big Rock they suddenly rushed at full speed
through the bush and in a few leaps reached the top, where
they settled among the boulders. I scrambled after them as best
I could, but Elsa made it quite plain that I should now leave
them alone. She always knew exactly how much she felt it
was fitting for her to give to each of her two worlds, so I

confined myself to taking some photographs of her guarding her cubs.

George arrived about teatime with a suitcase full of mail. While we strolled about picking flowers for Christmas decorations, he told me of the enquiries he had made about finding a new home for Elsa and the cubs. He thought that the Lake Rudolf area would be the place in which the lions would be safest from human interference. He had obtained permission from the authorities to take them there if the need arose, and was soon going to reconnoitre the region to find a suitable spot.

This part of Kenya is very grim and conditions are tough there, so I felt depressed at the prospect. To make matters worse Elsa chose this moment to join us on our way home; behind her the cubs were playing happily along the road, and I could not bear to visualize them roaming on the wind-swept, lava-strewn desert which surrounds the lake.

After we reached camp we gave the family their supper which kept them occupied while I arranged the table for our Christmas dinner. I decorated it with flowers and tinsel ornaments and put the little silver Christmas tree I had kept from last year in the middle and a still smaller one which had just arrived from London in front of it. Then I brought out the presents for George and the boys.

Jespah watched my preparations very carefully and the moment I turned my back to get the candles he rushed up and seized a parcel which contained a shirt for George, and bounced off with it into a thicket. Gopa joined him immediately and the two of them had a wonderful time with the shirt. When at last we rescued it it was in no state to give to George.

By now it was nearly dark and I started to light the candles. That was all Jespah needed to make him decide to come and help me. I only just managed to prevent him from pulling the tablecloth, with the decorations and burning candles, on top of himself. It needed a lot of coaxing to make him keep away so that I could light the rest of the candles.

When all was ready he came up, tilted his head, looked at the glittering Christmas trees and then sat down and watched the candles burn lower and lower. As each flame went out I felt as though another happy day of our life in the camp had passed. When all the lights had gone out the darkness seemed intense and as though it were a symbol of the darkness of our future. A few yards away Elsa and her cubs rested peacefully in the grass, hardly visible in the fading light.

Afterwards George and I read our mail. It took us many hours to do so, during which our imaginations travelled across the world and brought us close to all the people who were wishing Elsa and her family and us happiness.

Mercifully it was one of the last envelopes I opened which contained an order from the African District Council for the removal of Elsa and her cubs from the reserve.

PART THREE

23. The Deportation Order

The reason given by the council was that since Elsa was used to our company she might become a danger to other people.

We were amazed; the local authorities themselves had helped us to choose the area for her release, and up to now had regarded her as a great asset to the reserve.

Now, with the arrival of the deportation order, all we could do was to try to make this removal as little harmful to the lions as possible and find a satisfactory new home for them.

We wrote to friends in Tanganyika, Uganda, the Rhodesias and South Africa, enquiring what the chances were of finding a good territory for the family in their countries but, before finally deciding to remove Elsa and her family from Kenya, George wished to carry out a reconnaissance along the eastern shores of Lake Rudolf in the north of Kenya.

I was distressed by this plan. The country there is very grim, and I feared that game around the lake might be so scarce that Elsa and the cubs would become dependent upon us for their food supply. Besides this, the area is so remote that in case of an emergency we should be very lucky if we were able to get any help.

To make the removal we would first build a ramp and then place a five-ton lorry against it so that its floor was level with the top of the ramp; in the lorry we would place the lions' dinner. Once the cubs had got used to their new feeding place we could build a strong wire enclosure over the lorry and make a trapdoor to it, which we would close when the cubs were feeding, thus converting the lorry into a travelling crate.

We dug the ramp at the salt lick near the studio. My heart was

267

heavy as I watched the cubs; they were excited by the unusual activities taking place on their playground, sniffed the freshly dug soil curiously, found it great fun to roll on the loose earth, and seemed to think that all this work was being done to amuse them.

On 28 December George started off on the recce to Lake Rudolf. That afternoon I met the family near the river, and after the usual friendly greetings from Elsa and Jespah, we went together to the water's edge. The cubs plunged in at once, ducking and chasing each other; Elsa and I watched them from the bank. While they were in the river she guarded them in a dignified manner, but when they emerged dripping wet she joined in their games and helped them to look for a new playground. A nearby tree provided what was needed; the cubs struggled up its trunk but were soon overtaken by their mother, who in a few swift movements leapt high above them. I gasped as she went higher and higher, the slender upper branches bending alarmingly beneath her weight, finally she reached the crown of the tree. What, I wondered, was she doing? Teaching her children the proper way to climb trees, or just showing off? When she found that the boughs were no longer strong enough to support her, she turned with great difficulty and, cautiously testing each branch, began her descent. She managed to make her way down but her landing was by no means dignified, then, as though to suggest that the tumble was a joke, she at once began to jump around the cubs. They chased her, and all the way home played games of hide-and-seek or ambushes, in which I was often the victim.

Next day, at teatime, Elsa showed me very clearly what a wonderful mother and companion she was to her cubs. The family appeared on the far bank of the river opposite the studio. I had seen a six-foot crocodile slither into the river at their approach and was therefore not surprised when the cubs paced nervously up and down the rocky platform by the river's edge, obviously frightened to jump into the deep pool beneath.

Elsa licked each in turn, then they all plunged in together and swam safely across in close formation. When the cubs relaxed and began to chase each other so as to get dry, Elsa joined in. She took Jespah's tail in her mouth and walked round in circles with him, obviously enjoying the clowning as much as he did.

Eventually Jespah sat down close to me, turning his back to me. This he did when he wanted to be petted; he seemed to realize that I was always a little afraid of being accidentally scratched by him because, unlike his mother, he had not learnt to retract his claws when playing with human beings.

When I went for an afternoon stroll, the lions joined me; I welcomed this new habit of a family walk; it gave me a chance to observe the cubs' reactions to everything we met on our way and also allowed me to spend more time with Elsa, of whose company I had been to a considerable extent deprived since the birth of the cubs. When we reached the Big Rock, Gopa and Little Elsa stayed behind; I tried to induce them to follow us but they would not. Elsa walked along as if she knew that no harm would come to them. She had lately kept her children on a longer leash and did not seem to worry when they showed independence. Jespah, however, was plainly very anxious; he ran backwards and forwards between us and only eventually and with reluctance decided to follow his mother and me.

We walked for about two miles; when it grew cooler, Elsa and Jespah began to play; it was very funny to see each trying to outwit the other as they gambolled about like kittens.

On our way back I saw Gopa and Little Elsa on a rocky outcrop of the main ridge, silhouetted against a magnificent sunset. They watched me aloofly as I passed below them. Elsa and Jespah climbed to the top of the Big Rock and called softly. Lazily the two cubs stretched and yawned and then joined their mother.

All through the evening I waited with a carcase, but there was no sign of Elsa or of the cubs. Late at night I heard the whuffings of the cubs' father which explained their absence. Next morning, to make sure that all was well, I went with Nuru to the rock; at the base we found the spoor of a large lion.

For two days Elsa and the cubs kept away from the camp, and during this time I repeatedly heard their father roaring. When Elsa returned it was late in the evening. Only her sons were with her, but she did not seem perturbed at Little Elsa's absence, and after a large meal they all went back to the rock.

Early next morning I followed up their spoor until I saw Gopa and Little Elsa on the rock; then, assuming that their father might be nearby, I went home.

Later in the afternoon the whole family appeared along the road. Gopa and Little Elsa were panting; they had been chasing a jackal which I had heard calling some way off. While Elsa greeted me, I signalled to Nuru to return to camp and prepare a carcase, but Jespah decided that Nuru was to play hide-and-seek with him and, until his mother intervened, Nuru had to use all his wits to dodge the cubs. Elsa then took her offspring in hand, played with them and kept them busy until Nuru's task was accomplished; she so often acted in this way that it was impossible not to conclude that she did so deliberately. When we arrived in camp, the cubs pounced on their dinner, but their mother seemed to be very nervous and after several short reconnaissances disappeared into the bush, leaving them behind.

On 1 January I felt very apprehensive. What would the New Year bring? As if to cheer me up, Jespah came close and, taking up his 'safety position' (i.e. the one that ensured my safety from his claws), invited me to play with him. I stroked him affectionately, but suddenly he rolled over and instinctively I jerked back. He looked bewildered, then again rolled into his safety position and tilted his head. Plainly he could not understand my fear of his unretracted claws; repeatedly he invited me to play with him, and I wished I could explain to him that when his mother was a tiny cub I had been able to teach her to control her claws, and that was why I could play with her fearlessly, but not with him.

The following day the same thing happened: Jespah wanted a game and I wanted to play with him, but when I came within reach of his claws I was obliged to break off. Elsa watched the scene from the top of the Land Rover. She seemed to be aware of Jespah's disappointment at my cautious behaviour, for she came down and licked and hugged her son until he was happy again. Meanwhile Little Elsa sneaked around nervously, hiding in the grass and obviously too frightened by my presence to come out into the open. Elsa went over to her and rolled about with her until she too was quite at her ease. When Jespah and Gopa joined in the fun Elsa retired to her sanctuary on top of the Land Rover; I went up to her, intending to stroke her to make up for the apparent unfriendliness I had shown towards her son; but when I approached she spanked me, and during the whole of that evening she remained aloof.

On 2 January, Ken Smith and Peter Saw, both Game Wardens from adjoining districts, arrived in a lorry. They had come with the consent of the Game Department to offer their help in moving Elsa and the cubs. Ken took some measurements for fitting the ramp to a four-wheel-drive Bedford lorry belonging to the Government, which he proposed to lend us for the move. He also offered to order a lion-proof wire enclosure to fit it, and to send us our old Thames lorry until the adjustments to the Bedford were completed. This would make it possible for us to accustom the cubs to feeding in a lorry with the minimum loss of time.

Ken had been on the lion hunt which brought Elsa into our life and had visited her twice since then, but he had never seen the cubs, so, after we had dealt with the measurements, we all went off to look for the family. We found them in the studio lugga ('lugga' is Somali for dry riverbed), but at the sight of two strangers the cubs bolted. Elsa greeted Ken as an old friend, but paid no attention to Peter. She put up with being photographed, but when our guests came close to her, Jespah peeped anxiously through the foliage, obviously prepared to defend his mother if the need arose. Eventually he came into the open, though he kept at a safe distance from Ken and Peter.

As we did not want to upset the cubs, we returned to camp and sent the lorry a few hundred yards down the track. A little later Elsa arrived alone. She watched us for some time and then, still ignoring Peter, she gripped Ken firmly around the knee with her paw; we guessed she wanted to show him that she thought it was time for him to go. Ken took the hint and they left, and immediately the cubs came bouncing along and began to play. This showed us that they were becoming increasingly shy of strangers. Jespah had overcome his suspicion of George and myself, but he didn't trust anyone else.

He showed his confidence in me on the following day, when he allowed me to remove a tick from his eyelid and rid him also of a couple of maggots. These maggots, which are found in great numbers in most game animals, though themselves harmless, weaken the condition of their host and render it susceptible to other illnesses.

Jespah kept absolutely still while I attended to his maggots, then he licked his wounds and placed himself in his safety position, inviting me to pat him. For the first time, he even allowed me to touch his silky nostrils; perhaps he wanted to show me that he was grateful for my help.

That evening he came alone into the tent, squatted in his safety position, and kept quite still until I stroked him. His demands for affection posed a serious problem: I hated to disappoint him but, on the other hand, apart from my fear of his claws, we wanted the cubs to develop into wild lions, and Jespah's friendliness was already jeopardizing his future. Gopa and Little Elsa were different; their reactions were always those of wild animals.

Jespah was the leader of the cubs. One afternoon I found him in great distress; he was alone on the far bank of the river, which the rest of the family had just crossed; he was pacing up and down looking anxiously at the water, obviously scared by the presence of a crocodile. I tried to help him by throwing sticks and stones into the deep pool across which he had to swim, but he only pulled faces at the invisible reptile. After a time, however, he made up his mind, plunged in and swam as fast as he could, deliberately churning up the water. Elsa, standing quite still a few yards off, had watched my attempts to frighten the crocodile away. When Jespah had landed safely, she came over and licked me affectionately; he too was particularly friendly all that afternoon.

Later, as we were walking up the narrow path to the tents, Gopa ambushed me, growling savagely; I was quite frightened, and could not think what had caused him to be so cross, until I saw that he had taken his dinner to this spot, and realized that when I passed within a few feet of the kill he had felt obliged to defend it.

The next day the Thames lorry arrived. We gave it a thorough wash and then parked it at the ramp, but it smelt of petrol, oil and Africans, and nothing would persuade the cubs to go near it. Even Elsa would not follow me into it, although I tried every trick I could think of to persuade her, in the belief that her example would encourage the cubs. There was nothing to be done except to wait until the lions had overcome their suspicion of the lorry, and remind myself that since the cubs so far had never been inside a vehicle I was asking a lot of them.

*

On 8 January, about lunchtime, I heard the excited chatter of baboons coming from the bank opposite the studio. This usually meant that the family were around, so later on I went to the studio lugga with my sketchbook. I found Elsa and her sons there and, as they were very sleepy, I had a splendid opportunity of drawing them. Poor Elsa was infested with maggots, but when I had tried to squeeze them out she flattened her ears and growled at me, so I was obliged to leave her alone.

When it got dark and there was still no sign of Little Elsa, I was anxious, but as her mother did not seem in the least apprehensive I decided not to worry, for I had discovered that Elsa's instinct was more reliable than mine. I am convinced that when there was a source of danger in the neighbourhood she had some means of sensing its presence, and also that she had a way, a quite imperceptible way, of transmitting her wishes to her cubs. We often watched attentively for any indication of a visible or audible sign of communication between her and her children, but were never able to observe one. Yet she was able to make her cubs stay put in the most varied circumstances. She could sense the presence of crocodiles under water, or of hidden beasts which might be a source of danger to her family. She knew when we arrived in camp, even if she were far away at the time, and even if we had been absent for a very long time. She also knew with unerring instinct whether the people she met genuinely liked her or not, and this quite irrespective of their behaviour towards her.

What faculty did she and other highly developed wild animals possess which could account for this? I think perhaps it is the power of telepathy, which we human beings too may have possessed before we developed the capacity to speak.

When I had finished sketching, we all returned to camp, and gave the lions their dinner. After the meal was over, Elsa suddenly got up, listened intently in the direction of the river, and began to walk towards it. I followed at a short distance. We went along the bank for a while, then she turned sharply, crossed the studio lugga, and crept on through the bush till she reached the water's edge. I caught up with her, and in the failing light was just able to see Little Elsa pacing up and down on the far bank, evidently frightened to enter the water, which was fairly deep at this point and where more than once I had seen a large crocodile. Elsa gave her low affectionate moan, moving quickly upstream and keeping her eyes fixed on Little Elsa as she did so. Along the opposite bank, the cub followed her. When they came to a shallow part of the river, Elsa stopped and her call changed, and finally her daughter plucked up enough courage to swim across.

By then it was nearly dark and so as not to add to Little Elsa's fears, I started to go home. To my surprise, when I emerged from the thick bush, I found Jespah and Gopa apparently waiting for the return of their mother and sister. I took a short cut home so that the family could join up without being disturbed by my presence. Later, Elsa came to my tent and rubbed herself affectionately against me as if to show me how happy she was to have all her family together again and how pleased she was that the anxiety we had shared was over.

But Elsa was to have another alarm before the day was over. While she was still rubbing herself against me, she suddenly stiffened and, her head level with her shoulders, trotted off into the dark. She soon came back, but only to rush off again. She did this several times until she finally settled down to her evening meal with the cubs. Soon afterwards I was startled by the roaring of the cubs' father who can only have been about twenty yards away. I counted the whuffs which followed his roar. There were twelve of them. While this went on, his family stopped eating and stood motionless between him and their dinner; they waited till he had left before they started to eat again. During the night they remained close to the camp, but went off early in the morning and did not return for twenty-four hours. When they came back we gave them some meat, but though the cubs dragged it into the bush they did not eat it; instead, they joined Elsa and myself at the salt lick.

It was six days since we had placed the lorry by the ramp at the salt lick and, so far as I could judge from the spoor, no lion had been near it. I went into the open truck and called to Elsa; after some hesitation she followed me, but placed herself broadside on to the entrance, thus preventing me from getting out or Jespah, who was following her, from coming in. After a time she went back to the tents and hopped on to the roof of the Land Rover. The cubs began to eat and I went over to their mother and started to play with her; as I did so, I noticed that two of the maggot swellings had gone septic. I wanted to deal with them, but each time I touched her she withdrew, and when on the following day I again tried to help her she seemed to be even more sensitive.

I always carry a little sulphanilamide powder with me to disinfect insect bites or scratches but George believes that, while they are very effective for human beings, in the case of animals one should not give such drugs unless there is proof that their own antibodies are not strong enough to effect a natural cure. Because of this, I did not give Elsa sulphanilamide, relying on her natural resistance and thinking that she would lick her wounds clean, as she had often done before when she had been plagued by the maggots.

The lions spent the next day in the kitchen lugga where Nuru and I found them in the afternoon. I sent him off to prepare a carcase at the camp – Elsa managed to keep the cubs away from the goats, even though they were developing an increasing interest in them. Had she not always shown such a co-operative attitude our peaceful truce could never have been maintained.

On this day, too, she showed her usual tact and sense of fair play when the cubs started to ambush me. All they wanted was a friendly game, but their claws were very sharp. Elsa came to my rescue, cuffed her children, gave me too a mild spanking, and generally saw to it that the cubs' surprise at my reluctance to play with them did not develop into animosity.

There could be no doubt about her wish to maintain good relations between all of us. I had another proof of it on the following afternoon. Nuru and I spotted the lions on the Whuffing Rock. As soon as I called to her, Elsa came and joined us and was most affectionate to me – indeed, she seemed to be making the most of the few moments in which we were alone; as soon as Jespah appeared she became aloof. She was plainly determined not to arouse her cubs' jealousy, was always careful in Jespah's presence, and when Gopa and Little Elsa were about it was an understood thing that no demonstrations of affection were ever to take place between us, for they, more than Jespah, had a tendency to be very jealous of me.

We crossed the thick bush towards the river, and Nuru had a difficult time with Jespah, who took advantage of every piece of cover to pounce out at him and try to get his rifle. It was only because Elsa often stood between her son and him that any progress was possible.

When we reached the river, I told Nuru to take a short cut home and get the lions' dinner ready. He sneaked away as quickly as he could, but Jespah was not going to be deprived of his fun, and stealthily followed him. My 'No's' were without effect; luckily I knew I could rely on Nuru's tactics to get him out of his difficulties. He has a unique way with animals and can always be relied on to be kind to them. How often I have watched him using all sorts of tricks to divert their interest when they were being naughty, rather than resort to force or punishment. In all the years he has been in daily contact with them, he has never once suffered so much as a scratch, and there is no doubt he is genuinely fond of his charges. I would rather have him than anyone else to deal with lions.

While Nuru was making his way home, I took the rest of the family back by the river. When we reached the studio lugga Jespah joined us, and by his spirited prancings I could just imagine what fun he had been having with poor Nuru. When we got to camp the cubs pounced on their dinner and Elsa stepped carefully up on to the roof of the Land Rover. Her maggot wounds seemed to be hurting her a great deal, but she would not allow me to touch the swellings, much less press the maggots out.

24. Elsa Is Ill

George had now been away for two weeks on the recce to Lake Rudolf. He had been joined by Ken Smith as well as by the Game Warden for the area. I expected them back any day but almost dreaded to hear the noise of the car, for I feared it might mean the end of Elsa's happy life. What would await her in her new home? How many lionesses might she have to conquer before her territory was safe for the cubs? She loved her home and here she had at least established her rights. She and her children would need to forget this ideal environment and all that was familiar to them before they could begin to be happy in another place. If man with all his capacity to reason often gives tragic proof of his inability to adjust himself to exile, how could one expect wild animals, who are more conservative and more dependent on their territory, to adjust themselves to something completely strange?

Now the lions were in the studio lugga which, flanked by thick bush and overshadowed by large trees, was one of their favourite lie-ups; it provided a cool shelter from the hot sun, soft sand to doze on and usually a slight breeze swept up to it from the river. The family had been there since morning: at teatime I joined them with my sketchbook. As I drew I listened to the chirping of many birds and the soothing bubbling sound of the river. How peaceful it all was, and how contented we were.

When it got cooler, Elsa woke up, stretched herself, walked over to Jespah and licked him; he rolled on his back and hugged her with his paws. Then she came over to me, rubbed her face against mine and licked me too; afterwards she went over to Gopa and repeated her demonstrations of affection, and then went on to Little Elsa. She had greeted each of us in turn, beginning with the one closest to her and ending with the one farthest away. This was her signal that she thought it time to go home. She started off for camp, looking back every few yards to make sure that we were following. We were not very quick off the mark, for first Jespah wished to investigate all my paraphernalia, and I had only just time to rescue my sketching materials and cameras, put them into bags and hang them on a branch out of his reach. Gopa and Little Elsa had gone ahead, and when I followed they blocked my way so cunningly that there was nothing for me to do but sit down and pretend that I wasn't interested in their antics. It was dusk and the mosquitoes had become very active and rendered my involuntary rest rather disagreeable. Luckily for me, Elsa noticed what was happening and came to my rescue. She cuffed her children playfully, after which they forgot about me and followed her, prodding and chasing each other, which enabled me to make my way home.

That evening, for the first time, I saw Gopa show a sexual impulse, first when playing with Elsa and later with Jespah. It was only play and no doubt he was simply moved by a strange instinct, the significance of which he did not understand. I was surprised that this should happen at such an early age; the cubs were only twelve and a half months old and still had their milk teeth.

During the night I heard the family around the camp, and it was not until after breakfast that they scampered towards the doum-palm logs beyond the salt lick, where Elsa stood contemplating the lorry. Very soon she stepped cautiously on to the roof of the cabin and sat down. For ten days I had been waiting for her to do just this, but now I felt sad to see her sitting so trustingly on the lorry which was to take her away from her home.

I joined her and tried, without success, to deal with her maggots. She was licking them, and I saw that she had seven swellings, but, as at times she had had as many as fifteen, I was not unduly alarmed.

After a while, the cubs went off to the bush and Elsa followed; in the afternoon they came back and began playing on the logs. Elsa was very impatient with her children, and eventually took refuge on the cabin roof of the lorry to escape their teasing. It would have been easy for them to follow her, but they preferred to make a wide detour whenever they passed the truck.

All that afternoon Elsa rested on the cabin roof, from which she watched her cubs and me. When I went for a short walk she did not follow me, and when I came back I found her still in the same position. After it got dark she came and lay in the grass in front of my tent, but made no attempt to hop on to the roof of the Land Rover as she usually did. I walked up to her, but was charged by Gopa and Jespah who had been resting nearby in the tall grass.

Early next morning I heard Elsa calling to the cubs in her soft moan, 'Mhm, mhm, mhm'; it was a most comforting sound and always had a very soothing effect on me.

Soon they all disappeared in the direction of the studio lugga; in the afternoon I took a sketchbook and went there. Elsa welcomed me gently and affectionately, and even Gopa showed a sign of friendliness by tilting his head towards me. We spent another lovely afternoon, the cubs playing as I drew. I would have been completely happy but for the apprehension which nagged at me when I thought of the cruel move from which only a miracle could save us. I hoped that Elsa didn't sense my wretchedness and anxiety; she was ill enough as it was with her maggot sores.

When she thought it was time for us to go home she gave us her usual signal by licking each of us in turn. I wondered how long she would be able to maintain the friendly relations which existed between the five of us. For how much longer would I be accepted as a member of the pride? If we succeeded in enabling the cubs to live natural wild lives this would in any case bring the relationship to an end. Our intimate life with the lions had only lasted as long as it had because the threat of attack by poachers had compelled us to stay with the family to protect them. On the other hand, if the lions were not removed to Lake Rudolf the possibility of their taking up a full wild life would be delayed or even become impracticable. This might be inevitable, but for them to be denied their natural life simply so that I should retain my position as part of the pride was too high a price to pay for my privilege.

Elsa was constantly licking her wounds; I hoped this would help to heal them quickly. That night she again stayed in the grass outside my tent and refused to eat. As I was watching her, Gopa came up to me and wished to make friends. This was unusual, and I wanted to respond, but, like Jespah, he had not learned to retract his claws when playing with human beings, so reluctantly I had to disappoint him. I squatted near him, looking him in the face, calling him by his name and hoping that he would understand that even if I would not play with him, all the same I loved him. Jespah brought this awkward situation to an end by bouncing on his brother. The manes of the two lions had grown a lot lately; Gopa's was much darker and nearly twice the length of his brother's; his growl was deep and sometimes threatening. In every way he was a powerful young lion.

Next afternoon I again found the family in the studio lugga. I had brought my sketchbook, but preferred to sit near Elsa and comfort her by stroking her head. She lay quite still and allowed me to pat her, but when I touched her back, or my hand came near one of her sores, she growled and made it very plain that she did not want me to interfere. Her nose was wet and cold; a sure sign that she was ill. Two of the wounds were festering and pus was oozing out of them. I hoped that this meant that they would drain. I still refrained from giving her sulphanilamide, so as not to weaken her natural resistance, and I was so convinced that the maggots were responsible for her condition that I never thought of taking a blood slide and having it analysed to see whether she had any other infection.

When it got dark, Elsa moved into the bush a few yards from the lugga, and when I left for camp she remained there with the cubs. After waiting for some time to see her appear, I became anxious and began to call her. To my relief she soon came up, walked slowly into my tent and gently licked me. Afterwards she went out into the dark and I did not see her or the cubs again that evening.

In the morning, I followed their spoor till I saw the lions on top of the Whuffing Rock. As I did not want to disturb them, I painted the rock from a distance until a cloudburst put an end to my efforts.

In the afternoon I returned and, through my field glasses, saw two cubs on the rock. There was no sign of Elsa and, assuming that she and Jespah, though hidden from my view, were close by,

I called, but there was no response. The lions did not come to the camp that night. This was not unusual, but I felt worried on account of Elsa's condition, so, at first light, I went to the rock. There I was relieved to see all the family on the ridge. I called to Elsa and she raised her head; the cubs didn't move.

At teatime I went back with Nuru; Elsa at once came out of the bush below the rock, followed by Jespah. She greeted us affectionately, but I noticed that she was breathing heavily and that every movement seemed to require an effort. Jespah acted like a bodyguard and made it difficult for me to stroke her. I sat close to her till Gopa and Little Elsa joined us and then we all started for home. Elsa was very impatient with the cubs and evidently extremely sensitive to being touched. If one of her children brushed against her, she flattened her ears and growled. She did not, however, object to my walking beside her and flicking off the tsetse flies, but got really angry when one of the cubs tried to prod her. I had never before seen her react like this. She sat down repeatedly during the short distance through the bush to the car track, but after we reached the track the going was easier. When we got to the camp she went straight to the Land Rover and lay down on the roof very carefully to avoid putting pressure on her sores. She stayed in this position all through the evening. I brought her some marrow, a thing she loved, but she only looked at it and turned away, and when I tried to stroke her paws she moved them out of my reach.

I awoke to hear the cubs chasing each other round the tents, but there was no sign of Elsa. I waited for her familiar moan, but heard only Jespah's high-pitched 'tciang'. I saw him peep through the gate of the enclosure, and as I came out caught sight of Gopa standing on the river bank, about to cross to the far side. When he saw me he gave a startled whuff, plunged in and soon I heard the others greeting him.

Soon it would be four weeks since we had received the

deportation order and it was already three since George had gone on his recce to Lake Rudolf. Before he left, we had planned to start the move on 20 January; today was the 19th; never once had the cubs entered the Thames lorry; the Bedford had not arrived, Elsa was ill, we had not yet found a new home for the cubs or a way of moving them. Plainly, we were going to be far behind our schedule.

25. Elsa's Death

That evening George arrived, but his news was not good.

He and Ken Smith, driving two Land Rovers and a lorry, had first gone to Alia Bay, immediately north of the Longendoti Hills. Alia Bay was the place to which we had taken Elsa on the foot safari which I described in *Born Free*. From this range some secluded valleys run down to Lake Rudolf, and it was one of the areas in which George hoped that we might find a suitable home for Elsa and the cubs. Up to now no one had ever reached these valleys by motor, so the first need was to find a possible route.

George made a pretty comprehensive recce, and his opinion was that Moite offered the only hope, and this only if he could find or make a passable track to it and get permission to rent some land there.

Before returning to Isiolo, he discussed with the District Commissioner of Marsabit the possibility of leasing some land round Moite, and asked for his co-operation to build a sixty-mile road and clear the ground for an airstrip. The District Commissioner gave his consent. We, of course, were to provide the necessary cash. Since the sum involved was considerable, George said he would wait to take a decision until he had discussed the matter with me.

This was the story of his recce.

The prospect of settling the lions near Lake Rudolf seemed very unsatisfactory to me. So I was much relieved that, in the mail which George had picked up on his way to camp, we found letters from the Rhodesias, Bechuanaland and South Africa in reply to our enquiries, all offering alternative possibilities.

Since we had no idea whether the ecological conditions in these areas would be suitable for our lions, George suggested that I should go at once to Nairobi and ask the advice of Major Ian Grimwood, our Chief Game Warden, who knew these localities well. If he should consider them unsuitable, then I would telegraph to the District Commissioner at Marsabit asking him to start work at once on the new road and the clearing of a site suitable for an airstrip. During my absence, George would train the cubs to feed in the Bedford, which was due to arrive, complete with wire enclosure, within a few days.

As there was so little time left, I agreed to go, provided that Elsa was well enough for me to leave her. That evening we did not see the lions, but heard them on the far side of the river. Early next morning we waded to the opposite bank and found the family a few yards from the water. Elsa broke through the dense undergrowth and rubbed herself affectionately against me. I scratched her on the head and behind the ears. Her coat was like velvet and her body hard and strong. I stroked her for a long time; then she greeted George and Nuru, and finally returned to the bush where her cubs were hiding.

George did not think she looked any worse than she had on earlier occasions when she had been infested with maggots, and this relieved my anxiety. However, as she had not eaten for two days, before I left, we placed meat on the river bank; while we did this Elsa watched us from the far side. As she made no attempt to come over and collect it, George floated it across; he had to put it right in front of her before she rose and, without eating anything herself, dragged it up the steep slope and into the thicket where the cubs were.

With this last picture of Elsa helping her children, I reluctantly left the camp for Nairobi; there I received a telegram from George: Elsa worse. Has high fever. Suggest bring aureomycin.

The message had been telephoned through from Isiolo by Ken, who had asked Major Grimwood to tell me that he had already sent the drug to George.

I was terribly worried, but since help was already on the way I decided, in view of the urgent need to make arrangements for the move, to stay one night in Nairobi.

Major Grimwood told me that in the homes offered in the Rhodesias and Bechuanaland the ecological conditions would not suit Elsa or the cubs, therefore he advised us to move the lions to Lake Rudolf. He also suggested that the wire enclosure in the lorry had better be partitioned, since, if we transported the family in a communal crate and one lion were to panic, it might hurt the others.

I telegraphed to the District Commissioner at Marsabit asking him to start on the work which George had discussed with him.

Next morning I got up early, as I had some urgent matters to attend to before leaving Nairobi. When I came downstairs I found Ken waiting for me. He looked tired and dusty, having just arrived from Isiolo with a message from George that Elsa was now desperately ill. George had sent an SOS at midnight, asking for me to return and for a vet to come at once. Ken had got in touch with John MacDonald, the vet at Isiolo, who had left immediately, then Ken had driven the 180 miles to Nairobi to give me George's message. How grateful I was to him.

I chartered a plane and soon Ken and I were on our way to the small Somali village which was the nearest landing strip to the camp, at which we might be able to hire a car for the rest of our journey. We were lucky enough to find an old Land Rover and in it drove the last seventy miles.

We arrived at the camp about teatime, leaving the car some distance away so as not to alarm Elsa. I rushed to the studio. George was sitting there alone, and looked at me without saying anything. His expression told more than I could bear.

When I had recovered from the shock he took me to Elsa's grave.

It was under a tree close to the tents, overlooking the river and the sandbank where Elsa had introduced me to her children. This was the tree on whose rough bark the cubs had learned to sharpen their claws and under the shade of which the family had so often played and where, last year, Elsa's mate had tried unsuccessfully to get his Christmas dinner.

George told me all that had happened while I was away. This is what he said:

After you had left I moved my tent near to the ramp and waited for the family to appear, but that night they did not come. In the morning I was obliged to visit a game post higher up the river, so it was not until the afternoon that I was free to look for Elsa. I saw the cubs playing on the far bank, and then found Elsa lying under a bush a little farther up the river. She got up and greeted me and Makedde. The cubs came along and played around their mother.

I then went back to camp; that night again no lions appeared. Before breakfast I went to look for Elsa; she was lying alone near the place where I had left her the night before. She replied to my calls, but did not get up to greet me. Her breathing was laboured and she seemed to be in pain; she was obviously ill. I returned to camp and at once dispatched the Thames truck to Isiolo with the telegram to let you know that Elsa was worse and asking you to send aureomycin. I also sent a letter explaining the situation.

Then I went back to Elsa with water and a plate of meat and brains into which I had mixed sulphathiazole. She drank a little water but, even in spite of her liking for brains, did not eat anything. I then put some sulphathiazole into the water, but she refused it.

Later I went back and had lunch; afterwards I returned to Elsa and found that she had moved a little way and was lying in long grass. I felt very much alarmed, for she was steadily growing weaker; she would not look at food, and only drank a little water which I offered her in a basin.

To leave her alone for the night was unthinkable, for in her weak state she might have been attacked by hyenas, buffalo, or by a lioness. I therefore decided to spend the night with her, and got the boys to bring my bed over from the camp, also the remains of the goat and a pressure lamp. I spent the night in the bush and kept the lamp burning. The cubs came up from the stream and ate the goat; afterwards Jespah tried to pull the blankets off my bed. Elsa seemed to be a little better. Twice she came up to my bed and rubbed her head affectionately against me.

Once during the night I woke up and found the cubs on the alert looking intently behind my head. Next I heard a loud snort and flashed my torch and a buffalo crashed away into the bush. Elsa lay close to my bed. The cubs were in a playful mood and wanted their mother to join in their game, but every time they came near her she growled.

At dawn Elsa seemed fairly comfortable, so I went back to camp for breakfast and then did some typing.

About ten o'clock I began to feel anxious, and went to look for Elsa. I could not find her; there was no answer to my calls and no sign of the cubs. For two hours I searched up and down the river and at last I found her lying half in the water by a little island near the camp. She looked desperately ill, her breathing was very fast and she was extremely weak. I tried to give her water in my cupped hands but she could not swallow.

I stayed with her for an hour. Then Elsa suddenly made an immense effort and went up the steep bank on to the island, where she collapsed. I called Nuru and got him to cut a path to a place from which it was easy to cross the river. Then, I left Nuru in charge, and went back to camp and improvised a stretcher out of my camp bed and tent poles. When this was ready I carried it back to the island and laid it beside Elsa, hoping that, since she always liked lying on a bed, she might roll on to it. If she did this, I meant, with the help of the men, to carry her across the river to my tent. But Elsa did not attempt to get on to the bed. About three o'clock she suddenly rose to her feet and staggered to the river. With my help she waded across it to the bank below the kitchen. She was completely exhausted by the effort and lay for a long time on the bank. At least now she was on our side of the river and close to the camp. The cubs appeared on the island, having no doubt followed their mother's scent, but they seemed nervous of crossing over.

Stopping twice to rest, Elsa made her way to the sandbank below our tents.

I showed some meat to the cubs, who followed my progress along the other side of the river as I dragged their dinner to the sandbank. Jespah and Little Elsa swam across, but Gopa hesitated until he saw his brother and sister eating, then he ventured to swim over and was ambushed by Jespah as soon as he landed.

For the next two hours Elsa lay on the sandbank with Jespah close to her. Twice she got up and went to the water's edge to drink, but she could not swallow. It was a pathetic sight. I tried pouring water from my cupped hands into her mouth but it just dribbled out again. When it got dark she walked up the narrow path and lay down at the place where my tent used to stand before I moved it up to the ramp.

I tried to give her a little milk and whisky by squirting it into her mouth with a syringe; she managed to swallow some of it. Then I covered her with a blanket and hoped she would not move. I was in despair, feeling sure that she would not last out the night, anxious to send a message to you and worried because the truck was very much overdue. I realized that the only hope of saving her was to get a vet as quickly as possible; on the other hand, I did not want to leave her in case she wandered off in the darkness, in which case it might have been impossible to find her.

In the end, I decided to risk leaving her for an hour and a half, the time it would take me to go to and from a bad ford where I thought the truck might be stuck. Less than two miles from camp I met the truck which had got stuck both going to and returning from Isiolo. The driver had brought the drug for Elsa. I wrote a letter to Ken, telling him that Elsa was in desperate need of a vet and asked him to get in touch with you. Then I sent the driver straight back to Isiolo in my Land Rover.

Fortunately Elsa had not moved. The cubs had arrived and I gave them some meat.

It was impossible to get Elsa to swallow the drug. She had become very restless, would get up, move a few paces and then lie down again. All my attempts to make her drink failed.

At about eleven at night she moved into my tent near the studio and lay there for an hour. Then she got up, walked slowly down to the river, waded in and stood there for several minutes making attempts to drink but unable to swallow.

Eventually, she returned to my tent and again lay down in it.

The cubs came to the tent and Jespah nuzzled his mother, but she did not respond.

At about a quarter to two in the morning, Elsa left the tent and went back to the studio and into the water. I tried to stop her, but she went resolutely on till she reached the sandbank under the trees where she had so often played with the cubs. Here she lay on the sodden mudbank, evidently in great distress, alternately sitting up and lying down, her breathing more laboured than ever.

I tried to move her back to the dry sand of the studio, but she seemed beyond making any effort. It was a terrible and harrowing sight. It even crossed my mind that I ought to put her out of her misery, but I believed that there was still a chance that you might arrive with a vet in time to help her.

At about 4.30 I called all the men in camp and with their help put Elsa on the stretcher and with much difficulty carried her back to my tent. She settled down and I lay beside her, completely exhausted.

As dawn was breaking, she suddenly got up, walked to the front of the tent and collapsed. I held her head in my lap. A few minutes later she sat up, gave a most heart-rending terrible cry and fell over.

Elsa was dead.

The cubs were close by, obviously bewildered and distressed. Jespah came up to his mother and licked her face. He seemed frightened, and rejoined the others who were hiding in the bush a few yards away.

Half an hour after Elsa died, John MacDonald, the Senior Veterinary Officer from Isiolo, arrived. Although George hated the idea, he agreed in the interests of medicine and of the cubs themselves, that a post-mortem should be carried out to establish the cause of death.

When this was over, Elsa was buried under the acacia tree where she had often rested (it stands on the river bank, close to the camp); at George's command the Game Scouts fired three volleys over the grave. The reports echoed back from Elsa's rock; perhaps somewhere in the sea of bush her mate may have heard them and paused.

It was 24 January, 1961.

26. Guardians of Elsa's Children

Now we were the guardians of Elsa's children.

After sunset, I went to the river and sat on the sandbank where, a year ago, Elsa had introduced her cubs to me. I sat there for a long time. Suddenly, from the other side of the river, I heard a faint 'tciang'. Instantly I gave all the calls which I hoped the cubs might recognize, and eventually, through the darkness, caught a glimpse of Jespah peeping between the undergrowth; but he vanished as quickly as he appeared.

I placed some meat in the open where the cubs could see it, but they did not come, nor did they give any response to my calls. The only sound I heard was the howling of an unusual number of hyenas. Later, we secured the carcase near George's tent; but the cubs did not come during the night and as we listened to the sinister chorus of hyenas we became very anxious, for we did not think that they would stand a chance if they were attacked by such powerful predators.

Next morning, we continued our search. We followed the spoor which Jespah had left on the previous evening. It led upstream, to the place near the island where Elsa had collapsed on the day before she died. We took some meat with us, hoping to tempt the cubs back to camp by giving them only a little at a time, but when we saw Jespah, hiding in a thicket and looking hungrily at the meat, we dropped the whole lot. He grabbed it at once, and ate it ravenously. Then I heard a rustling noise and saw Little Elsa about twenty yards away, but as soon as we looked at each other she bolted.

Haunted by the thought of the many hyenas we had heard during the night, we wanted to make the cubs stay close to the camp, so we did not provide them with any more food, hoping that hunger would force them to come to us.

Then, as Ken had to return to Isiolo, we went to see him off. When we returned we took out a ration of meat for Little Elsa and Gopa, but when we reached the place where we had left Jespah, he bounced out of a bush and seized the meat before we could stop him. Feeling sorry for Little Elsa and Gopa, who must, I knew, be terribly hungry, we went back and fetched the remains of the carcase. Attracted by it, Gopa appeared. We then dragged the meat towards the camp and were followed by all three cubs, who were obviously very nervous. We floated the carcase over the river, but the cubs remained on the far bank. For two hours they watched us guarding the meat and calling to them, but made no attempt to swim across. So we fastened the carcase to a tree and returned to camp. Meanwhile, the men had collected three lorry loads of stones from the Big Rock; these we piled above Elsa's grave in a large cairn and we cleared the surrounding ground of grass.

At dusk, George and I went to see what was happening to the cubs. Jespah and Little Elsa were resting placidly by the meat, but Gopa was still on the far bank. Suspecting that he might come over to defend the kill, George began to drag it towards the camp, but was stopped by Jespah, who bounced on it. We returned to the tents, hoping that Gopa might eventually pluck up courage to come over and get his share.

Later, when we were sitting outside George's tent, which was still pitched close to the ramp, we heard Jespah's 'tciang'. Quickly we told the boys to bring another carcase. When they did so, Jespah stalked them but made no attempt to touch the meat and, as soon as it was placed near the tent, he disappeared. We had left the only chain with which we could secure the carcase at the place where we had seen the cubs during the afternoon, so we went to fetch it, but found both chain and meat gone.

When we got back to camp all three cubs were tearing at the kill, but bolted at our approach. Evidently Jespah had come to reconnoitre and then called his brother and sister to join in the meal. From the moment of Elsa's death he always acted as leader and protector to them. It was only after we had gone to bed that the cubs came back and finished off the carcase. At dawn I went in search of them and found all three on the Whuffing Rock; though they saw me they did not answer my calls. I collected George and we stopped on the ridge which faced the rock but was divided from it by a wide chasm, hoping that this would reassure the cubs. They reappeared and for two hours just sat looking at us without stirring. All our attempts to talk to them were met only by their scrutinizing gaze, and I began to feel as though I were on trial for murder. We had to return home alone; and it was long after dark before the cubs arrived. Jespah took immediate possession of the meat and dragged it over to the others who were hiding nearby in a bush.

I went close to them and called softly 'Jespah, Jespah!' He came up to me and allowed me to pat him. I was happy to find myself trusted as I used to be. After this he returned to Little Elsa and Gopa, then I got a stick and, hoping he might play with it, swung it round; he came up and we had a tug-of-war, at the end of which he proudly carried the stick to the other cubs.

They stayed all that night in the camp; whenever I woke up I heard them moving around and also the sardonic laughter of the hyenas.

In the morning, George had to go upriver to inspect a Game Scout post. I decided to keep the cubs company, hoping to gain their confidence by getting them accustomed to my presence during the heat of the day, when they were less active. I found Jespah on the opposite side of the river; he had been dozing under a bush and allowed me to come within a few yards, but watched very alertly every movement I made. After about an hour, he got up and went off. I followed his spoor, which led me to a tree with a large fork which stood on the bank of a deep lugga. Here I caught a glimpse of the other two cubs bolting round a bend.

Suddenly I had a strong feeling that I was being watched. I looked up and saw Jespah sitting in the fork of the tree. He jumped down and ran off to join Gopa and Little Elsa. I stayed for an hour under the tree, so as to give the cubs time to settle down, then I followed and found them at the bend of the lugga, Jespah keeping the rearguard. I approached to within ten yards, then sat down and kept still for another hour, after which I cautiously moved to within three yards of him. Jespah promptly bolted, but when I called to him, he turned, and came very close and looked me straight in the eyes, after which he left the lugga.

It was impossible to see spoor in the long grass, so I walked downstream. Again I had the sensation of being watched and, turning, saw Jespah crouching behind me. I sat down, hoping to encourage him to do the same, but he retreated as quietly as he had approached. I stayed where I was for two hours, and then noticed a slight movement some twenty yards away and immediately afterwards observed two cubs dozing under a bush. None of us moved till teatime, when George arrived, then the cubs disappeared and we caught a glimpse of Jespah running as fast as he could through the dense bush.

All this made us realize that it was entirely due to Elsa that her cubs had ever tolerated our presence. Since her death, they not only refused to answer our calls, but bolted every time they heard or scented us. So as not to frighten them away from camp by our presence, we placed some meat on the sandbank below our tents, and then went in search of plants for Elsa's grave.

Early in the morning, we were woken by the excited chatter of baboons coming from the far side of the river, and got up and crossed to the opposite bank to see what it was about. We soon saw the cubs; they were hiding. We had brought two pieces of meat with us, one of which we gave them; the other we held up for them to see and then carried it back to our side of the river, placing it in their view. I spent the whole morning guarding it against vultures, while the cubs watched me but made no attempt to swim over.

At midday, knowing how hungry they must be, I could bear it no longer and floated the meat across. Jespah at once dragged it into a thick cluster of palm trees. I waded back and, having hidden myself from them, watched the cubs eating voraciously and sometimes going down to the water for a drink. Every time they came into the open they looked round nervously. When the meal was over, I saw Jespah bury the stomach contents and then climb up into a tree. He spent a long time there before joining the others in the bush.

About teatime, George and I went to have another look; we saw the cubs, but they ran away as we approached. After dark the hyenas began howling from across the river and I worried about the cubs, until about midnight I heard their father call. He started from high upstream and gradually came nearer, until I heard him just opposite Elsa's grave. He roared three times, at short intervals. Was he calling Elsa?

It was a clear night, the stars seemed very large and the Southern Cross stood right above Elsa's grave. When their father roared the cubs must have been close to him, for at dawn we found their spoor leading from the camp across the river. We spent all the next day following their pugmarks but did not find the cubs; just before dark, at a point far from the camp, we recognized the spoor of the cubs' father and those of the cubs were beside his.

The next day was occupied by a fruitless search, during the course of which we ran into several buffalo and rhino and were charged by a porcupine. In the way of spoor we noticed only those of a single lion, far downstream, and of a lion and lioness upriver. We wondered whether these might have been made by the fierce lioness and her mate?

In the evening, we tied a carcase to the Land Rover and hoped the cubs might come to it, but we waited in vain.

It was just a week since Elsa had died. We had expected her children to become dependent upon us, but in fact they had avoided us as far as hunger permitted. Looking back, it seems to me as though there had been a pattern running through Elsa's life of which even her untimely death was a part. While she was alive her stigma of being semi-tame was bound to react upon her cubs and diminish their chances of living a natural life. It was because of their mother that they were to be expelled from their home and obliged to live on the grim shores of Lake Rudolf. Now that she was dead, it seemed possible that they might either be adopted by wild lions and allowed to remain where they were or, if not this, then at least permitted to live in a game reserve or a national park, from both of which Elsa herself would have been banned on account of her friendship with human beings. The cubs were just the right age to adapt themselves to either alternative. I wondered whether Elsa, as so often in the past, had not solved a problem in her own way?

Worried by the problem of how to regain the trust of the cubs, who would need our help for at least another ten months, I lay awake that night. It was exactly a year since Elsa had brought them over the river to introduce them to us.

I did not feel well enough to go in search of them again until the following afternoon, then Nuru and I circled the rocks, fruitlessly; on our way home, we tracked a hyena spoor which led to the doum-palm logs near the camp, and there we found the cubs. Jespah followed me back to the tents and allowed me to stroke him while the boys were getting meat for him. When it appeared he pounced on it and dragged it quickly to the other cubs who were hiding. Then, before starting his own meal, he returned to me and placing himself in his safe position, invited me to play with him. He tilted his head and rolled on his back, but as I came up to him made a lightning swipe at me; instantly I jerked back. I had often watched him playfully pressing his sharp claws into his mother's pelt – how could he know that my skin was different? To console him, I rolled an old tyre towards him and offered him a stick, but though he made an attempt to play with these lifeless toys, he soon got bored and went back to the other cubs.

Hoping to find him in a quieter mood after his meal, I waited for a couple of hours and then approached him. Again he gave a quick swipe with his paws, which made any further advances on my part impossible. I tried talking softly to Gopa, but he only growled at me and moved off with flattened ears. Jespah followed him, and then placed himself between the two of us, obviously protecting his brother. Suddenly we were interrupted by a snort from the salt lick. While I collected my torch, Jespah removed the carcase into a thorn thicket.

Although so young, and himself in need of help, he was proving a responsible leader of the pride, always ready to care for his brother and sister.

At teatime George arrived from Isiolo.

We had now received the result of Elsa's post-mortem. She

had died of an infection by a tick-borne parasite called babesia, which destroys the red blood corpuscles. The 4 per cent infection which they found had proved fatal because of the weak condition to which she had been reduced by the bites of the mango flies.

It was the first time that such an infection had been found in a lion.

27. Plans to Move the Cubs

On the day of George's return the cubs only came into camp after dark, Jespah first, followed later by Gopa and Little Elsa. Again Jespah invited me to play with him, and now that George was back I felt that I could risk a scratch, so, overcoming my fear, I held my hand out. Before I knew what was happening Jespah tore open one of my finger joints. It was not a serious wound, but it was bad enough to make me realize sadly that we two could never play together.

George brought the news that Major Grimwood would be passing through Isiolo the next day, so I decided to meet him there, since we wanted to discuss the cubs' future with him. If it were necessary to move them we hoped that he would help us find a home for them in an East African game reserve.

Major Grimwood proved most sympathetic, and promised to contact the authorities of the National Parks of Kenya and Tanganyika.

I brought an old crate back to camp with me. It had originally been made to take Elsa to Holland. Now I hoped to induce the cubs to feed inside it.

This was our plan: the cubs must get accustomed to feeding

in the large communal crate, placed on the ground. Then, one day, when all three were inside, we would close the door and, disguising the tranquillizer in marrow, we would administer a dose in each of the three pie dishes. We would push the dishes through a second door, small enough to prevent the cubs from escaping through it. The cubs would be safe inside the crate during the time the drug was taking effect. This was important, for we didn't want them to wander about in a state of semi-unconsciousness and perhaps become a prey to predators. As soon as they had been immobilized by the drug, we intended to transfer them to three separate crates, specially designed to fit the back of a five-ton lorry.

I arrived about midnight and found all the cubs guarding their meat close to the tents. They did not mind the glare of the headlights, even when I turned them in their direction. We had noticed that though they were so nervous during the day, they showed little apprehension when it was dark. George had to return next morning to Isiolo, so I once more found myself in charge of the camp. I always slept inside my Land Rover when I was alone, and parked it close to the meat as a guard against predators.

On the evening of 10 February, I was very happy to see the cubs chasing each other round the tents after their evening meal, for they had been distressingly subdued since their mother's death, and up to now had kept quiet after eating, just sitting still and watching.

The following evening I placed the crate in position and secured the meat near to it. When the cubs arrived at their usual time, Jespah, after a few suspicious sniffs, went into the crate. Then he came out and settled down near the meat with Gopa and Little Elsa. I talked to them in a low voice, hoping they would gradually learn to associate food with my presence. I now prepared three pie dishes every day, filling each dish with a mixture of cod-liver oil, brain and marrow, hoping in this way to train the cubs to eat separately so that when the time came to give them tranquillizers for the removal trip they would each get their ration of the drug, concealed in the titbits, and avoid the risk of any of them getting an overdose.

During the next three days, the lions kept to their routine – spending the day across the river, at the place where they had last been with their mother, and coming into camp after dark for their dinner. I did not interfere with their routine in any way, hoping that this would reassure them and make them trust me. I felt that I was succeeding when one evening Jespah crossed the river very early, about six, and licked the pie dish clean while I was holding it in my hand. Whenever I said the word Elsa – which I did every time I called her daughter – Jespah looked up very alertly. He and Gopa knew their own names very well. That their sister should share their mother's name was confusing, but I felt that they must get used to it. In case of an emergency it was essential that Little Elsa should know that I was calling her.

After a peaceful evening together I retired into the Land Rover. At about three o'clock in the morning I heard the cubs' father calling in a low voice from across the river. It sounded as though he were talking to the cubs. Later I heard him calling again from the Big Rock, and in the morning Nuru told me that he had found the cubs' pugmarks leading to the rock.

In the afternoon I went out with Nuru to examine the pugmarks and saw that those of the cubs soon joined up with their father's spoor. I did not want to disturb them, so came back and watched two parrots until it became dark.

Jespah arrived about 8 p.m. and was soon followed by the other cubs; until the early hours of the morning I watched them eating and playing and I wondered whether their father was ever going to feed his cubs or teach them to hunt.

George's return on the following day coincided with Jespah's first meal inside the crate. Gopa and Little Elsa watched him but showed no desire to emulate him. However, after we had gone to bed, they plucked up courage and both ventured into the crate to get their dinner. This was a great relief to us. Now that we knew that they were able to overcome their fear of this strange object, we felt that we must at once order the kind of crates in which they could be moved.

We decided to have three sides of the crates made of iron bars, so that during the journey the cubs would be able to see each other and, without being able to do any harm, could give each other moral support. There was, of course, a greater risk that they might get chafed against the bars, but we felt that this physical damage would heal more easily than a mind which had been injured by panic – which might arise when travelling in a dark box. The fourth side of the crates was to consist of a wooden trapdoor.

Having made up our minds about this, I set off to Nanyuki, 220 miles away, to order the three travelling crates. On the way home I passed through Isiolo, where I found a message from a pharmaceutical firm offering to supply medicine which might help the cubs to overcome their present state of anxiety. Since Elsa's death we had received many letters of sympathy, letters which proved how well she had been loved by people all over the world; various officials connected with zoos had suggested taking the cubs, but this was the first practical offer which took their immediate condition into account. I waited in Isiolo until I could meet the representatives of the firm and was much touched by their gift of the antibiotic terramycin in powder form which they believed would strengthen the resistance of the cubs.

I was also extremely grateful for their advice on tranquillizers. Our enquiries had suggested that Librium was the only one which we could risk giving the cubs. Lions are not only highly sensitive to drugs, but are also apt to react to them individually, and therefore unpredictably.

When I got back to camp, George told me that he had had an exciting time while I was away. On the first day the cubs had come in in the late afternoon and, though a lion had called, they had remained by the tent all night. On the following afternoon, he had followed their spoor to the Whuffing Rock, climbed up it and called to them. Finally, Jespah had appeared, sat down near him and allowed George to scratch his head. Then Little Elsa came into view, but remained some distance away; as for Gopa, all he saw of him were the tips of his ears, sticking up behind a rock.

On the way home, George put up three buffalo and one rhino, and was glad that the cubs were not with him. After dark they came into camp and fed off some meat which was chained outside the crate, until Jespah dragged it inside. After this meal the cubs crossed the river and spent the next twenty-four hours playing on the other side. George saw them climbing trees and noticed that they managed to get quite high up. They didn't come in that evening for a meal, so next morning Nuru took the uneaten meat towards the studio, intending to hang it up in his cool bush-fridge there. As he was climbing down the tree, Jespah jumped at the meat and narrowly missed him. Soon afterwards, George arrived and saw Jespah tearing at the hanging meat watched by Little Elsa from the branch of a tamarind tree on the far bank. When Jespah went to have a drink George took the opportunity to cut the meat down; on his return Jespah dragged it to the river and floated it across to his brother and sister.

About teatime George surprised the cubs on a sandbank. Gopa and Little Elsa bolted, and were followed by Jespah. An hour later he waded over and spent twenty minutes calling to the cubs without getting any response, then he noticed a movement high up in the tamarind tree and looking up, saw a leopard perched on one of the top branches; it was busy eating the remains of the meat which it had stolen from the cubs.

Jespah now appeared and started to climb up towards the leopard, who spat and snarled at him. As the thinner top branches were too weak to sustain the cub's weight, Jespah found himself obliged to settle in a fork nearer the ground.

To get a better view, George began to climb up the bank; at this moment the leopard sprang down, passing within a few feet of Jespah. After landing, he made off as fast as he could, with all three cubs in pursuit. George followed their spoor down river until he came upon Jespah, who was looking intently at the treetops around him; but as George could not see any sign of the leopard he decided to leave him and return home.

Long after dark the cubs came into camp and Jespah took his cod-liver oil from a pie dish which George held out to him. Gopa ate his dinner inside the crate. I had arrived by then, and was glad to see that he was getting used to the idea of eating it there.

We were both very proud of Jespah: leopards and lions are natural enemies. Of course a leopard would stand no chance against a fully grown lion and so would give way to it; but for a young cub to tackle a leopard was quite another matter, and Jespah had shown great pluck in the encounter.

I was woken in the morning by soft moans that sounded very familiar – indeed, I could hardly believe that it was not Elsa calling. But in fact it was Jespah telling his brother and sister to stop their morning chase round the tents and follow him over the river. Not long afterwards I heard all three splashing across and then two lions roaring upstream.

Very late that night Jespah appeared for a brief moment: evidently he had come as a scout to make sure that all was safe, for soon he returned with Gopa and Little Elsa. He took the cod-liver oil and let me pat him on the head, muzzle and ears, standing quite still as I did so. After the lights were out George saw Little Elsa join her two brothers in the crate which, with the three cubs and the kill inside it, was rather crowded.

On the following day I again found myself in charge, as George had to leave for Isiolo. In the afternoon, when I saw the cubs on a sandbank near the studio, I observed that Gopa's mane was now very well defined. It was about two inches longer and much darker than Jespah's blond ruff.

All I heard that night were heavy splashings, which sounded like buffalo in the river, and there was no sign of the cubs until the following evening. They were all very hungry, and Little Elsa cuffed her brothers and made it quite plain that she did not intend to be deprived of her share of the cod-liver oil which as a rule they licked up before she had a chance to get near it.

They all still found difficulty in opening a carcase, and as the boys had forgotten to do so that day I waited my opportunity and then went to the cubs' assistance. When Jespah saw me interfering with their kill he charged me. The situation was tricky for a moment as the carcase and I were inside the crate and the cub blocked the exit. Luckily he seemed to realize that I was trying to help them, and waited till I had finished the job; in this he gave proof of a degree of intelligence and good nature which reminded me very much of his mother.

More than twenty-four hours passed before I saw the cubs again; then in the early hours of the morning I heard their father's call, first from close by, and finally from near the Big Rock; and soon afterwards I heard the cubs lapping water out of the steel helmet which was still their favourite drinking bowl. I climbed out of the car to open the crate and give them access to their dinner, but they paid no attention to me and walked off determinedly towards the Big Rock, obviously more interested in joining their father than in having a meal. Was he, I wondered, perhaps helping to provide food for them? During the rest of the night I heard repeated whuffings from the rock, and next morning found the spoor of all the lions leading to it. To my disappointment, by next evening their father had deserted the cubs again; I heard him roaming round, and they came into camp very hungry. In spite of this they waited patiently for me to open the crate and rushed at the meat after I had got inside my 'sleeper'. They finished every scrap I had prepared for them before crossing the river at dawn.

28. Have the Cubs Found a Pride?

One evening, the cubs, for the first time, rested near Elsa's grave. It was a month since it had been made, but although it used to be their favourite playground we had never seen them there or found their pugmarks near it since their mother's death.

This may have been coincidence, or due to the strong sense of smell that lions possess. On the other hand, there is evidence which suggests that animals with a highly developed intelligence appear to have some conception of death.

This is particularly true of elephants. There was, for instance, an elephant who was apparently highly esteemed by his companions. When he died of natural causes two bull elephants stayed by the body for several days, then drew out the tusks and deposited them a little distance away from the body. Another curious occurrence took place when George was obliged to kill an elephant which had become dangerous. He shot it at night in a garden at Isiolo. Next day the carcase was moved because of the smell. On the following morning he found that the shoulder blade of the dead animal had been brought back by his companions and laid on the exact spot at which he had been killed.

We have also come across several instances in which elephants appeared to be concerned about the death of a human being.

On one of our safaris we were told by the local tribesmen that a man had been killed a few days earlier by an elephant and that since then the animal had come each afternoon to stand for an hour or two over the place where the tragedy had occurred. We investigated the facts and they appeared to be true.

On 27 February we found the cubs on top of the Whuffing Rock resting in the shade of some candelabra euphorbias. Jespah came when we called to him, sat close to me and tilted his head, but kept his eyes fixed on Gopa and his sister. After a time Little Elsa came a little nearer to us, but Gopa kept aloof and behaved as though we did not exist. I saw an unusually large tick on Jespah and I was alarmed, fearing that it might carry babesia, but however cunningly I tried to remove the parasite he prevented me and interpreted my actions as an invitation to a game. It was a lovely afternoon, peaceful and timeless; everything around us held memories of Elsa, and how like her Jespah was, with his intelligent expression and friendly, responsible nature. We took many photographs and only went home after the sun had turned a deep red.

As soon as we had come down from the rock Gopa and Little Elsa joined Jespah, and all stood silhouetted against the sunset. They seemed to be watching us intently, but perhaps they were really watching the buffalo who broke cover from the base of the rock as soon as we came near it and crashed past within a few feet of us, fortunately as anxious to avoid an encounter as we were. The cubs remained standing on the top of the rock until finally we were unable to make them out in the fading light.

During the next two nights the cubs stayed away from camp. After hearing a lion calling from the far side of the river, George followed their spoor, discovered that they had drunk at the point where the river comes nearest to the Whuffing Rock, and that after drinking they had crossed to the other side. The next day he found their pugmarks about two miles downstream, close to those of a lion and lioness. All led to the rocky ridge to which Makedde had traced Elsa's spoor last July, after she had been absent for sixteen days.

George circled the ridge and observed that the cubs' spoor stopped at one end of the rocks, while the pugmarks of the lion and lioness stopped at the other.

I could not join George in these searches, for the state of my leg made walking impossible. It was three weeks since I had cut open my shin on a tree stump. At first the wound seemed to be healing, but then it got worse and by now it looked alarming and was very painful. I decided to seek help from the mission hospital in the nearby hills and set off with Ibrahim very early in the morning. As soon as the doctor saw my wound, he took me straight to the operating theatre and he and the matron looked after me with great kindness for two days, and by then I had recovered sufficiently to return to camp. Ibrahim had come to the mission each day with notes from George giving me news of his search for the cubs.

3rd March. The cubs did not turn up yesterday nor during the night. Set off about 7 a.m. down river on the far bank. Saw no fresh spoor until Nuru and I got to the crossing below cataract. There I waded over and saw all three cubs. Jespah came up and sat close to us while the others hid in the bush. We started back towards camp, but as it was the heat of the day I thought the cubs would lie up in the thick under-growth. I returned to the camp, got there about 11.30 a.m. to find that Ibrahim had arrived with news of your operation. He told me that at about 5 p.m. just after crossing the small river between here and the hospital, he saw a big lion and three cubs sitting beside the road. Two of the cubs were male and one female – the same age as Elsa's cubs. Naturally Ibrahim thought they were hers, together with their father.

He stopped the car a few yards away from them. The lion and two cubs moved off a short distance; the third cub sat still beside the road. Ibrahim called 'Jespah, Jespah! Cu-cu-ooo!' The cub tilted its head. Ibrahim opened the door and half got out – still the cub sat. Meanwhile the rest of them appeared and sat down on the other side of the car. Is it not an extraordinary coincidence? If it had not been for having seen our cubs at midday, I would have been convinced that he had seen Elsa's children and would have driven at once to the river. It is almost uncanny. The cubs appeared about 7.30 p.m. not at all hungry. They stayed all night and went in the morning towards Whuffing Rock. Heard two more lions calling up river.

4th March. About 5 p.m. I went to the top of the Whuffing Rock and found the cubs there. Little Elsa was the only one who came out and sat about forty feet from me until sundown. I returned to camp. By 11 p.m. cubs had not arrived, so went to bed. 12.30 a.m. I woke up to find Jespah in my tent. Got up and gave him cod-liver oil and brain, and other cubs ate goat inside the crate. Went back to bed. About 1.30 a.m. was aroused by a startled 'Whuff-whuff' from one of the cubs – a sure sign that other lions were in camp. As I got up, heard growls and squabbling in the nearby bush – then full-throated roars of two lions a few yards away. They roared for a long time in and around camp, until one of them went to the studio, calling in a low tone, and then back along the track towards the Big Rock. More growls and squabbling. Later they moved off towards the kitchen lugga. Afterwards I heard a single moan which sounded like a cub from near the kitchen. A few minutes later the lions were back in camp, and after more roaring I heard them finally splashing through the river and their roars receded downstream.

5th March. At dawn found lion spoor all round the camp and through it. The lions had apparently chased each other on the sandbank where Elsa lay at the time of her death. I followed up the spoor of two cubs on opposite side of river up the ridge towards the Shamba Rock. Lost it and came on the tracks of a big lion going up a gully. Near the rocks where Elsa used to lie I found the spoor of a lioness and cub.

There are two alternatives: the cubs panicked when lions appeared and bolted across river, or they joined up and have gone off with them. The fact that the cubs did not appear in camp until 12.30 a.m. and that they might have come across the river would suggest that they had been with the lions before coming into camp, and that later the lions followed them.

George had to leave for Isiolo on 5 March, the day I returned from hospital. That night no cubs appeared and I did not know whether to be pleased or worried. If they had joined up with a pride and were being taught to hunt by a lioness, then they would go wild before the question of deporting them arose; and this would probably be the best thing that could happen. On the other hand, they might have been driven away from the camp by the wild lions and be in desperate need of help.

The state of my leg made it impossible for me to join Makedde and Nuru in searching for the cubs. I tried to make the best of my handicap by telling myself that it would at least prevent me from interfering, and that this was a good thing because if the cubs had been adopted by a pride any disturbance might cause their foster-parents to abandon them. Still, I did not *know* that they had joined up with a pride and the uncertainty was distressing.

Another two days and nights passed without news of the cubs, then George returned. He at once made a search which proved fruitless. Next morning he and Nuru set out again and found that the cubs had joined up with a young lion or lioness. Feeling sure now that the cubs had been adopted by a pride, George did not pursue them for fear of upsetting the foster-parents.

We began to believe that they had themselves solved the problem of their future, for we had not seen them for twelve days.

29. The Cubs in Trouble

On 16 March George and Nuru left early for their daily search.

I was alone in camp when two Game Scouts and an informer arrived to report that during the night of 13–14 three lions had attacked the bomas of tribesmen on the Tana River and mauled four cows. The Africans had tried to drive them away with stones, fire and wooden clubs, but they had persistently returned. They believed that the raiders were Elsa's cubs and they begged George to come and dispose of them.

I immediately sent the men to contact George, which they eventually did by firing shots. They all returned to camp and after lunch set off for the scene of the raids.

In all there were eight bomas within a short distance of each other; they consisted of groups of small circular mud huts protected by a shoulder-high thorn fence some six feet wide. The country surrounding the bomas was dense bush, which meant that a lion could approach the huts without being seen. The bomas were close to the Tana River, where the tribesmen watered their stock.

George saw the spoor of a lioness; she had entered an almost impenetrable thorn enclosure and then forced her way out of it. He then tried to examine other lion spoor, but had difficulty in doing so as most of the pugmarks were obliterated by cattle tracks. However, he managed to trace the lions back to the place on the river bank where they had drunk. He continued down river expecting to find fresh spoor where they had probably drunk during the preceding night, and was not disappointed, for he came upon new pugmarks recently made by three lions.

With two scouts and a guide he took up this spoor. About an hour later they were casting about in a dry watercourse covered with thick vegetation when suddenly about ten feet away he saw a lioness lying asleep, partly concealed by the trunk of a tree. He watched her for several minutes; she looked like a mature lioness. A scout who was a few paces behind signalled to George and tapped his rifle. He looked at it and found that he had forgotten to load it. Even the clatter of the bolt as he loaded it failed to wake the sleeping animal. In a whisper the scout urged George to shoot, saying that it was a full-grown lioness. It would have been very easy to put a bullet into her brain. But something made George hesitate. Suddenly, the lioness sat up and looked straight into his eyes. She wrinkled her face into a snarl, and, giving a low growl, dashed off. Simultaneously, he heard two other lions break away. He felt convinced that these were not our cubs, but was glad all the same that he had not fired, for how could he be quite certain? He called the cubs by name, but there was no response. Facts which helped to strengthen his belief that these raids were not the work of our cubs were the cunning manner in which the lions had attacked the village and forced their way through the particularly strong thorn fence, and also the apparent ease with which the two fully grown cows had been killed. All this suggested the work of experienced lions.

George told the tribesmen to report any further raids immediately, and then returned to camp.

On the following morning George and Nuru went off in the direction of the mouth of the elephant lugga; he saw two cubs resting on an island in the river, but they bolted before he could focus his field glasses. Simultaneously, he heard more lions breaking away. Following their spoor, he came upon the carcase of a young buffalo which must have been killed the night before. Five lions had feasted on it. George felt sure these must have been Elsa's cubs and their foster-parents. He called to Jespah, and went on doing so for a long time, and thought he heard a faint moan from the far side of the river, but no cub came in sight, so he returned to camp.

The next day a terrible thunderstorm struck and all through that night the downpour continued, and by the morning the river was only just fordable. Nevertheless, an informer managed to get across. He brought a message from the headman of the Tana settlement stating that their stock had again been raided by lions.

On hearing this news George set off in his Land Rover for the scene of the raid. It had been raining so heavily that he was obliged to take a circuitous route. I remained in camp to keep a lookout in case the cubs were still in our area.

Two mornings later I went to Elsa's grave, and while I was there noticed some movement on the Big Rock. Looking through my field glasses, I saw two lions basking on top of the rock. I walked towards them as fast as my injured leg allowed, and soon distinguished three adult lions and three cubs exactly the size of Elsa's children. They were on top of the ridge, outlined against the sky. I watched them for several minutes; they were resting quietly together, one lioness licking the cubs who were rolling on their backs and playing. I took some photographs, but fearing that the distance was too great to get good results, even with my telescopic lens, I cautiously advanced towards the pride. When I was within about four hundred yards of them, the lions became alarmed and one after the other disappeared into the gap where Elsa had started her labour. Only one cub remained behind. It crouched with its head on its forepaws, watching me. This behaviour made me think that it was probably Jespah. Unfortunately, as it sat right against the morning sun, I could only see its silhouette and could not pick out any details to confirm its identity with Jespah. When I tried to come nearer, the cub sneaked away.

The idyllic family scene I had witnessed made me feel happier than I had felt since Elsa's death. Though I could not be quite sure that these were her children with their foster-parents, it seemed too great a coincidence that a pair of lions with three cubs exactly the same age as hers should suddenly have appeared near the camp.

When I returned to the tents I was greeted by two Game Scouts with a letter from George. This is what he wrote:

Got to the settlement on the evening of Sunday 26th, after travelling forty miles over bad roads and eight through thick bush. Managed to get a carcase and sat over it close to a Boma which the lions had raided. No lions came that night. In the morning I made camp some two miles from the village on the banks of the Tana and walked down the river to look for spoor. Saw nothing fresh. Later the Scouts arrived to report that the lions had tried to enter another boma during the night but were driven off. The Scouts had followed their spoor but lost it. Yesterday evening I again sat up over a carcase in a clearing half a mile from this other boma. About 11 p.m. without any warning, Little Elsa suddenly appeared and pounced on the carcase which was fastened to a tree stump. She was followed immediately by Jespah, who had an arrow, fortunately not poisoned, sticking in his rump. Both started to eat. Presently I saw Gopa lurking in the distance. Finally he also came to the meat. They were extremely thin and looked starved. They showed no fear when I talked to

Elsa's grave – we piled up stones in a large cairn and cleared the surrounding ground of grass.

My last day with the cubs at their original home.

Above and below: The crates and arrival in the Serengeti.

Release of the cubs.

Jespah taking cod-liver oil. They had become so greedy for it that we
had been obliged to ration them, in order not to overfeed them.

Jespah with George in the Serengeti.

Jespah on the Land Rover.

A cheetah.

A leopard and its kill.

Left: Elsa's grave after its repair.

Main photo: Zebra.

Opposite page, right: Our last view of the cubs.

Far right: George winches the Land Rover out of a lugga during our search for the cubs – no one could remember such awful rains.

In every lion I saw during our searches I recognized the intrinsic nature of Elsa, Jespah, Gopa and Little Elsa, the spirit of all the magnificent lions in Africa.

Joy and George.

them and finished off the diminutive goat in an hour. They frequently came up of their own accord to the bowl of water I had placed close to the back of the car. I am confident that they recognized my voice and I am sure that they will come again tonight. There is no doubt that it is the cubs that have been raiding the bomas. We will have to pay lots of compensation. Send Ibrahim with your Land Rover at once with all my goats, some more food for me, also my small tent, table, chair and my boxes. I must immediately take on a gang of local men to cut a track, and then we will have to move the whole camp and get a lorry here with crates and finally move the cubs out of this district. But the most urgent thing is to send the goats with Ibrahim. If the river is too high, he will have to go the long way round, but he *must* get here today. The cubs are very hungry and will certainly raid the boma unless I feed them. There is no doubt that all the trouble has been caused by the Fierce Lioness who must have chased the cubs away from Elsa's camp on 4th March.

Yours, G. Please send all my ammunition.

30. Crisis

When I read this I felt as if all my blood were draining away from me. At first I could not get over my surprise at the extraordinary coincidence that a pride with three cubs of the same size as Elsa's should arrive in the area just now and thus deceive us into thinking that Jespah, Gopa and Little Elsa were still around the camp.

Then I remembered the pride to which Elsa, when she herself was pregnant, had given her goat and acted as aunt. Was it possible that the Fierce Lioness was the mother of these cubs, born perhaps just before Elsa's? If so, it seemed likely that the area around the camp had been the territory of this lioness before Elsa's release there. In this case, when the Fierce Lioness discovered a rival – and one that kept strange company with human beings – she might have withdrawn up river and brought up her cubs there. I remembered the day last July, when we were looking for Elsa and thought we saw the family near a baobab tree upstream and were astonished at their strange behaviour. Now I wondered whether we might not have mistaken this lioness, whom we have come to call the Fierce Lioness, and her cubs for Elsa's family. When, later, she had reconnoitred the camp, she had always come from up river. She had come alone, but she might well have preferred to leave her cubs in safety when she was on a scouting expedition. If this supposition were true, then the Fierce Lioness's attacks on Elsa were no doubt an attempt to re-establish her right to her old home. On these occasions she had found us in residence as well, and had retreated. But now that Elsa was dead what could be more probable than that she had jumped at the opportunity to chase her rival's cubs away and take possession of her old territory? However this might be, it seemed almost certain that the pride, this morning, I had taken to be Elsa's cubs was the family of the Fierce Lioness.

This was an anticlimax to the happiness I had felt a few hours earlier, when I believed the cubs were safe and well and exonerated from raiding the Tana bomas.

How they had managed to survive on their own for several weeks, I could not imagine. They were too young to know how to hunt wild animals successfully and they must have gone through a ghastly period of starvation before they came upon the goats which they would regard as their natural food. The angry reception from the enraged tribesmen must have terrified them.

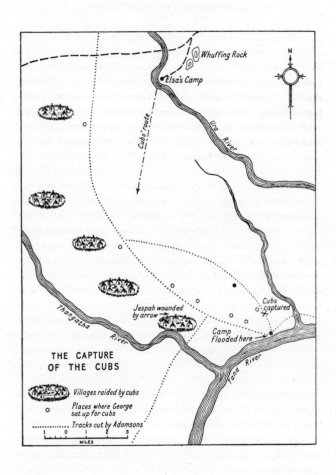

Whuffing Rock

Elsa's Camp

Ura River

Cubs' route

Thangatha River

Jespah wounded by arrow

Cubs captured

Camp flooded here

Tana River

THE CAPTURE
OF THE CUBS

Villages raided by cubs

○ *Places where George
sat up for cubs*

.... *Tracks cut by Adamsons*

1 0 1 2 3
MILES

N

The only hope now was to pay such heavy compensation that they would not be in too great a hurry to get rid of the cubs, and at the same time to find a safe place for the family with the least possible delay.

Since there was no longer anything to keep me in camp, I immediately set off with Ibrahim, a scout as a guide, five goats and all our essential camping material. We were very cramped, and the second scout and the rest of our staff had to take the short cut through the bush on foot.

We jolted along over very rough tracks; the country around looked as though some giant had amused himself by throwing rocks about at random. Now and then we passed small African settlements nestling among enormous boulders; the round earth huts resembled mounds and blended perfectly into the landscape.

We reached the Tana just before dark.

From this point the scout had to guide us on foot over the last eight miles, for the bush was so thick that it was impossible to see any distance ahead or to avoid obstacles.

After two long hours of crashing through the bush, we found ourselves on the bank of a fast-flowing river some 150 feet wide. We took the fanbelt off and plunged down a steep bank, and after a lot of pushing knee deep in water, reached the other side.

Here we found the boma of the headman, but we went on another two miles to George's camp. There we were told that he was sitting up for the cubs. I dropped all my kit and drove on to join him, arriving at about 9 p.m.

While we waited for the arrival of the cubs, intermittently switching on a powerful spotlight to guide them, George told me about Jespah's wound.

On the night of the 25th a number of tribesmen set out to kill the lions. They cornered one of them (in fact Jespah) in the thorn enclosure which protected a flock of goats. The lion had killed two of the goats but before it could get away with its spoil it was surrounded by a band of angry tribesmen, armed with bows and poisoned arrows. The lion took cover in the thick thorn fence, and into this the Africans shot about twenty poisoned arrows. Luckily the fence was so thick that the arrows did not penetrate. Only one shot loosed by a toto found its mark. Fortunately the arrowhead was not lethal, as the toto was too young to be trusted by his elders with the deadly poison.

The arrowhead had luckily not penetrated deeply into Jespah's rump. The barb and three inches of the shaft could clearly be seen running under the skin, one inch of the shaft hung downwards. George hoped that its own weight might cause the head to fall out and, as Jespah could easily lick the wound, there was a good chance of his keeping it free from infection. It did not seem to hinder his movements, nor could it be causing him any pain, since George had often seen him lie on it. The cubs were very friendly and did not object to his presence, but of course there was no question of Jespah allowing him to remove the arrowhead.

George had engaged thirty Africans to cut an eight-mile track along the river; this enabled us to bring up our whole camp in the lorry.

Later we moved the camp, taking care not to site it on the hippo paths.

We then made plans for solving our immediate problem. George decided to sit up at night inside his Land Rover on routes which he thought the cubs would take to reach the bomas; he would have meat placed ready for them. I would do the same at the camp, while the scouts, equipped with thunder-flashes, would protect the various bomas. Should any of us see the cubs we would warn George by firing shots: one if the scouts sighted them, two if I did.

When it got dark, George left for his vigil, but on this night the cubs took a different route, raided a boma and mauled a sheep; before they were able to feed they were driven off by the scouts' thunderflashes.

It rained during the night, which made tracking difficult next day. Hoping to guide the cubs to his Land Rover, George dragged a carcase through the bush to it, thinking they might pick up the scent; but next morning it turned out that only hyenas and jackals had come for the meal. Consequently, next night the cubs tried their luck at yet another boma and mauled two goats; again before being able to eat they were chased off.

The rains were due to start very soon and we were worried because, when this happened, we would be immobilized if we did not have a four-wheel-drive lorry. The old Thames lorry was useless in virgin bush and we could not borrow Ken Smith's Bedford truck for an indefinite time. We also needed a lorry to bring up our camp kit, to help the labour gang and, above all, for the final move when we had caught the cubs. Indeed, for this we should need two lorries; for we saw the convoy as comprising a lorry for the lions, a lorry for our camp kit, and two Land Rovers to carry our personal luggage. It was essential that these cars should not be overloaded in case they were required to tow the lorries through bad patches.

Having talked this over, I decided that I had better go to Isiolo and order a new Bedford lorry, the same size as Ken's, on which the three travelling crates, already ordered, could be loaded.

Next morning, after hearing that the cubs had tried to raid two bomas but had been driven off before doing any damage, I started off with our faithful Ibrahim.

When I enquired about ordering a new Bedford lorry, I was told that delivery would take about three weeks. This was very inconvenient, so I asked if in case of an emergency we could hire a truck from a safari firm. This I was told was possible, and after making the necessary arrangements I started back in Ken's truck to Elsa's camp to pick up the kit we had left behind and to sleep there.

The night was very still and the soft moonlight blended everything into a peaceful harmony. I lay awake and late in the night heard the cubs' father circling the camp, whuffing, and afterwards moving to the Big Rock, finally crossing the river. This was the last night I spent in our old camp, which had been like a home to me.

We arrived about teatime, at the Tana, and George greeted me with the news that although he had tracked every day and sat up every night he had not once seen the cubs, but each night they had raided a boma.

George looked worn out with sleepless nights, anxiety and the worry of knowing that his work was piling up at Isiolo, but while the present crisis lasted he could not leave the Tana for a single night.

Next morning a tracker reported the spoor of a single lion heading in the direction of Elsa's camp, but he had lost the pugmarks eventually by the river opposite the scout post.

That evening about 9 p.m. as George was sitting up over the meat, he suddenly saw Jespah and Little Elsa. They were terribly emaciated and the arrow was still in Jespah's rump. Neither, however, seemed nervous, and Jespah licked the cod-liver oil out of the pie dish which George held out to him. They ate ravenously and did not leave till 5 a.m. After this, we thought it likely that Gopa had deserted his brother and sister and that it was his spoor the tracker had seen heading in the direction of the old camp.

George spent the rest of the day paying out heavy compensation to the tribesmen; in the evening he waited at a place close to where he thought the cubs were lying-up. It rained all night; the cubs did not appear. Instead, they had gone to the spot where they had seen him the night before, and not finding him there had raided three bomas, killed two goats and mauled six others. In the morning the trackers who were following the spoor caught sight of two bolting cubs.

Later a scout arrived from Elsa's camp and reported that during the night of 5/6 April a young lion had been there and left pugmarks all over the place where George usually pitched his tent; afterwards he had gone off towards the Big Rock. On the following night he had returned in the company of a big lion. The latter did not come into camp but crossed the river. The young lion had gone first to the tree we used as a 'bush-fridge', then to Elsa's grave, and finally into the old crate. This confirmed our belief that it must be Gopa. No doubt disgusted at being chased out of the bomas before he could get a meal, hunger had prevailed over his natural timidity and he had made the journey home on his own, hoping to find us in camp with a square meal ready for him.

If Gopa were to act as a guide to the other cubs and induce them to return to Elsa's camp, this would greatly facilitate our task.

That night the cubs passed within a hundred yards of George, on their way from a boma where they had eaten part of a dead goat which the tribesmen had thrown out. We were desperate. All we could do was to reinforce the thorn enclosures around all the bomas and set scouts to guard as many of them as possible.

During the next day the atmosphere was heavy with rain and after I went to bed it started to pour. I felt worried about George, sitting up in this deluge in his small tent surrounded by lions; also the hippos' booming sounded very much closer to my tent than I cared for. But in spite of these anxieties, I dozed off.

I woke suddenly, conscious of a rhythmic swish-swishing noise, but as it was mixed up with the drumming of the rain on the canvas of my tent and the roaring of the flooded Tana a few feet away, I could not make out what it was – perhaps a broken branch brushing against my tent. I paid no further attention to it. Then one of my tent-poles collapsed. I flashed my torch and saw that the swishing noise was made by waves lapping against my tent.

We had pitched camp about nine feet above the normal water level; within three hours the waters of the Tana had risen by this amount. In whatever direction I looked I could see nothing but water. By the beam of my torch I could see that the hinterland was already a swamp pocked with deep pools, and this was the only place to which we could move – if the river did not get there first; another foot rise, and the water would sweep over it.

I was near to panic. I yelled to the boys, but their tents were about two hundred yards away, and in the thundering roar of the Tana they could not hear me. I ran over to them as fast as I could. The flaps of their tents were tightly fastened and they were all sound asleep in what were now proper traps. Indeed, if I had not reached them when I did, they might all have been drowned.

As soon as they staggered out, they realized the danger. First they pulled down George's large tent, which held our rifles, medicines, food and kit. It was already half-flooded, so we dumped all we could snatch in the hinterland and then pulled down my smaller tent. My torch was the only one which worked, but soon this too dropped into the water and was useless. I thought how lucky it was that Ibrahim was here, for he organized the panic-stricken men and got most of our kit out of the torrent.

We were safe for the time being, but I realized that unless a miracle happened it would only be a matter of minutes before the hinterland, our only refuge, was also flooded.

I stuck a stick into the mud to mark the water level, and watched it anxiously. I could hardly believe my eyes when I saw that the water remained at the same level; the flood had reached its full height just before it would have carried our camp away.

Quickly, we set about rescuing George's Land Rover, which was temporarily out of action and half covered by the flood. Luckily it was close to a tree and, with an improvised pulley, we were able to hoist it and keep it suspended above the water, so that it could not be swept away. Again, I was glad that Ibrahim was there to help with the operation. When it was completed we waited, drenched and exhausted, for dawn to break.

At first light George arrived, stiff, cold and wet. He told us that before the rain started Jespah and Little Elsa had arrived and eaten an enormous meal and left soon afterwards. When the downpour began all the tent-poles gave way and the tent collapsed on top of George. For the rest of the night he had huddled beneath the wet canvas. He felt very uneasy, for if the cubs had returned to investigate the wreckage he would have been quite helpless. But Little Elsa and Jespah were, as it later proved, otherwise occupied, for in spite of having eaten so heartily they had gone off to a boma and killed a goat.

By breakfast-time the river had fallen six feet. Scanning the lashing waves with field glasses, I saw amongst the debris a dinghy perched upside down on the top of a tree growing on one of the islands. I also observed a beautiful Goliath heron on the opposite bank; he was smashing a fish in rapid strokes against a rock. I thought how hard he had to work to prepare his breakfast.

31. Preparations for Trapping the Cubs

I laid out our soaked belongings to dry in the sun, while George went in search of the cubs. He did not find them but that night, as he sat up in my car with a meal ready, Jespah and Little Elsa arrived, ate ravenously and stayed till 11 p.m. In the early hours of the morning George heard both cubs roaring. So far as he knew, this was their first attempt, and though the sound was a little immature, it was quite a creditable performance. We wondered whether they were calling to Gopa – or asserting their right to their new territory.

On the following night the two cubs came in early, ate half the meal George had prepared for them, and then, when it started to rain, went off and apparently out of sheer devilment attacked a boma, killing three goats and mauling four more.

The next evening, on his way to the cubs, George got bogged down in the mud. When he arrived he found Jespah and Little Elsa waiting for him, and for some time he sat in the dark and heard them contentedly eating the meal he had provided. Later, when he switched on his headlights, he was surprised to see three cubs. Gopa must just have arrived, for he was formally greeting his brother and sister. When this ceremony was over, he got down to the meat and would not let the other cubs come near it. He must have been very hungry, but looked fit. He had been away for over a week, and George thought that during this time he must have had at least two good meals or he would not have been in such good condition. All the cubs took their cod-liver oil, after which they went off in the direction of the bomas. George fired a warning shot, so the scouts were on the alert when the cubs arrived and greeted them with thunderflashes which scared them off.

Although, up to now, the cubs had not collaborated in our plans to catch them in the crates, we thought it essential that everything should be ready for their capture. Day by day the weather was getting worse, and it was vital that we should get the crates up before the rain made transport by lorry impossible.

To collect all the things we required, I set off with Ibrahim for Isiolo; there I heard from Major Grimwood that after negotiating with a number of game reserves he had obtained permission for us to take the cubs to the Serengeti National Parks in Tanganyika. I was most grateful to him and extremely pleased, for the Serengeti is famous for lions and an abundance of game; I felt that we could not have found a better home for Elsa's cubs.

I wrote to the Director of the National Parks, thanking him for his generous offer and pointing out that for a month or two at least the cubs would still need our help, since they were only sixteen months old; and a short time ago still had their milk teeth and would not be able to hunt independently until they were two years. Of course I also mentioned that Jespah had an arrow in his rump.

It rained without stopping while I was at Isiolo and I itched to get back before we were cut off by the floods. When I finally arrived, complete with three crates and a lorry, George told me that the cubs had come to him during each of the four nights I had been absent, and that though they had tried to make some raids they had been driven off before any damage was done. The precautions he had taken – reinforcing the thorn enclosures, guarding the most vulnerable homes with scouts and giving a warning shot when he suspected that the cubs were bent on mischief – had proved successful.

George described how on one occasion he had given the cubs two guinea fowl. This had immediately started a fight; with guinea fowl available they showed no interest in the carcase he had put out for them. He said that Little Elsa was limping badly, probably from a thorn in one of her pads, but as she was as wild as ever he could do nothing to help her.

The cubs were now in excellent condition. Jespah still carried the arrowhead in his rump, but it did not appear to cause him any discomfort or interfere with his movements. They had recovered their trust in George and were quite at ease as he walked amongst them while they fed, refilling their water bowl and their pie dishes of cod-liver oil. Nor was it only during the hours of darkness that they proved trustful. The day before, in broad daylight, George had come upon them asleep under a bush. They had shown no alarm and only slowly moved a short distance before settling down to sleep again.

This was certainly an improvement, but we still felt as though we were living on a volcano. The bush all round us was swarming with herds of goats and sheep and these herds were in the charge of small children. The sooner the cubs were captured and removed the better for everybody.

To this end, we cleared an opening in the bush close to the place where they were in the habit of lying-up during the day. There we placed the three crates side by side. George suspended their trapdoors by ropes running through pulleys fastened to a straight tree-trunk which he had secured horizontally above the crates by driving both ends into the forks of the two trees between which the crates stood. Having done this, he then brought the ends of the three ropes together and spliced them into a single rope; this he tied with a slip knot to a tree about twenty yards in front of the crates where he intended to wait inside his Land Rover. Thus, if the three cubs entered separate crates, all he had to do was to release the rope and all three trapdoors would fall simultaneously.

The first thing to do was to accustom the cubs to feed in the crates, and then wait for the critical moment. For eleven nights now they had come more or less regularly to be fed by George, so to entice them from the vicinity of the bomas and in the direction of the traps, he gradually moved the place at which he fed them towards the crates. When he had lured the cubs to within a quarter of a mile of them he attached two carcases to the Land Rover and when the cubs appeared slowly towed the meat towards the box-traps.

The cubs did not show any fear of the large boxes – Gopa even sat inside one of them while he ate his meal.

At last it looked as though we might capture the cubs fairly soon.

Meanwhile, we wanted to remove the arrowhead from Jespah's rump. George had asked the elders who could still remember tribal warfare how they used to extract arrows embedded in flesh. They said that they twiddled the shaft and thus loosened the barb with less damage to the flesh than if it were pulled straight out. We didn't think that Jespah would allow us to do much twiddling, so George invented a device consisting of a larger copy of the barb, with razor-sharp edges. This he hoped to slip under the arrowhead and then pull both out together without enlarging the wound more than was necessary. To do this would involve confining Jespah in a crate and then using a local anaesthetic of the freezing-spray type. George hoped that it could be done after the three cubs were trapped and before they started the journey to the Serengeti. So, to get the spray, and some chains for our four-wheel-drive vehicles, I set off for Isiolo with Ibrahim. We travelled in Ken's Bedford lorry which needed repairs and had some nasty moments when the huge five-ton truck skidded on the wet road. The sky was black and there was plainly more rain coming, so I was in a great hurry to get back before conditions got any worse.

Luckily it only took me one day to make my purchases. I also rang up Julian McKeand who promised to join us next morning to help with the capture. Then I rang up John Berger the Naro Moru vet and one at Nairobi, both living along the route we should take with the cubs, and asked them if they would operate on Jespah if we passed at a convenient time, for I was doubtful whether the freezing spray would take effect on Jespah's thick pelt and didn't want to risk an operation that might be a failure.

When Julian arrived, I told him how we planned to capture the cubs. He advised fetching the large communal crate from Isiolo. He thought it might be much easier to catch the cubs in this and afterwards move them into separate crates, for he doubted whether they would each simultaneously enter a separate crate. We could not of course risk trying to capture them separately, as the first to be caught would be certain to warn the others.

So we loaded the lorry with the cumbersome communal crate, filled with as many goats as it would hold; Julian took his Land Rover so that he could move independently.

During the night the rain poured down as though it were coming through a hose. All along the road cars were slithering about in and out of deep ruts, their drivers fighting to avoid landing in a ditch or colliding with other vehicles; sudden cloud-bursts made the situation still worse. Long before we reached the river, the roaring of its torrent told me that we were not going to be able to get across. Nearly nine feet of raging water was flowing between the steep banks. All we could do was to camp beside the river for the night and hope that by next day the level would have fallen.

But in the morning we saw that the water instead of falling had risen to a still higher level. There was nothing to be done except send two scouts across country – a distance of not more than fifteen miles in a straight line through the bush – to tell George of our predicament and to ask him to send us his Land Rover along the newly cut track and, when the water receded, to tow us across. We then settled down to wait for our rescue party.

32. The Capture

Among the mail I had collected at Isiolo I found press-cuttings with most alarming headlines. *Elsa's cubs may have to be shot. Death threat to Elsa's cubs. Elsa's cubs sentenced to death.*

I was terrified. The reports stated that Major Grimwood had told reporters in Nairobi that he had instructed George to try to capture the cubs and transfer them to a game reserve, and that if he failed to do so he must shoot them. That Major Grimwood should tell the press that he was giving such an order without first informing us was utterly unlike him. I felt sure then, as I afterwards discovered to be true, that the press had misunderstood what he had told them.

I knew, of course, that if the cubs scratched anyone, even slightly, they would be sentenced to death; mercifully they had not done so, but it was vital to move them as soon as possible, and meanwhile we had to remain inactive, facing the unfordable river.

Suddenly the rain stopped. Ibrahim and I anxiously watched the water slowly subsiding. As I feared that the scouts, making their way on foot to the camp, might have been delayed, I suggested that Julian should drive as near to the camp as he could, taking Ibrahim with him so that when they could go no farther in the Land Rover Ibrahim could walk the rest of the way and deliver my message to George.

They set off, and after the car had reached its limit, Ibrahim plodded for many miles waist-deep through slush and, as I expected, reached the camp long before the scouts turned up. George sent Ibrahim back to us in his Land Rover, and at noon the next day we saw him waving cheerfully to us from the opposite bank.

When we reached the far bank we left the lorry and driver behind to follow later, squeezed into the Land Rover, and were soon bumping along the newly cut track.

Soon after his arrival, George took us to see the box-traps and demonstrated his device. We were very much impressed when, as soon as he released the rope, the three doors crashed down simultaneously like guillotines, leaving a small gap to accommodate a protruding tail if necessary. No professional could have designed a better way of trapping the cubs, and I felt very proud of him.

He told us that the cubs had come every night and that each had entered a crate to eat the meat he had placed in it. Jespah had even spent a whole night inside one of them. The trouble was that sometimes two cubs would go into the same box; or if all three were in different crates, then a head or a rump would protrude beyond the door, making it impossible to use the guillotine device. Would they ever, all three, be at the same time in a position which would make it possible for us to capture them?

We were full of hope that our anxieties might be nearing an end when the mail brought us a bombshell. George received a letter from the District Commissioner in whose area we now stayed, containing an ultimatum to capture the cubs within a stated period. The DC added that he was sorry to have to give this order, but since the situation was being exploited politically he could not give us his support after this date.

We were most distressed; for although we believed that we were nearing the time when we might hope to capture the cubs, we were working under great handicaps: my injured leg, sickness amongst our staff, the fact that though George had recently handed in his resignation, so as to be able to spend all his time with the cubs, this could not take immediate effect and he might be obliged to return to Isiolo, then Julian had had to leave and, finally, there was the possibility that at any moment heavy rains might stop us. The one satisfactory thing was that for the last nine days the cubs had ceased raiding bomas and had come every night to George for their food.

It was 24 April. I had not seen them since 27 February, when Jespah had played with me on the Whuffing Rock. In the hope of seeing them again I joined George and after parking my car close to his, I prepared lumps of meat in which I concealed doses of terramycin and placed them inside the crates with the carcases. Then we waited inside our Land Rovers.

Soon after dark I felt something brush against my car – it was Jespah. Silently he went straight to the crates, apparently unperturbed by finding a second car on the scene. He ate two of the titbits containing terramycin and then walked over to George, who was standing outside his car holding out a pie dish of cod-liver oil. The cub licked it clean and then returned to his dinner. He showed no surprise at seeing me, and when I called 'Cucucoo' very softly, only cocked his ears for a moment and then went on with his meal. He had grown enormously and filled out, though he remained, like Elsa, a lion of slender build. The arrow was clearly visible under the skin of his rump, and the open wound was discharging a little, but it was not swollen and looked clean. From time to time he sat down and licked it. I was glad that it did not seem to hinder his movements.

Suddenly I heard a rustling in a bush behind my car and, flashing my torch, caught a glimpse of Gopa, some twenty yards away. For a quarter of an hour he remained there in hiding, then he was joined by Little Elsa. I called 'Cucucoo' to them, but so far from encouraging them, this caused Gopa to bolt twice, but in the end he could not resist the smell of the meat and cautiously sneaked up to the crates. He ate the lumps of meat and cleared out both pie dishes of cod-liver oil before he started on the carcase. Little Elsa was extremely shy, and it was long after midnight before she ventured to approach the crates. By then all the terramycin and the cod-liver oil had been eaten by her brothers.

All the cubs were in good condition. Having seen the photographs George had taken of them when he had first found them on the Tana, which showed them as pathetic skeletons, I realized what an incredible job he had done. That they were now in splendid health and that their trust in us had been restored was entirely due to his patience and ingenuity. We watched them eating until 4 a.m. when they departed with heavy bellies.

Next morning we were obliged to send Ibrahim to Isiolo with urgent mail; the weather looked forbidding and we could only hope that he would not be too long delayed by his 400-mile journey over slippery tracks.

That evening the cubs did not appear. We tried not to worry by reminding ourselves that after last night's large dinner they did not need one this evening. During the night I heard a lion roar. We could not go out spooring next morning because heavy rain had washed away all pugmarks. I was relieved when Jespah arrived at dark; but he paid us only a fleeting visit and about an hour later I heard him calling from far away. Meanwhile Gopa had put in a short appearance and hearing the call – trotted off. Eventually all three cubs arrived. Soon afterwards a lion roared, but they paid no attention to him. Jespah and Little Elsa were inside separate crates busy with their dinner. Gopa visited them in turn, but finding himself unwelcome, sat down sulkily at the entrance to the third crate. Would he enter it? Should we be able to release the trap-doors and capture the cubs? The suspense was nerve-racking and increased by our fear that the lion we had recently heard might in time induce the cubs to follow him. If they did we should be unable to protect them from the death warrant or from the tribesmen's arrows.

The following night we again had cause to worry for at the first roar the cubs stopped eating, listened intently, dropped the meat and rushed off in the direction from which the calls came. They all returned later to finish their meal; but we could not help wondering whether they would always come back.

Ibrahim returned with the news that the new Bedford would not be ready for ten days. Another new worry was that whenever heavy rains fell – and they fell frequently – the roads were now to be officially closed to traffic.

Meanwhile our trackers had come in and reported that the cubs' spoor led in the direction of the wild lion. If we waited for the weather to improve and for the Bedford to arrive when the roads were reopened, the cubs might well by then have wandered off with the local lion and run into disaster.

That night they did not appear. I could imagine them having fun with their new friend, but I could also visualize the period of their reprieve running out. The one good factor was that in our area it had not rained for two days. The official closing of the roads operated on the basis of local conditions so that, if the rain held off and if the cubs *did* enter the crates, the weather at least would not prevent us from moving them from this area.

We spent the day improving the trapping device, rehearsing our parts in the capture and sharpening the scalpel with which George hoped to extract the arrowhead. In spite of these occupations the hours seemed to drag until it was time to sit up for the cubs.

I had barely finished putting the terramycin into the meat lumps when Jespah appeared. He ate two of them and then came and sat in front of our cars and watched us. Meanwhile his brother and sister entered separate crates. A little later they came out and lay near Jespah. They looked very lovely in the bright moonlight and I longed to remove them from the dangers which were increasing. But as if to mock me, the lion chose this moment to roar, and the cubs went off like a flash. I heard a hearty curse from George's car; another of the few remaining nights was lost. Resigned, I went to lie on my bed, asking George to call me when it was my turn to keep watch, or before that, if anything should happen. I felt very depressed but was so tired that I dozed off.

Suddenly I was woken by the crashing of the crate doors. A deathly silence followed; it was as if all life had suddenly stopped. After a short time the struggle inside the crates began.

Simultaneously George and I ran to them, quickly removed the wooden blocks we had placed below the doors to prevent any damage to protruding tails, and closed the narrow slits so as to remove any opportunity for leverage and make an attempt to escape impossible.

Although it was an immense relief to know that the cubs were now safe, both George and I felt disgusted at the deception we had practised on them. Very grateful for the way in which George, single-handed, had effected the difficult capture, I kissed him, but he only gave a sad smile.

33. The Journey to the Serengeti

Now there was no time to lose if we wished to reduce the cubs' time of discomfort and bewilderment to a minimum. George remained on guard and I went back to camp, woke the men, told them the news, then, together, we hurriedly packed up, so as to be ready to hoist the cubs on to the truck at first light.

Dawn crept across the still moonlit sky and a new day began which was to mark a great change in all our lives.

When all was ready we drove the five-ton Bedford to the crates. George told me that after Jespah had recovered from the shock of finding himself trapped, he had calmed down and spent most of the night sitting quietly in his box. Little Elsa had followed his example, but Gopa had gone on fighting for a long time. Now he was growling savagely at our boys, who had come to help in hoisting the crates on to the truck.

Although we had told the tribesmen not to come near the lions, a chattering crowd soon collected. This terrified Gopa, who in his struggles broke one of the ceiling planks of his cage and split two others. We immediately covered the gap with a groundsheet, fixed iron bars across it and tied them on with thick ropes. Then we hoisted the crates, each of which weighed well over 800 lb. During this operation the Africans to induce the necessary impetus shouted in rhythm, which terrified the excited cubs. As the heavy boxes, lifted by block and tackle, dangled in the air, the horrified lions paced to and fro, causing the crates to sway alarmingly. We hoisted Little Elsa first; her crate placed lengthwise to the side of the truck filled half its breadth. Gopa we placed alongside her, and his crate filled the other half. Both their wooden doors faced the back of the driver's cab. Jespah's crate we placed broadside across the end of the lorry. In this way the cubs had the fullest view of each other, only separated by the bars of the cages. It also had the advantage of making it possible to get at Jespah easily from the rear of the truck, so that we could try to extract his arrowhead as soon as an opportunity arose. For the moment there was no question of operating on him, as he was far too excited, but we hoped that later on either we or a vet might be able to remove it.

In their present state the cubs would not touch any food, so there was no chance of giving them tranquillizers. Luckily we knew that they had all had a good meal, and we had secured meat in each crate, as well as a water container which we refilled before covering the lorry with a groundsheet to protect the cubs from any low branches which might hit the truck during the journey.

We were ready to move; I took a last look to make sure that everything was in order: Jespah's expression of despair was almost unendurable. Leaving the jabbering crowd behind, we proceeded in convoy.

The first fourteen miles were very rough, the trucks bumping over boulders as they wound their way through dense shrub along the newly cut track. In spite of the shaking the cubs lay down and took the drive well.

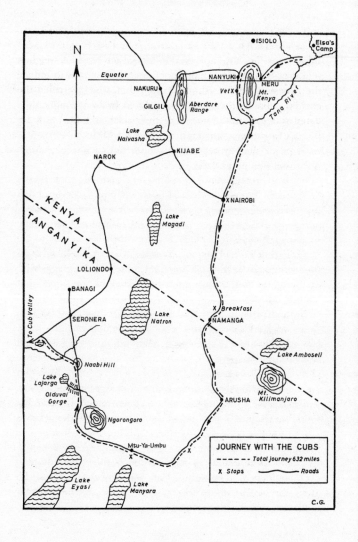

JOURNEY WITH THE CUBS
- - - - Total journey 632 miles
X Stops ———— Roads

We found the river still in flood, but just fordable. My Land Rover and the lion lorry crossed safely, but messed up the banks so badly that the other cars couldn't make the gradient and had to be towed by the lion truck.

Heavy rain clouds were gathering on every side; we were surrounded by a threatening black wall. Skidding through mud, we raced this colossal storm for sixty miles and won only by a hair's breadth. At dusk we reached the District HQ, left a message for the District Commissioner telling him our good news, and then pressed on.

When we passed the boundary of the district I took a very deep breath: the cubs were now outside the jurisdiction of the death sentence. Looking back at the deluge which was following close behind us, I realized how narrowly we had escaped being imprisoned by floods.

Altogether we had about 700 miles to travel. From now on most of the way lay through highlands which rose to 7,500 feet. We had started at an elevation of 1,200 feet, and had now reached an altitude of 7,000 feet. Although we were actually crossing the Equator, it was bitterly cold. Above us, Mount Kenya's ragged, ice-covered peaks rose to 17,000 feet; they were covered with heavy cloud and drizzling rain fell upon us as we went along its base.

Up to now our little convoy had kept close together, and if one vehicle lagged behind we waited for it. It was nine in the evening before we reached a little township where there was the vet who might be able to operate on Jespah.

Even though the hour was so late, John Berger very kindly offered to try to extract the arrowhead there and then; but he was unable to do so because Jespah, when he saw the stranger, got into a rage and would not allow him to come near enough to administer the anaesthetic. The vet comforted me by saying that he thought if we waited for two or three weeks the arrow might well slough out by itself. In any case, the wound was only skin-deep, looked perfectly healthy and was not interfering with any vital function. In case the arrow did not come out of itself, he lent me some extra long bullet forceps, gave me some antiseptic, and suggested that we might be able to pull it out later on, if Jespah allowed us to perform the operation. We gratefully accepted the vet's offer of coffee, as we had had nothing to eat or drink since breakfast.

Warmed up, we pushed on. The weather got worse, the drizzling rain turned to a real downpour and it became icy cold. We stopped often to fasten the flapping tarpaulins to the cubs' lorry, and I felt very sorry for them when I saw them crouching in the farthest corners trying to avoid the drenching rain. All through the night we were at an altitude of 5,000 feet, and I feared they might develop pneumonia. Twice we were held up by Askaris (African police) who were searching for a criminal, and it took us some time to convince them that there was no one concealed in our lorries – only three lions who had never harmed a human being.

We reached Nairobi at 3 a.m. and filled up the tanks. When the sleepy staff at the petrol station saw our lions they seemed to think they must be dreaming, and I didn't like to imagine what our passage through towns during daylight was going to be like.

The hours between 3 a.m. and daylight were a great strain on all of us. As we crossed the Kajiado Plain there were gusts of icy wind and several cloudbursts. Our drivers were worn out by their efforts to keep their vehicles on the slippery road. I took over from George, who couldn't keep his eyes open. This part of the journey must have been torture to the cubs.

Dawn found us a few miles short of Namanga, close to the Tanganyika border. Here we allowed ourselves a brief rest and warmed ourselves with hot tea. The cubs were completely exhausted and lay apathetically in their cages, their faces chafed by the constant friction against the bars. The meat inside the crates was very high and covered with maggots, so we tried to remove it with iron scrapers which we had equipped ourselves with for the purpose, but the carcases had been so securely fastened to the bars that we could not move them. All we could do was to give the cubs fresh meat and water, in which they showed no interest.

To reduce the length of their misery as much as we could we decided that I should drive full speed ahead to Arusha, a hundred miles distant, announce our arrival to the Director of the National Parks, and find out the location of the release point in the Serengeti. (Because our move was taking place over a weekend, we had had no chance of sending a warning telegram.) George would follow with the cubs at a slower pace and we would meet at a short distance outside the town, where we should avoid a crowd of curious spectators.

It was a lovely morning, and I watched last night's clouds disperse, to disclose Mount Kilimanjaro rising above the early mist. Its cap of newly fallen snow looked so ethereal in the soft morning light that it was difficult to believe that it was a glacier-crowned volcano. I have often admired Kilimanjaro from a distance, and I have climbed to its summit, but today more than ever it seemed a manifestation of glory, remote from the troubled world of man; part of the grandeur of an unspoiled creation of which animals were an integral part. With this thought in my mind, I was sorry to see only three giraffe and a few impala antelope on plains where a few years ago wild life abounded. The increasing traffic along the new tarmac road had driven the animals away, and I reflected that at the moment I myself was one of these destructive motorists; but at least my presence was justified by the hope of providing the cubs with a natural life, unthreatened by man. I thought too that the length of time during which sanctuaries such as the national parks will be able to give refuge to wild animals will depend not only on the sympathy and active help of a few dedicated people, but on the support of all who live in Africa, whatever their race may be. This made me all the more determined to use the money coming to me from the sale of books about Elsa and her cubs to subsidize preservation schemes.

At Arusha, I saw the Director of the National Parks and we discussed the locality of the release point. I was surprised when he suggested Seronera as it is the HQ of the park and where all the park staff live and is also a centre for tourists. I pleaded for a more remote location, and the director agreed that we might take them farther afield to an area near a river which never went dry. He very kindly promised to send a radio message to one of the park wardens asking him to meet us on our way and guide us to this spot. He also offered us any further help we might need.

After leaving the director it took me five hours to find George who had driven the lorry sixty miles beyond Arusha. This meant that we should not be able to reach the Serengeti by nightfall; so we camped at Mtu-Ya-Umbu at the foot of the Manyara escarpment.

The cubs were in a pitiful state. Their faces were bruised and battered and the bony parts of their bodies were chafed; the decomposing meat inside the crates attracted a swarm of blue-bottles which buzzed over their sores. They tried unsuccessfully to protect themselves by putting their paws over their faces; I could not bear to watch their suffering.

As the men were as tired as the rest of us, we decided not to pitch camp, and slept in the open. George and I put our beds close to the crates, and all through the night I heard the cubs moving about restlessly. At first light I roused the camp, which did not make me popular, but I was determined that the cubs should be released from their misery as soon as possible.

Soon, as we began to climb up the escarpment which towered above us, we saw Lake Manyara, until now hidden from our view by miles of virgin forest. This lake is one of the great attractions of Tanganyika. Its shallows are covered with flamingos and other water fowl, while out of the lush forest elephant, buffalo and lion come to drink its waters.

We had no time to enjoy these sights for the sky was overcast and small showers warned us of more rain to come. Concentrating on speed, we climbed steadily into the 'Highlands of the Giant Volcanoes'. Unfortunately, drizzling rain soon reduced visibility to a few yards, so we were unable to see the volcanoes and Ngorongoro, the world's largest crater, which has a diameter of ten miles. We could only guess at the steep gradient of the slopes into which the road was cut by seeing, level with its verge, the tops of giant lobelias, a plant which grows to a height of nine feet.

The higher we climbed, the thicker the fog grew and it began to penetrate icily through our clothes. The men, who had never been at such a high altitude, looked blue under their dark African skins. Many droppings told us that this was not only a highway of tourists but also for buffalo, elephant and other wild beasts, and once an elephant stepped out of the thick bush and we had to stop abruptly.

At last we reached the rim of the Ngorongoro crater. On an earlier visit, I had looked down it and seen a multitude of game grazing some 1,500 feet below, but today nothing was visible but billowing clouds. For a few miles we crawled cautiously along the slippery road round the rim, then, all of a sudden, the mist lifted; it was as though a curtain had suddenly been raised on a new scene and we saw, far below us, the Serengeti Plain bathed in warm sunlight.

Ahead of us lay undulating slopes, so profusely covered with bright yellow senecios that they might have been made of gold. Among this mass of flowers grazed great herds of zebra, wildebeest, Thomson's gazelle and cattle herded by Masai tribesmen. It was strange to see wild and domestic animals feeding side by side, a circumstance only made possible by the fact that the Masai do not poach ungulates.

We came down rapidly to an altitude of 5,000 feet, at which level the sun was so warm that we were able to shed some of our clothes. After passing the famous Olduvai Gorge, we knew that we now had only some seventy miles to go. The road had been fair so far; suddenly it deteriorated into one of the worst tracks we had ever travelled over. The ruts were knee deep with lava dust, and rattling along them we stirred up a choking cloud which penetrated everything.

As the heat increased we removed the tarpaulins which covered the lorry, to prevent the cubs from suffocating, but this resulted in their raw wounds being covered with dust; they were indeed having a terrible time for they were bounced about mercilessly as the lorry lurched from one pothole to another. We had to stop often to jack the vehicles out of deep holes and replace broken springs. I did not know which was worse for the cubs, the icy wet and cold we had just left behind, or the infernal heat and appalling dust of the next fifty miles. We were two hours late when we reached Naabi Hill at which we were to meet the park warden; the poor man had spent the time watching our convoy creeping along like a caterpillar, raising a trail of dust in its wake.

We had to cut our greeting short, for heavy storm clouds were gathering and we still had a long way to go through black cotton soil, the worst ground to cross when wet. On our way we passed vast herds of wildebeest and zebra; these were only the forerunners of the annual migration, but neither of us had ever before seen such an assembly of wild animals. Dodging between the herds and avoiding swampy patches we reached the release point in the late afternoon.

34. The Release

The cubs' new home was a very beautiful place lying at the head of a broad valley some forty miles long. On one side, a steep escarpment rose to a plateau, on the other, there was a succession of hills. Close by was a river which gradually wound its way to the centre of the valley and flowed down it. Its banks were covered with dense undergrowth and fine trees, which provided perfect cover for all kinds of animals. The valley looked like a park, with clusters of thorn trees and bush which higher up the hills increased in density. But for the mosquitoes and the tsetse flies, it was a paradise – and perhaps we ought to have regarded the tsetse as its winged guardians, for they are the best protectors of wild animals: since they are fatal to men and to their livestock, they cause them to keep away.

Our first thought was to see what we could do to make the cubs more comfortable. We chose a stout acacia tree, attached the block and tackle to one of its branches, and swung the crates to the ground. It was three days since the cubs had been captured and they had almost reached the limit of their endurance. Their eyes were deeply sunken and they lay apathetically on the floor of their cages, apparently too tired to take the least interest in their surroundings. How glad we were that we had decided to bring the cumbersome communal crate in which they would be able to recover from the strain of their journey.

After opening the back of it, we placed Little Elsa's and

Gopa's boxes with their doors opposite the opening, then with block and tackle we raised the trap-doors of the cages.

For a few moments nothing happened, then, suddenly, Gopa rushed into Little Elsa's box; he sat on her and they licked and hugged each other, overwhelmed with joy at being reunited. Quickly we closed the door behind them and replaced Gopa's empty crate by the one containing Jespah. The instant we opened this door he was out like a flash, and covered his brother and sister, as if to protect them from further disaster, and started to lick and embrace them.

As we watched them we became more than ever convinced that we had done well to move the cubs in crates which allowed them to see each other. This had probably resulted in some extra chafing, but it would be easier to heal wounds than broken spirits. We were delighted to see that in spite of all they had gone through the cubs were as friendly as they had always been.

Now we had to see that they got rested and made up for their lost meals. We put a carcase into the communal crate, told our men to camp a little way off and parked our Land Rovers right and left of the crate to protect the cubs from any prowlers that might come by night.

By 9 p.m. all this had been done, and we were ready for a good sleep. But Gopa soon became restless and often during the night I heard him shifting about, and the crunching of bones. Next morning I was glad to see that there was nothing left of the meal we had prepared the night before. The cubs had gone back into the filthy travelling crates; they seemed to cling to them as the one familiar place which gave them a sense of security in their strange surroundings. As a result we were unable to remove the rotten meat.

Until they became less bewildered it was plain that we must keep them confined; to entice them into the communal crate we put some fresh meat into it. We thought it very important to leave them undisturbed, so we gave strict orders to our staff to keep away from the crates, and we ourselves went to find a camping site at least a mile away. After pitching our tents we came back and saw that the cubs had not moved out of their dirty cages which were buzzing with flies. Ignoring their protests, we cleaned out the crates as best we could. It was not an easy task, for the cubs defended their little territory, growling and scratching. Both George and I were sick several times as we scraped out the filth, so when the repulsive operation was completed, we went back to the camp to have a bath and the first hot meal we had eaten for four days.

While we were eating the park warden came to discuss our camping arrangements. The park authorities had kindly given us permission to look after the cubs until they had settled in their new home and could fend for themselves. The park warden told us that meanwhile we could feed them on game animals shot outside the Serengeti Park.

When we got back to the cubs we found all three lying in the communal crate. Their faces were a shocking sight, for the big cage was made of weld-mesh wire which chafed them even more than the iron bars of the travelling crates. Every time they pressed against it their wounds reopened, and they made matters worse by using their paws to try and keep the flies off their sores. Poor Gopa was the most battered and he and Little Elsa growled savagely whenever we came close to the crate. Jespah did not mind our presence and even allowed us to pluck at the arrowhead; but we failed to extract it.

We settled down for the night, the communal cage sheltered between our two cars; soon afterwards we heard the first lion approaching. The whuffing came rapidly nearer, until we could distinguish several animals circling round our little sanctuary and then saw their eyes reflecting the light of our torches. The cubs listened intently to their grunts, while we shouted at them trying to shoo them away. When all was quiet again, I called the cubs softly by their names and soon afterwards heard them tearing at their meat. I was disturbed to notice that one of them was breathing heavily and I feared it might be going to develop pneumonia. But when it became light I was pleased to see that, in spite of the heavy dew, none of the cubs seemed to be seriously ill – in fact they looked very content and their bellies were full.

The morning was brisk and fresh; even at this altitude – about 3,500 feet – the air was much cooler than at Elsa's camp. In the evening we had covered the crate with a tarpaulin; now we removed it as the sun was rising. As soon as it got hot the horrid flies appeared and literally covered the cubs. Poor Jespah kept brushing one front paw against his sores, while with the other he hugged Little Elsa.

After breakfast, George drove off to shoot a kill outside the Serengeti while I remained with the cubs. Whenever he gave me an opportunity to do so I tried to remove the arrow from Jespah's rump. He did not mind even when I pinched the skin and tugged as hard as I could, but the barb remained jammed. Jespah had been hit five weeks ago and I did not like the look of the wound; but as the vet had advised against operating for a few more weeks, I had to resign myself to waiting.

Later in the morning the plague of flies made the cubs very restless; they paced up and down, rubbing their heads against the wire and reopening their wounds, but in the end cuddled up together, looking at me reproachfully. In spite of being caged, dirty and covered with bleeding wounds, they were as dignified as only lions could be under such conditions.

I knew that the Serengeti was far the best home we could have found for them, but the climate and the ecological conditions were very different from those of their old home and most of the local animals belonged to species unknown to them. Even the local lions were of a different sub-species from theirs. What would their mutual reactions be and what trouble might arise over territorial rights? Since there was so much game about that every animal could be assured of an ample food supply, I could only hope that the lions of the Serengeti were more tolerant than the Fierce Lioness who had attacked Elsa.

When George returned about 3 o'clock with a carcase we discussed the question of releasing the cubs. We had intended to keep them confined for another day or two so as to build them up, but the torment of the flies made us change our minds and we decided to release them then and there.

It was a good time of day, since during the hot hours the cubs were less energetic, therefore less likely to bolt or panic; moreover, at this hour there was less danger of their meeting wild lions. After placing the carcase between the cage and the river, we hoisted one of the travelling boxes, thus opening an exit. When they saw us doing this, the cubs rushed in terror to the farthest corners of the communal crate and huddled close together. After some time, Gopa suspiciously investigated the opening, cautiously retreated several times, and then walked out in a most dignified manner. He took no interest in the kill but continued slowly towards the river. After about a hundred yards he stopped, hesitated, and then walked calmly on.

Jespah and Little Elsa held each other close; they had puzzled expressions as they watched Gopa walking away. Then Jespah went up to the exit and moved out. He too went very slowly towards the river, pausing several times to look back at his sister.

Meanwhile Little Elsa rushed frantically up and down the crate or stood upright against it, plainly desperately anxious to join her brothers and not knowing how to do so, till at last she found the way to freedom and trotted quickly after Jespah, and all three cubs disappeared into the reeds. Almost immediately a cloudburst screened them from our view.

35. The Migration

As soon as the grey curtain lifted we searched the place where we had last seen the cubs through our field glasses but there was no trace of them. I was glad that at least they had walked straight to the river, since this meant that they would know where to get a drink.

Although the river was not so lovely as the one at Elsa's camp, it provided for all the cubs' needs; its bed carried a slow-flowing stream of fresh water, and even in the dry season a few pools, milky and stagnant, would remain; and beyond the far bank a chain of hills concealed an extensive salt lick which was frequented by many animals. We were happy to think that if only our cubs were accepted by the local lions they were not going to find life too difficult here.

To avoid quarrels one of our first tasks would be to find a feeding place, where the cubs could eat without the local lions or other predators interfering with them. To secure their meat inside the communal crate would be risky, for in a confined space the cubs might be cornered. What we needed was a shelter for the kill which provided an easy exit for the cubs in case of danger. We placed the communal crate near a large tree; on either side we parked our two cars, thus making an open square. Across a thick branch we hoisted the kill by a block and tackle, which we attached to one of the cars; this would make it easy to lower the meat during the night if the cubs appeared, and while they were absent the carcase would dangle out of reach of thieves. We did not expect the cubs that night, for until they were hungry we did not think they would return to the crates in which they had been trapped.

349

Soon after dark a pride of three or more lions came so close that the light from our torches was reflected in their eyes. It was easy to know when a lion was around for he always announced his arrival by a low grunt, but the lionesses sneaked in silently and I only became aware of them when I heard the breathing and by then they were crouching by my car. However, in spite of their cunning they never got at the kill, which we protected.

Early next morning we screened the river banks through our field glasses, but saw no sign of the cubs. It was only when the first rays of the sun touched the water that we spotted them coming out of the bush, very close to the place at which they had disappeared the night before. They walked halfway up the hill, stopping often, until they reached a thicket; there they lay down. When I called to them they looked at me but did not move. Then a troop of baboons came in sight, and the cubs walked at a leisurely pace to the top of the hill with the baboons close behind them. Finally the whole party disappeared over the crest.

Hoping to be able to follow the cubs' movements, we drove across the river and along the far side of the hill, but we did not see them. On our way we were overtaken by a Land Rover which had brought a radiogram saying that our new Bedford was now ready and could be collected at Nairobi. Mail in the Serengeti was dependent on occasional transport, but telegrams were transmitted twice daily by radio from Arusha HQ.

We sent Ibrahim to Nairobi to return the truck, which Ken and Downey had so kindly hired us at a low price; he was to bring back the Bedford.

Next evening the cubs arrived at about 9 p.m. They ate hungrily but when George switched on his headlights, bolted and did not return for an hour. This time they settled down to their dinner. Jespah even asked for two rations of cod-liver oil and took it in his usual way out of the pie dish which George held out to him, so we knew that in spite of everything he had lately suffered he still trusted us.

In the early hours of the morning I heard one of the cubs moving towards the river; it gave a series of short roars, but I noticed that these were not followed by the whuffs with which a lion's roar should end.

Little Elsa made the most of her brother's absence and ate heartily at the kill. Later, all three cubs had a good fill-up for the day, and left at dawn. As soon as they had gone a lion roared loudly; he was alarmingly close and soon I saw a splendid dark-maned lion clearly silhouetted against the blood-red morning sky. He sniffed in the direction of the kill, then walked to the back of George's car and watched the mosquito net flapping inside. When he showed an inclination to investigate the carcase, we shouted at the top of our voices, and though we couldn't compete with his roars we did succeed in startling him and he trotted off in the direction of the camp. As soon as he had gone, we hoisted the kill beyond his reach and then drove to the camp to warm ourselves with some hot tea.

When we got there we saw this dark-maned lion standing within a hundred yards of the excited boys who, from their refuge on top of the lorry, were trying to warn us of his presence. Poor lion, he must have wondered what to make of such an unexpected invasion of his territory.

Towards evening we went back to our post near the kill. Gopa arrived at dusk, but hid in the tall grass until he thought it was dark enough to be safe for him to come to his meal. Jespah soon followed him, but Little Elsa did not appear. Instead, the dark-maned lion and his two lionesses turned up. They crouched within eight yards of my car while, on the other side of it, Gopa and Jespah crunched their dinner. I was sorry I had not got a flashlight and could not take a photograph of this absurd party; three hungry wild lions crouching in the grass, only separated from the cubs by my car. Jespah and Gopa were not in the least worried by the proximity of the local lions, indeed, they must have felt perfectly safe and have had complete confidence in our ability to protect them, for when they were full up they rolled on their backs.

Suddenly there was a faint call from over the river; perhaps it was Little Elsa for instantly the brothers sneaked off behind George's car, avoiding the wild lions. We hoisted the kill and spent the rest of the night keeping the wild pride at bay.

On 7 May, George left early to get a new kill outside the Serengeti. The track to the border was rough and I did not expect him back till the afternoon. About lunchtime the clouds gathered threateningly over the camp; as the first drops fell a Land Rover unexpectedly appeared, bringing the Chairman of the Trustees of the National Park and his party which included the park warden. We hurried into the tent to avoid a drenching. The chairman told me that he appreciated the publicity the cubs were giving to the Serengeti, but went on to say that by the end of May we must leave, as the tourist season opened in June and our camping out and feeding the lions might arouse criticism. I was horrified, and I stressed that we really could not abandon them until they were able to fend for themselves. I suggested, to avoid the difficulties he foresaw, that we should move our camp to some place far from the tourist tracks, and I promised to be very discreet about feeding the cubs, but pointed out that by the end of May they would only be seventeen months old and that as a rule lions of that age are not yet able to hunt on their own.

At this moment George returned, and supported my view. The chairman did not agree to our proposal and left us dismayed. The cubs had only been released a few days; up till then they had been dependent upon us, and we felt it would be monstrous just to dump them and hope that they would manage somehow.

We were still discussing the situation when more visitors arrived. These included Lee and Matty Talbot, American scientists engaged in ecological research. Their views were most stimulating, they shared many of our interests and we soon became friends.

When we took up our night station we found the cubs already waiting for us. George was tired after his long drive, so he went to sleep and I sat up to guard the cubs. Jespah came several times to the back of my car asking to be patted and remained quite still while I stroked him. This was the first time he had done such a thing since he had left Elsa's camp. In spite of what had happened, perhaps because of his mother's example, he still trusted us and acted as liaison between his brother and sister and ourselves. We were both sure that without him neither Gopa nor Little Elsa would have put up with us. Gopa had the strength and independence to be the leader of a pride, but he lacked the qualities of affection and understanding which distinguished his mother and his brother. Although it was Gopa who left the Tana, made his way back to his old home and spent a week there on his own; although he was the one who first took the risk of making his way to freedom out of the communal crate and claimed the lion's share of every meal – yet, when he was distressed or frightened, Gopa at once rushed to Jespah for comfort and support, as he used to rush to his mother.

Jespah appeared to provide the moral backbone for the trio, which was probably what caused him to become the leader, even though he was less powerful than Gopa. From a very early age he had always protected his mother and since her death he had taken charge of his brother and sister. It was always he who went out to reconnoitre and see if there was danger around, and if a threat arose it was he who challenged it and recently whenever Little Elsa bolted he had run after her, comforted her and brought her back.

The cubs spent the night devouring the fresh kill. At dawn they walked off, their bellies swinging heavily from side to side. They were in perfect condition, except for some sores from chafing, and of course Jespah still had the arrowhead in his rump.

During the next two nights there was no sign of the cubs and as my injured leg still prevented me from taking long walks, George went off to search for them. He found their spoor leading across the valley towards the escarpment, where rocks offered them good shelter. We thought that they probably felt safer at a distance from the local lions, even if this meant that they had to walk two miles to get their dinner.

The following night the cubs arrived soon after our vigil had begun. They seemed unusually nervous and bolted the moment they heard a lion calling, even though he was far away. They did not return till three in the morning, then gulped their food and left. We appreciated the reason for the hurry when soon afterwards a chorus of lions started to roar quite close to us.

The next night the same thing happened, and Little Elsa was in such a state of nerves that she even bolted when we used our torches.

It rained all day and we went early to the kill. When we reached it we saw Jespah balancing on the branch from which his dinner was hanging; he was trying to get at it from above, while the other cubs, half hidden in the grass, watched him. As soon as we lowered the carcase they all rushed at the meat and spent the night gorging. By morning there was nothing left but a few bones; this meant that we must again drive outside the Serengeti and go hunting for them.

Quite close to the camp we passed the dark-maned lion and his two girlfriends. We had always supposed that lions like to pass their honeymoon in privacy and were therefore surprised to see this lion making love to one of the lionesses in the presence of the other. Not more than a mile farther on we saw a magnificent blond-maned lion sunning himself on the open plain. He paid no attention to us or to the clicking of our cameras and stretched and yawned as though we weren't there. After that, I had hardly time to change my film before we ran into another pair of lovesick lions. They lay as close together as they could, seemed very tired, and ignored us.

The farther we drove, the more wooded and hilly the country became and the more the herds of animals increased. When we neared the border we might have been passing through a gigantic cattle sale such as the stock-rearing tribes hold on the northern frontier. Mile after mile under every tree groups of wildebeest and zebra crowded together to the limit of the shade; whilst, in the blazing sun, animals unable to find shelter wandered about aimlessly. The noise was deafening. When I closed my eyes I might have been listening to a chorus of bullfrogs, and only the high-pitched barking of the zebra reminded me that we were not in a swamp but amongst thousands upon thousands of animals assembled in preparation for their great annual migration towards Lake Victoria and the adjoining Mara reserve. We were very lucky to have arrived in the Serengeti in time to see this unique sight.

When we returned to the cubs' feeding place with our kill, we found Jespah and Gopa doing acrobatics along the branches of the acacia tree and we saw Little Elsa hiding nearby. Suddenly Gopa listened in her direction, and began to scramble down. When he had nearly reached the ground he jumped and fell heavily; then he got to his feet, looking rather foolish, and trotted over to his sister. Jespah remained on his branch till I showed him the pie dish, then he too came down and almost toppled over in his eagerness to get at the cod-liver oil. I was glad to see that his sores were nearly healed and that a fine fluff was growing over the scars, but the wound made by the arrowhead was discharging and looked very nasty.

When it was quite dark Little Elsa came to the meat, but seemed terribly nervous, so I tried to reassure her by calling her name. Later we did our best to scare off the wild lions and hyenas but in spite of this the cubs left and did not return.

After breakfast we went off to see more of the migration. On our way we passed the mating lion and his lioness again. Although they were lying in the open and must have seen us, they allowed us to approach to within twenty-five yards of them, and were so little disturbed by our arrival that eventually the lion sired his mate, an act which lasted three minutes and ended by his giving her a gentle bite on the forehead to which she responded with a low growl. After a quarter of an hour he approached her again, but this time she dismissed him with a sweep of her paw. This was repeated three times before she permitted him to sire her again and, as before, he bit her forehead. We continued to watch them, and after about twenty minutes the lion sired her a third time, releasing her only after giving her a slight bite in the neck; after this both went to sleep. There was no sound to be heard and time seemed to stand still on this vast plain. When we started up the car, the lioness raised her head and blinked at us through half-closed eyes, but the lion never stirred.

We had been told that in the Serengeti there were many more lionesses than lions. This no doubt accounted for the unusual number of love-making pairs we saw. Lions nearly always keep a harem, and can manage a large family successfully since a lioness spends two years looking after her cubs and does not allow herself to be sired during this time. But here, the males being vastly outnumbered by females, a good many of the lions we saw looked rather thin. We thought this was partly because a lion's honeymoon usually lasts four or five days, and during this time the couple do not eat and seldom drink, and here there were not enough lions to satisfy the demands of so many lionesses, so the lions often went hungry.

During the next three nights the cubs failed to turn up, but hungry predators were very active. In particular, the dark-maned lion and his pride remained close and were plainly not prepared to allow the cubs to take over their territory.

This made us realize that we must establish a new feeding place for the cubs – but first we had to find them.

We were told that during the season of the migration many lions simply followed the column of moving animals, since they found it easier to kill stragglers than to hunt in the usual way. All we could hope to do was to discover where the more conservative prides had established their rights and remove our cubs to another area.

We spent the next days scouring the country, but the long grass and dry ground made spooring difficult.

As for lions, we had never seen so many: we walked past a pride of five sitting on a rock, and a short distance away from them we saw a pride of seven lying on a hillock, who looked us up and down but didn't move, even when we had to pass within four yards of them. As we went on we came upon a third pride consisting of a lioness, two small cubs, two half-grown cubs and two magnificent lions, and only a short distance away two dark-maned lions were stalking a topi up a hill; as it was getting hot and they were not very enthusiastic he got away. Later we were several times surprised to see two fully grown lions together but were told that in the Serengeti a pair of lions will sometimes remain together for many years.

We went to a small lake to watch the flamingos who were standing on its edge and noticed a hammer-headed stork pecking at its food in the shallows, close to a sleeping monitor. The lizard was rather a large specimen, about four feet long. As we were looking at it a jackal approached the monitor from behind – obviously not with the best intentions. We had been told of jackals eating puff adders, and of lions around Lake Rudolf killing crocodiles, but neither George nor I had ever seen a carnivore kill and eat a reptile. The monitor seemed completely unaware of danger until the jackal was near enough to make a bite at him, then he lashed his tail threateningly and his attacker leapt into the air and bolted. The monitor went to sleep again, but the jackal was not to be put off so easily. He returned to the attack this time approaching the monitor from the front. He was greeted by a loud hiss, which sent him dashing off into the grass, where a lioness suddenly sat up in front of him, her two cubs peeping out to right and left of her, and the jackal nearly fell backwards in his hurry to be off. Seeing this the lioness strolled down to the water and began to drink quite close to the monitor, who waddled away very quickly. None of this disturbed the hammer-headed stork, who went on pecking industriously, completely disregarding lion, jackal and monitor.

When the cubs had been missing for six days we became anxious. We had expected them to become independent only gradually, and this sudden disappearance didn't seem natural. We wondered whether they might share the homing instinct with cats. If so, they might now be travelling to their old homes – 400 miles if they went in a straight line; 700 if they followed the route by which they had come. That they should follow the road seemed unlikely, but we decided to investigate it and drove back thirty miles to the hill, to where we had first met the park warden. We saw no sign of the cubs. On our way we passed through vast herds of migrating animals and saw one column three miles long of Thomson's gazelle walking in single file, advancing as if drawn by a magnet. In spite of the easy hunting, we did not think it probable that the cubs would have gone into this country, for the open plain offered no shelter and they were used to thick bush-cover. All the same, we made a careful search in the rocks and vegetation of the hill before we gave up and returned to camp.

The next morning we took a map and drew a straight line between the Serengeti and Elsa's camp.

As soon as it left the Serengeti the line entered an area inhabited by the Masai tribe which is noted for lion hunting. Before the time of the European administration each young warrior of this tribe was obliged, in order to prove his manhood, to spear a lion, whose mane he converted into a headdress which he thereafter wore on special occasions as a proof of his courage. Lion spearing was now forbidden by the game laws but still went on secretly, so we did not think that we should count on getting news of our cubs in this area. We therefore thought of sending Makedde who, though himself a Turkana, could speak Masai, to camp among the tribesmen and see whether in casual conversation he could pick up any news of the cubs. If they had raided stock he would perhaps be able to prevent them from being speared.

On our way to the border we stopped at Seronera to call on the director. He said he was sorry that we had run into difficulties, but made it clear that we should be obliged to leave the Serengeti by the end of the month. This left us only ten days, an alarmingly short time. We passed through country where there were many lions. In one pride five lionesses were suckling eight cubs of varying ages. The cubs went from one mother to another and the lionesses showed no wish to distinguish between their cubs and others.

I planned that next morning I would drive Makedde and his kit into the Masai area and try to find a family who would take him in, while George would go on searching the valley near the camp.

As soon as we got back I packed, to be ready for an early start. Since we had so little time left, George decided to start searching the valley at once. Next morning he arrived grinning; he had found the cubs, or rather they had found him.

He had driven six miles down the valley and parked the car where the headlights could be seen over a great distance and at intervals he had flashed the spotlight to all the points of the compass.

About 9 p.m. the cubs arrived. They looked fit and were not hungry, but they were so thirsty that the brothers lapped up all the water George could give them, leaving nothing for poor Little Elsa. All were very friendly and Jespah even tried to enter George's car. They remained there through the night, eating little of the very high meat he had brought them but amusing themselves by chasing hyenas. When, soon after dawn, they left, they went towards a little valley. George had hurried back to bring me the good news and stopped me going to the border. It was obvious that, after their experience with the Fierce Lioness at Elsa's camp home, the cubs were scared of all the lions round the release place and had gone to find a more secluded area where they could stake out their own territory.

We decided not to move the main camp but to go every evening to the 'cub valley' and spend the night there in our cars. The glen they had chosen for their home was at the foot of the escarpment and above the tsetse belt; it was about a mile and a half long and two narrow ravines led into and out of it. One of these provided a particularly safe refuge. It was about half a mile long, its vertical walls were nine feet high and it was five feet wide; above it almost impenetrable vegetation provided a thick canopy which turned it into a cool shelter during the hot hours of the day.

Any approaching danger could be heard from a long way off, so, if need be, the cubs could retreat inside the ravine and up one of the sheer cliffs which broke off the escarpment. Here among overhanging rocks and dense undergrowth they would be in a strong strategic position to sight and avoid an enemy. From the top of the escarpment there was a splendid view across the vast, undulating hinterland of woods and parkland to the river, another valley through which it ran and beyond it to hills and other valleys which stretched out to the horizon. The course of the river was marked by a green belt which wound along the valley till it was lost in a haze. We thought that the cubs had found a much better home for themselves than the one we had chosen for them.

When we first arrived at their valley it was late afternoon, we took up our post under a large tree between the escarpment and the river and hoisted up the meat. One cub soon emerged from the ravine but hid in the grass. When it grew dark all three appeared and went straight to the water bowl. They were very thirsty and we had to refill the basin many times before they were satisfied. We observed that all three were in good condition, and the sores due to the chafing were healing well. The arrowhead in Jespah's rump, however, showed no sign of coming out and though he drank his cod-liver oil from the pie dish I held out to him he would not allow me to pull at the arrow. When they had quenched their thirst the cubs went off into the darkness and did not come back for their supper until George switched off the headlights of the car. We realized they had not changed their purely nocturnal habits and in general only appeared at night and left at dawn.

36. The Ravine

As soon as we had found the cubs George sent the news to Seronera.

Later we met the director and discussed the cubs' future with him. He suggested that we should now go away but when we argued that they were not yet able to fend for themselves and that we were worried about Jespah's arrow wound, he agreed that we should stay on until the end of May to help them.

That evening Jespah and Gopa came from the ravine at dusk, but Little Elsa did not appear. Gopa tore greedily at the meat while Jespah went back to his sister and the two of them remained outside the range of lights until George turned them out, when they came up and joined Gopa.

Next day we went to have another look at the migration; it was a truly fantastic sight. The migrating herds spend several weeks assembling; during this time they churn up the plain and after a couple of days the three-foot-high grass is reduced to bare stalks of only about four inches. The actual move lasts only a few days and its drive and urgency is something which has to be seen to be believed.

We watched in amazement the herds advancing in tens of thousands and sometimes had the impression that it was the ground itself that was moving. The wildebeest kept in groups of ten to one hundred or walked in single file along well-trodden paths; the zebra, whenever possible, kept close to the water; these two species predominated, but there were also great herds of Thomson's gazelles, also many smaller ones of Grant's gazelles, kongoni and topi, and we counted one herd of two hundred eland antelopes. On the periphery of the herds were hungry jackals and hyenas watching for the chance to pick up a straggler. In whatever direction we looked the plain was covered with animals whose number it was impossible to estimate.

During the cool hours they were full of energy. We were particularly amused by the behaviour of the shaggy wildebeest. The bulls chased any of their cows which strayed off, and challenged rivals to a fight, while the cows tossed their heads and kicked out with their hooves at too persistent suitors. Many times an army of them passed by, covering us with dust. I became very anxious for our cameras, so I covered them up and in consequence got no pictures. Once a herd of many hundred zebras galloped past our car, their thundering hooves stirring up a pall of dust; when they had almost passed by, through the cloud of dust I saw a lion leaping upon the last of the zebras; he missed his prey and so did a second lion who sprang a second later.

When the dust settled we saw the two lions sitting under a tree and noticed that one of them was very old and thin. We thought it possible that he was dependent for hunting on his companion who was in his prime.

That evening when we returned to the ravine we found the cubs looking very tired. Jespah was particularly lethargic and rested near my car, and whenever Little Elsa came by he licked her and later joined her when she went a little distance away and embraced her. Gopa was already at the meat but it was only after Little Elsa plucked up courage and started on her supper that Jespah came for his cod-liver oil. After this he spent the night close to my car.

Next morning we decided to explore the forty-mile valley in which was the cubs' ravine. For a while we were able to follow a car track, then it faded out and we were obliged to plough our way through shoulder-high grass and whistling thorns.

In the circumstances, we naturally saw very little game; only rhino seemed to favour this spiky wilderness, and how we envied them their pachydermatousness.

The valley ended in a wide open plain in which stood a solitary borassus palm, a species which usually grows near water; beside it was a herd of topi, which we estimated to number over 3,000 head. We had never before seen so large a herd, though we were later told that in this plain, which is their favourite concentration ground, up to 5,000 have been counted.

It was late afternoon when we got back to the cub valley and we were delighted to find the cubs waiting for us. We hoped it might be a sign that they were abandoning their purely noc-turnal habits and learning to behave like the lions of the Serengeti, which, assured of their safety, spend their days in the open. If our cubs were able to adapt themselves to a different ecological environment this would not only benefit them, but also make a precedent for moving other doomed lions into new areas with good hope of the success of such releases. It was a cold night and the cubs went off at 10 p.m.

When we returned to camp we found a letter from the director in which he confirmed that we must leave the Serengeti on 31 May and added that between now and then we were not permitted to bring any more meat into the camp to feed the cubs.

We drove up the ravine and found the cubs waiting for us. Jespah was off his feed, did not touch any of the meat and seemed listless. We wondered whether, although it appeared healthy, the open wound round the arrowhead had become infected. Another possibility was that like Elsa at the time of her first release in country very similar to the Serengeti, he had developed an infection due to tsetse fly or ticks and was suffering from fever. He had been listless for a couple of days; now his condition was alarming.

Next morning, feeling anxious about him, we walked along the edge of the cubs' ravine and looked through our field glasses to see if we could catch sight of him amongst the thick canopy of vegetation. In time we did see the cubs but they spotted us and, alarmed by our presence, rushed towards the cliff. I called to them but they went off. So we set off for home.

The few miles that lay between the cubs' ravine and our camp was the most attractive part of the valley.

As we picked our way across the black rocks it struck me that one of these smooth slabs would make a perfect tombstone for Elsa's grave, and I thought it fitting that her slab should come from the cubs' new home. To test its durability I scratched a slab with a piece of quartz but could hardly make any impression. Later when a stone-mason engraved Elsa's name on one of these slabs he broke five chisels and told us that neither granite nor marble was so hard and that he would never work again on such a rock.

Next evening the cubs only appeared after dark. This was disappointing as it showed that they were not yet prepared to abandon their nocturnal habits.

After one lap of cod-liver oil Jespah retired behind the car; when the other cubs had eaten they went over to him and tried to make him play with them, but, though he licked them, he wouldn't move.

At dawn Gopa and Little Elsa had another meal and then went over to Jespah and tried to prod him into going to the ravine with them. After a time he rose slowly and began to follow them. I called and he returned and stood in front of me. I pointed to the meat and talked to him, as I did when I wanted Elsa to eat, and he reacted as his mother used to – went over to the kill and began his meal. It was the first time in three days that we had seen him eat.

Each time Gopa and Little Elsa called him, he looked up and only started eating again when I said: 'Come on, Jespah, *nyama* [meat], *nyama*, eat a little more.'

Eventually Gopa came back, and jumping on to Jespah's rump persuaded him to go to the ravine with the others.

Having found I still had some terramycin I decided to start treating Jespah with it that evening. It was lucky that only he was prepared to take his cod-liver oil from the dish I held out for him. Otherwise, no doubt Gopa would have got most of it.

The remains of the carcase were already very high and the cubs, accustomed to fresh meat, sniffed at it with expressions of disgust.

The widespread belief that lions purposefully leave meat in order to allow it to become putrid before eating it is erroneous, though of course when desperately hungry they will eat anything. I could only hope that our cubs would soon learn the art of providing themselves with fresh food; and as I was thinking this Little Elsa walked off determinedly and looked as though she might be going off to search for a kill. Gopa followed her, but Jespah lay still, only occasionally raising his head. When his brother and sister returned he played with them as best he could but it was only too evident that he was ill.

It was unthinkable that we should leave him in this state. So we sent Ibrahim to Seronera with a letter to the park warden explaining the situation and asking for a few days' extension of our permit to stay in the Serengeti. Meanwhile we had no food to give him. So, as we were very short of time, George took it upon himself to drive forty miles outside the boundary of the park to shoot a kill. We realized that this was contrary to our instructions but we hoped that in the circumstances we might be forgiven. Near the border we noticed a low-flying aircraft which was, we imagined, carrying out a migration census. On our return to camp the park warden who had been a passenger in the plane and had seen George's kill met us and asked us to explain why we had shot an animal in defiance of the prohibition. We apologized, told him of the circumstances and begged him to extend our permit to camp near the cubs. He said that he was not in a position to grant the extension and advised us to get an interview with the director at Arusha. The warden offered to hire a plane for me by radio from Nairobi. It was to collect me next morning. That night we spent as usual with the cubs. Next day I flew across fascinating country to Arusha where I had been invited to lunch with the director. He was displeased at George's shooting of the last kill against his orders. I apologized and explained our predicament. He then suggested that if we were not happy about the situation, we might recapture the cubs and move them to one of two game reserves in Tanganyika where we would not be subject to the regulations of the national parks and could stay with the lions if they were ill. I was not anxious to move the cubs a second time and after we had looked at a map I was convinced that on other grounds as well the plan was not advisable: both the suggested areas were very narrow and I realized that the cubs might easily cross the protecting boundary and enter thickly populated country. After I had rejected this proposal the director agreed to extend our permit to enable us to stay eight more days with the cubs and to allow us to make three more kills outside the Serengeti between now and 8 June when we had to leave. To avoid any misunderstanding he put this in writing and left it to us to decide whether to remove the cubs from the Serengeti or after 8 June let nature take its course. He also offered to arrange a meeting between ourselves and the chairman of the trustees if we wanted to put our case before them and ask for more help than he himself could give us.

I arrived back at the camp in a heavy rainstorm feeling depressed and rather ill. All the same, I went up at once to the ravine to join George but no cubs appeared that night and all we heard was the barking of zebra. Next morning I had a high temperature. In spite of this we searched for the cubs in the morning but found no trace of them.

The cubs arrived only after dark and made straight for the cod-liver oil. Lately they had become so greedy for it that we had been obliged to ration them, in order not to overfeed them.

When I held out the dish which contained meat mixed with terramycin to Jespah he lifted his paw to push it nearer to the ground, then stopped and kept his paw suspended in the air while he ate up the meat. I wondered whether he sensed my fear that if his sharp claws touched my hand I should get scratched.

Later a faint lion call attracted the cubs' attention and they went off in the direction it came from.

During their absence we were kept busy chasing hyenas away from the carcase; but they only left when the cubs returned. They quickly ate some more of the meat and then retired into the ravine. As soon as they had gone the hyenas came back and stayed till we hoisted the kill out of their reach. On the following night the lion called again, and the cubs who had hardly touched their dinner went off in his direction. On the third evening Gopa and Little Elsa were very hungry and ate ravenously, but Jespah didn't eat. His condition, thanks no doubt to the terramycin, had improved but he was still far from well.

In view of this, I decided to visit the chairman and put our problem to him. I pointed out that Jespah's arrow wound might require to be operated, and that in his present low state he needed our help, and I stressed that if we abandoned the cubs before they became competent hunters, the rehabilitation was not likely to be a success. My arguments failed to convince the chairman or to make him relent over the date fixed for our departure.

This meant that we had only three days left, but, on my way home, it suddenly occurred to me that no one could prevent me from staying on in the Serengeti as a tourist.

I would have to camp at the official sites and this would entail a long daily drive to see the cubs. I would not be able to feed them, or to go out at night; still, it would enable me to keep in touch with them. I therefore changed direction and drove straight to Seronera to book a camping site. There I was told that my request would have to be submitted to the director. This surprised me, but I put it in, hoping for the best.

Eager to make the most of the few days that remained, we drove to the ravine but the cubs didn't appear till the evening.

While we were waiting we watched a solitary impala ram which we had noticed on each of our visits to the glen. He never joined a herd of impala and took no notice of the cubs who for their part never attempted to stalk him. We were astonished at this truce which as it turned out was to last for all the time we spent in the Serengeti.

When Jespah arrived he took his medicine, Gopa rushed at the meat and Little Elsa went off after some zebra which were barking in the distance. She came back very hungry and cuffed Jespah when he tried to share the meal, so he went away good-naturedly and sat a little way off till she had finished; then he took the bones in his paws, and rolling his head from side to side scraped a meagre meal from them. He was generous and unselfish as Elsa used to be.

George went next morning to get the last kill we were allowed to shoot for the cubs.

When we returned to the ravine and produced the meat the cubs pounced on it. I hated to think that from now on they would have to go through a period of starvation before they had grown into competent hunters. At least Gopa and Little Elsa were in good condition but I felt very concerned about Jespah.

When it started to rain the cubs disappeared and George hoisted the kill, but they had not gone far. When they saw what was happening they rushed back to the meat and hung on to it till we feared the rope would break. When George lowered it they at once seized the carcase by the throat, trying to suffocate the animal as though it had been a live beast. This was reassuring for it showed that they knew at least the first rule of killing.

On 7 June I went to Seronera where I learned that so long as I behaved as an ordinary visitor I could stay on.

While returning to the camp I saw the dark-maned lion again; he was accompanied by his mate and another lioness who had two cubs; they looked about five weeks old. I felt sure that this was the pride which had chased our cubs from the release point some weeks ago.

We passed the last night we were to be allowed to spend in the open, shivering in the car under a deluge of rain. The noise was so loud that it drowned our calls to the cubs. Even after the rain stopped they failed to appear and, given the cubs' nocturnal habits, it might well be the last chance we should have of seeing them. It was therefore with great sadness that I heard the sleepy twitter of awakening birds and saw dawn break.

A flock of starlings were making their breakfast off the kill and went for George when he began to lower the carcase. We broke up the larger bones and scraped out the marrow of which the cubs were so fond, then we dragged all the meat into the ravine and covered it with branches, hoping that no hyena would discover it before the cubs arrived. Then we searched for them; slowly we went along the ravine calling all the familiar names, but saw no sign of the cubs.

While we were packing up I scanned the surroundings through my field glasses and saw two bateleur eagles soaring high up in the sky. I had noticed them some days earlier gliding through the air, hardly ever changing the perfect curve of their wings. Evidently their territory lay above the cubs' ravine.

George had already started up the engine of his car when on top of the escarpment I noticed a yellow speck which I soon recognized as Jespah's head. I called and in response Gopa and Little Elsa showed up. We couldn't go away without saying goodbye to the cubs, so George switched off his engine and we climbed the escarpment.

Gopa and Little Elsa, unused to being followed into their fortress, bolted for the cover of the ravine, but Jespah sat calmly waiting for us and allowed us to take some photographs of him. Then he slowly went off to join the others, stopping several times to look back at us. Should we ever see the cubs again?

37. I Become a Tourist in the Serengeti

It took most of the day to pack up the camp and it was after teatime before we reached Seronera, where the three wardens and their families live close to the lodge which provides accommodation for tourists. If visitors prefer to camp they can do so in an authorized area about a mile away. I chose to live in the open and watch the dawn from my bed in the tent.

After George had gone we began to pitch camp when a cloudburst soaked most of our possessions. During the night several hyenas prowled around and a lion came so close to my tent that I could hear his breathing; luckily the boys were sleeping in the lorry so I did not have to worry about their safety.

Later in the day I went to Seronera to make arrangements for my stay and found that I had to hand in our firearms as it was against the regulations for visitors to keep them.

When I asked the warden what I should do if lions visited me during the night he grinned and replied: 'Shoo them off!' And certainly by the time I left the Serengeti I became quite an expert at the 'shooing off' technique.

Early next morning I went with Nuru and a local driver to look for the cubs; it was a twenty-five-mile drive over skiddy roads to the ravine. We found the three of them lying under a large tree. It was nine o'clock by then and I had never before seen them in the open at such a late hour; I wondered whether they might have been awaiting our return. The cubs never tried to find us but had always waited for us to come and look for them. This was just what Elsa used to do. Indeed, after her release she always treated us as visitors to her territory. I thought that the cubs' present behaviour might show that they did not feel

371

deserted and were sufficiently settled in their new environment to feel at home: in fact, that the rehabilitation had been a success.

I called to the cubs, but they did not move, and when I got out of the car they bolted. I followed them in the car until Gopa and Jespah settled under a tree; by then Little Elsa had disappeared. Next I went to the ravine to see what had happened to the last kill, but could find no trace of the meat.

After this I returned and seeing the two brothers still under their tree, I showed myself and called to them, but they just sat watching me and didn't stir, so I settled down to write letters. Later Gopa went down to the river and after a while was followed by Jespah moving slowly. Two hours later a zebra thundered past, followed by a herd of impala racing as though in flight. Thinking that the cubs must be chasing them I drove to the place where I had seen Jespah disappear and nearly collided with a young blond-maned lion and farther down the valley I saw a full-grown lioness and later two others; but there was no sign of the cubs.

By this time it was necessary to start back for Seronera if we were to be there before dark. We had trouble with the car and next morning by the time the garage had put it right it was 10 a.m., so I had little hope of finding the cubs in the open at the hour at which we would reach the ravine.

As we were driving along I saw a magnificent rufus-maned lion replete and sleepy at a kill; three jackals were also tucking into it but the lion never so much as flicked an ear. Nor did he pay any attention to two young lions with blond ruffs which were sitting some hundred yards away under a tree.

When we reached the ravine it was deserted except for the lone impala ram.

Thinking that the cause of the cubs' nervousness yesterday might have been due to the presence of a strange driver, whom

I had engaged, I had taken only Nuru with me, but we had no luck and had to start back for Seronera after a blank day. The blond-maned lion and his party had not moved from the place where we had seen them in the morning.

On our way to the ravine next morning I noticed a dozen spotted hyenas moving in one direction; farther away I saw a dark mass of animals which seemed to be in a heap. Taking my field glasses I observed six wild dogs on a kill. When they moved aside for a moment I was able to distinguish a hyena cub struggling to its feet, but a second later the dogs were on it again. I couldn't watch six dogs tear a cub to pieces, so I drove ahead as fast as I could and the dogs retreated. I manoeuvred the car between them and the cub until it was able to walk slowly over to the hyena pack. The little hyena had some bleeding scratches on its back but did not seem to be in pain or seriously injured. It stopped often to look back at the dogs. When a second cub advanced towards them I didn't know in what direction to move the car or how to head it off quickly enough to protect both cubs simultaneously; but eventually the adult hyenas took over and kept the youngsters safely in their midst. The dogs then developed another interest and, seeming to play, jumped on their hind legs at each other as they cunningly manoeuvred close to a few Tommies. Suddenly four of the hyenas rushed at the dogs which, to my surprise, ran away. Certainly hyenas have strong jaws and as a pack can be very dangerous, but I would never have expected wild dogs to abandon a victim whose blood they had already tasted when attacked by an inferior number of hyenas.

Among the animals we met that morning were a herd of fifty head of impala. With their lyre-shaped horns, slender well-proportioned bodies and rich red colouring, they are amongst the most beautiful antelopes. At our approach one bounded away gracefully in long leaps, and soon the whole herd was jumping rhythmically. This time they had an excuse for their movement, but often they leap about just for the fun of it. At this season the herds were composed of both sexes, but during certain months, the females keep apart and the males form bachelor herds. We have counted up to forty old and young rams in a single herd and up to seventy ewes, sometimes guarded by a single male.

At the entrance to the cubs' valley I recognized the two pairs of mating lions that I had seen there before and when I arrived at the ravine I found the jaw bone of an impala which had recently been killed. I looked round anxiously for the solitary ram and was glad to see him watering a short distance away. I called to the cubs but saw nothing but a hyena sneaking off.

That day too we drew a blank with the cubs. The driving was rough and we went into several ant-bear holes which were hidden by the grass and had to jack the wheels.

Every morning we left early for the cub valley. The sun was still low and the plains were a sea of sparkling dew from which a mist arose. Wherever we looked we saw animals sleek or fluffy, striped, spotted or plain; with horns and bodies of infinite variety, all leaping and gambolling with a gaiety which was most infectious. Many were conservative in their habits and we got to know a number of individuals quite well.

One day we spent some time observing three lions which resembled ours so much that Nuru could not be persuaded that they were not Jespah, Gopa and Little Elsa. To prove to him that he was wrong I called to them but got no response and finally I put a dish of water near the car to test them. When he saw it the leader of the two male cubs growled at me and moved off. It was odd that three cubs about the same age as Elsa's should also have lost their mother, odd too that the lioness not only looked like Little Elsa but behaved much as she did, though she did not, when sitting, tuck her head between her shoulders as Little Elsa did, and neither of the male cubs had an arrow wound like Jespah or a potbelly like Gopa. After watching them for several hours I was pretty certain they were a strange pride, yet after we had driven away I began to have doubts, so we returned to have another look at them which confirmed my certainty that they were not our cubs.

Since I was fairly sure that Jespah, Gopa and Little Elsa would not quickly adapt themselves to the tsetse fly or to the proximity of a lot of lions, I searched for them along the base of the escarpment and in ravines farther down the valley where there were no tsetse and fewer lions. One deeply eroded lugga looked particularly promising, for protected by its steep walls I thought the cubs would feel that they could go more safely to the river than by crossing the valley to reach it. There were so many impala near this lugga that we called it the impala lugga. At its far end by the river a pride of lions had their territory. The first time we met them was during the hot hours of the day. We saw a lioness and two almost fully grown female cubs asleep. Nearby was a kill, which though replete they were guarding. A tree above the kill was thick with vultures, and on one of its branches a third female cub sprawled. After a while she stretched herself, yawned, climbed slowly to the ground and flung herself against her mother.

It was very hot and all the lions were panting. Suddenly two of the cubs moved over to a small, bushy tree and climbed on to its slender branches, which shook alarmingly under their weight, but undeterred the lionesses remained aloft, no doubt enjoying the breeze.

On another occasion we came across the same four lionesses making their way to a stagnant pool in the riverbed. The mother walked ahead, at each step cautiously testing the mud with one paw. When she could go no farther without the risk of getting stuck, she consoled herself for not being able to reach the water and drink by looking about for a place to her liking and then resting on the cool mud. Two of the cubs followed her example. We had often seen Elsa acting with the same caution. Lions are always very careful to avoid getting caught in the mud and I cannot recall a case of a lion getting fatally trapped.

This is unfortunately not the case with elephant which during droughts, when crazy with thirst, often become bogged; the harder they struggle to get out the deeper they sink into the sucking mud. We have often tried to rescue elephant from this horrible lingering death. Sometimes several get trapped in the same place. It is possible that a disaster of this kind involving a number of elephant has given rise to the myth of elephant cemeteries. Hippo, rhino and buffalo, on the other hand, all heavy animals which enjoy wallowing in the mud, never seem to get stuck and appear to know by instinct which places are safe for mud bathing and which should be avoided.

A few days later we again met the four lionesses in the same area and also a very large lion. I thought that we had better pursue our search farther down the valley, since it was unlikely that our cubs would stay in the territory established by such a pride. We drove the forty miles to the end of the valley where we saw a vast congregation of wildebeest and zebra; they were plagued by swarms of tsetse, which made me think that this also was a place that the cubs would not choose as their home. The only area we had not so far searched was that of the hills on the far side of the river opposite the cubs' ravine and the hinterland of the escarpment.

The hills were a hopeless proposition since there was no way of driving up them, but I hoped we could reach the edge of the escarpment by making a long detour into the hinterland and reaching the gentler slopes which led up the back of it. To do this, we spent several days bumping over very rough country. Eventually I decided to give up the attempt to reach the escarpment; for one thing, I could not afford to have a break-down in this remote area.

Each morning we started out full of hope and each evening returned defeated.

On our homeward journey the sun was behind us and we could watch the animals in a perfect light.

The evening scene appeared very peaceful, yet I knew it was the pause before each predator set out to kill and fill his belly, and there were plenty of hyenas prowling about to remind one of the fact. Unlike the cats which make a straight kill, hyenas either try to benefit by the kill of other predators or make for a newly born antelope calf or some other victim which is unable to defend itself.

My nights in camp were often exciting. I could hear lions prowling round and got to recognize the voices of most of them. Once I awoke to hear lapping noises and, being half asleep, listened for some time before I realized that a lioness was inside my tent drinking out of my basin. I had nothing but a table between me and Africa so I shouted at her and urged her to go away which obligingly she did. This incident I reported to the park warden who told me that the lions of the Serengeti were known occasionally to go into tents, pluck at a groundsheet and take a look round to see what was going on.

Although some of my nocturnal visitors made my heart beat fast, the roaring of the lions in the stillness of the night never seemed to me a blood-curdling noise, but a most wonderful sound and often appealingly gentle. The lions close to Seronera, having been used to visitors since cubhood, were particularly friendly. Many had been surrounded by cars while suckling their mothers and therefore had come to regard human beings and motors as a natural feature in their lives.

Except in areas in which people have hunted or shot from cars, the wild animals seemed to consider cars as some kind of fellow-creature with strange habits and a peculiar scent, but nevertheless harmless. So long as passengers do not talk too much or move, they too, if they remain inside, do not cause alarm, but when they get out, the animals panic and race away.

Every day we met many lions – but there was never any trace of our cubs. About this time the director paid a short visit to Seronera. I asked him if I might be allowed to spend a few nights inside my car, near to where I thought the cubs would be. I explained that it seemed hopeless to look for them by daylight but that they would probably be attracted by my headlights. He did not, however, feel able to grant me this permission so I carried on as before.

We now searched as close as we could to the hills on the far side of the river.

The dry season had come and the animals were now dependent on waterholes and such rivers as did not dry up.

This was the time of year when poachers' activities were at their height. Since they knew exactly where the animals must pass to quench their thirst, the wardens worked very hard to counteract their activities and it was horrifying to see the number of snares, poisoned arrows and spears which they confiscated and to realize how small a proportion of the total of weapons and traps these represented: wire for snares is cheap and can be bought from any Indian trader.

All over East Africa poaching, drought, floods and the legal destruction of wild animals to make place for men and their crops, threaten the survival of wild life. The idea that they may one day become extinct appals me. The longer I live among animals the more I want to help them and the more I believe that in helping them we also help man, for if we exterminate all the wild animals we shall upset the balance of creation of which we ourselves are a part. A Quaker paper has made a very apposite remark on our relationship to animals, saying that we are apt to overlook the fact that when in the beginning man was said to have been given dominion over the animals he was without sin, for he had not then disobeyed God, and he lived in daily communion with him.*

As I drove out daily in search of the cubs, I had plenty of time to wonder why man should be divorcing himself from natural life; yet the many letters I received about the Elsa books assured me that an immense number of people would in fact like to live a life which kept them in relation with nature and wild animals; I thought how much they would enjoy seeing, instead of only reading about, the lioness and her cubs which at that moment were blocking our track, stretching out lazily in the sun and not showing any intention of letting us go by (and whose track was it anyway?).

As the days passed in fruitless search, I became more and more depressed and finally wrote to George asking him to come back and help me to find the cubs.

A few days later the director and a park warden visited my camp. I took the opportunity to renew my previous request to be allowed to spend a few nights out in the car in the hope that the cubs would be attracted by the headlights and I also asked if I might be allowed to walk up the escarpment and in the hills, if necessary escorted by an armed African ranger. I stressed again the condition of Jespah's wound and the youth of the cubs. The director replied that at the trustees' next meeting he would put my requests before them; meanwhile he suggested that I should write the chairman. This I did.

One evening while I was typing I was startled by hearing an English voice and looking round saw three men. They were farmers from Kenya who were on holiday and they had pitched their camp within a few hundred yards of mine. Seeing

*'Eastward to Eden', *The Friend*, 5 August 1960

379

my light they had walked across to invite me to have a drink with them.

I was startled that they should have crossed even this short distance without a light, and I pointed out that there were lions about and plenty of cover for them. The men laughed at my anxiety, but accepted my lamp to guide them back.

The next night I dined with them and was astonished to see that they had no tent and slept in the open on camp beds only five inches off the ground. When I asked them what they would do if a lion called on them while they were sleeping they laughed and obviously regarded me as a nervous woman.

Next morning we met again at the rivulet below the camp site; we had to stop as our path was barred by a pride of thirteen lions, which kept us waiting a long time. Eventually the pride moved off and we were able to go on. The farmers left that day and when I returned in the evening I found a bottle of wine and a letter telling me to cheer up and stop worrying about who called in after dark. I hoped they were right but still thought it asking for trouble to sleep in the open on such low camp beds.

On 1 July I received a telegram from George saying that he would arrive on 4 July. Meanwhile I went on searching.

On my way home I was stopped by a safari party who told me that, the night before, a pair of lions had passed within a few yards of their tent and that one of them was limping.

On my return I found George in camp. He had been away nearly a month and had now taken ten days' leave and so anxious was he not to waste a moment of it that he had driven all through the night.

In spite of lack of sleep he was ready to start off at once in search of the cubs, but first he gave me the director's reply to our appeal to the trustees asking for permission to sleep out. It only said that the trustees had discussed our letter and that he was writing officially to let us know what they decided. He added that he hoped we would feel that they had not been unsympathetic in the matter. This didn't tell us much but made us hopeful.

Knowing that the park warden had been to Arusha and was expected back that evening I called on him. He had brought the letter from the director; this stated that if we agreed to certain conditions we could sleep out for not more than seven nights, offer the cubs water and cod-liver oil, walk where we liked, at our own risk, and George could carry firearms for self-defence. The director added that he had obtained permission to move the cubs to Mkomazi Game Reserve in Tanganyika, where, since it was not a national park, we should be able to stay on with them; he however left it entirely to us whether to move them or not.

The conditions referred to were: that we immediately send cages to the area in which we were searching; if and when we found the cubs come to a decision about moving them or leaving them where they were; if they were not to be moved then we were to leave the park and expect no more exceptions to be made for us; if we decided for the move, we were to let the park warden know immediately; we were to make no kill without permission from the park warden, and were to keep him informed every other day about what was going on.

Driving back to camp I passed a safari party which had just arrived and had pitched their tents a few hundred yards from ours. They also were farmers from Kenya.

We then packed our cars for a week's absence. As a result of camping out among wild animals for many years I have become a light sleeper and that night I woke to hear the distant engine of a car. Some moments later the park warden arrived and told us to move at once into the cars as a lion had taken a visitor from a camp near ours and was still prowling around. He asked if we had any morphia with us as there was none in Seronera. The man had been badly mauled. Luckily George had two ampoules, so we gave the warden these and all our supply of sulphonamide.

He told us that there was a charter plane in the area which could take the injured man at first light to Nairobi, then assuring us that there was nothing we could do to help, he left and not long afterwards we heard the plane take off.

Meanwhile George had told Nuru and the rest of our staff to light lamps and keep awake.

Very early we went to the scene of the incident, only three hundred yards from our camp, to find out whether the friends of the unfortunate man needed any help. Our spooring revealed that the two lions had come past our camp and gone along the car track leading to the next camp and had stopped abreast of it. The spoor was that of two male lions; one was considerably larger than the other. The bigger lion had gone up to the camp fire, seized a large enamel jug and bitten through it, an indication of the capacity of his jaws. The camping party had consisted of five people, a married couple who had a tent of their own, the entrance flaps of which they had closed for the night, and three men who shared a tent. The night was warm so the men had not put up their mosquito nets and had placed their low camp beds in a row. They lay with their heads at the entrance of the tent which they left open. One had placed a basin set on a stand behind his head, the man next to him had the middle tent pole as a protection but the third had nothing between him and the world outside. During the night the farmer in the middle bed, woken by a low moaning sound, noticed that his neighbour's bed was empty and disarranged. He switched on a torch and, fifteen yards away, saw a lion with his friend's head in its mouth. He roused the camp, and two African servants very courageously rushed towards the lion; one flung a panga (a long knife) at it. Possibly this hit the lion for he dropped the man, bit viciously at the handle of the panga and moved a short distance away. The injured farmer was quickly rescued. Meanwhile the lion continued to circle the camp and was only kept off by having a car driven towards him.

Among the visitors at the lodge there was a European dresser who was able to attend to the farmer's wounds, and then the park wardens and their wives cared for him until the plane was able to take off and fly him to Nairobi; unfortunately his wounds proved fatal and he died on the operating table.

This was the first fatal accident to take place in the Serengeti since it became a national park. That morning two of the park wardens shot both lions. The larger one was found to have a septic wound in his shoulder, which no doubt was a serious handicap to his hunting activities. In such circumstances any lion in any part of Africa will not hesitate to kill a human being.

38. We See the Cubs Again

The director arrived by plane that morning and we had a talk with him. He confirmed the concession to sleep out in the cub valley for seven nights but so far as preparing for feeding the cubs should we find them emaciated, he advised us not to cross our bridges before we came to them, and added that in an emergency the park warden might be able to help us. George had only eight days' leave left so we decided that we would not have time to collect the crates though this was a condition mentioned in the letter. In any case we could not know whether or not they would be needed. Before we could start we had to move our camp to Seronera, as in view of the accident no more camping was to be allowed till security measures had been taken.

As a result it was late in the day before we set off to the cub ravine. When we got there we parked our cars in the middle of the small plain where George had seen the cubs in May.

No cubs showed up during that night.

Early in the morning we drove near to the cubs' ravine and climbed the escarpment above it where nearly a month ago we had seen the cubs. We walked along its crest for nearly three hours, calling repeatedly but in vain. Then we came down into the next valley and walked back to the car. As we reached the top of a rise which led into the cub ravine George grabbed me by the shoulder. There were all three cubs sitting by the cars waiting for us. They behaved in the most matter-of-fact manner as though we had never left them. Jespah came to greet us giving the soft moans with which Elsa always welcomed us. He allowed me to pat his head and then sat and watched us as we went over to the other cubs. They went off as we approached and settled under a tree. But when we offered them cod-liver oil and water they came and lapped it up quickly. They were thin but in fair condition though Jespah and Gopa had now completely lost their ruffs and looked like lionesses. Jespah's coat was no longer shining and he still carried the arrow. The wound was discharging a thin serum which attracted flies and which he licked repeatedly; he also had some small scars probably gained in combat with other animals. He was very friendly and came close to us but would not allow us to pull at the arrowhead.

It was wonderful to see the cubs again and as we watched them we discussed several puzzling questions. Why had the lions lost their ruffs? We knew that under stress domestic cats sometimes moult. Could Jespah and Gopa have become maneless owing to the strain of adapting themselves to a new environment? Why had they turned up today? Had they seen the light during the night and realized that we were there? Or had they been hiding when I searched in the cub valley and been too frightened by the presence of the strange driver to come into the open?

Though previously they had always taken cover during the hot hours of the day, now they stayed in the light shade of a tree while we lunched. When George went off to collect the second car which we had left in the plain, this didn't disturb them and for all the rest of that day they remained in the open. In fact they seemed to be adopting the habits of the Serengeti lions.

The solitary impala ram was present all the time. Towards dark he moved in a leisurely way down the hill grazing as he went. Little Elsa stalked him and after a while Jespah followed. So long as the ram was feeding they crouched low and wriggled towards him but when he looked in their direction they froze. Gopa remained behind watching the hunt. Finally, the impala dashed off and the cubs returned.

We had stored some of our kit beside our camp beds inside the cars and the rest on the roof. Jespah inspected these objects hoping perhaps to find his dinner, and even Gopa and Little Elsa came close to us, but we had nothing for them but cod-liver oil. We allowed them to drink as much of this as we thought good for them, then they settled close to our car and during the night we heard them playing. Jespah visited us several times, no doubt puzzled that we had not given him any meat.

After the weeks of anxiety it was a tremendous relief to know that the release had proved a success and that the cubs were in relatively good condition: the only worry was Jespah's discharging wound and his dull coat. We could not consider moving the cubs again after all they had been through, nor did we want to remove Jespah separately if he could be operated on in the Serengeti. So we decided to use our week to try to get him into better condition and then try to make arrangements to have him operated upon. The day now at our disposal did not allow us time to do this.

Next morning we found the cubs under a bush about four hundred yards down the hill. Jespah came at once and placed himself between us and his brother and sister and I gave him his cod-liver oil. That morning his coat was much worse than it had been when we first saw him and he was covered with swellings the size of peas. This worried us but we did not wish to raise a false alarm about it until we were sure what the swellings were due to; they looked rather similar to swellings which Elsa had sometimes developed after rolling on ants. However, we could not be sure that this was what they were and would have to keep Jespah under observation. This meant feeding the cubs who would otherwise need to go off hunting.

George therefore drove off to Seronera to get permission to feed the cubs and to send a cable to the publishers of the Elsa books to give them our good news.

In his enthusiasm he worded this telegram and also a similar one to the director at Arusha over-optimistically: 'Cubs found in excellent condition.' This wording caused a false impression and later gave rise to a grave misunderstanding. While George was away I watched the cubs dozing under a bush.

About lunchtime a herd of some 120 Tommies appeared together with the impala ram. On seeing me they stopped, turned towards the cubs and began grazing within twenty yards of them. One cheeky Tommy even went up to their bush and indeed the whole herd behaved as though no lions were about. The cubs sat on their haunches, heads on their paws, watching. This went on for half an hour, then, suddenly, Little Elsa rushed full speed at the herd which fled into the valley except for some twenty-five Tommies which got cut off and remained behind. A little later she chased these too, but plainly only for the fun of it. Neither side took the game seriously until Gopa and Jespah joined in the hunt, when the Tommies clattered over the rocks and up the hill, all except one small fawn and its father, which stood quietly watching the proceedings and only left after the cubs had returned. Then they walked slowly down the valley to rejoin the others. Halfway there they were met by the fawn's mother who licked it and guided it safely back to the herd.

George returned without a kill; the park warden had been absent, so he had waited till the afternoon when he could speak to the director over the radio. He obtained permission to buy two goats at a small village outside the park, some sixty miles away, but since he could not get there and back in the day he had to put off getting the goats till the next day.

At dusk the cubs came looking for their dinner but as we had only cod-liver oil to give them they left early. Next morning George drove off to get the goats and I sorted out our kit and aired our bedding. The cubs arrived while everything was still laid out on the ground. This provided them with a splendid game, but they were very good-natured and in the end allowed me to collect all our possessions undamaged. After this they retired into the shade of a bush where they spent the rest of the day.

George arrived at 6 p.m. with the goats. The moment he saw the meat, Jespah seized it and raced away with it; Gopa and Little Elsa chased him and there was a scrimmage. The three cubs sat, noses together, holding on to the carcase, tempers grew hot and there were growls and spittings; for an hour the deadlock went on and not one of them would give way. Then Gopa made a try to go off with the meat, but Jespah grabbed it instantly and another deadlock ensued. With ears flattened and giving angry snarls the brothers faced each other while Little Elsa quietly gnawed away. Finally Jespah and Gopa relaxed and the three cubs ate amicably together.

The second carcase we placed on the roof of the car, thinking it would be safe there till tomorrow, as the cubs had never tried to get on to the cars. But early in the morning I was woken by a heavy thud and found the car rocking violently. The next moment I saw Jespah jump with the carcase from the roof on to the bonnet and make off with it to the ravine followed by the other cubs.

A couple of hours later he reappeared and leapt on to the roof of the car where we had stored our surplus kit and found a lot of things there to delight him: cardboard boxes filled with bottles, my plant press, a rubber cushion, a folding armchair. Busily he emptied the boxes, clattering their contents on to the ground. Then he tried to get at the blotting paper inside the plant press and when defeated threw it overboard. He also ransacked the rest of our kit. When he had finished he rested his head on his paws and blinked at us. His brother and sister had watched him intently but had not ventured to join him; now they went off to play on a fallen tree where Jespah soon joined them. The three cubs prodded each other playfully for a while and then disappeared into the ravine.

We noticed a lot of vultures circling above the crest of the nearest hill and supposed they were leaving a kill, probably one made by the lion which I had heard roaring close by during the night. After lunch we went to look for the cubs and found them asleep in the dense cover at the base of the cliff. Next to them was the carcase of a freshly killed reedbuck. Whether they had killed it or stolen it from a leopard we couldn't tell. That a kill should have taken place so close to us without our hearing a sound was odd enough.

In the evening we went back to the cubs and found that they had practically finished the reedbuck and had dragged what remains were left into cover. We could hear the lions breathing in the thicket but we could not see them. It seemed extraordinary that such large animals could hide themselves so completely – particularly as we knew to within a few feet where they were. Later the coughing of a leopard told us who had made the kill.

When it was dark the cubs came for a drink and spent the night near us but by the morning they had gone off. After lunch they emerged from the ravine and Jespah hopped on to the roof of my car, while Gopa and Little Elsa lay under the shade of a tree some fifty yards away. I wondered why Jespah preferred to get on my car rather than George's. Had he got used to thinking it was *his* car, or did it look to him the more comfortable of the two? Elsa had always preferred George's car.

The impala ram was present as usual; he gave snorts and grunts but the cubs took no notice of him. Little Elsa spent some time stalking Tommies but was evidently not out for a kill and soon settled down. I sat close to Jespah and whenever my position allowed I tried to pull at the arrow. He made no objection to my twiddling the protruding shank, but it was firmly fixed as ever and there was no sign of its sloughing out. The point of the arrow was just below the skin and a small slit might well suffice to pull it out point first. The swellings, probably due to ant bites, had disappeared, but his coat looked dull and shabby. But when the setting sun turned it to gold, his features and his expression were so like his mother's that when he looked at me intently, as she used to do, I suddenly had the impression that Elsa had returned. While he allowed me to pat his paw and stroke his nostrils he shut his eyes and I closed mine. Then I felt certain that Elsa was there. After I opened my eyes again I felt strangely free.

When night came we retired to our cars. Very soon the canvas roof of mine sagged under Jespah's weight and from my bed I was able to pat him through the canvas. Later George was woken by the swaying of his car and found Jespah leaning over the tail-board looking at him as though he wanted to come in. There was no sign of the others and Jespah himself left at dawn.

We spent the morning looking for the lions and found no trace of them; but at teatime they came up from the valley in which we had been looking for them and Jespah seated himself on the bonnet of my car. I made a last attempt to move the arrow but without success.

Tomorrow we should have to leave the cubs and we could have been fairly happy about them had it not been for Jespah's wound. However little it seemed to encumber him at the moment, it had obviously weakened his condition and was a source of infection as his dull coat proved. In combat with a prey the skin might get torn or the arrowhead packed deeper and either of these possibilities might cause serious damage which would ultimately impair his capacity to hunt. In the circumstances the sooner he could be operated on the better. We discussed the situation and decided to cut our time with the cubs short and leave as early as was possible the next morning, so that we could speak over the radio to the director and get permission to carry out the operation. For this we should need a crate in which to confine Jespah and a veterinary surgeon to give the anaesthetic and perform the operation. George was sure that his leave would be extended for the time necessary to make the arrangements and get the operation performed.

When it was dark Jespah came for his cod-liver oil. There was not much left in the gallon tin we had opened six days ago and I wanted to divide it equally among the cubs. When Jespah saw me holding the tin he tried to seize it. I said 'No, Jespah, no,' and looking puzzled and hurt he at once turned away. After this I poured the oil into three dishes. Gopa and Little Elsa drank theirs up at once, but Jespah was offended and would not come near the dish I held out to him. I dared not put it on the ground for then the others would have finished it off, so I tried my best to get into favour again. But Jespah looked stonily in the opposite direction and ignored me.

We passed the evening watching the cubs licking each other and rolling about affectionately together behind the cars. They left about 11 p.m. This was the last we were to see of them though at the time we expected to return soon with a vet.

Later in the night we heard some lions calling in a low voice to each other and hoped it might be our cubs hunting.

Next morning we left for Seronera, hoping to arrange facilities to operate on Jespah at once. These were denied. On our way through Arusha we approached the director again. He advised us to appeal to the trustees who were holding the next meeting in August. With a heavy heart we left Tanganyika.

39. The Long Search

When we got to Nairobi we heard the good news that Ken Smith could now take over as Senior Warden of the NFD, leaving George free to help with the cubs. We wrote to the director of the Tanganyika National Parks, asking him to submit our request for permission to operate on Jespah to the trustees at their mid-August meeting.

I went first to Isiolo to move our furniture out of the Government house in which we had been living and into one which we had rented from the National Parks of Kenya and which was about eight miles from our old home. Meanwhile, George set off to help to move a herd of Thomas kob which were living in an area where their presence clashed with human interest, to a game reserve, 300 miles away. This operation was being financed partly by the Game Department, partly by the Elsa Appeal and partly by royalties from the Elsa books. These Thomas kob are not only beautiful antelope, but their herd which numbers about 500 head is the only one of the species in Kenya.

Towards the end of August Billy Collins paid another visit to East Africa. He came in the hope of getting a last sight of the cubs and to attend the Arusha Conference. This conference was the first to which people from all over the world, who were interested in the preservation of wild life, had been invited to come together to discuss the conservation of game in East Africa.

Billy Collins's arrival in Nairobi coincided with the receipt of a telegram from the director, informing us that the trustees had refused permission for an operation to be performed on Jespah.

Doctor T. Harthoorn, of Makerere Veterinary College, one of the most distinguished veterinary surgeons in Africa, had already agreed to do the operation, should Jespah be found in a state which demanded an intervention. As he happened to be in Nairobi at this time we were able to talk over with him, and also with Noel Simon, Founder and Chairman of the East African Wild Life Society, and Major Grimwood what, in view of the new blow to our hopes, we should now do.

We decided that Billy and I should go to the Serengeti and spend a week there trying to find the cubs and that Billy would see the chairman in Arusha and try to persuade him to change his mind, and allow Dr Harthoorn to operate, if this were possible and if he considered it necessary.

On our way through Arusha, Billy called on the director and discussed our wish to be allowed to sleep out in order to find the cubs and to have permission to operate on Jespah, if when we found him this seemed necessary. This conversation did not result in any change of attitude on the director's part; but they agreed that after our search for the cubs, Billy should see the chairman and talk the matter over with him.

Early in the morning after our arrival at Seronera, we set off for the cubs' release point. We found it occupied by a party of surveyors who had been living there for the last month. We asked them what lions they had seen. They had seen many, but could not, of course, know whether the cubs had been among them.

Then we went up to the cub ravine and I called Jespah, Gopa, Little Elsa, but there was no response. So we continued up the valley. Every time we saw trees covered with vultures, we drove up to them, hoping to find the cubs on a kill but were always disappointed. We found several pride of lion and at one point came very close to a herd of 200 buffalo and were obliged to drive off very quickly indeed. We stayed as late as was possible if we were to comply with the regulation that compelled tourists to be back at Seronera before dark.

For the next days we searched along the river where, owing to the drought, there was a bigger concentration of animals than I had ever seen before. Finally we went back to the ravine and called for a long time but saw no sign of the cubs. On our way home we saw a beautiful cheetah on his anthill and at a big pool a leopard and a saddlebill stork quenching their thirst.

By the fourth day Billy was obviously unwell. He had been unmercifully bitten by tsetse, his arms and legs were very swollen and I was thankful that a doctor happened to be staying at the lodge. He diagnosed an allergy, prescribed remedies and advised Billy not to go back to the tsetse-infected area.

One evening we dined with the park warden and his wife and met the director who suggested that on the following day we should witness the release of a rhino which had been brought to the park from an area where it interfered with a settlement scheme. It was the first release of this type.

A great many people arrived to see the release. When the doors of the crate were opened and the rhino became visible a din arose. The bewildered beast walked towards a saloon car, whose owner, startled by warning shouts, moved it quickly; then the rhino turned and passed close to the chairman's car, went slowly towards the river and finally disappeared into a thicket. I was relieved to see its good behaviour, as rhinos particularly when provoked are most unpredictable beasts.

Billy took this occasion to give the chairman a letter asking him to allow the operation on Jespah to be performed. Soon afterwards we left the Serengeti.

When we reached the Manyara Escarpment on our way to Arusha, the sun was setting; in the fading light the expanse around us seemed boundless. Suddenly we heard a sound of humming and the notes of an instrument, which sounded like a xylophone, and there, walking across the immense plain, was a small toto playing a home-made instrument, consisting of a few bars of thin metal of differing lengths fixed across a hollow wooden box. As the little boy walked out into the darkness, it seemed to me that Africa was his, or he was Africa – maybe he was.

The next day, various people who had been attending the conference lunched with us; they included the chairman. We all did our best to persuade him to agree that Jespah should be operated on if this became possible and necessary. We did not succeed. Noel Simon, who was particularly unhappy at our failure, afterwards wrote on behalf of the East African Wild Life Society to the chairman suggesting that Dr Harthoorn should accompany George on a ten-day search for Jespah and if they found him, perform the operation if he thought it advisable. I agreed not to accompany George and Dr Harthoorn, thus giving proof that my insistence that Jespah should be found did not arise from a selfish motive. Then we motored to Nairobi and Billy caught his plane for Europe.

When I got back to Isiolo I found George there who had news that Elsa's grave had been wrecked by elephant and rhino, so we set off to investigate, taking with us the slab of stone on which her name had been cut and a bag of cement to make the cairn elephant-proof.

When we got there we found the damage much less than we had expected. But rhino had obviously used it as a resting place, two of the euphorbias and all the aloes had been eaten, and the bush along the riverbank and in the studio had been trampled flat. I found elephant and rhino droppings everywhere. I had dreaded going back, but now felt strangely at peace, almost as though I had come home.

Next morning we drove to the Big Rock and collected lorry-loads of large slabs, which we broke off the surface of the rock and rolled down the steep slopes. We wanted to build up the cairn, cover the stones with slabs and cement the whole invisibly together. At the head of the grave we intended to place the black slab on which Elsa's name and the dates were engraved. For a week we worked at Elsa's grave and during this time the unusual silence seemed unbearable.

We waited until the end of October to learn the trustees' decision. When it came it was a refusal. Determined to find Jespah, we decided to return immediately to the Serengeti although this meant that we should have to race against the rains and search for him under tourist conditions.

In the NFD the rains had already started and we had a lot of difficulty in getting our two Land Rovers and the Elsa lorry along the flooded road which led to Tanganyika.

When we reached the Serengeti we found an overcast sky which threatened to release floods at any moment.

We camped at our former site. The plains were teeming with large herds of wildebeest and zebra and there were many foals and calves amongst them. When we went to the cub valley we were held up at its entrance by a lioness who was blind in one eye and whom we had seen before. She lay in the track and wouldn't move, so we were obliged to drive round her. In the ravine we found no trace of lion but when we drove on to the parkland valley, we saw a pride of five at a zebra kill and among them two young lions, one with a short blond mane and another with one

395

equally short but darker. We remained there for four hours watching the pair until we were quite sure that they were not Jespah and Gopa.

We thought that one way of attracting our cubs might be by leaving our empty car out overnight by the ravine. The familiar sight might attract them and if it did so, next morning we would recognise the spoor; or they might even wait for us. We therefore placed my car where it could be seen from a long way off and then went home in George's.

That night it poured which delayed our start next morning and later we were held up by finding four lionesses with six very small cubs at a kill near the head of the cub valley. We stopped to watch them and soon noticed that we ourselves were being watched by a fifth lioness who was hiding behind our car. We had never seen so many female lions together but assumed that the male must be close by.

On our arrival at the ravine we found no lion spoor near the car and decided to leave the Land Rover where it was for some time so we protected the wheels with thorns and removed the spare tyre, because hyenas are not averse to eating rubber.

By now the rains had set in properly and flooded the country. In spite of the difficult conditions we went every morning first to the ravine, crept up valleys and into the hinterland beyond the escarpment, but we never saw a sign of the cubs. We covered about one hundred miles a day.

Soon the rains increased and it was no longer possible to drive along the river and even the high ground along the base of the escarpment was in a bad state. Sometimes we got stones to put into ruts; at others we were able to find a termite hill and place its hard cement-like substance under the wheels. Often George had to harness himself to the block and tackle; one end of the rope would be tied to a tree while the other cut deeply into his shoulder, as he heaved the car out of the mud.

To avoid getting bogged, we kept, as much as we could, to the tops of the ridges and found that the few animals which were about were doing as we were.

However, a moment came when we were obliged to cross a lugga. Almost at once, the car got completely stuck in muddy water right at the bottom. All day we worked to get it free, but without success.

Just before it got quite dark, George decided to have a last try at heaving us out. But as he pulled with all his strength on the rope, it broke and he somersaulted backwards into the icy water.

All we could do now was to spend the night where we were.

George settled himself in the back of the car and I made myself as comfortable as I could on the front seat, from which I kept an anxious eye on the water which was still rising and was by now about at the level of the seats. Luckily we had a Primus stove with us. George lit it and dried his soaking clothes on a line over it. We spent a most disagreeable night and the irony of it was that, after pleading for so long to spend a night in the open, so as to attract the cubs by keeping our headlights on, now that an accident had obliged us to pass a night in the open, our position at the bottom of the lugga was such that our lights could not be seen at any distance.

About 11 o'clock the next morning we heard the vibrations of a car engine and hoped this meant that someone was looking for us, but very soon the noise faded away. Soaked to the skin, we went on working in the pouring rain till 3 p.m. when we decided that as after twenty-eight hours we hadn't managed to move the car one inch we had better start walking back to Seronera. We were exhausted and it would be a long and dangerous walk, but better than spending another night in such awful conditions. We were just starting off when a Land Rover arrived and out got an American who had camped near us at Seronera two days before.

He told us that when we didn't return our boys gave the alarm and two cars set out in search of us, but the heavy rain had obliterated our spoor. It was one of these cars which we had heard during the morning. Now even with a lot of pushing and towing it took us two hours to get clear, before the cars splashed home to Seronera. That evening we celebrated our return with our last bottle of sherry.

No one could remember such awful rains and it was estimated that 75 per cent of the animals had moved to the higher slopes of the Ngorongoro crater to escape from the swampy plains. We knew that lions were taking part in the exodus and wondered whether our cubs were among them. The unprecedented floods often imprisoned us for days on end and camp life became very uncomfortable.

The weather continued to be appalling; there was very little game about and the lions near the lodge had to go considerable distances to find prey; as a result the cubs who were too young to accompany their mothers were often deserted for as long as forty-eight hours. When the lionesses as well as the cubs became emaciated the park warden sometimes shot a buck to prevent the mother from having to abandon her children while hunting. This helped the Seronera prides but I wondered how many new-born cubs far away from the lodge would survive these conditions.

As I was suffering from toothache and anxious to see a dentist in Nairobi I was glad that a plane could land in such weather and that I was able to get a seat on it.

I spent five days in Nairobi and then flew back bringing a winch with me; next day when we went to the cub ravine it proved its worth, for we were able to extricate the car from any hole in a short time and could therefore drive along places which we had till then thought too dangerous to risk.

It was a month since we had left my car in the ravine but as the rains had washed away all spoor we could not tell whether the cubs had been to inspect it. Hoping for better luck we left it where it was.

We drove ten miles down the valley but saw no game except buffalo. Tsetse were present in swarms and the canvas of the car was black with them. We disproved the theory that they only follow moving objects for even when we stood still we were covered with them and however long we waited they showed no sign of taking off.

On 6 December two park wardens called to tell us that in connection with a visit Prince Philip was making to the Serengeti on the 11–12 December we must leave Seronera from the 8th to the 13th and suggested that we should spend this time at Banagi, eleven miles away. We asked whether we might not be given special permission to continue to look for the cubs during the days that the Duke was not spending in the park, but the director did not grant it. So we moved to Banagi.

Until Seronera was built this had been the headquarters of the Serengeti and the house was now used as temporary accommodation for people doing research work in the park. In memory of Michael Grzimek a laboratory has been built near to the house which it is hoped will one day become a centre of scientific research. Both buildings stand on a small hill over-looking the river which one has to cross to reach them. A cement causeway makes the crossing easy in dry weather but when there are floods communication with Seronera is only preserved by a bamboo bridge which hangs from trees that grow on opposite banks.

All we could do there was to write our mail and listen to the wireless on which we heard an appeal from the small Somali village near Elsa's camp for help in fighting the floods.

After our return on 13 December we went to the cub ravine where we saw a lioness with an injured eye; she watched us calmly for a quarter of an hour. She didn't look like Little Elsa but to make sure we called all the familiar names and waved her pie dish at her. But she only continued to look at us and finally she disappeared into the ravine. It was strange that a wild lioness should have remained so long watching us, but probably she had cubs in the ravine which she was guarding.

Now I must confess that during my last visit to Nairobi I had been so depressed about Jespah that for the first time in my life I had consulted a fortune-teller, a man of great repute. He told me that on 21 December my stars would change and with them my luck and that I should be unexpectedly successful. (I assumed in finding the cubs.) He added that during the critical period I was to wear something blue, for this was my lucky colour. I was rather ashamed of myself and didn't tell George what I had done but I did keep a blue handkerchief on me by day and by night, and on the 21st I felt excited. That morning we decided to try to reach the ravine but came upon a vast lake which formed over a salt lick. George tested it by wading in up to his thighs, then he took off the fan belt and drove the car into it. Almost at once, we stuck and the water rushed up to the level of the seats. As fast as I could I took off my clothes, grabbed the cameras and waded out. In my hurry I forgot my blue talisman and when I looked back I saw my handkerchief floating away and with it my belief in fortune-tellers. We spent all the rest of the day working to get the car out, so it was not till next morning that we were able to go to the ravine. We found my car still there; we checked it, and then drove fifteen miles down the valley, but saw only a giraffe and a couple of hyenas. The tsetse were in full force and the going was so rough that the back axle of the car broke. When in the evening, rattling and slushing through the mud, we reached Seronera, we were greeted with cries of 'Here comes the submarine', a name which stuck to George's car. I went to bed early but woke at about 5 a.m. and heard two lions whuffing near the kitchen. I turned quickly so that I could watch the opening of my tent. A few moments later a heavy body brushed against the canvas and pulled out several tent ropes, then a large lion came in and stood within a few feet of my bed; with his great mane he looked like a giant powder-puff. Luckily there was a camp table between us which gave me time to yell. At my shouts the lion jumped back, went out and rejoined his friend. Both trotted past George's tent, but kept on whuffing for a long time; they were probably intrigued by the light of our torches which we focused in their direction. On the following night the pair came again to visit us but I heard them in time to shout and prevent them from calling on me. They walked between our tents and then disappeared into the night.

George's car had to go to the workshop for much-needed repairs, so on Christmas Eve we got our lorry to take us to the cub ravine where my car was still stationed. When we reached it the driver went home in the truck and we drove on in my car.

It rained without stopping and we saw no sign of the cubs, so, towards evening, turned home very dispirited. When we came to the river we found that it had risen rapidly and was now eight feet deep. This meant that we were cut off from Seronera and should have to spend the night out. It would be very uncomfortable but perhaps it might give us the chance we had waited for for so long, of attracting the cubs with our headlights. We parked in the open as far as we could from the river and left the lights switched on.

They attracted millions of mosquitoes and other insects, and, as we had no aerosol, we were completely at their mercy. All I could do was to put a cloth we had used for cleaning the windows of the car over my face to protect it.

Twice we heard lions roar and hoped the cubs might come. But only a hyena appeared. She showed great interest in our rubber tyres and was not at all alarmed by our shouts, but bolted when she got our scent. I lay on the front seat remembering how we had spent the last two Christmases. Christmas Day 1959, when Elsa had suddenly reappeared for the first time after giving birth to her cubs and had swept our Christmas dinner off the table in her joy at seeing us again; and Christmas Eve 1960, when she and the cubs had watched me light the candles with so much interest and Jespah had gone off with my present for George and I had opened the envelope which contained the deportation order.

Today bore no resemblance to those days and in the morning when I wished George a Happy Christmas, he looked surprised and asked: 'Is today Christmas Day?' All the same, I was glad I had spent last night in the car rather than in camp; but George felt that we should try to get back to Seronera at once, so as to prevent a rescue party from setting out to look for us and wasting petrol of which there was very little left.

The river had fallen during the night and with some trouble we managed to cross it; soon afterwards we plunged into a deep hole and I hit my head so hard that I saw stars, but not the favourable stars which the fortune-teller had promised me.

When we arrived in camp the boys told us that all through the night lions had been around, and the ample spoor we saw corroborated this story.

A big Christmas mail was waiting for us; presents had come from all over the world: several of the donors had taken the conditions in which we were living into account, so besides having many nice things to take back to Seronera, our camping from now on would be much more comfortable.

It was a lovely evening and we saw a strange phenomenon which we had sometimes observed in the semi-desert areas of the NFD. As the rays of the setting sun faded out in the west, in the east there appeared a reflection of the sunset, rather blurred but otherwise an exact replica.

We continued hunting for the cubs from dawn to dusk, and

observed that the wild animals were gradually returning to the valley. Among them were three lionesses with five cubs. Thereafter we met them so often that they became quite accustomed to us and one afternoon when the lionesses went off to stalk a buffalo they left the cubs to stay put so close to the car that we could easily have picked them up.

For a short time the weather improved, then the rain returned with renewed force. Our only chance of finding the cubs was to look for them on the higher levels. So, as far as the floods permitted, we decided to make a thorough search of the hilly area. To reach it we would drive across the plains, keeping where possible to the ridges.

The ground was terribly soggy and as disagreeable to the animals as to ourselves; we had proof of this one morning when we saw a lioness and her two cubs high up in a tree obviously trying to keep dry. As we came up to take a photograph, the little ones fell to the ground, then the lioness jumped down but immediately led them up another tree. On this trip we also saw a very amusing sight: three jackals being chased by angry guinea fowl. Whenever the jackals turned the cackling birds flew over the trio or pecked at them. At this the jackals rushed off with their tails between their legs to a safe vantage point from which a little later they made a counter-attack, but the fowl grew so aggressive that finally the jackals bolted.

During all these weeks the rains never ceased and our submarine gradually fell to pieces; the centre bolt went, the U-bolts, the brake pipe, the starter, finally the exhaust pipe broke off, yet, in spite of this, the car continued to carry us until the day when we were again marooned in our camp by the floods. Then I used the car as a bedroom, for my tent was leaking like a sieve and anyway perhaps it was prudent to sleep there, as a pride of lions with five cubs had settled very close to the camp.

40. The Price of Freedom

We had now struggled for months against the worst possible weather, wrecking our car, putting important work aside and doing no good to our health and all this under conditions which greatly reduced our chances of finding the cubs. So, when on 2 February the director came to Seronera, I wrote to him repeating my plea to be allowed to sleep out since this was our best hope of seeing the cubs. He replied that it was not within his competence to give us such permission but that he would place my request before the trustees at their March meeting if I wished him to do so. By then Jespah, if he were still alive, would have carried the arrowhead for a year, unless it had sloughed out. Since, for the time being, we could do nothing more than obtain the permission we needed we continued our search, trying desperately to find a route by which we could reach the escarpment and its hinterland. But only when the rains had decreased did we eventually succeed in reaching the top of the escarpment and driving along it. The early morning and late afternoon were the most probable times for seeing the cubs but it was difficult for us to reach the area where they might be early enough, or to leave late enough because of the need to obey the park regulation, to be at Seronera during the hours of darkness.

One evening the director visited us and I suggested that as a possible way of breaking the deadlock between the park authorities and ourselves I would be ready to attend the March meeting of the trustees if it were thought that by doing so I could clarify the position. The director promised to let me know if this could be arranged. The camp manager, who had come with him, told us that two days earlier when he had approached the shed in which he kept his Land Rover a lioness had jumped out of the open back of his car and that today she had repeated her performance. Evidently she was seeking shelter from the rain; but in future the camp manager proposed to keep the canvas drawn over the back of his car.

After some days I learned that the trustees had agreed that I should appear at the meeting, so, when the time came, I started off for Arusha, leaving George to search for the cubs. As I drove across the plain I saw that great herds of wildebeest and zebra were returning to it from the high ground. While it had been devoid of game we had not searched the area, but I thought that when I returned we must see whether our cubs might not be among these herds.

The executive committee of the Board of Trustees consisted of the chairman, three trustees and the director; a veterinary surgeon was there as a guest. I asked to be permitted to sleep out and if we did find the cubs to be allowed to decide afterwards what it would be best to do about Jespah. My request was turned down on the advice of the veterinary surgeon who had never seen Jespah, and on the evidence of the telegram George had sent in July, saying that we had found the cubs in excellent condition. I pointed out that as soon as we had time to observe the cubs more closely we had retracted this statement as far as Jespah was concerned, and I stressed that many people who were well qualified to judge the case of a lion carrying an arrowhead had supported our view that an intervention might be essential. I added that these were people who would not risk their reputation unless they were sure of their facts. It was all of no avail so we found ourselves back where we had been for the last nine months. Before I left, my attention was drawn to the fact that the Serengeti would be closed during the next rainy period – April and May – but that should we wish to come back in June as ordinary visitors, there would be no objection.

When I told George the outcome of the meeting he decided to appeal to the Minister of Lands, Forests and Wild Life of Tanganyika, and wrote to Minister Tewa asking for permission to sleep out and also to continue our search in the Serengeti during the rainy period. The reply was negative.

During the time that was left we determined to concentrate our searches in the areas which were free of tsetse and should it prove necessary, we would return in June and continue to look for Jespah. When the park warden returned from a safari he told us that he had seen the lame young lion which a white hunter had also recently seen. He was still in company with another lion who was plainly providing him with food, since he could not hunt for himself. The park warden had shot two Tommies to help him out, but doubted if he would recover and said he meant to keep an eye on him and put him out of his misery if it seemed necessary. On hearing this, even though the warden had assured us that the lion could not be Jespah as he had no wound or scar, we set off at once to find the injured animal. On our way we met a safari party who told us that they had seen two very thin young lions one of which limped. We did not think this could be the warden's pair for they were ten miles away from where he had observed them and the lame animal could hardly have covered such a distance.

Within a few hundred yards of Naabi Hill were some rocks and a few trees which provided shade and made the spot an ideal lie-up for lions; from here they could watch the surrounding plain which was now teeming with game.

We found the rocks occupied by two young lions. George had seen them before; then one of them had been ill, but now both were in fine condition. They rubbed their heads affectionately against each other just as our cubs always did. Nearby was a fully grown lioness; when we stopped the car to take a photograph of her she rolled on her back with her four paws in the air and yawned lazily.

One morning we saw a young blond lion and three lionesses on a kopje; they let us come close to them, and the lion, though he seemed older than Jespah, looked tantalizingly like him and I could only hope that one day he too would have his harem and be equally happy. When we saw the pride again late in the afternoon they were in the plain and evidently selecting a prey for their evening meal from among a group of three zebra and a foal which were grazing unsuspectingly about four hundred yards away.

One of the lionesses advanced, her belly close to the ground; after thirty yards she stopped to let the rest of the pride catch up with her; the lion brought up the rear. Then a different lioness took the lead and led the party forward another thirty yards. They were within seventy yards of their prey before one of the zebra noticed them. The lions, seeing that they had been spotted, froze; the zebra looked calmly at them and continued feeding. Meanwhile the foal moved towards the pride as it grazed. Everything around was quiet and peaceful and it was distressing to see the little zebra so innocently approaching the lions; they seemed to be in no hurry and just sat in a line, watching. Well, the lions had to live and who was I to criticize them for killing in order to survive; indeed, I could remember a time when I thought it great sport to shoot a defenceless deer. That was long ago and after I had lived for some time close to animals in their natural environment I could no longer imagine how I had once been capable of taking the lives of harmless creatures simply to provide a trophy for my vanity.

When the light faded we had to drive home so were spared seeing the end of the stalk, but perhaps the foal escaped, for next day when we came to the place expecting to find the pride on a kill, there was no carcase nor were there any lions to be seen. A few miles farther away, we found three lionesses devouring a freshly killed wildebeest. One of them was carefully removing the hairs of the beard and spitting them out. She reminded me of Elsa, who always detested tickling hairs and feathers and although she loved guinea fowl refused to eat one unless we had first plucked it for her. In the afternoon we had a chance of seeing the ceremony observed by wild dogs on rejoining their pack. We came upon eight at their burrow and noticed a ninth rushing towards them. He arrived panting, greeting each member of the pack in turn by rubbing himself against it; when he had finished his round he moved away and defecated. Then he came back to rest with the other dogs. Later four more arrivals took place; each dog behaved exactly in the same manner. We were therefore convinced that this greeting to all members of the pack by a returning dog and the marking of the burrow with excrement, must be customary with wild dogs.

Circling round Naabi Hill on our way back, we saw a pride of eight lions and stopped the car; immediately a young male rushed up and sat close looking at us. He was so strikingly like Jespah that we even wondered whether he might be our cub, but he showed no scar and his expression was different. All the same we wanted to test him, but could not wait to do so because of the need to be back at Seronera by nightfall.

Very early next morning we set out to look for him again. The pride had only moved a short distance into the plain; they were dozing and too replete to bother about us, except for the young lion who came up, circled the car and behaved in such a friendly manner that doubts again assailed us. Could he be Jespah? The pie dish would be the conclusive test. We held it out: the cub looked at it with complete indifference. Then his brothers and sisters plucked up courage and came to play around the car and we had to resign ourselves to the fact that these were not Elsa's children, though the largest male cub had many characteristics in common with him, including the habit of keeping watch over the pride whilst the adults rested and recovered their energy for the night's hunting. Once this young lion had satisfied himself that we were harmless he went over to his father and snuggled up to him but, head on paws, continued to watch us through half-closed eyes, long after the rest of the pride had gone to sleep.

By now we had almost given up hope of finding the injured lion, though we were anxious to do so, to make quite certain that he was not Jespah; one day, we found him by a rain pool. His companion was with him, and not far away were two young lions with short ruffs. The four seemed to have formed a bachelor party; we hoped it was for the purpose of helping the sick lion. At our approach he pulled himself up into a standing position, but carefully sat down again for obviously it hurt him to put weight on the injured leg. His rump was withered, he was very thin, and the expression of his eyes showed that he was in pain. A first glance had told us that he was not Jespah, but I was tormented by the idea that our cub might be in a similar state.

We had not much time left before we should be forced to leave the Serengeti for two months, so as we knew that by now we had investigated the lion population round Naabi Hill pretty thoroughly, we decided to spend our last days examining the cub valley.

On our way home, one day we noticed some circling vultures and driving in their direction, came upon a couple of lion on a buffalo kill. They were mature lions and if it had not been for this difference in age we should have been convinced that they were Jespah and Gopa, for the blond lion had the same narrow, long muzzle, golden eyes and an equally good-natured and dignified expression as Jespah, while the darker of the two had a squint like Gopa. But they were at least four years old, with fully developed manes, so it was impossible that they should be our cubs.

During our final days in the park we drove non-stop from

sunrise to dark hoping that we might still get a sight of the cubs before we had to leave. We had spent five months in the Serengeti, much of it under appalling weather conditions, we had driven ceaselessly, making demands on our bodies and on our vehicles that they were scarcely able to endure, we had searched every accessible place in which we thought the cubs might be. It had all been fruitless. The only positive results were that we had got to know the wild animals in the area and been able to study their behaviour during the rains and we left a network of car tracks that would be useful to the wardens in reaching hitherto inaccessible parts of the Serengeti.

On our last day we were again guided by vultures to a buffalo kill near to the place where five days previously we had seen the two lions that looked so like an older Jespah and Gopa.

The dark lion who resembled Gopa, replete to bursting point, was guarding a new buffalo kill against three cheeky jackals, who seized every opportunity to sneak a bite, till a growl sent them running off to avoid a cuffing. The blond lion took no part in the defence, but lay in the shade of a tree, his mane ruffled by the morning wind.

How splendid these lions were – aloof, but friendly, dignified and self-possessed. Looking at them it was easy for me to see why the lion has always fascinated man and become a symbol of something he admires. The king of animals, as they have called him, is a tolerant monarch; true, he is a predator, but predators are essential to keep the balance of wild life and the lion has no wish to harm, he does not attack man unless he is persecuted for his skin or when he is too infirm to find other more active prey. He never kills except to satisfy his hunger as is proved by the unconcern with which herds graze around a pride when they know that the lions' bellies are full.

How I loved watching this scene in front of us. I thought of Elsa's children. Where would they be at this moment? My heart was with them wherever they were. But it was also with these two lions here in front of us; and as I watched this beautiful pair, I realized how all the characteristics of our cubs were inherent in them. Indeed, in every lion I saw during our searches I recognized the intrinsic nature of Elsa, Jespah, Gopa and Little Elsa, the spirit of all the magnificent lions in Africa. May God protect them from any arrow and bless them all and their kingdom.

Serengeti, June 1962

THE END

MAPS

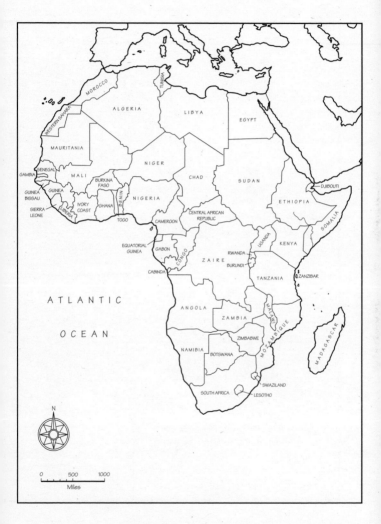

Political map of Africa at the time

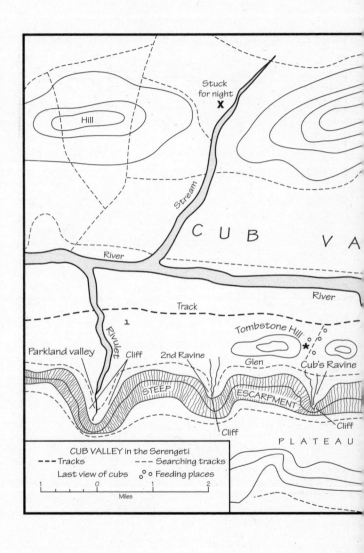

CUB VALLEY in the Serengeti

- - - Tracks   - - - Searching tracks

Last view of cubs   °°° Feeding places

Miles

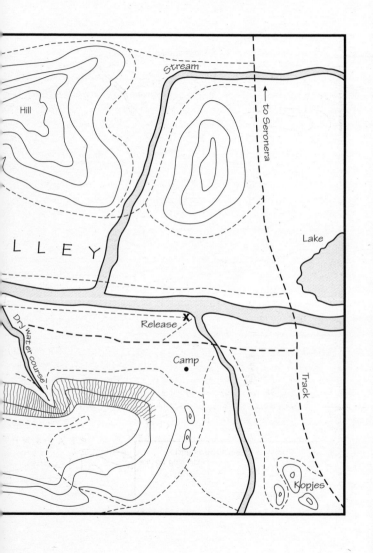

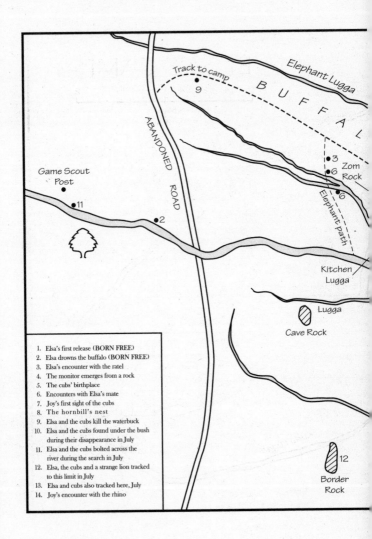

Elephant Lugga

Track to camp

B U F F A L

ABANDONED ROAD

9

Game Scout
Post

3
Zom
6 Rock

6

Elephant path

11

2

Kitchen
Lugga

Lugga

Cave Rock

12

Border
Rock

1. Elsa's first release (BORN FREE)
2. Elsa drowns the buffalo (BORN FREE)
3. Elsa's encounter with the ratel
4. The monitor emerges from a rock
5. The cubs' birthplace
6. Encounters with Elsa's mate
7. Joy's first sight of the cubs
8. The hornbill's nest
9. Elsa and the cubs kill the waterbuck
10. Elsa and the cubs found under the bush
    during their disappearance in July
11. Elsa and the cubs bolted across the
    river during the search in July
12. Elsa, the cubs and a strange lion tracked
    to this limit in July
13. Elsa and cubs also tracked here, July
14. Joy's encounter with the rhino

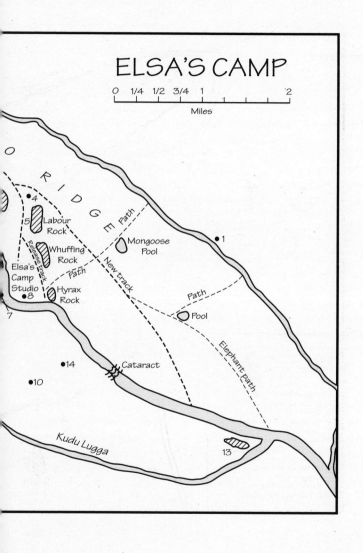

ELSA'S CAMP

0   1/4 1/2 3/4 1   2

Miles

O R I D G E

4

5 Labour
   Rock

Path

Mongoose
Pool

1

Whuffing
Rock

Release track

Elsa's
Camp
Studio

Path

New track

8 Hyrax
   Rock

7

Path

Pool

Elephant path

14   Cataract

10

Kudu Lugga

13

the dam busters

Ⓟ Ⓐ Ⓝ ⑦ Ⓜ Paul Brickhill

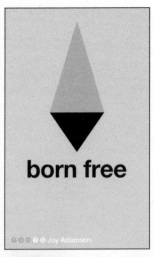

born free

Ⓟ Ⓐ Ⓝ ⑦ Ⓜ Joy Adamson

england, their england

Ⓟ Ⓐ Ⓝ ⑦ Ⓜ A.G. Macdonell

it shouldn't happen to a vet

Ⓟ Ⓐ Ⓝ ⑦ Ⓜ James Herriot

jaws

◉ ◉ ◉ **7** ◉ Peter Benchley

the pan book
of horror stories

◉ ◉ ◉ **7** ◉ Selected by Herbert van Thal

not a penny more,
not a penny less

◉ ◉ ◉ **7** ◉ Jeffrey Archer

ten stories

◉ ◉ ◉ **7** ◉ Rudyard Kipling

the
hitchhiker's
guide to the
galaxy

Douglas Adams

the lost world

Sir Arthur Conan Doyle

childhood's end

Arthur C. Clarke

the
time
machine

H.G. Wells

The Hitchhiker's Guide to the Galaxy – Douglas Adams

Born Free – Joy Adamson

Not a Penny More, Not a Penny Less – Jeffrey Archer

Jaws – Peter Benchley

The Dam Busters – Paul Brickhill

The Thirty-Nine Steps – John Buchan

Childhood's End – Arthur C. Clarke

Savages – Shirley Conran

The Provincial Lady – E. M. Delafield

Last Bus to Woodstock – Colin Dexter

The Lost World – Sir Arthur Conan Doyle

Eye of the Needle – Ken Follett

It Shouldn't Happen to a Vet – James Herriot

Dead Simple – Peter James

Ten Stories – Rudyard Kipling

England, Their England – A. G. Macdonell

Gone with the Wind – Margaret Mitchell

The Time Machine – H. G. Wells

The Lady Vanishes – Ethel Lina White

The Pan Book of Horror Stories